DATE DUE			OCT 04
GAYLORD			PRINTED IN U.S.A.

Table of Contents

by
Osamu Tezuka

translation
Frederik L. Schodt

lettering and retouch
Sno Cone Studios

Dark Horse Comics®

publisher
MIKE RICHARDSON

editor
CHRIS WARNER

consulting editor
TOREN SMITH for STUDIO PROTEUS

collection designers
DAVID NESTELLE and LANI SCHREIBSTEIN

English-language version produced by DARK HORSE COMICS and STUDIO PROTEUS

ASTRO BOY® VOLUME 16

The artwork of this volume has been produced as a mirror-image of the original Japanese edition to conform to English-language standards.

Published by
Dark Horse Comics, Inc.
10956 SE Main Street
Milwaukie, OR 97222

www.darkhorse.com

To find a comics shop in your area, call the Comic Shop Locator Service toll-free at 1-888-266-4226.

First edition: June 2003
ISBN: 1-56971-897-0

10 9 8 7 6 5 4 3 2 1
Printed in Canada

A NOTE TO READERS

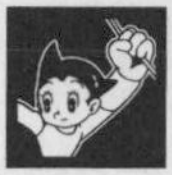

Many non-Japanese, including people from Africa and Southeast Asia, appear in Osamu Tezuka's works. Sometimes these people are depicted very differently from the way they actually are today, in a manner that exaggerates a time long past or shows them to be from extremely undeveloped lands. Some feel that such images contribute to racial discrimination, especially against people of African descent. This was never Osamu Tezuka's intent, but we believe that as long as there are people who feel insulted or demeaned by these depictions, we must not ignore their feelings.

We are against discrimination, in all its forms, and intend to continue to work for its elimination. Nonetheless, we do not believe it would be proper to revise these works. Tezuka is no longer with us, and we cannot erase what he has done, and to alter his work would only violate his rights as a creator. More importantly, stopping publication or changing the content of his work would do little to solve the problems of discrimination that exist in the world.

We are presenting Osamu Tezuka's work as it was originally created, without changes. We do this because we believe it is also important to promote the underlying themes in his work, such as love for mankind and the sanctity of life. We hope that when you, the reader, encounter this work, you will keep in mind the differences in attitudes, then and now, toward discrimination, and that this will contribute to an even greater awareness of such problems.

— Tezuka Productions and Dark Horse Comics

RED CAT

First serialized from May to November 1953
in *Shonen* magazine.

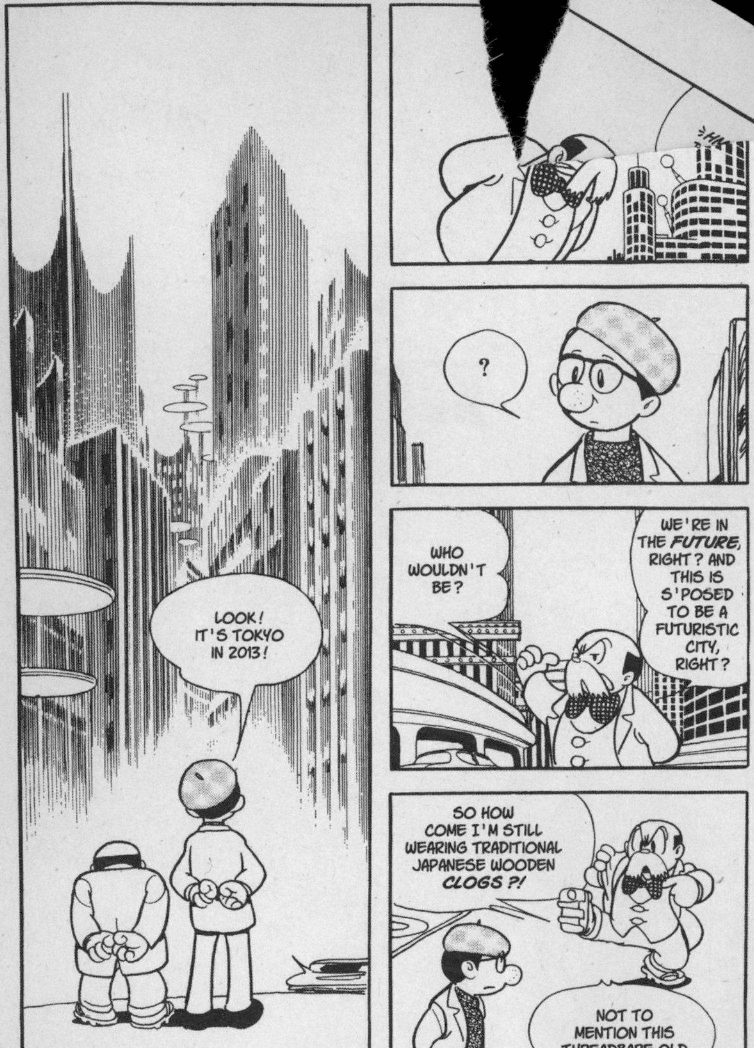
LOOK! IT'S TOKYO IN 2013!
?
WHO WOULDN'T BE?
WE'RE IN THE *FUTURE*, RIGHT? AND THIS IS S'POSED TO BE A FUTURISTIC CITY, RIGHT?
SO HOW COME I'M STILL WEARING TRADITIONAL JAPANESE WOODEN *CLOGS?!*
NOT TO MENTION THIS THREADBARE OLD SUIT!!

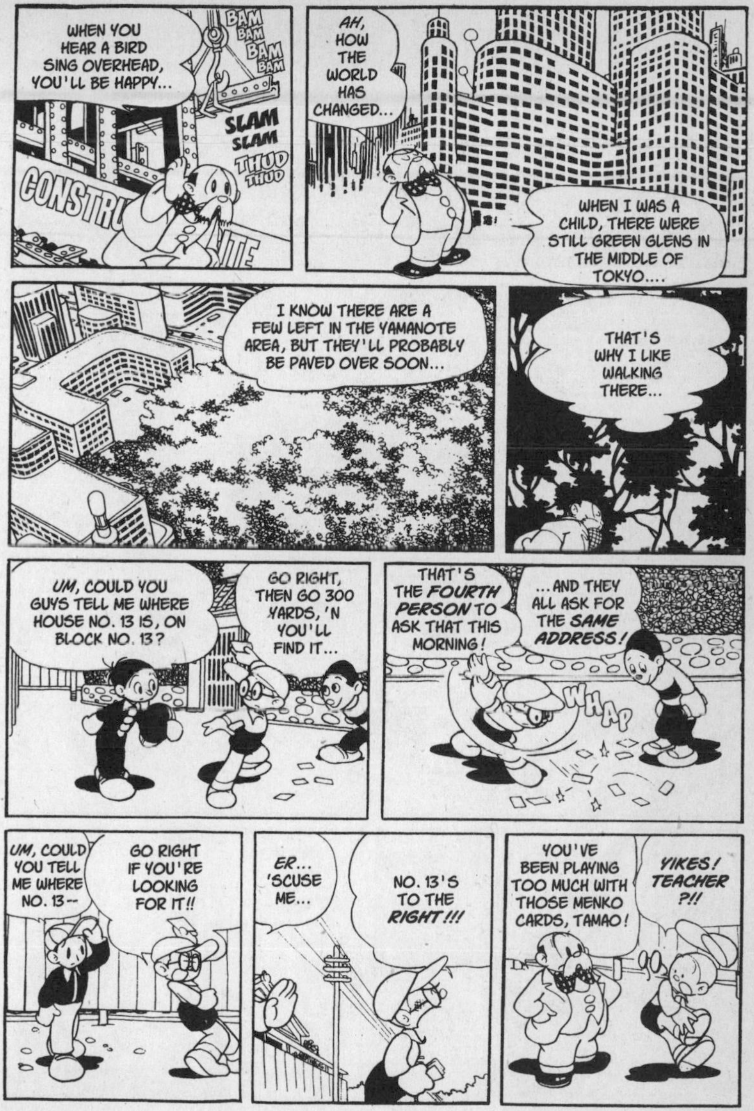
WHEN YOU HEAR A BIRD SING OVERHEAD, YOU'LL BE HAPPY...
BAM BAM BAM BAM
SLAM SLAM
THUD THUD
AH, HOW THE WORLD HAS CHANGED...
WHEN I WAS A CHILD, THERE WERE STILL GREEN GLENS IN THE MIDDLE OF TOKYO....
I KNOW THERE ARE A FEW LEFT IN THE YAMANOTE AREA, BUT THEY'LL PROBABLY BE PAVED OVER SOON...
THAT'S WHY I LIKE WALKING THERE...
UM, COULD YOU GUYS TELL ME WHERE HOUSE NO. 13 IS, ON BLOCK NO. 13?
GO RIGHT, THEN GO 300 YARDS, 'N YOU'LL FIND IT...
THAT'S THE FOURTH PERSON TO ASK THAT THIS MORNING!
...AND THEY ALL ASK FOR THE SAME ADDRESS!
WHAP
UM, COULD YOU TELL ME WHERE NO. 13--
GO RIGHT IF YOU'RE LOOKING FOR IT!!
ER... 'SCUSE ME...
NO. 13'S TO THE RIGHT!!!
YOU'VE BEEN PLAYING TOO MUCH WITH THOSE MENKO CARDS, TAMAO!
YIKES! TEACHER ?!!

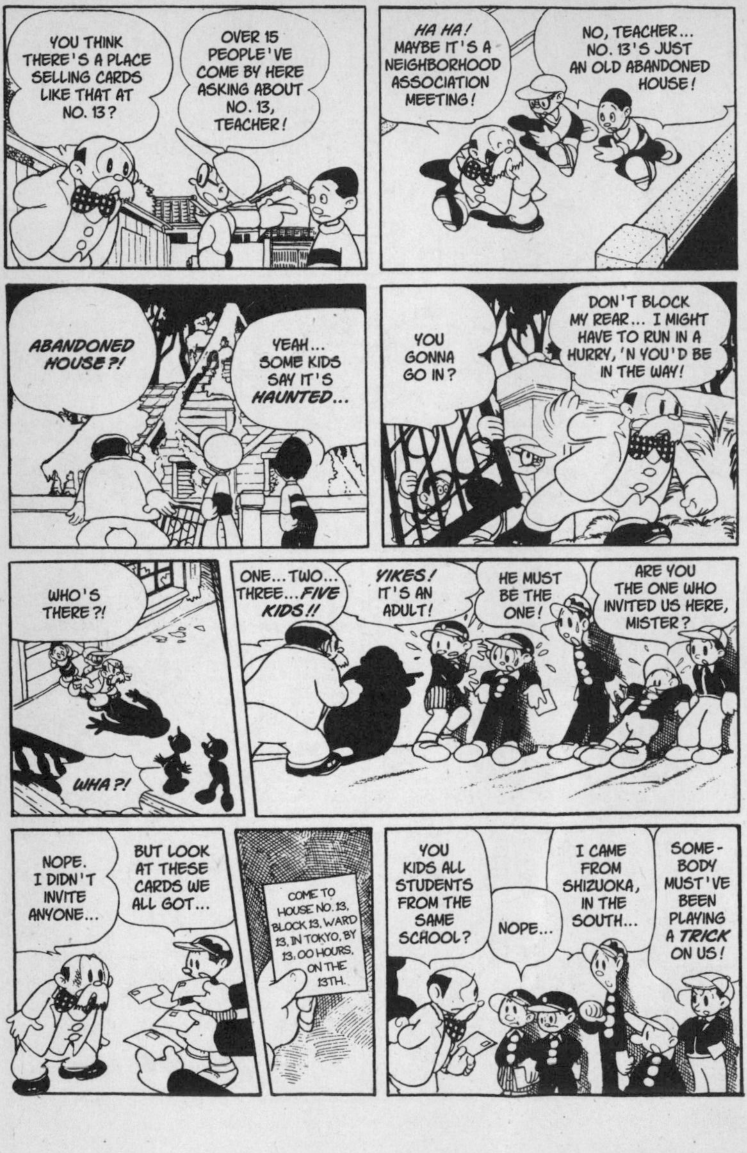
YOU THINK THERE'S A PLACE SELLING CARDS LIKE THAT AT NO. 13?
OVER 15 PEOPLE'VE COME BY HERE ASKING ABOUT NO. 13, TEACHER!
HA HA! MAYBE IT'S A NEIGHBORHOOD ASSOCIATION MEETING!
NO, TEACHER... NO. 13'S JUST AN OLD ABANDONED HOUSE!
ABANDONED HOUSE?!
YEAH... SOME KIDS SAY IT'S HAUNTED...
YOU GONNA GO IN?
DON'T BLOCK MY REAR... I MIGHT HAVE TO RUN IN A HURRY, 'N YOU'D BE IN THE WAY!
WHO'S THERE?!
WHA?!
ONE... TWO... THREE... FIVE KIDS!!
YIKES! IT'S AN ADULT!
HE MUST BE THE ONE!
ARE YOU THE ONE WHO INVITED US HERE, MISTER?
NOPE. I DIDN'T INVITE ANYONE...
BUT LOOK AT THESE CARDS WE ALL GOT...
COME TO HOUSE NO. 13, BLOCK 13, WARD 13, IN TOKYO, BY 13:00 HOURS, ON THE 13TH.
YOU KIDS ALL STUDENTS FROM THE SAME SCHOOL?
NOPE...
I CAME FROM SHIZUOKA, IN THE SOUTH...
SOMEBODY MUST'VE BEEN PLAYING A TRICK ON US!

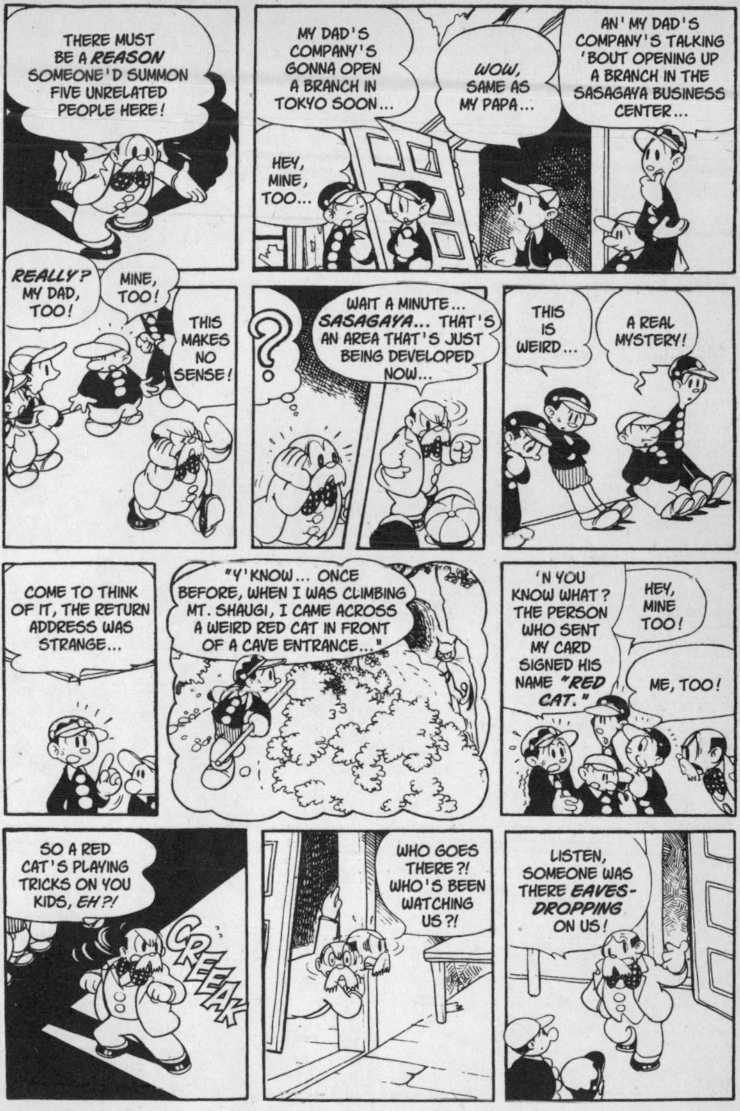
THERE MUST BE A REASON SOMEONE'D SUMMON FIVE UNRELATED PEOPLE HERE!
MY DAD'S COMPANY'S GONNA OPEN A BRANCH IN TOKYO SOON...
HEY, MINE, TOO...
WOW, SAME AS MY PAPA...
AN' MY DAD'S COMPANY'S TALKING 'BOUT OPENING UP A BRANCH IN THE SASAGAYA BUSINESS CENTER...
REALLY? MY DAD, TOO!
MINE, TOO!
THIS MAKES NO SENSE!
?
WAIT A MINUTE... SASAGAYA... THAT'S AN AREA THAT'S JUST BEING DEVELOPED NOW...
THIS IS WEIRD...
A REAL MYSTERY!
COME TO THINK OF IT, THE RETURN ADDRESS WAS STRANGE...
"Y'KNOW... ONCE BEFORE, WHEN I WAS CLIMBING MT. SHAUGI, I CAME ACROSS A WEIRD RED CAT IN FRONT OF A CAVE ENTRANCE..."
'N YOU KNOW WHAT? THE PERSON WHO SENT MY CARD SIGNED HIS NAME "RED CAT."
HEY, MINE TOO!
ME, TOO!
SO A RED CAT'S PLAYING TRICKS ON YOU KIDS, EH?!
CREEAK
WHO GOES THERE?! WHO'S BEEN WATCHING US?!
LISTEN, SOMEONE WAS THERE EAVES-DROPPING ON US!

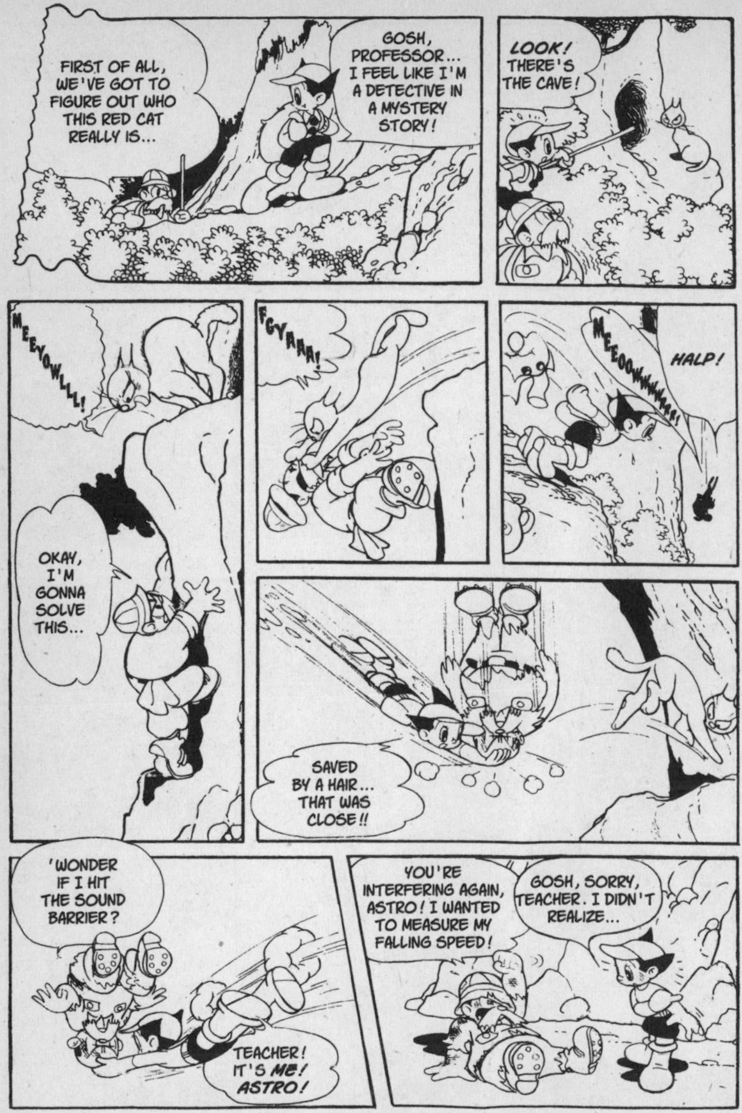
FIRST OF ALL, WE'VE GOT TO FIGURE OUT WHO THIS RED CAT REALLY IS...
GOSH, PROFESSOR... I FEEL LIKE I'M A DETECTIVE IN A MYSTERY STORY!
LOOK! THERE'S THE CAVE!
MEEYOWLLLL!
OKAY, I'M GONNA SOLVE THIS...
FGYAAAA!
MEEOOWWWWAAAA!
HALP!
SAVED BY A HAIR... THAT WAS CLOSE!!
'WONDER IF I HIT THE SOUND BARRIER?
TEACHER! IT'S ME! ASTRO!
YOU'RE INTERFERING AGAIN, ASTRO! I WANTED TO MEASURE MY FALLING SPEED!
GOSH, SORRY, TEACHER. I DIDN'T REALIZE...

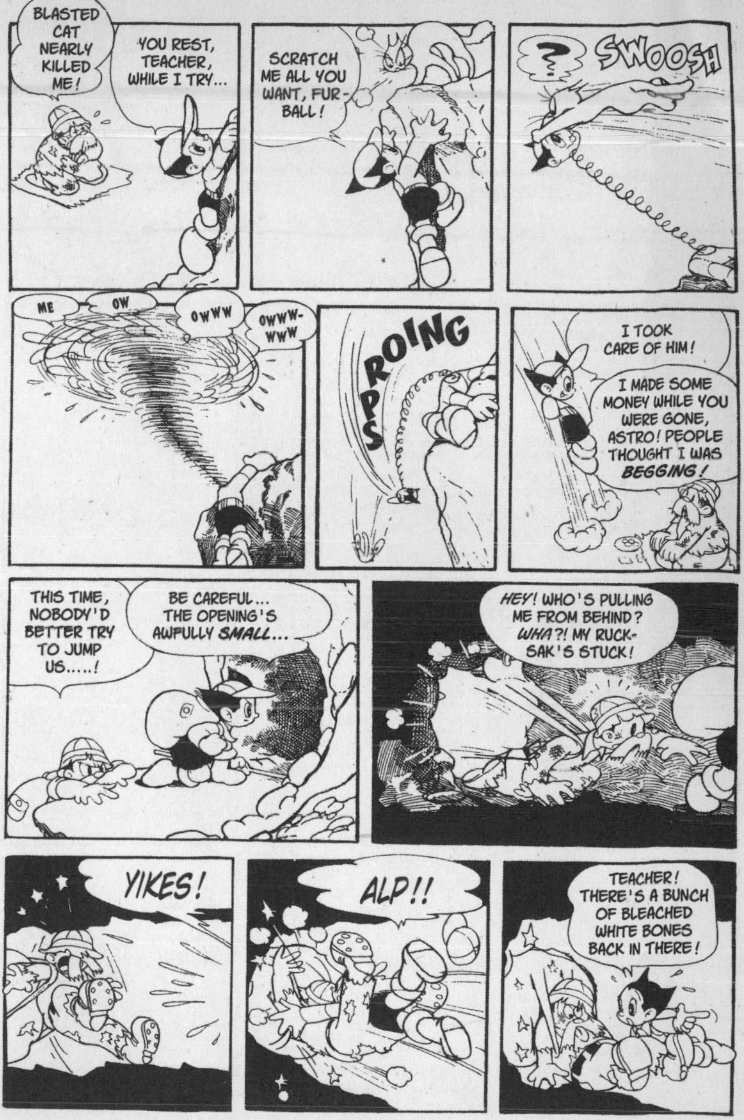
BLASTED CAT NEARLY KILLED ME!
YOU REST, TEACHER, WHILE I TRY...
SCRATCH ME ALL YOU WANT, FUR-BALL!
?
SWOOSH
ME
OW
OWWW
OWWW-WWW
SPROING
I TOOK CARE OF HIM!
I MADE SOME MONEY WHILE YOU WERE GONE, ASTRO! PEOPLE THOUGHT I WAS BEGGING!
THIS TIME, NOBODY'D BETTER TRY TO JUMP US.....!
BE CAREFUL... THE OPENING'S AWFULLY SMALL...
HEY! WHO'S PULLING ME FROM BEHIND? WHA?! MY RUCK-SAK'S STUCK!
YIKES!
ALP!!
TEACHER! THERE'S A BUNCH OF BLEACHED WHITE BONES BACK IN THERE!

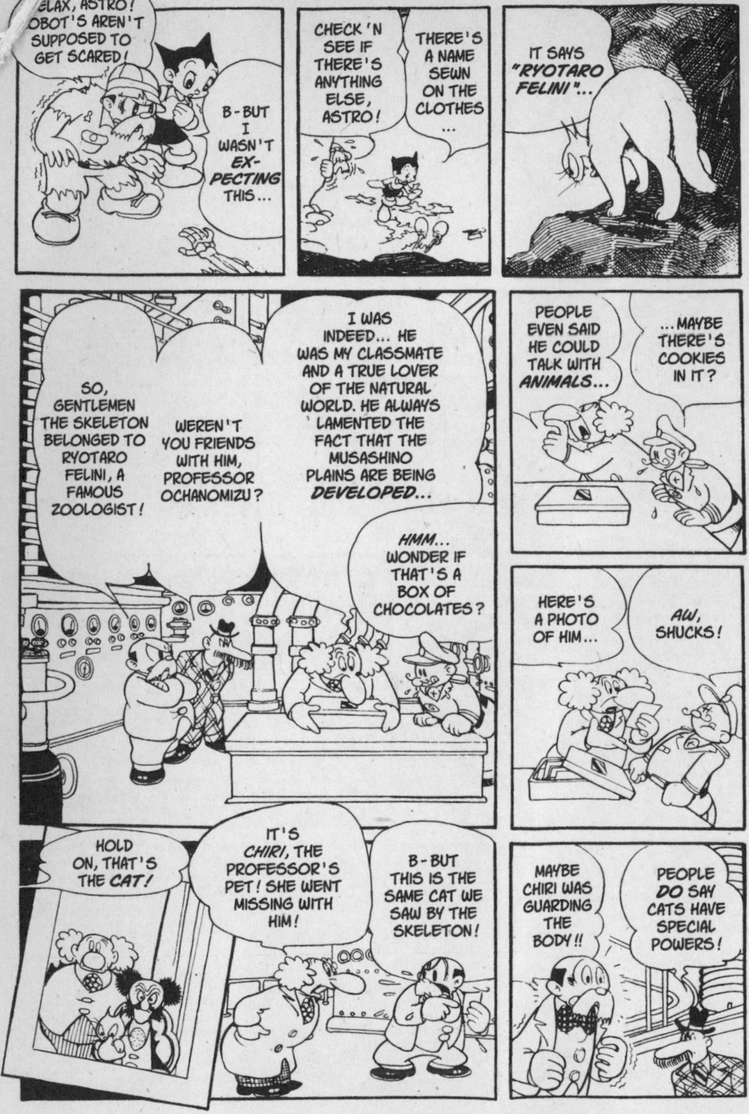
ELAX, ASTRO! OBOT'S AREN'T SUPPOSED TO GET SCARED!
B-BUT I WASN'T EX-PECTING THIS...
CHECK 'N SEE IF THERE'S ANYTHING ELSE, ASTRO!
THERE'S A NAME SEWN ON THE CLOTHES...
IT SAYS "RYOTARO FELINI"...
SO, GENTLEMEN THE SKELETON BELONGED TO RYOTARO FELINI, A FAMOUS ZOOLOGIST!
WEREN'T YOU FRIENDS WITH HIM, PROFESSOR OCHANOMIZU?
I WAS INDEED... HE WAS MY CLASSMATE AND A TRUE LOVER OF THE NATURAL WORLD. HE ALWAYS LAMENTED THE FACT THAT THE MUSASHINO PLAINS ARE BEING DEVELOPED...
HMM... WONDER IF THAT'S A BOX OF CHOCOLATES?
PEOPLE EVEN SAID HE COULD TALK WITH ANIMALS...
...MAYBE THERE'S COOKIES IN IT?
HERE'S A PHOTO OF HIM...
AW, SHUCKS!
HOLD ON, THAT'S THE CAT!
IT'S CHIRI, THE PROFESSOR'S PET! SHE WENT MISSING WITH HIM!
B-BUT THIS IS THE SAME CAT WE SAW BY THE SKELETON!
MAYBE CHIRI WAS GUARDING THE BODY!!
PEOPLE DO SAY CATS HAVE SPECIAL POWERS!

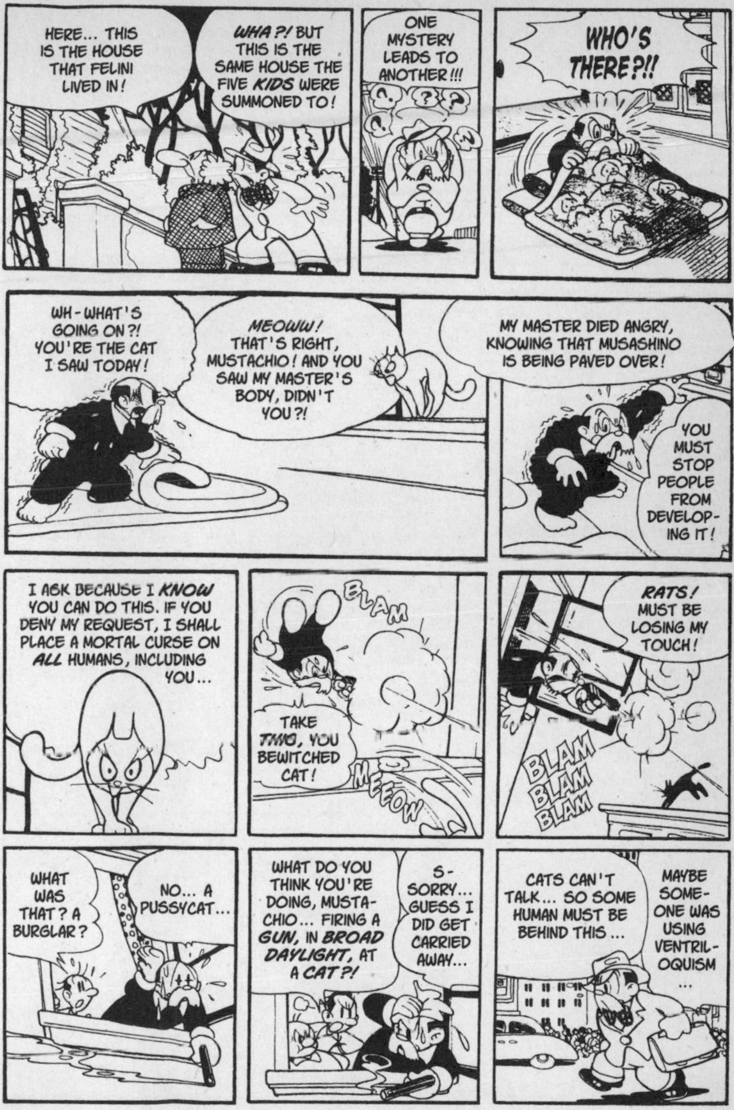
HERE... THIS IS THE HOUSE THAT FELINI LIVED IN!
WHA?! BUT THIS IS THE SAME HOUSE THE FIVE KIDS WERE SUMMONED TO!
ONE MYSTERY LEADS TO ANOTHER!!!
WHO'S THERE?!!
WH-WHAT'S GOING ON?! YOU'RE THE CAT I SAW TODAY!
MEOWW! THAT'S RIGHT, MUSTACHIO! AND YOU SAW MY MASTER'S BODY, DIDN'T YOU?!
MY MASTER DIED ANGRY, KNOWING THAT MUSASHINO IS BEING PAVED OVER!
YOU MUST STOP PEOPLE FROM DEVELOP-ING IT!
I ASK BECAUSE I KNOW YOU CAN DO THIS. IF YOU DENY MY REQUEST, I SHALL PLACE A MORTAL CURSE ON ALL HUMANS, INCLUDING YOU...
BLAM
TAKE THAT, YOU BEWITCHED CAT!
MEEOW
RATS! MUST BE LOSING MY TOUCH!
BLAM BLAM BLAM
WHAT WAS THAT? A BURGLAR?
NO... A PUSSYCAT...
WHAT DO YOU THINK YOU'RE DOING, MUSTA-CHIO... FIRING A GUN, IN BROAD DAYLIGHT, AT A CAT?!
S-SORRY... GUESS I DID GET CARRIED AWAY...
CATS CAN'T TALK... SO SOME HUMAN MUST BE BEHIND THIS ...
MAYBE SOME-ONE WAS USING VENTRIL-OQUISM ...

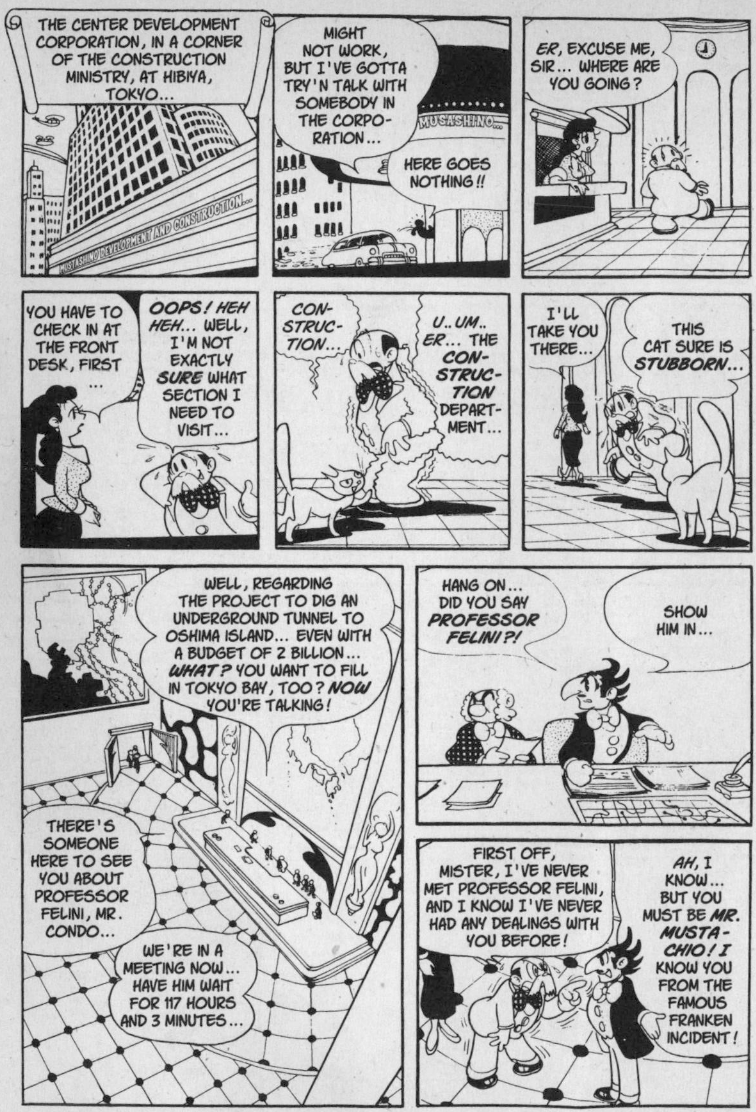
THE CENTER DEVELOPMENT CORPORATION, IN A CORNER OF THE CONSTRUCTION MINISTRY, AT HIBIYA, TOKYO...
MUSTASHINO DEVELOPMENT AND CONSTRUCTION...
MIGHT NOT WORK, BUT I'VE GOTTA TRY'N TALK WITH SOMEBODY IN THE CORPORATION...
MUSASHINO...
HERE GOES NOTHING!!
ER, EXCUSE ME, SIR... WHERE ARE YOU GOING?
YOU HAVE TO CHECK IN AT THE FRONT DESK, FIRST ...
OOPS! HEH HEH... WELL, I'M NOT EXACTLY SURE WHAT SECTION I NEED TO VISIT...
CONSTRUCTION...
U..UM.. ER... THE CONSTRUCTION DEPARTMENT...
I'LL TAKE YOU THERE...
THIS CAT SURE IS STUBBORN...
WELL, REGARDING THE PROJECT TO DIG AN UNDERGROUND TUNNEL TO OSHIMA ISLAND... EVEN WITH A BUDGET OF 2 BILLION... WHAT? YOU WANT TO FILL IN TOKYO BAY, TOO? NOW YOU'RE TALKING!
THERE'S SOMEONE HERE TO SEE YOU ABOUT PROFESSOR FELINI, MR. CONDO...
WE'RE IN A MEETING NOW... HAVE HIM WAIT FOR 117 HOURS AND 3 MINUTES...
HANG ON... DID YOU SAY PROFESSOR FELINI?!
SHOW HIM IN...
FIRST OFF, MISTER, I'VE NEVER MET PROFESSOR FELINI, AND I KNOW I'VE NEVER HAD ANY DEALINGS WITH YOU BEFORE!
AH, I KNOW... BUT YOU MUST BE MR. MUSTACHIO! I KNOW YOU FROM THE FAMOUS FRANKEN INCIDENT!

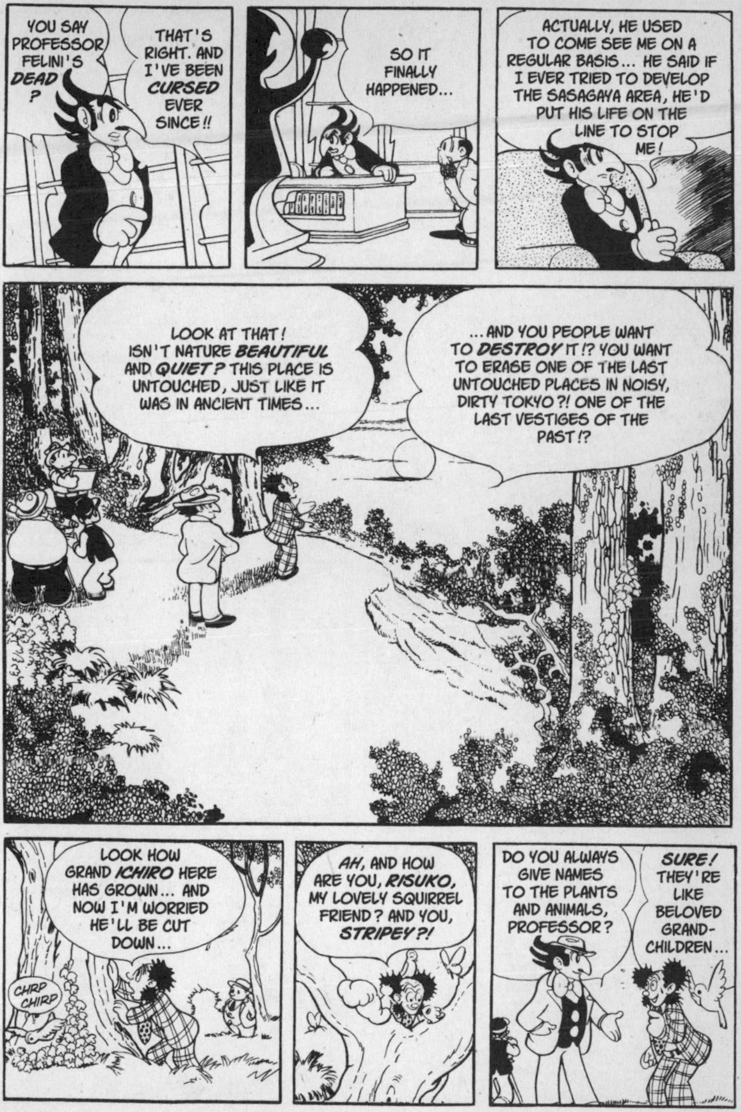
YOU SAY PROFESSOR FELINI'S DEAD ?
THAT'S RIGHT. AND I'VE BEEN CURSED EVER SINCE !!
SO IT FINALLY HAPPENED...
ACTUALLY, HE USED TO COME SEE ME ON A REGULAR BASIS... HE SAID IF I EVER TRIED TO DEVELOP THE SASAGAYA AREA, HE'D PUT HIS LIFE ON THE LINE TO STOP ME!
LOOK AT THAT! ISN'T NATURE BEAUTIFUL AND QUIET? THIS PLACE IS UNTOUCHED, JUST LIKE IT WAS IN ANCIENT TIMES...
...AND YOU PEOPLE WANT TO DESTROY IT!? YOU WANT TO ERASE ONE OF THE LAST UNTOUCHED PLACES IN NOISY, DIRTY TOKYO?! ONE OF THE LAST VESTIGES OF THE PAST!?
LOOK HOW GRAND ICHIRO HERE HAS GROWN... AND NOW I'M WORRIED HE'LL BE CUT DOWN...
CHRP CHIRP
AH, AND HOW ARE YOU, RISUKO, MY LOVELY SQUIRREL FRIEND? AND YOU, STRIPEY?!
DO YOU ALWAYS GIVE NAMES TO THE PLANTS AND ANIMALS, PROFESSOR?
SURE! THEY'RE LIKE BELOVED GRAND-CHILDREN...

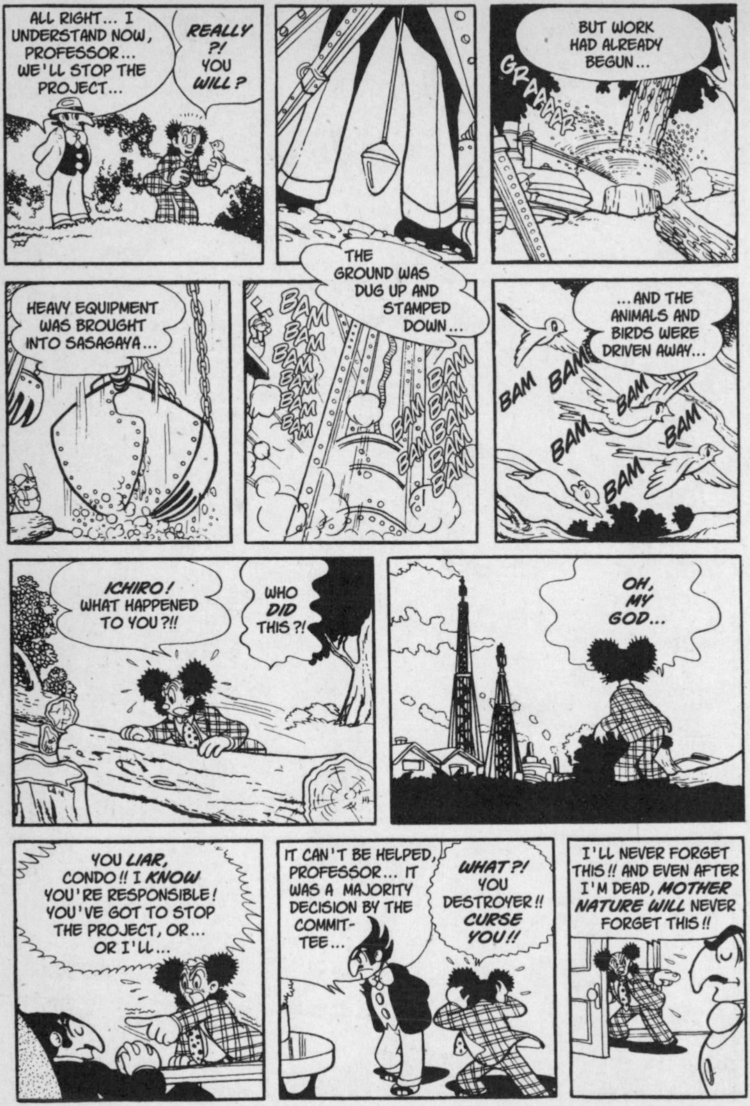
ALL RIGHT... I UNDERSTAND NOW, PROFESSOR... WE'LL STOP THE PROJECT...
REALLY ?! YOU WILL ?
BUT WORK HAD ALREADY BEGUN...
GRAAAAAR
HEAVY EQUIPMENT WAS BROUGHT INTO SASAGAYA...
THE GROUND WAS DUG UP AND STAMPED DOWN...
BAM BAM BAM BAM BAM BAM BAM
BAM BAM BAM BAM BAM BAM BAM
...AND THE ANIMALS AND BIRDS WERE DRIVEN AWAY...
BAM BAM BAM BAM BAM BAM
ICHIRO! WHAT HAPPENED TO YOU?!!
WHO DID THIS ?!
OH, MY GOD...
YOU LIAR, CONDO!! I KNOW YOU'RE RESPONSIBLE! YOU'VE GOT TO STOP THE PROJECT, OR... OR I'LL...
IT CAN'T BE HELPED, PROFESSOR... IT WAS A MAJORITY DECISION BY THE COMMIT-TEE...
WHAT?! YOU DESTROYER!! CURSE YOU!!
I'LL NEVER FORGET THIS!! AND EVEN AFTER I'M DEAD, MOTHER NATURE WILL NEVER FORGET THIS!!

...SO AFTER THAT, MR. MUSTACHIO, THE PROFESSOR COMPLETELY DISAPPEARED... OF COURSE, I DO HOPE HE'S ALL RIGHT... I'D FEEL VERY SORRY IF HE WERE DEAD...

WELL, THE PROFESSOR'S PET CAT HAS BEEN POSSESSED, AND NOW IT'S RUNNING AROUND YELLING *MEEYOOWGO*...

YOU MEAN, YOU THINK HE'S TRYING TO GET REVENGE FOR HIS MASTER'S DEATH?

MAYBE HE TAKES AFTER THE POSSESSED CAT IN THE FAMOUS PLAY ABOUT PRINCE NABESHIMA...

No.2 ANOMIZU ENTARY CHOOL

≥HMPH≥... LOOKS LIKE CONSTRUCTION'S REALLY UNDERWAY NOW IN SASAGAYA...

MUSTACHIO! MAKE SURE YOU TELL YOUR PUPILS NOT TO GO NEAR THE CONSTRUCTION SITE, OKAY?

YAZ-ZIR...

BOYS AND GIRLS.... I KNOW YOU'RE FAMILIAR WITH THE *SASAGAYA* AREA... WELL, DANGEROUS CONSTRUCTION'S GOING ON THERE, SO LIKE THE SAYING GOES, DON'T BE THE FOOLS WHO RUSH IN, WHERE WISE MEN FEAR TO TREAD...

B-BUT TEACHER... THAT'S WHERE WE ALWAYS *PLAY*! THERE'S NOWHERE *ELSE* FOR US TO GO!

YEAH! TELL IT LIKE IT IS, SHIB!

I'M AGAINST THEM MAKING ANY BUILDINGS THERE!

YEAH-- ME, TOO! ME, TOO!

WE OUGHTA HAVE MORE RIGHTS TO THE PLACE THAN ANYONE ELSE!

ENOUGH, SHIBUGAKI! YOU'RE NOT THE ONLY ONE IN THE WORLD!

I'M *KING OF THE MOUNTAIN*!

NYA NYA! HEY, YOU'RE NOT KING ANYMORE, SHIB!

21

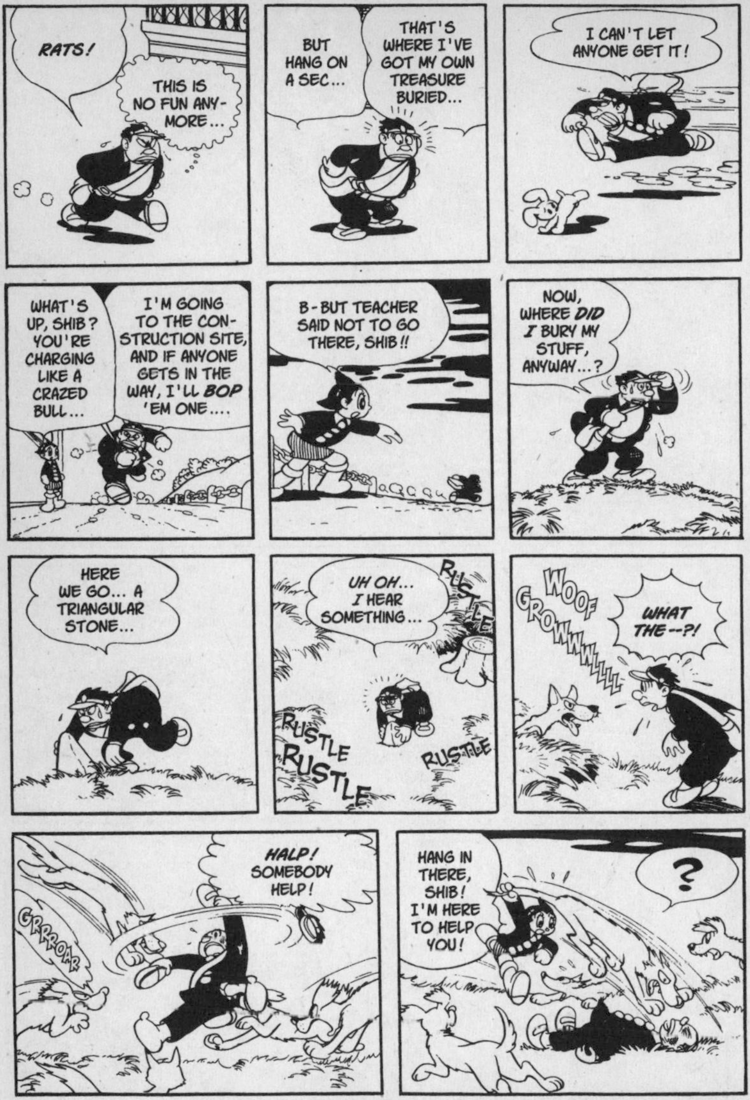
RATS!
THIS IS NO FUN ANY-MORE...
BUT HANG ON A SEC...
THAT'S WHERE I'VE GOT MY OWN TREASURE BURIED...
I CAN'T LET ANYONE GET IT!
WHAT'S UP, SHIB? YOU'RE CHARGING LIKE A CRAZED BULL...
I'M GOING TO THE CON-STRUCTION SITE, AND IF ANYONE GETS IN THE WAY, I'LL BOP 'EM ONE....
B-BUT TEACHER SAID NOT TO GO THERE, SHIB!!
NOW, WHERE DID I BURY MY STUFF, ANYWAY...?
HERE WE GO... A TRIANGULAR STONE...
UH OH... I HEAR SOMETHING...
RUSTLE
RUSTLE
RUSTLE
RUSTLE
WOOF
GROWWWLLLL
WHAT THE--?!
GRRROAR
HALP! SOMEBODY HELP!
HANG IN THERE, SHIB! I'M HERE TO HELP YOU!
?

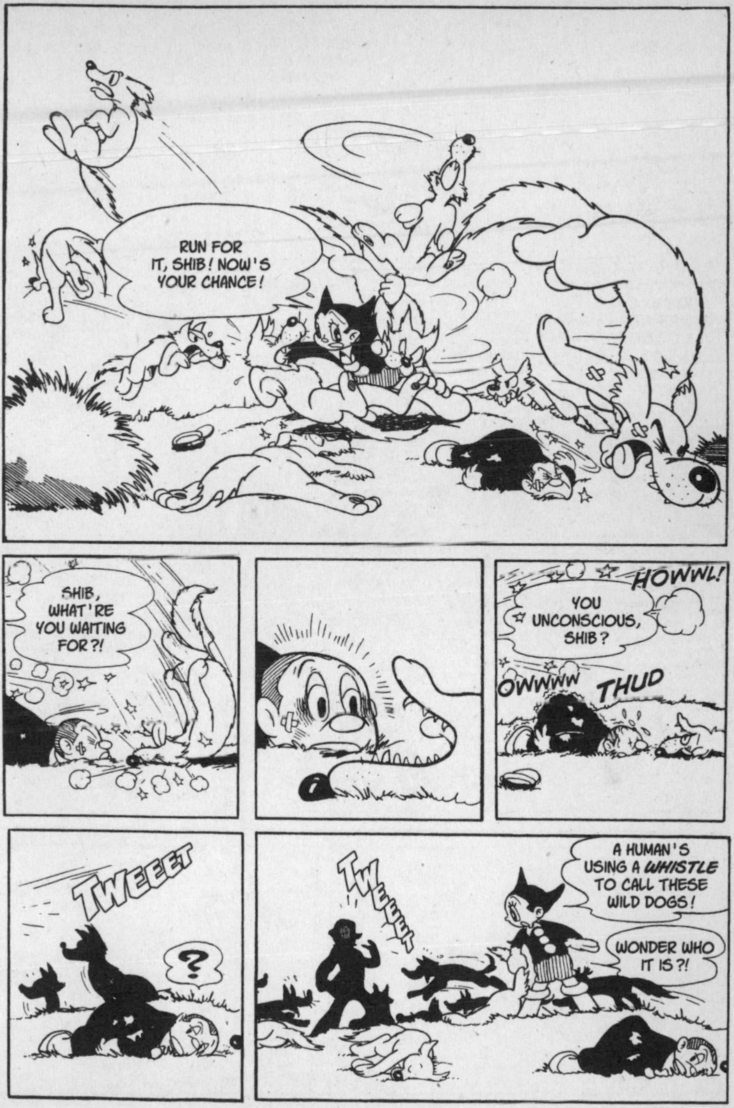
RUN FOR IT, SHIB! NOW'S YOUR CHANCE!
SHIB, WHAT'RE YOU WAITING FOR?!
YOU UNCONSCIOUS, SHIB?
HOWWL!
OWWWW
THUD
TWEEET
?
TWEEEEET
A HUMAN'S USING A WHISTLE TO CALL THESE WILD DOGS!
WONDER WHO IT IS?!

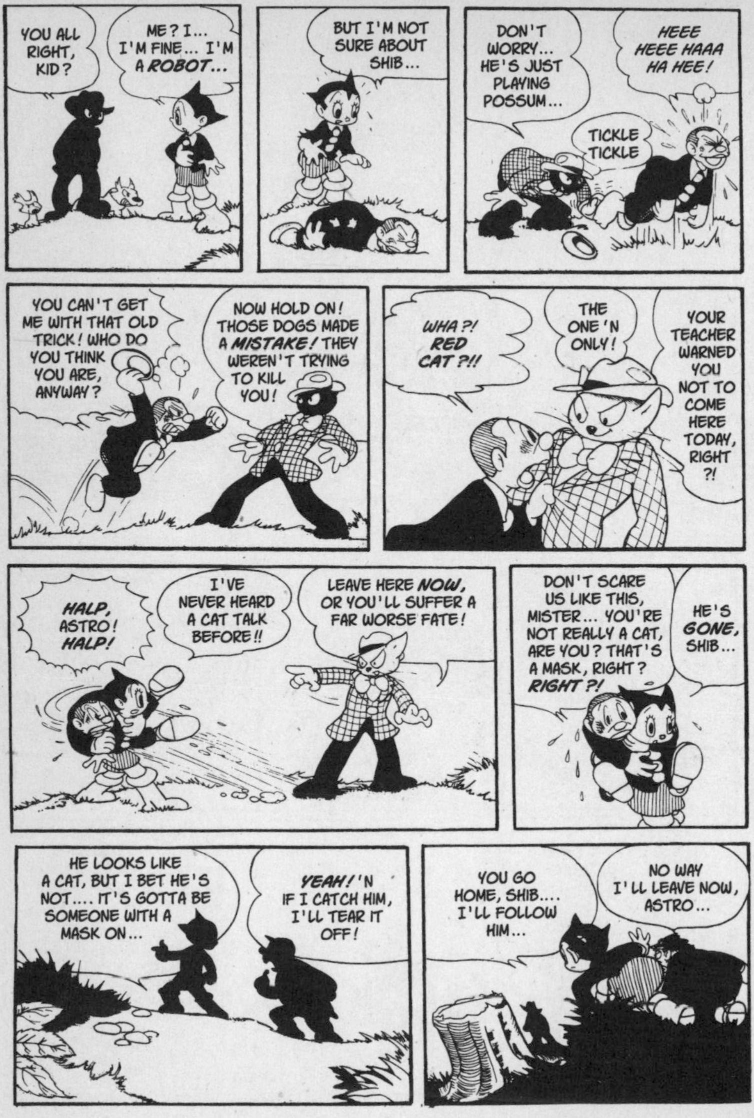
YOU ALL RIGHT, KID?
ME? I... I'M FINE... I'M A ROBOT...
BUT I'M NOT SURE ABOUT SHIB...
DON'T WORRY... HE'S JUST PLAYING POSSUM...
HEEE HEEE HAAA HA HEE!
TICKLE TICKLE
YOU CAN'T GET ME WITH THAT OLD TRICK! WHO DO YOU THINK YOU ARE, ANYWAY?
NOW HOLD ON! THOSE DOGS MADE A MISTAKE! THEY WEREN'T TRYING TO KILL YOU!
WHA?! RED CAT?!!
THE ONE 'N ONLY!
YOUR TEACHER WARNED YOU NOT TO COME HERE TODAY, RIGHT?!
HALP, ASTRO! HALP!
I'VE NEVER HEARD A CAT TALK BEFORE!!
LEAVE HERE NOW, OR YOU'LL SUFFER A FAR WORSE FATE!
DON'T SCARE US LIKE THIS, MISTER... YOU'RE NOT REALLY A CAT, ARE YOU? THAT'S A MASK, RIGHT? RIGHT?!
HE'S GONE, SHIB...
HE LOOKS LIKE A CAT, BUT I BET HE'S NOT.... IT'S GOTTA BE SOMEONE WITH A MASK ON...
YEAH! 'N IF I CATCH HIM, I'LL TEAR IT OFF!
YOU GO HOME, SHIB.... I'LL FOLLOW HIM...
NO WAY I'LL LEAVE NOW, ASTRO...

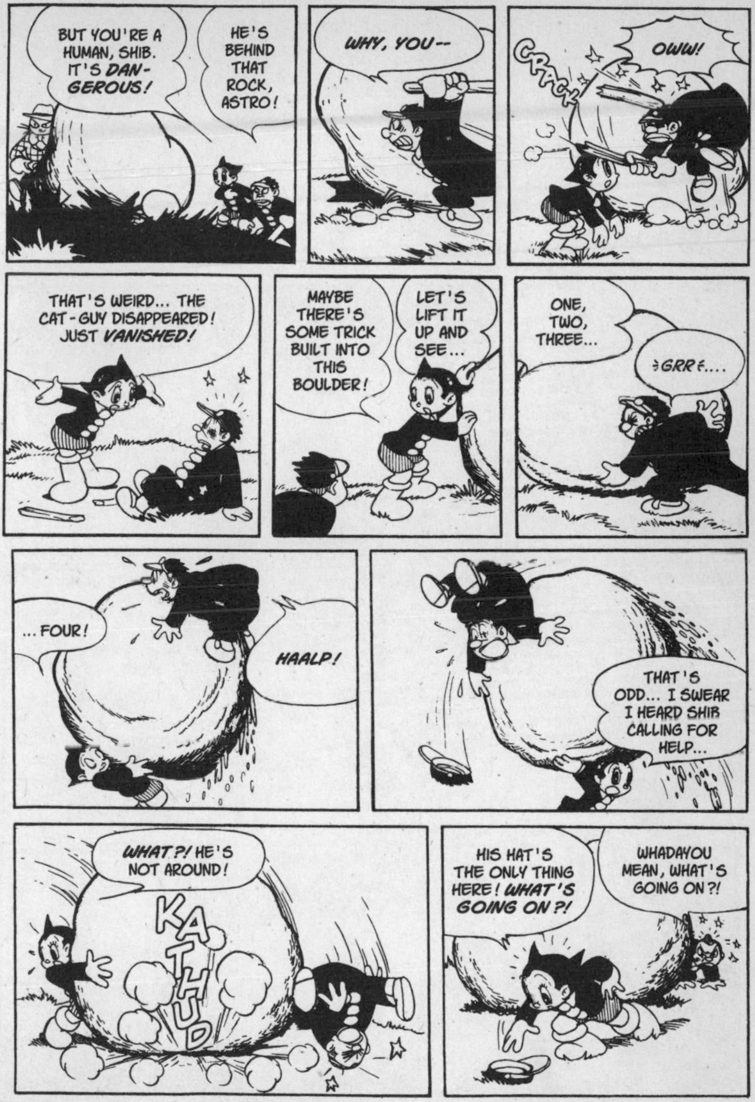
BUT YOU'RE A HUMAN, SHIB. IT'S DAN-GEROUS!
HE'S BEHIND THAT ROCK, ASTRO!
WHY, YOU--
CRACK
OWW!
THAT'S WEIRD... THE CAT-GUY DISAPPEARED! JUST VANISHED!
MAYBE THERE'S SOME TRICK BUILT INTO THIS BOULDER!
LET'S LIFT IT UP AND SEE...
ONE, TWO, THREE...
GRR....
... FOUR!
HAALP!
THAT'S ODD... I SWEAR I HEARD SHIB CALLING FOR HELP...
WHAT?! HE'S NOT AROUND!
KATHUD
HIS HAT'S THE ONLY THING HERE! WHAT'S GOING ON?!
WHADAYOU MEAN, WHAT'S GOING ON?!

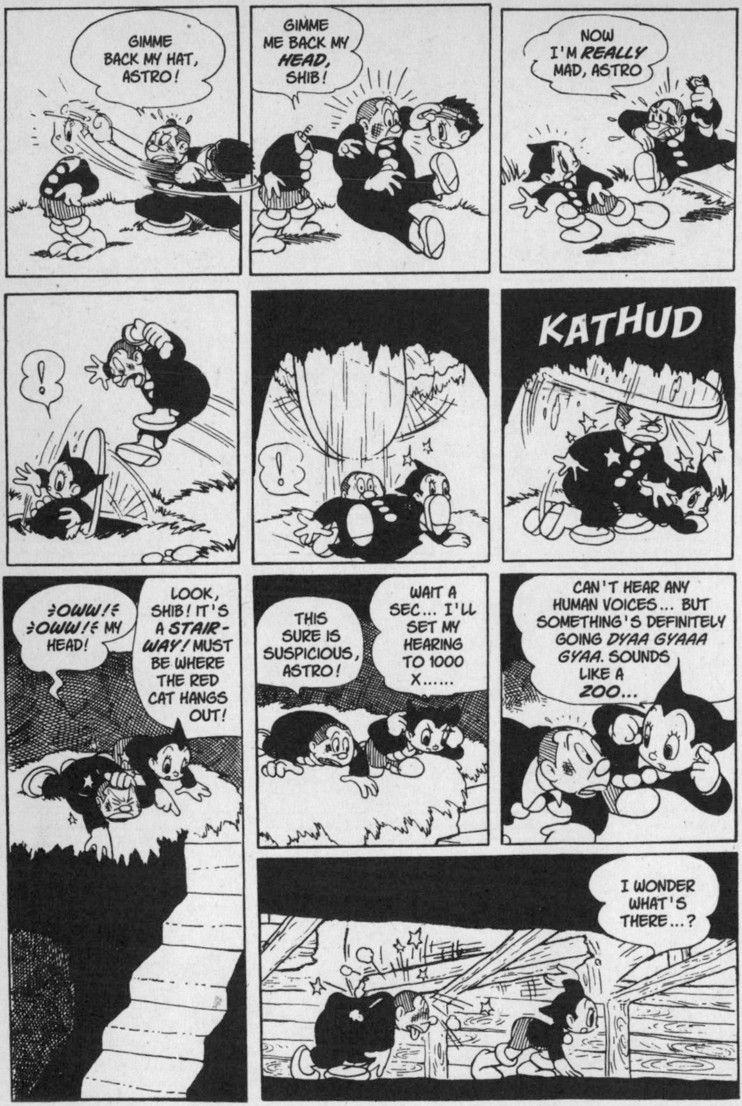
GIMME BACK MY HAT, ASTRO!
GIMME ME BACK MY *HEAD,* SHIB!
NOW I'M *REALLY* MAD, ASTRO
!
!
KATHUD
OWW! OWW! MY HEAD!
LOOK, SHIB! IT'S A *STAIRWAY!* MUST BE WHERE THE RED CAT HANGS OUT!
THIS SURE IS SUSPICIOUS, ASTRO!
WAIT A SEC... I'LL SET MY HEARING TO 1000 X......
CAN'T HEAR ANY HUMAN VOICES... BUT SOMETHING'S DEFINITELY GOING *DYAA GYAAA GYAA.* SOUNDS LIKE A *ZOO...*
I WONDER WHAT'S THERE...?

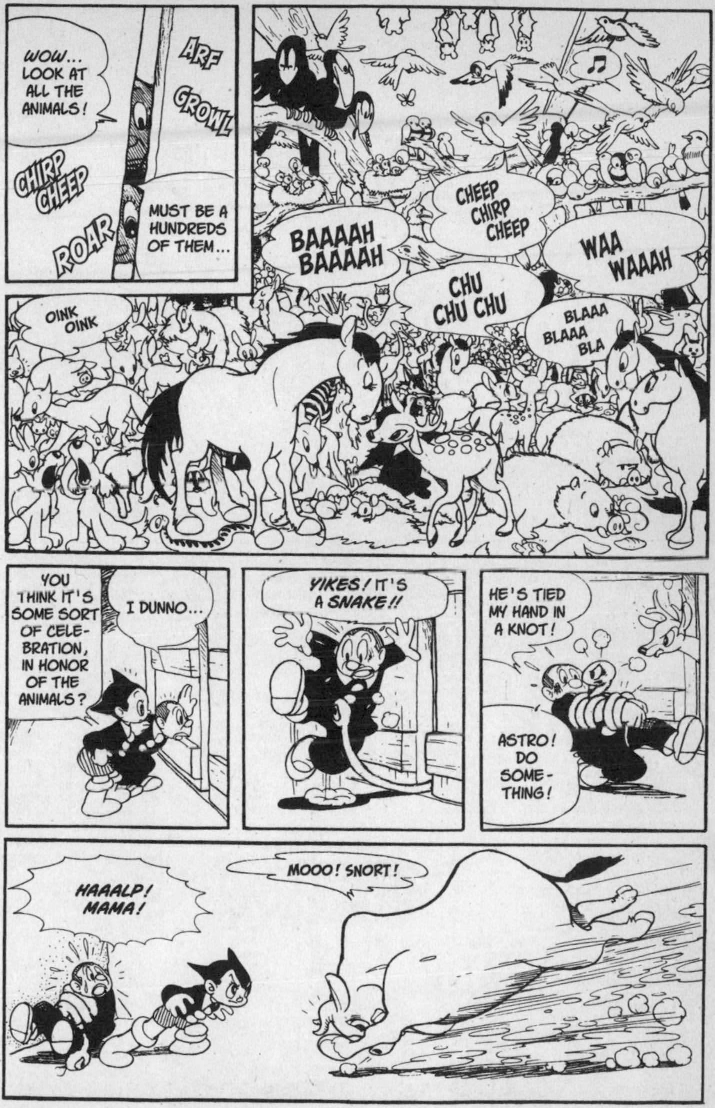
WOW... LOOK AT ALL THE ANIMALS!
ARF
GROWL
CHIRP CHEEP
ROAR
MUST BE A HUNDREDS OF THEM...
CHEEP CHIRP CHEEP
BAAAAH BAAAAH
WAA WAAAH
CHU CHU CHU
OINK OINK
BLAAA BLAAA BLA
YOU THINK IT'S SOME SORT OF CELE-BRATION, IN HONOR OF THE ANIMALS?
I DUNNO...
YIKES! IT'S A SNAKE!!
HE'S TIED MY HAND IN A KNOT!
ASTRO! DO SOME-THING!
HAAALP! MAMA!
MOOO! SNORT!

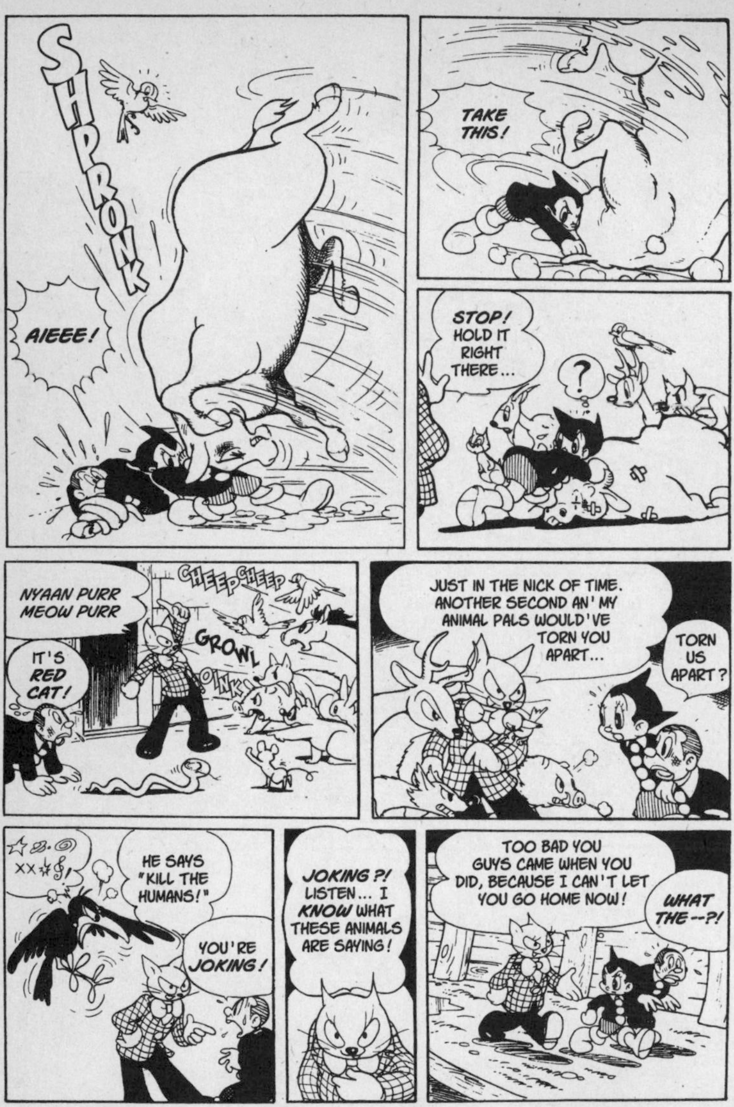
SHPRONK
AIEEE!
TAKE THIS!
STOP! HOLD IT RIGHT THERE...
?
NYAAN PURR MEOW PURR
CHEEP CHEEP
GROWL
OINK
IT'S RED CAT!
JUST IN THE NICK OF TIME. ANOTHER SECOND AN' MY ANIMAL PALS WOULD'VE TORN YOU APART...
TORN US APART?
HE SAYS "KILL THE HUMANS!"
YOU'RE JOKING!
JOKING?! LISTEN... I KNOW WHAT THESE ANIMALS ARE SAYING!
TOO BAD YOU GUYS CAME WHEN YOU DID, BECAUSE I CAN'T LET YOU GO HOME NOW!
WHAT THE--?!

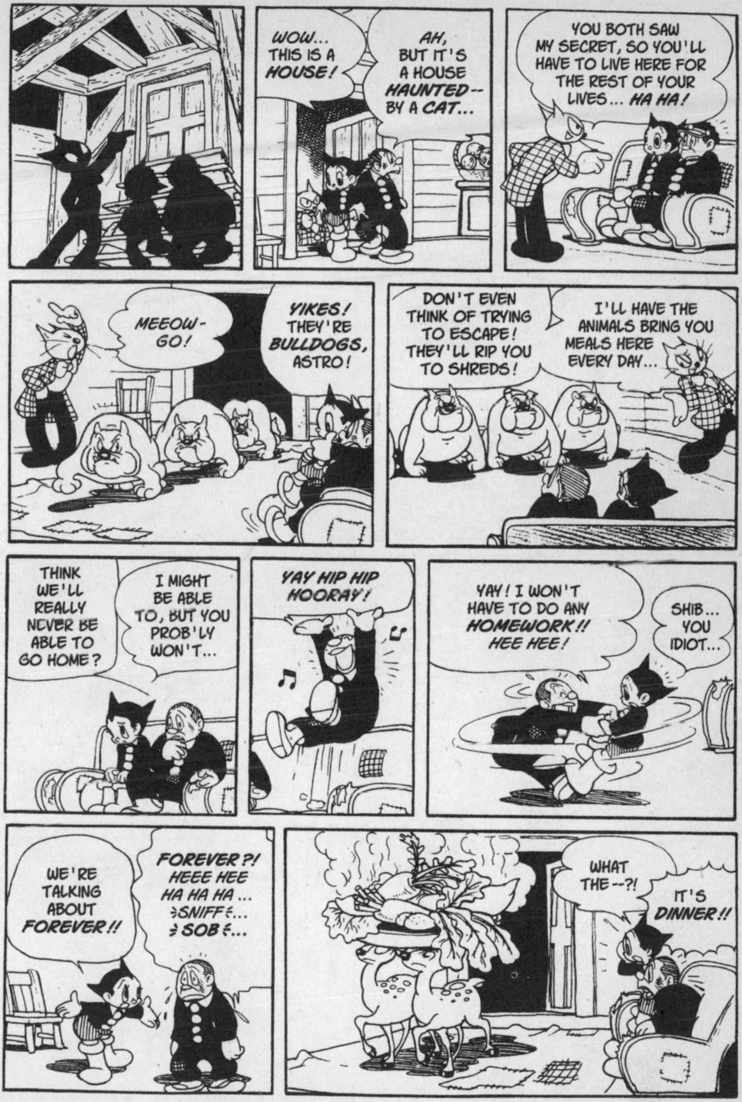
WOW... THIS IS A HOUSE!
AH, BUT IT'S A HOUSE HAUNTED-- BY A CAT...
YOU BOTH SAW MY SECRET, SO YOU'LL HAVE TO LIVE HERE FOR THE REST OF YOUR LIVES... HA HA!
MEEOW-GO!
YIKES! THEY'RE BULLDOGS, ASTRO!
DON'T EVEN THINK OF TRYING TO ESCAPE! THEY'LL RIP YOU TO SHREDS!
I'LL HAVE THE ANIMALS BRING YOU MEALS HERE EVERY DAY...
THINK WE'LL REALLY NEVER BE ABLE TO GO HOME?
I MIGHT BE ABLE TO, BUT YOU PROB'LY WON'T...
YAY HIP HIP HOORAY!
YAY! I WON'T HAVE TO DO ANY HOMEWORK!! HEE HEE!
SHIB... YOU IDIOT...
WE'RE TALKING ABOUT FOREVER!!
FOREVER?! HEEE HEE HA HA HA... SNIFF... SOB...
WHAT THE--?!
IT'S DINNER!!

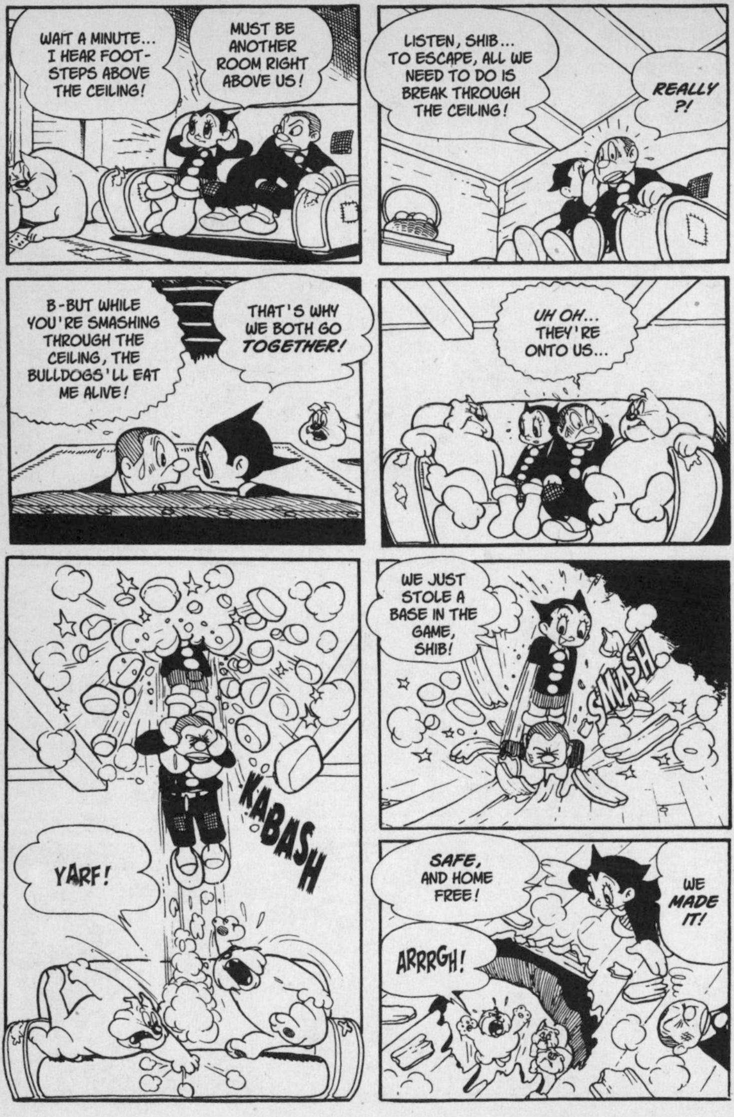
WAIT A MINUTE... I HEAR FOOT-STEPS ABOVE THE CEILING!
MUST BE ANOTHER ROOM RIGHT ABOVE US!
LISTEN, SHIB... TO ESCAPE, ALL WE NEED TO DO IS BREAK THROUGH THE CEILING!
REALLY ?!
B-BUT WHILE YOU'RE SMASHING THROUGH THE CEILING, THE BULLDOGS'LL EAT ME ALIVE!
THAT'S WHY WE BOTH GO TOGETHER!
UH OH... THEY'RE ONTO US...
KABASH
YARF!
WE JUST STOLE A BASE IN THE GAME, SHIB!
SMASH
SAFE, AND HOME FREE!
WE MADE IT!
ARRRGH!

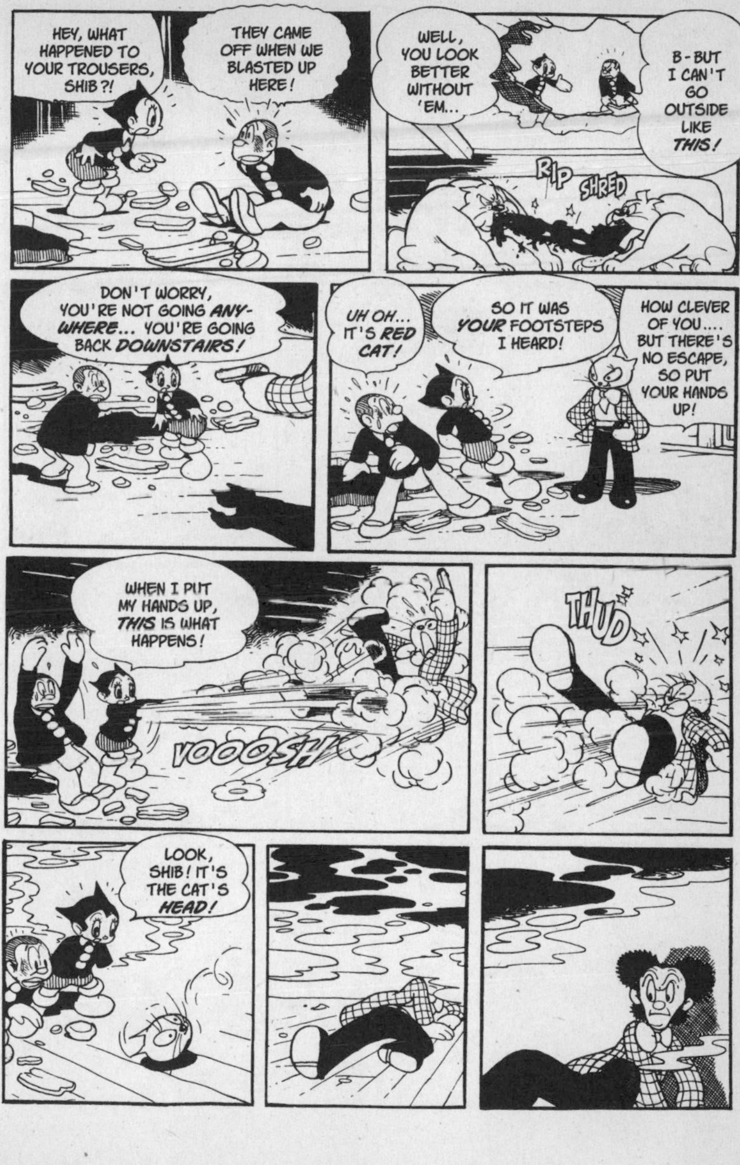

HEY, WHAT HAPPENED TO YOUR TROUSERS, SHIB ?!
THEY CAME OFF WHEN WE BLASTED UP HERE!
WELL, YOU LOOK BETTER WITHOUT 'EM...
B-BUT I CAN'T GO OUTSIDE LIKE THIS!
RIP
SHRED
DON'T WORRY, YOU'RE NOT GOING ANY-WHERE... YOU'RE GOING BACK DOWNSTAIRS!
UH OH... IT'S RED CAT!
SO IT WAS YOUR FOOTSTEPS I HEARD!
HOW CLEVER OF YOU.... BUT THERE'S NO ESCAPE, SO PUT YOUR HANDS UP!
WHEN I PUT MY HANDS UP, THIS IS WHAT HAPPENS!
VOOOSH
THUD
LOOK, SHIB! IT'S THE CAT'S HEAD!

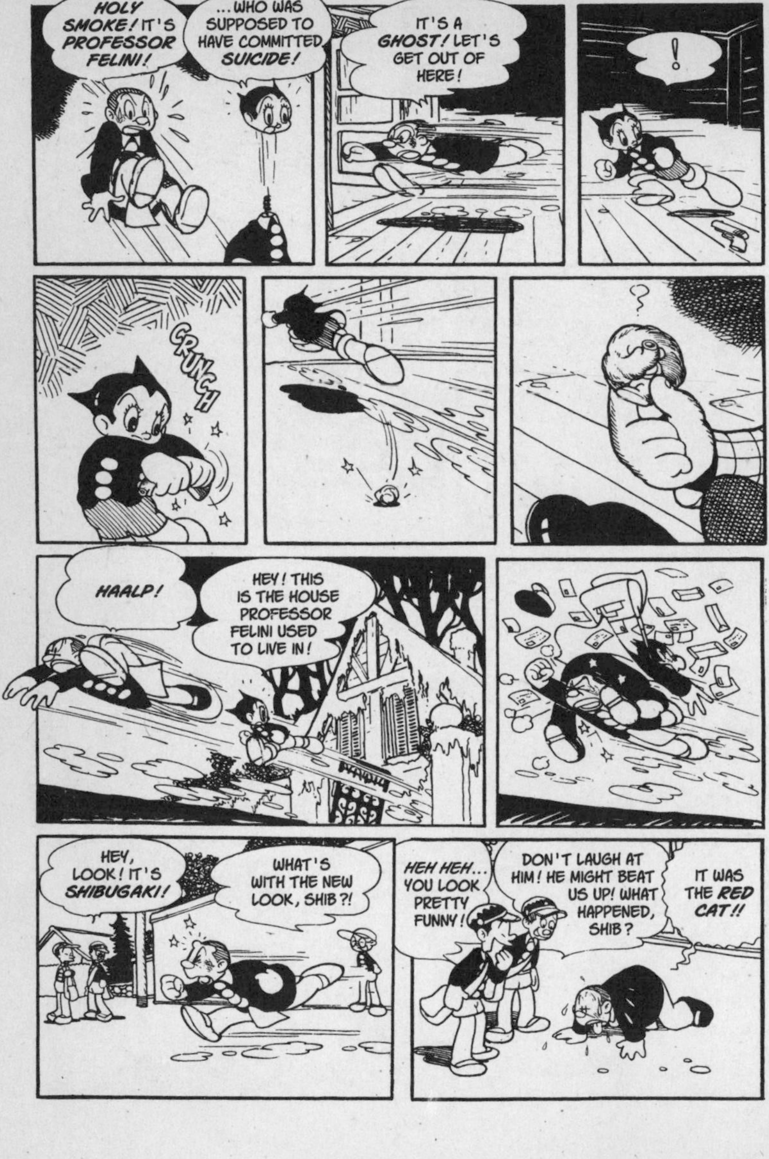
HOLY SMOKE! IT'S PROFESSOR FELINI!
...WHO WAS SUPPOSED TO HAVE COMMITTED SUICIDE!
IT'S A GHOST! LET'S GET OUT OF HERE!
!
CRUNCH
?
HAALP!
HEY! THIS IS THE HOUSE PROFESSOR FELINI USED TO LIVE IN!
HEY, LOOK! IT'S SHIBUGAKI!
WHAT'S WITH THE NEW LOOK, SHIB?!
HEH HEH... YOU LOOK PRETTY FUNNY!
DON'T LAUGH AT HIM! HE MIGHT BEAT US UP! WHAT HAPPENED, SHIB?
IT WAS THE RED CAT!!

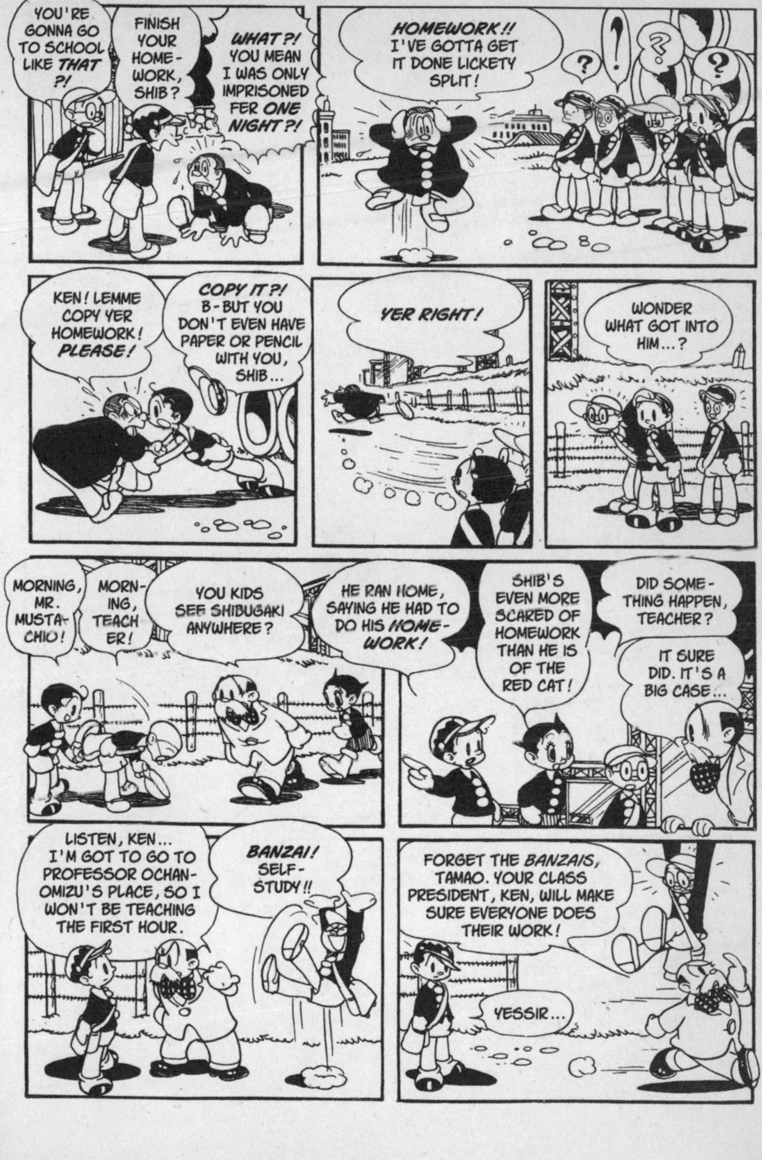
YOU'RE GONNA GO TO SCHOOL LIKE *THAT* ?!
FINISH YOUR HOMEWORK, SHIB?
WHAT?! YOU MEAN I WAS ONLY IMPRISONED FER *ONE NIGHT?!*
HOMEWORK!! I'VE GOTTA GET IT DONE LICKETY SPLIT!
KEN! LEMME COPY YER HOMEWORK! *PLEASE!*
COPY IT?! B-BUT YOU DON'T EVEN HAVE PAPER OR PENCIL WITH YOU, SHIB...
YER RIGHT!
WONDER WHAT GOT INTO HIM...?
MORNING, MR. MUSTACHIO!
MORNING, TEACHER!
YOU KIDS SEE SHIBUGAKI ANYWHERE?
HE RAN HOME, SAYING HE HAD TO DO HIS *HOMEWORK!*
SHIB'S EVEN MORE SCARED OF HOMEWORK THAN HE IS OF THE RED CAT!
DID SOMETHING HAPPEN, TEACHER?
IT SURE DID. IT'S A BIG CASE...
LISTEN, KEN... I'M GOT TO GO TO PROFESSOR OCHANOMIZU'S PLACE, SO I WON'T BE TEACHING THE FIRST HOUR.
BANZAI! SELF-STUDY!!
FORGET THE *BANZAIS*, TAMAO. YOUR CLASS PRESIDENT, KEN, WILL MAKE SURE EVERYONE DOES THEIR WORK!
YESSIR...

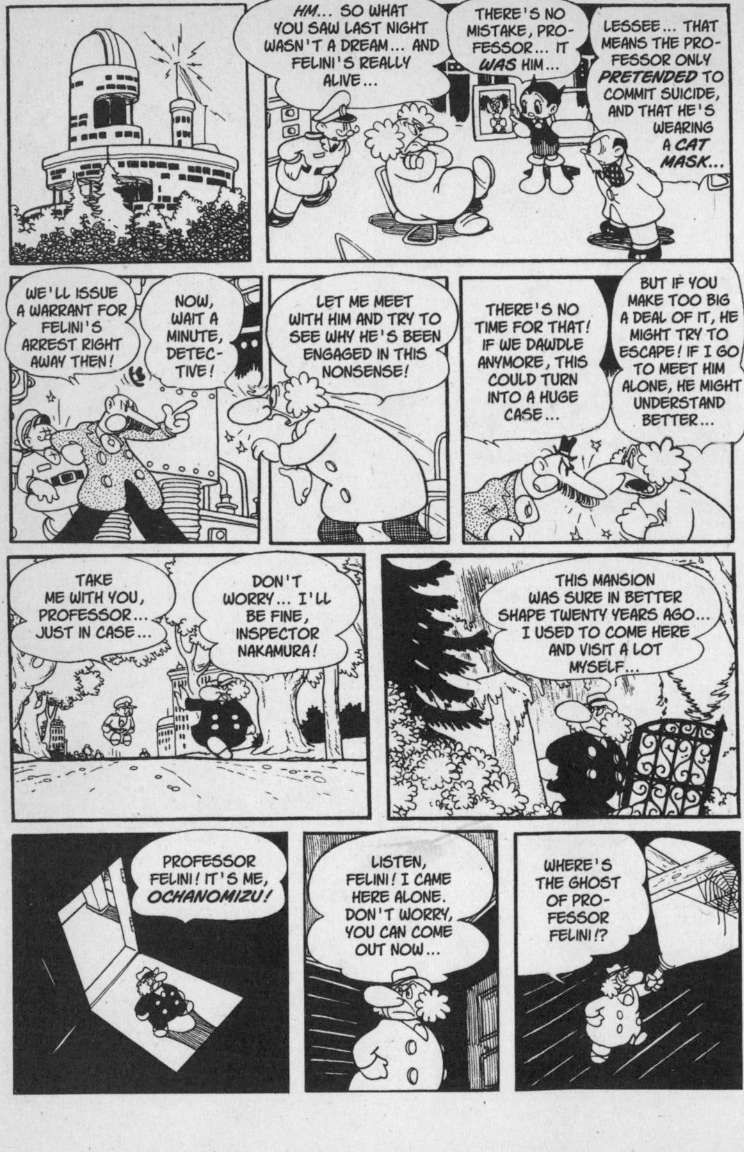
HM... SO WHAT YOU SAW LAST NIGHT WASN'T A DREAM... AND FELINI'S REALLY ALIVE...
THERE'S NO MISTAKE, PROFESSOR... IT WAS HIM...
LESSEE... THAT MEANS THE PROFESSOR ONLY PRETENDED TO COMMIT SUICIDE, AND THAT HE'S WEARING A CAT MASK...
WE'LL ISSUE A WARRANT FOR FELINI'S ARREST RIGHT AWAY THEN!
NOW, WAIT A MINUTE, DETECTIVE!
LET ME MEET WITH HIM AND TRY TO SEE WHY HE'S BEEN ENGAGED IN THIS NONSENSE!
THERE'S NO TIME FOR THAT! IF WE DAWDLE ANYMORE, THIS COULD TURN INTO A HUGE CASE...
BUT IF YOU MAKE TOO BIG A DEAL OF IT, HE MIGHT TRY TO ESCAPE! IF I GO TO MEET HIM ALONE, HE MIGHT UNDERSTAND BETTER...
TAKE ME WITH YOU, PROFESSOR... JUST IN CASE...
DON'T WORRY... I'LL BE FINE, INSPECTOR NAKAMURA!
THIS MANSION WAS SURE IN BETTER SHAPE TWENTY YEARS AGO... I USED TO COME HERE AND VISIT A LOT MYSELF...
PROFESSOR FELINI! IT'S ME, OCHANOMIZU!
LISTEN, FELINI! I CAME HERE ALONE. DON'T WORRY, YOU CAN COME OUT NOW...
WHERE'S THE GHOST OF PROFESSOR FELINI!?

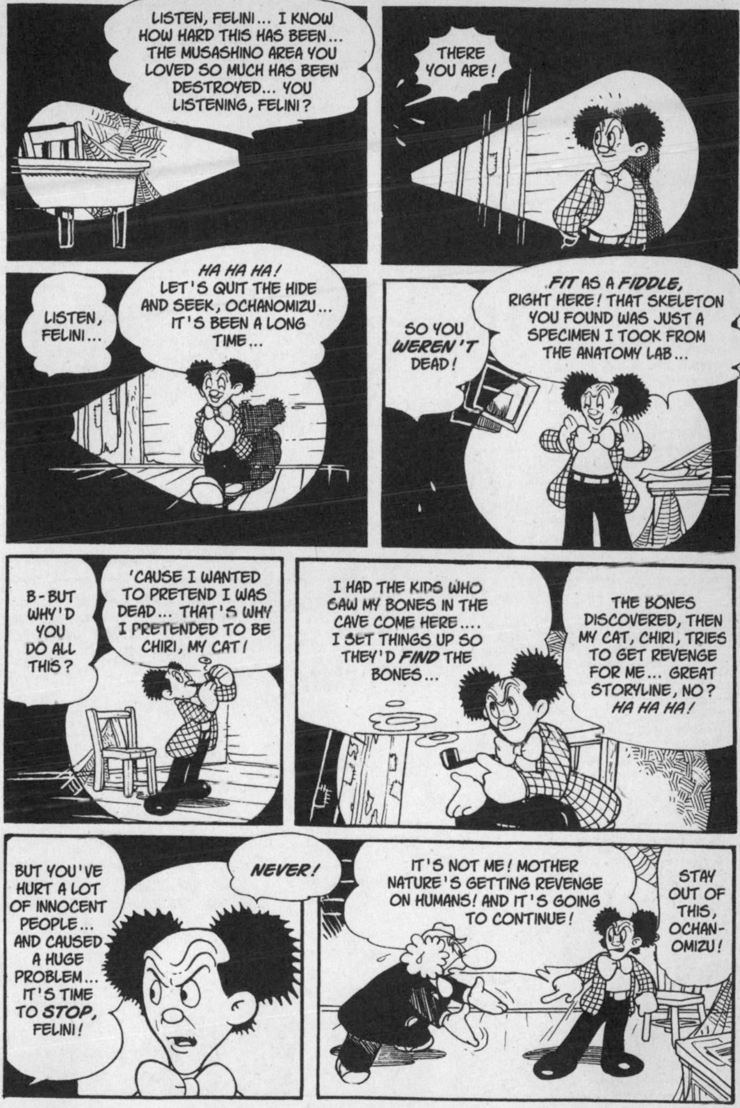
LISTEN, FELINI... I KNOW HOW HARD THIS HAS BEEN... THE MUSASHINO AREA YOU LOVED SO MUCH HAS BEEN DESTROYED... YOU LISTENING, FELINI?
THERE YOU ARE!
LISTEN, FELINI...
HA HA HA! LET'S QUIT THE HIDE AND SEEK, OCHANOMIZU... IT'S BEEN A LONG TIME...
SO YOU WEREN'T DEAD!
FIT AS A FIDDLE, RIGHT HERE! THAT SKELETON YOU FOUND WAS JUST A SPECIMEN I TOOK FROM THE ANATOMY LAB...
B-BUT WHY'D YOU DO ALL THIS?
'CAUSE I WANTED TO PRETEND I WAS DEAD... THAT'S WHY I PRETENDED TO BE CHIRI, MY CAT!
I HAD THE KIDS WHO SAW MY BONES IN THE CAVE COME HERE.... I SET THINGS UP SO THEY'D FIND THE BONES...
THE BONES DISCOVERED, THEN MY CAT, CHIRI, TRIES TO GET REVENGE FOR ME... GREAT STORYLINE, NO? HA HA HA!
BUT YOU'VE HURT A LOT OF INNOCENT PEOPLE... AND CAUSED A HUGE PROBLEM... IT'S TIME TO STOP, FELINI!
NEVER!
IT'S NOT ME! MOTHER NATURE'S GETTING REVENGE ON HUMANS! AND IT'S GOING TO CONTINUE!
STAY OUT OF THIS, OCHANOMIZU!

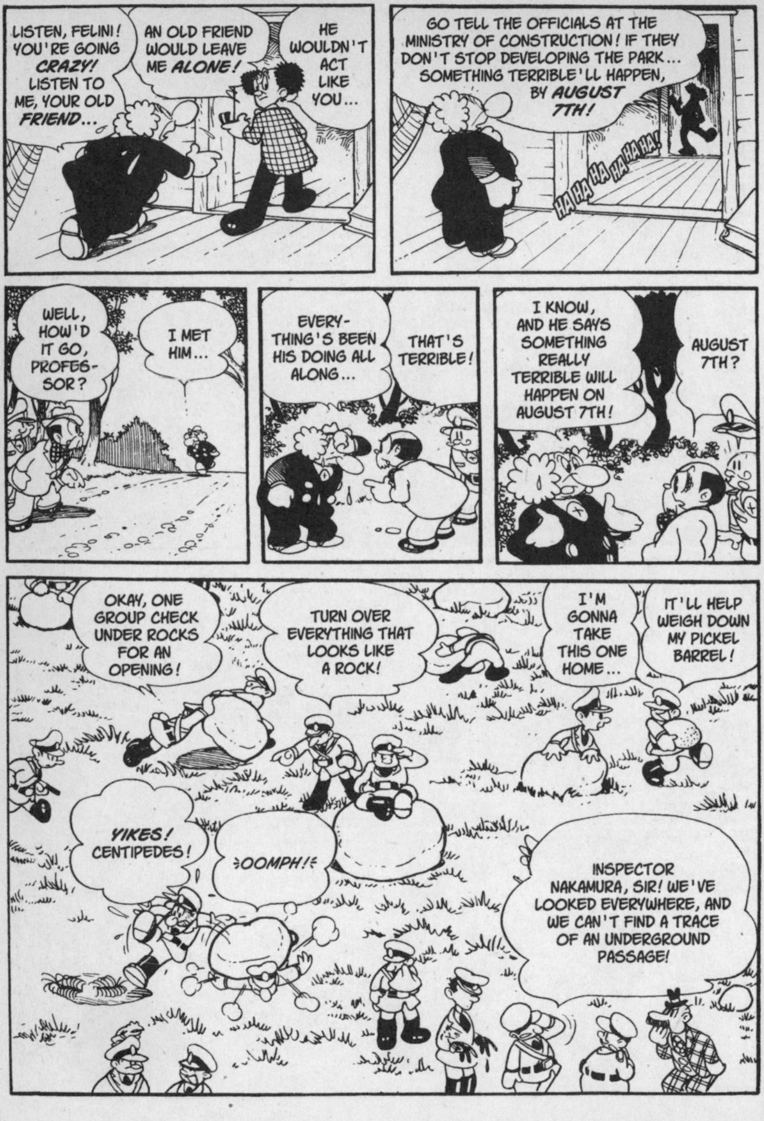
LISTEN, FELINI! YOU'RE GOING CRAZY! LISTEN TO ME, YOUR OLD FRIEND...
AN OLD FRIEND WOULD LEAVE ME ALONE!
HE WOULDN'T ACT LIKE YOU...
GO TELL THE OFFICIALS AT THE MINISTRY OF CONSTRUCTION! IF THEY DON'T STOP DEVELOPING THE PARK... SOMETHING TERRIBLE'LL HAPPEN, BY AUGUST 7TH!
HA HA HA HA HA HA!
WELL, HOW'D IT GO, PROFES-SOR?
I MET HIM...
EVERY-THING'S BEEN HIS DOING ALL ALONG...
THAT'S TERRIBLE!
I KNOW, AND HE SAYS SOMETHING REALLY TERRIBLE WILL HAPPEN ON AUGUST 7TH!
AUGUST 7TH?
OKAY, ONE GROUP CHECK UNDER ROCKS FOR AN OPENING!
TURN OVER EVERYTHING THAT LOOKS LIKE A ROCK!
I'M GONNA TAKE THIS ONE HOME...
IT'LL HELP WEIGH DOWN MY PICKEL BARREL!
YIKES! CENTIPEDES!
OOMPH!
INSPECTOR NAKAMURA, SIR! WE'VE LOOKED EVERYWHERE, AND WE CAN'T FIND A TRACE OF AN UNDERGROUND PASSAGE!

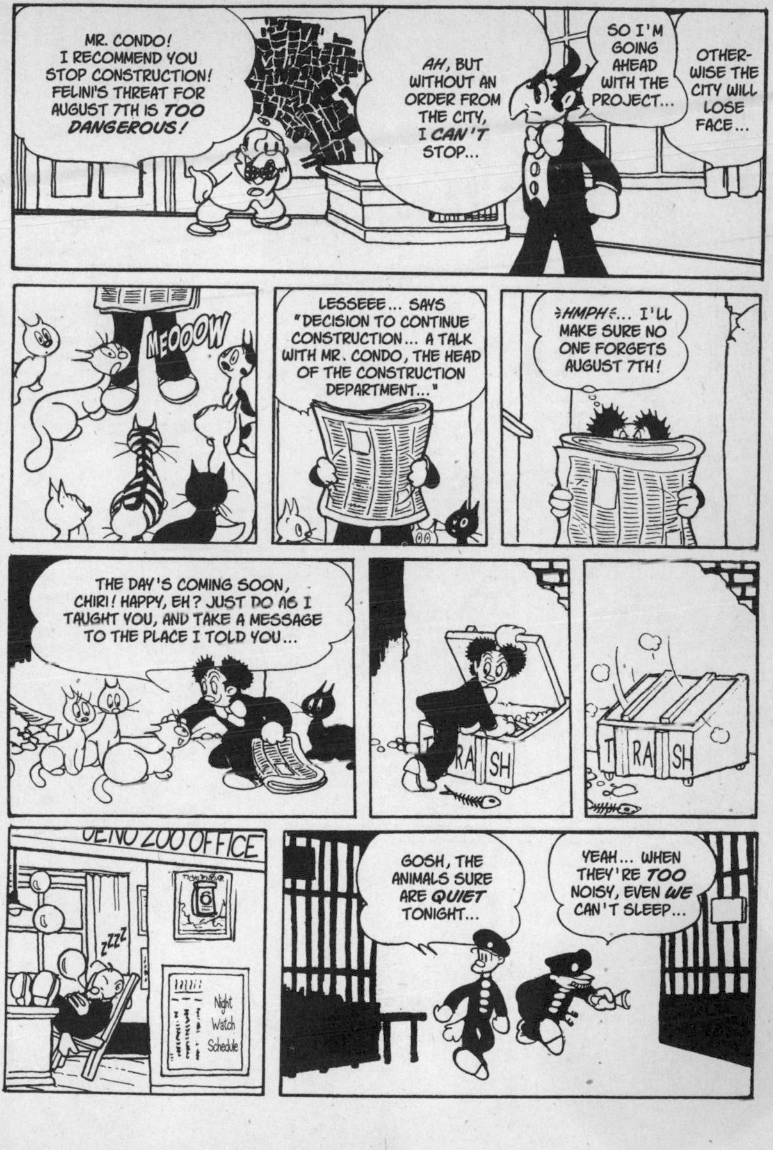
MR. CONDO! I RECOMMEND YOU STOP CONSTRUCTION! FELINI'S THREAT FOR AUGUST 7TH IS TOO DANGEROUS!
AH, BUT WITHOUT AN ORDER FROM THE CITY, I CAN'T STOP...
SO I'M GOING AHEAD WITH THE PROJECT...
OTHER-WISE THE CITY WILL LOSE FACE...
MEOOOW
LESSEEE... SAYS "DECISION TO CONTINUE CONSTRUCTION... A TALK WITH MR. CONDO, THE HEAD OF THE CONSTRUCTION DEPARTMENT..."
HMPH... I'LL MAKE SURE NO ONE FORGETS AUGUST 7TH!
THE DAY'S COMING SOON, CHIRI! HAPPY, EH? JUST DO AS I TAUGHT YOU, AND TAKE A MESSAGE TO THE PLACE I TOLD YOU...
TRASH
TRASH
UENO ZOO OFFICE
ZZZZ
Night Watch Schedule
GOSH, THE ANIMALS SURE ARE QUIET TONIGHT...
YEAH... WHEN THEY'RE TOO NOISY, EVEN WE CAN'T SLEEP...

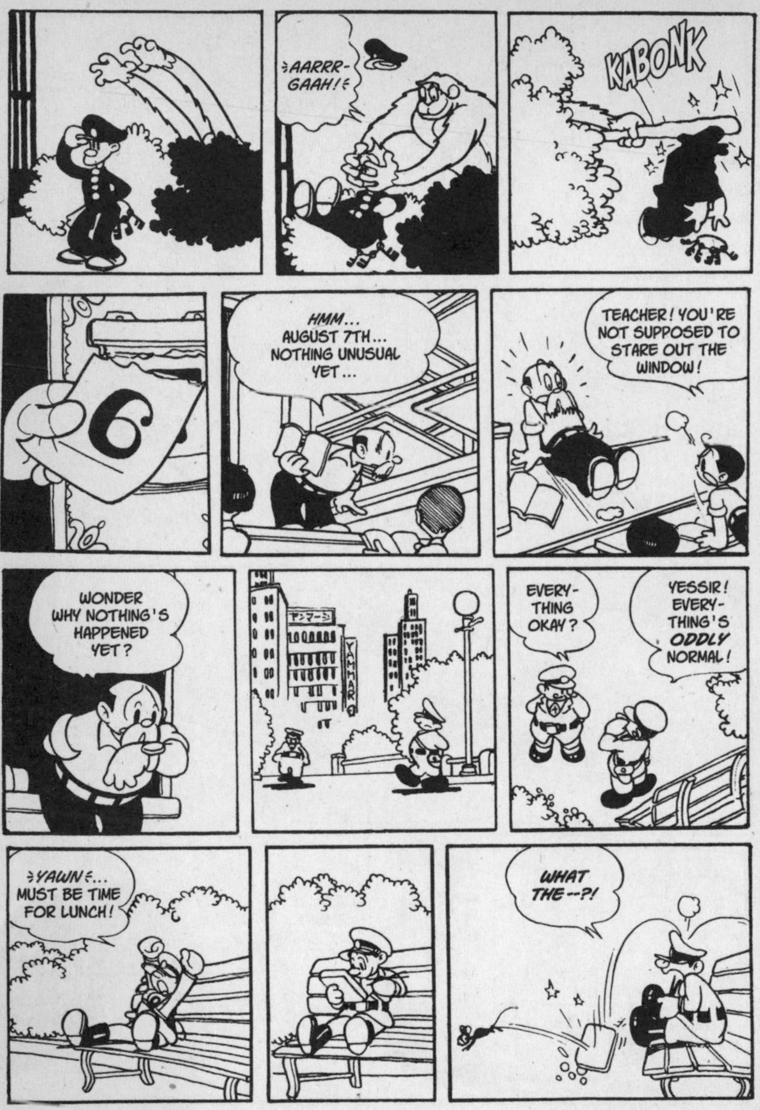
AARRR-GAAH!
KABONK
HMM... AUGUST 7TH... NOTHING UNUSUAL YET...
TEACHER! YOU'RE NOT SUPPOSED TO STARE OUT THE WINDOW!
WONDER WHY NOTHING'S HAPPENED YET?
ヤンマー
YANMAR
EVERY-THING OKAY?
YESSIR! EVERY-THING'S ODDLY NORMAL!
YAWN... MUST BE TIME FOR LUNCH!
WHAT THE--?!

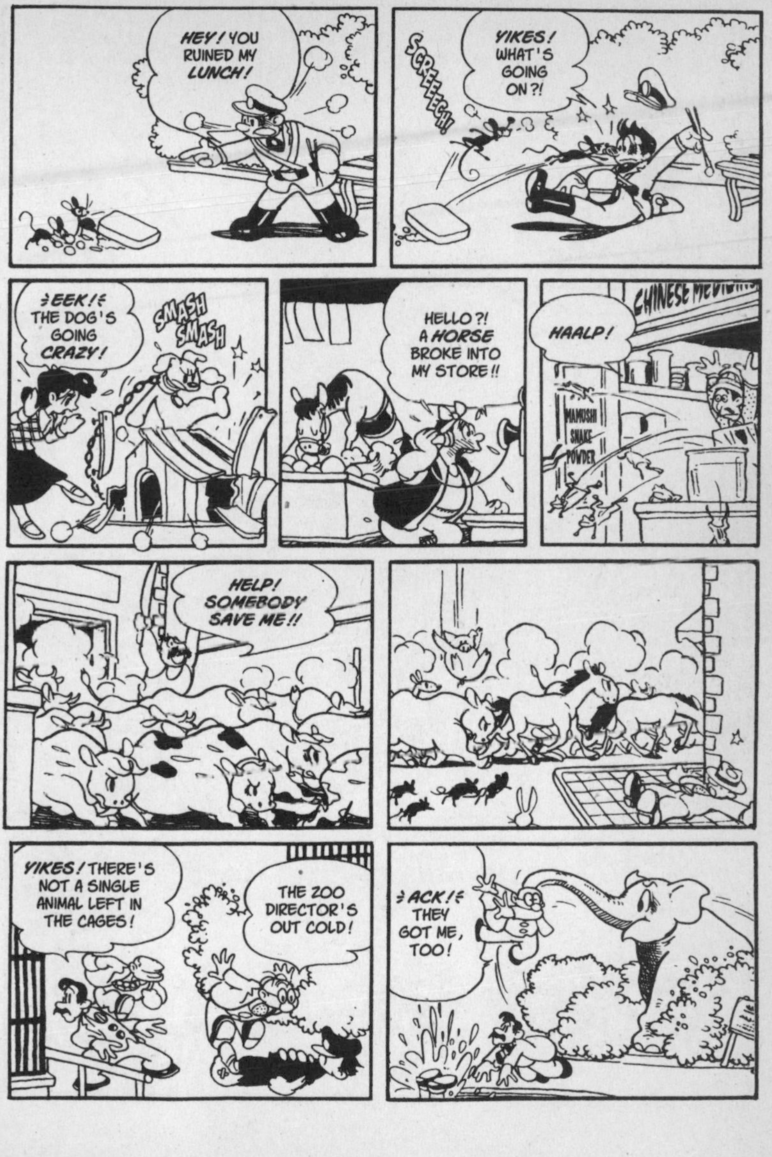
HEY! YOU RUINED MY LUNCH!
SCREEECH!
YIKES! WHAT'S GOING ON?!
EEK! THE DOG'S GOING CRAZY!
SMASH SMASH
HELLO?! A HORSE BROKE INTO MY STORE!!
CHINESE MEDIC
HAALP!
MAMUSHI SNAKE POWDER
HELP! SOMEBODY SAVE ME!!
YIKES! THERE'S NOT A SINGLE ANIMAL LEFT IN THE CAGES!
THE ZOO DIRECTOR'S OUT COLD!
ACK! THEY GOT ME, TOO!

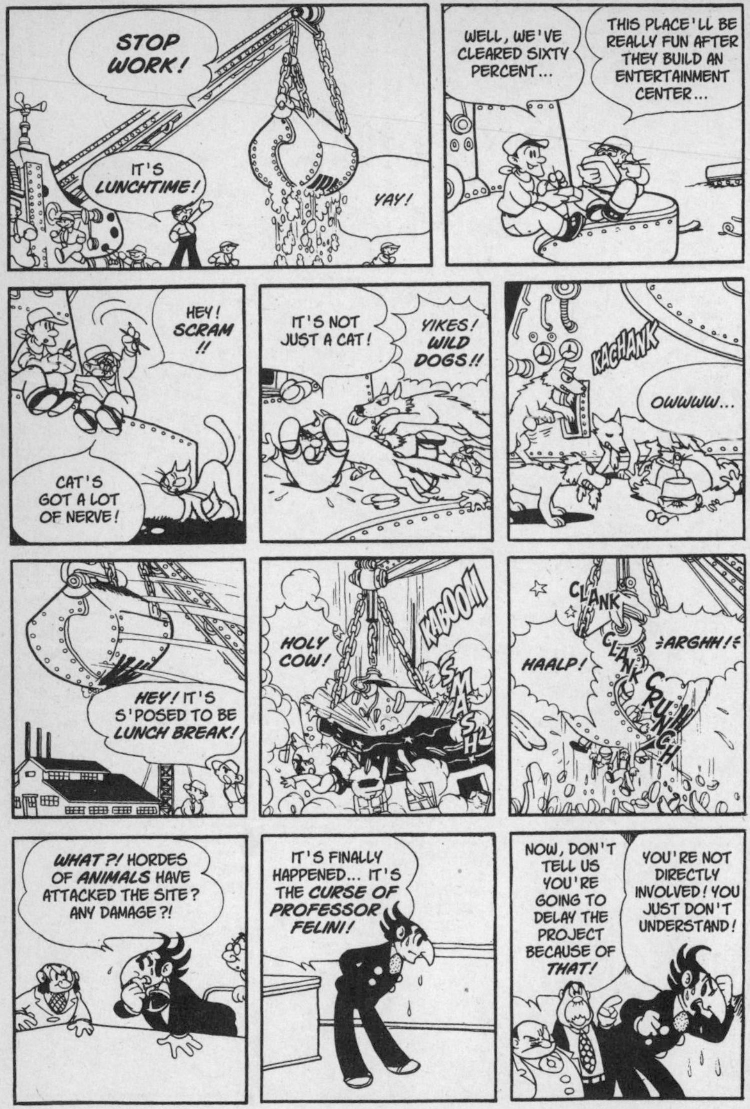
STOP WORK!
IT'S LUNCHTIME!
YAY!
WELL, WE'VE CLEARED SIXTY PERCENT...
THIS PLACE'LL BE REALLY FUN AFTER THEY BUILD AN ENTERTAINMENT CENTER...
HEY! SCRAM!!
CAT'S GOT A LOT OF NERVE!
IT'S NOT JUST A CAT!
YIKES! WILD DOGS!!
KACHANK
OWWWW...
HEY! IT'S S'POSED TO BE LUNCH BREAK!
HOLY COW!
KABOOM
SMASH
CLANK
HAALP!
CLANK
ARGHH!
CRUNCH
WHAT?! HORDES OF ANIMALS HAVE ATTACKED THE SITE? ANY DAMAGE?!
IT'S FINALLY HAPPENED... IT'S THE CURSE OF PROFESSOR FELINI!
NOW, DON'T TELL US YOU'RE GOING TO DELAY THE PROJECT BECAUSE OF THAT!
YOU'RE NOT DIRECTLY INVOLVED! YOU JUST DON'T UNDERSTAND!

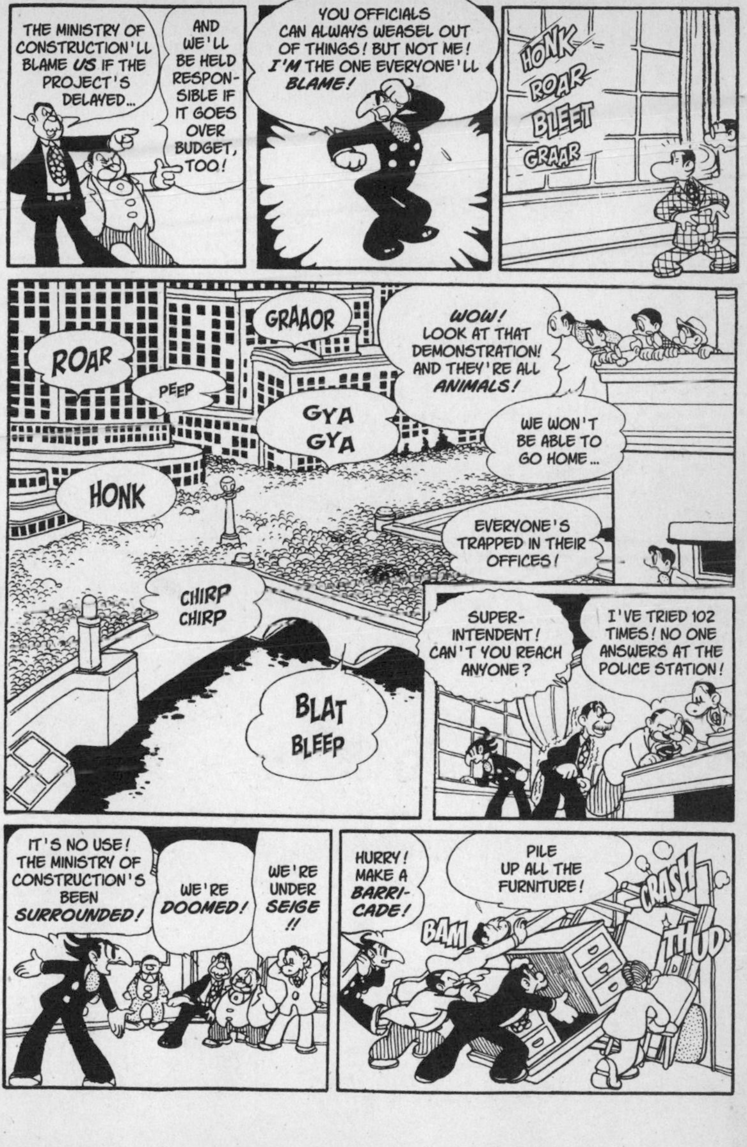
THE MINISTRY OF CONSTRUCTION'LL BLAME US IF THE PROJECT'S DELAYED...
AND WE'LL BE HELD RESPONSIBLE IF IT GOES OVER BUDGET, TOO!
YOU OFFICIALS CAN ALWAYS WEASEL OUT OF THINGS! BUT NOT ME! I'M THE ONE EVERYONE'LL BLAME!
HONK
ROAR
BLEET
GRAAR
ROAR
GRAAOR
PEEP
GYA GYA
HONK
CHIRP CHIRP
BLAT BLEEP
WOW! LOOK AT THAT DEMONSTRATION! AND THEY'RE ALL ANIMALS!
WE WON'T BE ABLE TO GO HOME...
EVERYONE'S TRAPPED IN THEIR OFFICES!
SUPER-INTENDENT! CAN'T YOU REACH ANYONE?
I'VE TRIED 102 TIMES! NO ONE ANSWERS AT THE POLICE STATION!
IT'S NO USE! THE MINISTRY OF CONSTRUCTION'S BEEN SURROUNDED!
WE'RE DOOMED!
WE'RE UNDER SEIGE !!
HURRY! MAKE A BARRICADE!
PILE UP ALL THE FURNITURE!
BAM
CRASH
THUD

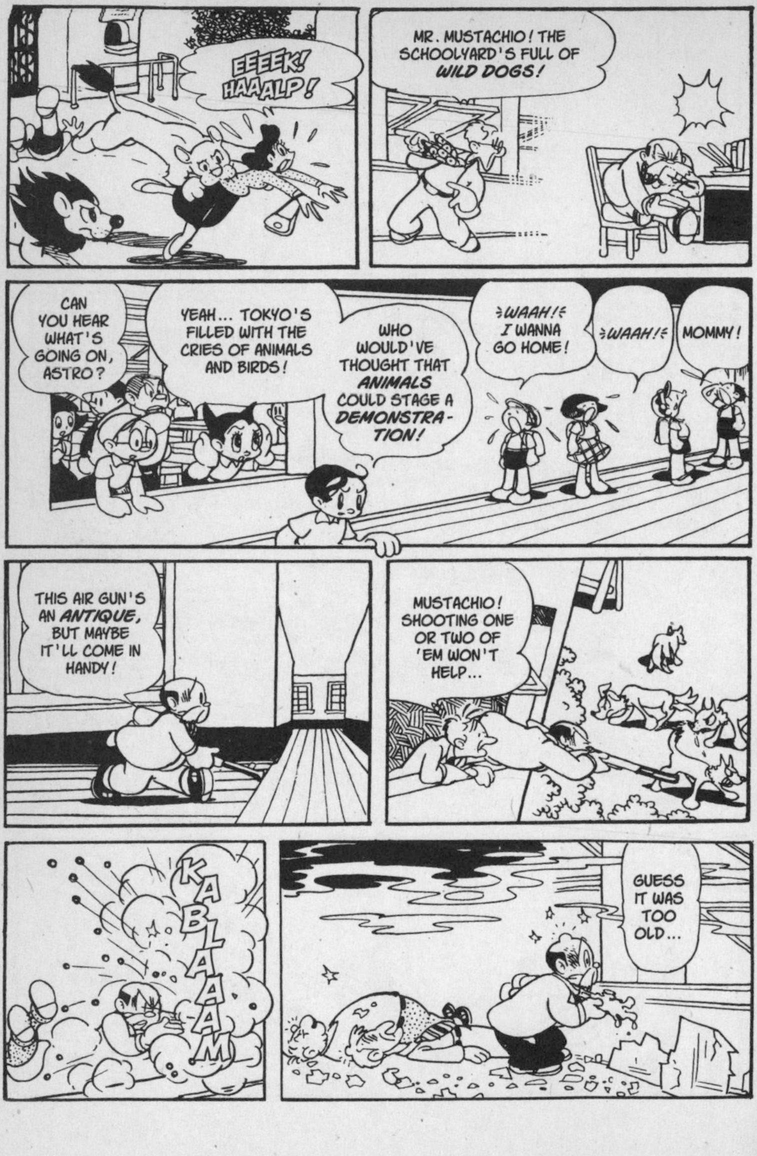

EEEEK! HAAALP!
MR. MUSTACHIO! THE SCHOOLYARD'S FULL OF WILD DOGS!
CAN YOU HEAR WHAT'S GOING ON, ASTRO?
YEAH... TOKYO'S FILLED WITH THE CRIES OF ANIMALS AND BIRDS!
WHO WOULD'VE THOUGHT THAT ANIMALS COULD STAGE A DEMONSTRATION!
WAAH! I WANNA GO HOME!
WAAH!
MOMMY!
THIS AIR GUN'S AN ANTIQUE, BUT MAYBE IT'LL COME IN HANDY!
MUSTACHIO! SHOOTING ONE OR TWO OF 'EM WON'T HELP...
KABLAAAAM
GUESS IT WAS TOO OLD...

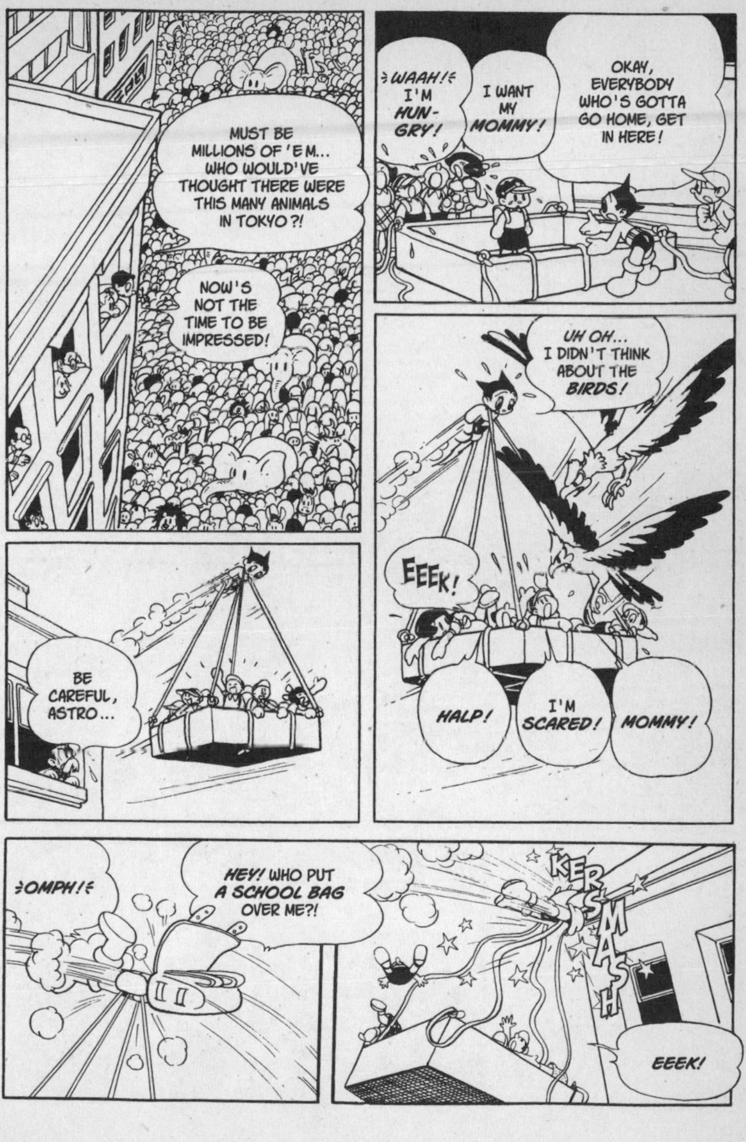
MUST BE MILLIONS OF 'EM... WHO WOULD'VE THOUGHT THERE WERE THIS MANY ANIMALS IN TOKYO?!
NOW'S NOT THE TIME TO BE IMPRESSED!
WAAH! I'M HUNGRY!
I WANT MY MOMMY!
OKAY, EVERYBODY WHO'S GOTTA GO HOME, GET IN HERE!
BE CAREFUL, ASTRO...
UH OH... I DIDN'T THINK ABOUT THE BIRDS!
EEEK!
HALP!
I'M SCARED!
MOMMY!
OMPH!
HEY! WHO PUT A SCHOOL BAG OVER ME?!
KERSMASH
EEEK!

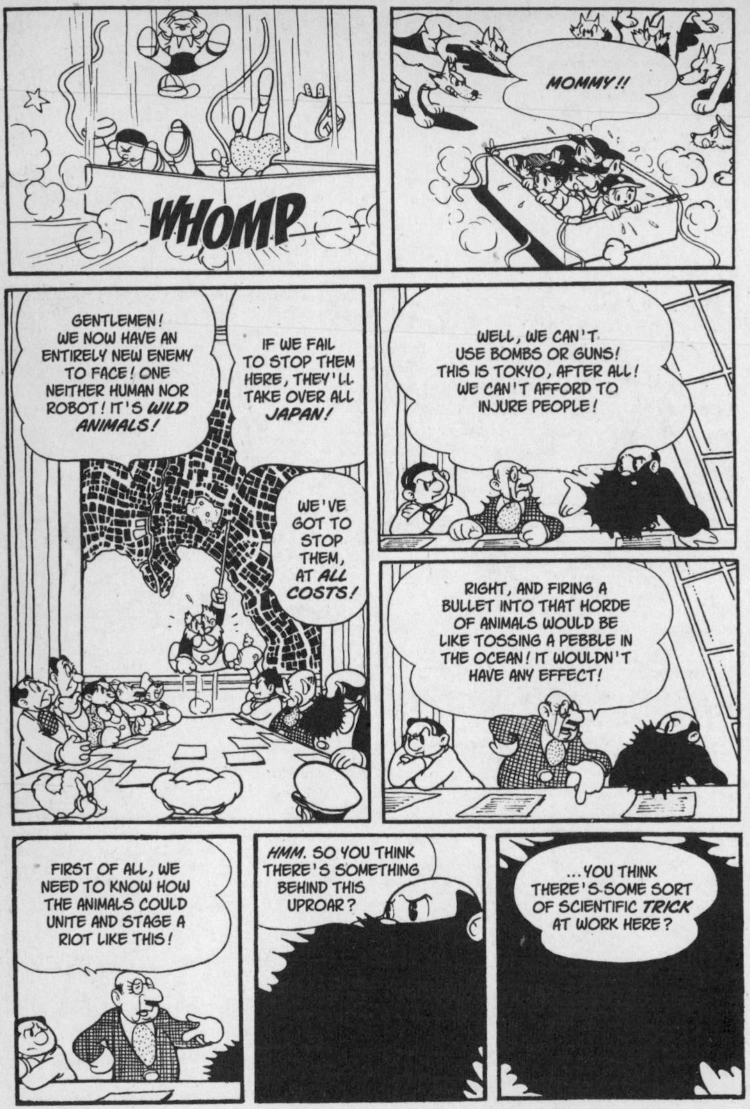
WHOMP
MOMMY!!
GENTLEMEN! WE NOW HAVE AN ENTIRELY NEW ENEMY TO FACE! ONE NEITHER HUMAN NOR ROBOT! IT'S WILD ANIMALS!
IF WE FAIL TO STOP THEM HERE, THEY'LL TAKE OVER ALL JAPAN!
WE'VE GOT TO STOP THEM, AT ALL COSTS!
WELL, WE CAN'T USE BOMBS OR GUNS! THIS IS TOKYO, AFTER ALL! WE CAN'T AFFORD TO INJURE PEOPLE!
RIGHT, AND FIRING A BULLET INTO THAT HORDE OF ANIMALS WOULD BE LIKE TOSSING A PEBBLE IN THE OCEAN! IT WOULDN'T HAVE ANY EFFECT!
FIRST OF ALL, WE NEED TO KNOW HOW THE ANIMALS COULD UNITE AND STAGE A RIOT LIKE THIS!
HMM. SO YOU THINK THERE'S SOMETHING BEHIND THIS UPROAR?
...YOU THINK THERE'S SOME SORT OF SCIENTIFIC TRICK AT WORK HERE?

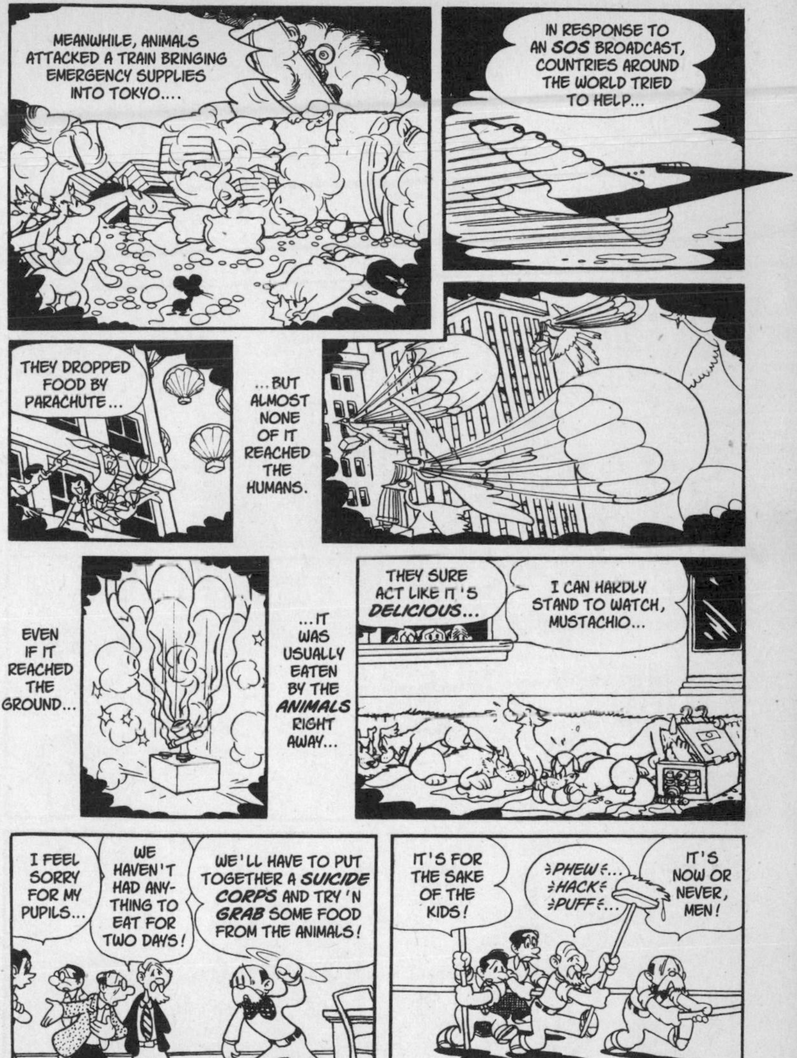
MEANWHILE, ANIMALS ATTACKED A TRAIN BRINGING EMERGENCY SUPPLIES INTO TOKYO....
IN RESPONSE TO AN SOS BROADCAST, COUNTRIES AROUND THE WORLD TRIED TO HELP...
THEY DROPPED FOOD BY PARACHUTE...
...BUT ALMOST NONE OF IT REACHED THE HUMANS.
EVEN IF IT REACHED THE GROUND...
...IT WAS USUALLY EATEN BY THE ANIMALS RIGHT AWAY...
THEY SURE ACT LIKE IT'S DELICIOUS...
I CAN HARDLY STAND TO WATCH, MUSTACHIO...
I FEEL SORRY FOR MY PUPILS...
WE HAVEN'T HAD ANY-THING TO EAT FOR TWO DAYS!
WE'LL HAVE TO PUT TOGETHER A SUICIDE CORPS AND TRY 'N GRAB SOME FOOD FROM THE ANIMALS!
IT'S FOR THE SAKE OF THE KIDS!
PHEW... *HACK* *PUFF*...
IT'S NOW OR NEVER, MEN!

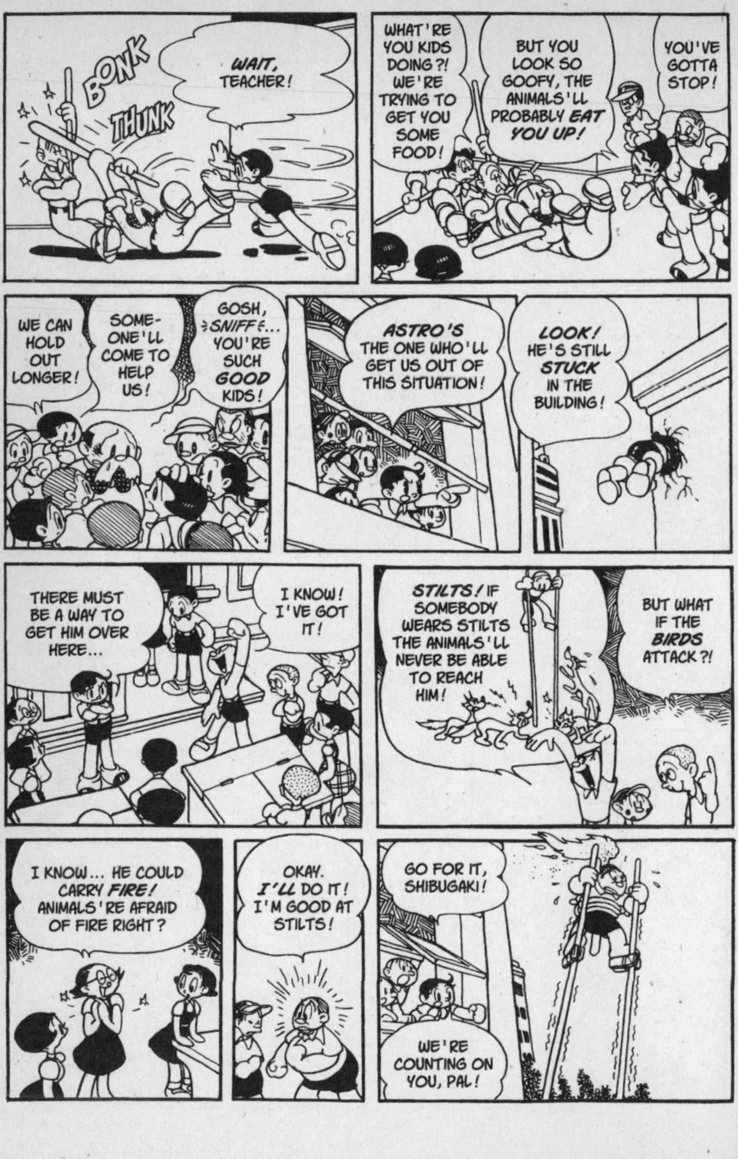
BONK
THUNK
WAIT, TEACHER!
WHAT'RE YOU KIDS DOING?! WE'RE TRYING TO GET YOU SOME FOOD!
BUT YOU LOOK SO GOOFY, THE ANIMALS'LL PROBABLY EAT YOU UP!
YOU'VE GOTTA STOP!
WE CAN HOLD OUT LONGER!
SOME-ONE'LL COME TO HELP US!
GOSH, SNIFF... YOU'RE SUCH GOOD KIDS!
ASTRO'S THE ONE WHO'LL GET US OUT OF THIS SITUATION!
LOOK! HE'S STILL STUCK IN THE BUILDING!
THERE MUST BE A WAY TO GET HIM OVER HERE...
I KNOW! I'VE GOT IT!
STILTS! IF SOMEBODY WEARS STILTS THE ANIMALS'LL NEVER BE ABLE TO REACH HIM!
BUT WHAT IF THE BIRDS ATTACK?!
I KNOW... HE COULD CARRY FIRE! ANIMALS'RE AFRAID OF FIRE RIGHT?
OKAY. I'LL DO IT! I'M GOOD AT STILTS!
GO FOR IT, SHIBUGAKI!
WE'RE COUNTING ON YOU, PAL!

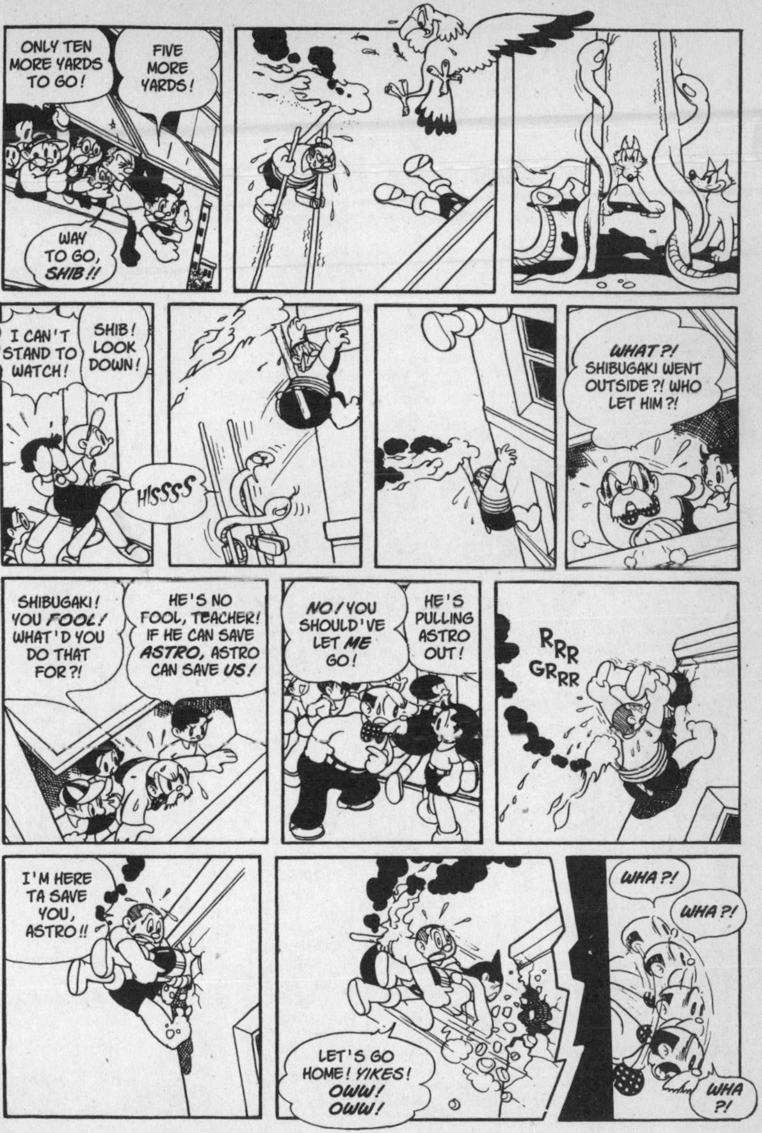
ONLY TEN MORE YARDS TO GO!
FIVE MORE YARDS!
WAY TO GO, SHIB!!
I CAN'T STAND TO WATCH!
SHIB! LOOK DOWN!
HISSSS
WHAT?! SHIBUGAKI WENT OUTSIDE?! WHO LET HIM?!
SHIBUGAKI! YOU FOOL! WHAT'D YOU DO THAT FOR?!
HE'S NO FOOL, TEACHER! IF HE CAN SAVE ASTRO, ASTRO CAN SAVE US!
NO! YOU SHOULD'VE LET ME GO!
HE'S PULLING ASTRO OUT!
RRR GRRR
I'M HERE TA SAVE YOU, ASTRO!!
LET'S GO HOME! YIKES! OWW! OWW!
WHA?!
WHA?!
WHA?!

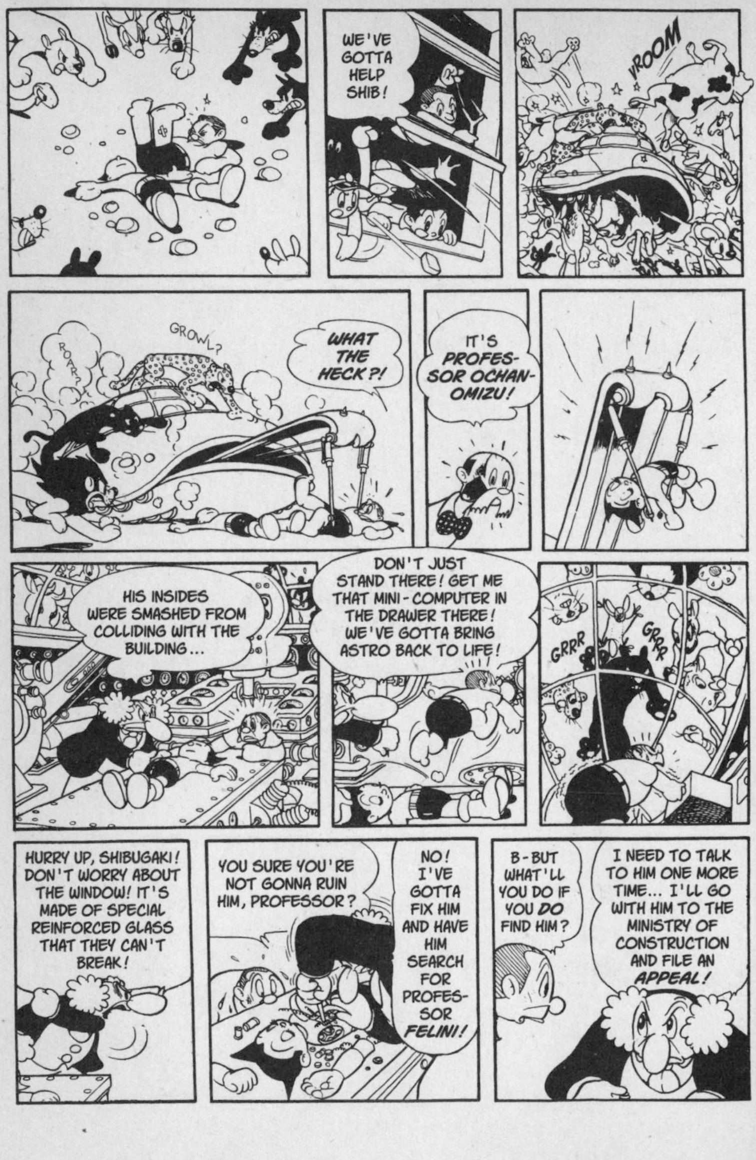
WE'VE GOTTA HELP SHIB!
VROOM
ROAR?
GROWL?
WHAT THE HECK?!
IT'S PROFES-SOR OCHAN-OMIZU!
HIS INSIDES WERE SMASHED FROM COLLIDING WITH THE BUILDING...
DON'T JUST STAND THERE! GET ME THAT MINI-COMPUTER IN THE DRAWER THERE! WE'VE GOTTA BRING ASTRO BACK TO LIFE!
GRRR
GRRR
HURRY UP, SHIBUGAKI! DON'T WORRY ABOUT THE WINDOW! IT'S MADE OF SPECIAL REINFORCED GLASS THAT THEY CAN'T BREAK!
YOU SURE YOU'RE NOT GONNA RUIN HIM, PROFESSOR?
NO! I'VE GOTTA FIX HIM AND HAVE HIM SEARCH FOR PROFES-SOR FELINI!
B-BUT WHAT'LL YOU DO IF YOU DO FIND HIM?
I NEED TO TALK TO HIM ONE MORE TIME... I'LL GO WITH HIM TO THE MINISTRY OF CONSTRUCTION AND FILE AN APPEAL!

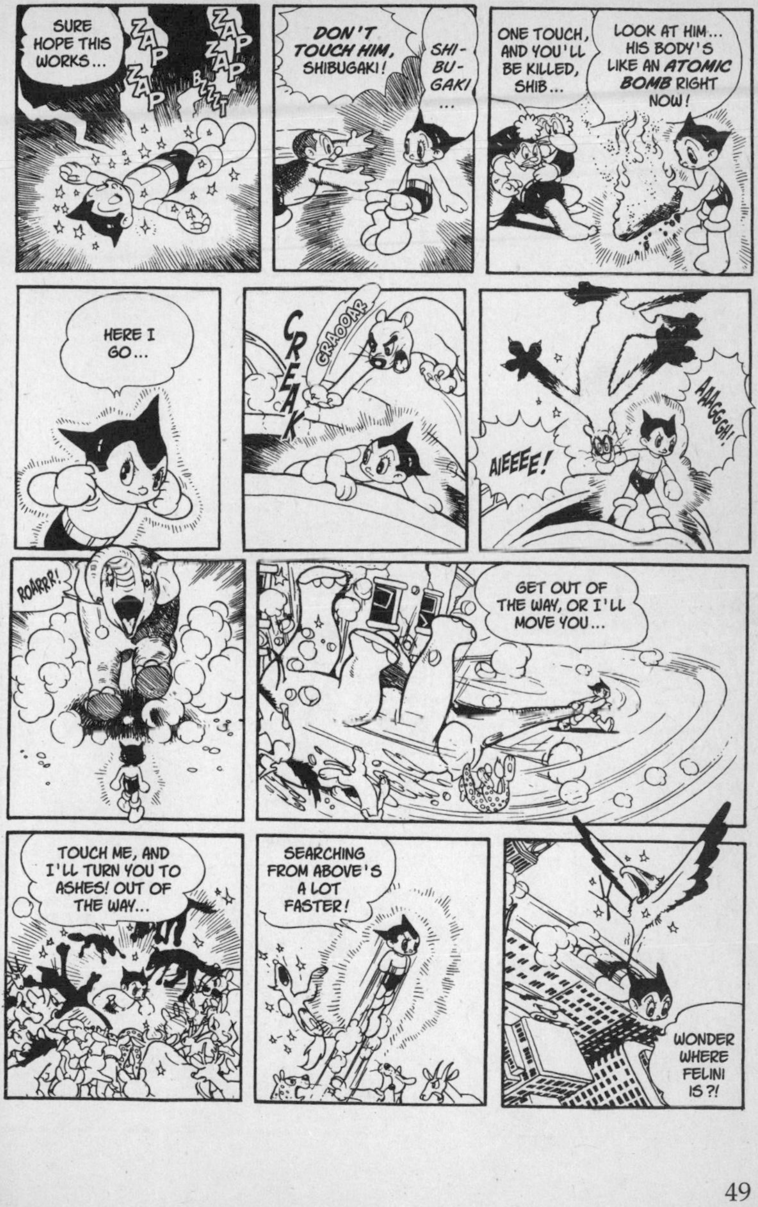
SURE HOPE THIS WORKS...
ZAP ZAP ZAP ZAP ZAP
BZZZT
DON'T TOUCH HIM, SHIBUGAKI!
SHI-BU-GAKI ...
ONE TOUCH, AND YOU'LL BE KILLED, SHIB...
LOOK AT HIM... HIS BODY'S LIKE AN ATOMIC BOMB RIGHT NOW!
HERE I GO...
CREAK
GRAOOAR
AIEEEE!
AAAGGGH!
ROARRR!
GET OUT OF THE WAY, OR I'LL MOVE YOU...
TOUCH ME, AND I'LL TURN YOU TO ASHES! OUT OF THE WAY...
SEARCHING FROM ABOVE'S A LOT FASTER!
WONDER WHERE FELINI IS?!

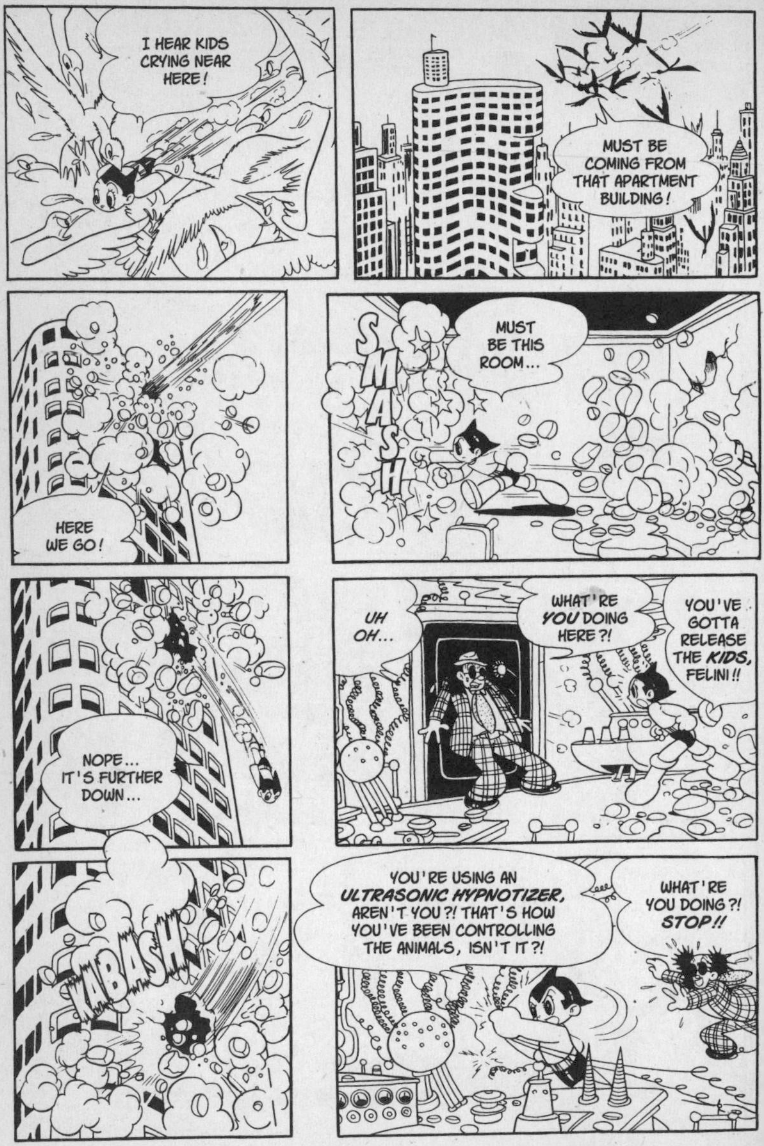
I HEAR KIDS CRYING NEAR HERE!
MUST BE COMING FROM THAT APARTMENT BUILDING!
HERE WE GO!
SMASH
MUST BE THIS ROOM...
NOPE... IT'S FURTHER DOWN...
UH OH...
WHAT'RE *YOU* DOING HERE?!
YOU'VE GOTTA RELEASE THE *KIDS*, FELINI!!
KABASH
YOU'RE USING AN *ULTRASONIC HYPNOTIZER*, AREN'T YOU?! THAT'S HOW YOU'VE BEEN CONTROLLING THE ANIMALS, ISN'T IT?!
WHAT'RE YOU DOING?! *STOP!!*

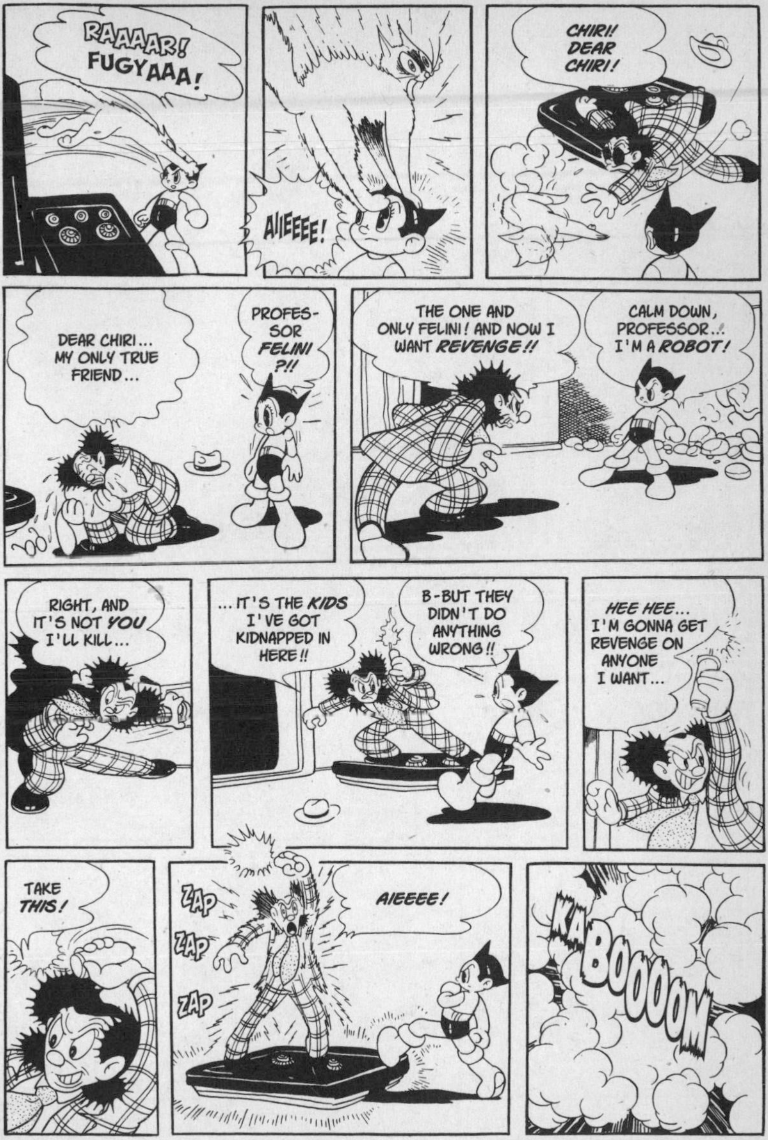
RAAAAR! FUGYAAA!
AIIEEEE!
CHIRI! DEAR CHIRI!
DEAR CHIRI... MY ONLY TRUE FRIEND...
PROFES-SOR FELINI ?!!
THE ONE AND ONLY FELINI! AND NOW I WANT REVENGE!!
CALM DOWN, PROFESSOR... I'M A ROBOT!
RIGHT, AND IT'S NOT YOU I'LL KILL...
... IT'S THE KIDS I'VE GOT KIDNAPPED IN HERE!!
B-BUT THEY DIDN'T DO ANYTHING WRONG!!
HEE HEE... I'M GONNA GET REVENGE ON ANYONE I WANT...
TAKE THIS!
ZAP
ZAP
ZAP
AIEEEE!
KABOOOOM

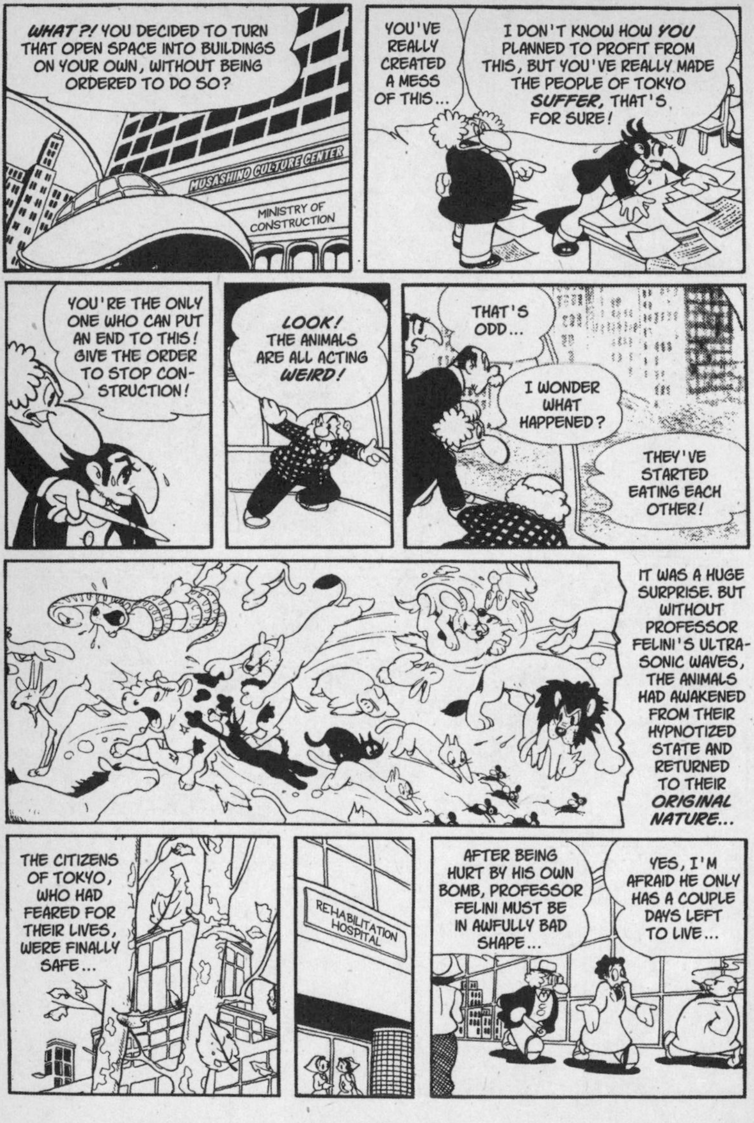
WHAT?! YOU DECIDED TO TURN THAT OPEN SPACE INTO BUILDINGS ON YOUR OWN, WITHOUT BEING ORDERED TO DO SO?
MUSASHINO CULTURE CENTER
MINISTRY OF CONSTRUCTION
YOU'VE REALLY CREATED A MESS OF THIS...
I DON'T KNOW HOW *YOU* PLANNED TO PROFIT FROM THIS, BUT YOU'VE REALLY MADE THE PEOPLE OF TOKYO *SUFFER,* THAT'S FOR SURE!
YOU'RE THE ONLY ONE WHO CAN PUT AN END TO THIS! GIVE THE ORDER TO STOP CONSTRUCTION!
LOOK! THE ANIMALS ARE ALL ACTING *WEIRD!*
THAT'S ODD...
I WONDER WHAT HAPPENED?
THEY'VE STARTED EATING EACH OTHER!
IT WAS A HUGE SURPRISE. BUT WITHOUT PROFESSOR FELINI'S ULTRASONIC WAVES, THE ANIMALS HAD AWAKENED FROM THEIR HYPNOTIZED STATE AND RETURNED TO THEIR *ORIGINAL NATURE...*
THE CITIZENS OF TOKYO, WHO HAD FEARED FOR THEIR LIVES, WERE FINALLY SAFE...
REHABILITATION HOSPITAL
AFTER BEING HURT BY HIS OWN BOMB, PROFESSOR FELINI MUST BE IN AWFULLY BAD SHAPE...
YES, I'M AFRAID HE ONLY HAS A COUPLE DAYS LEFT TO LIVE...

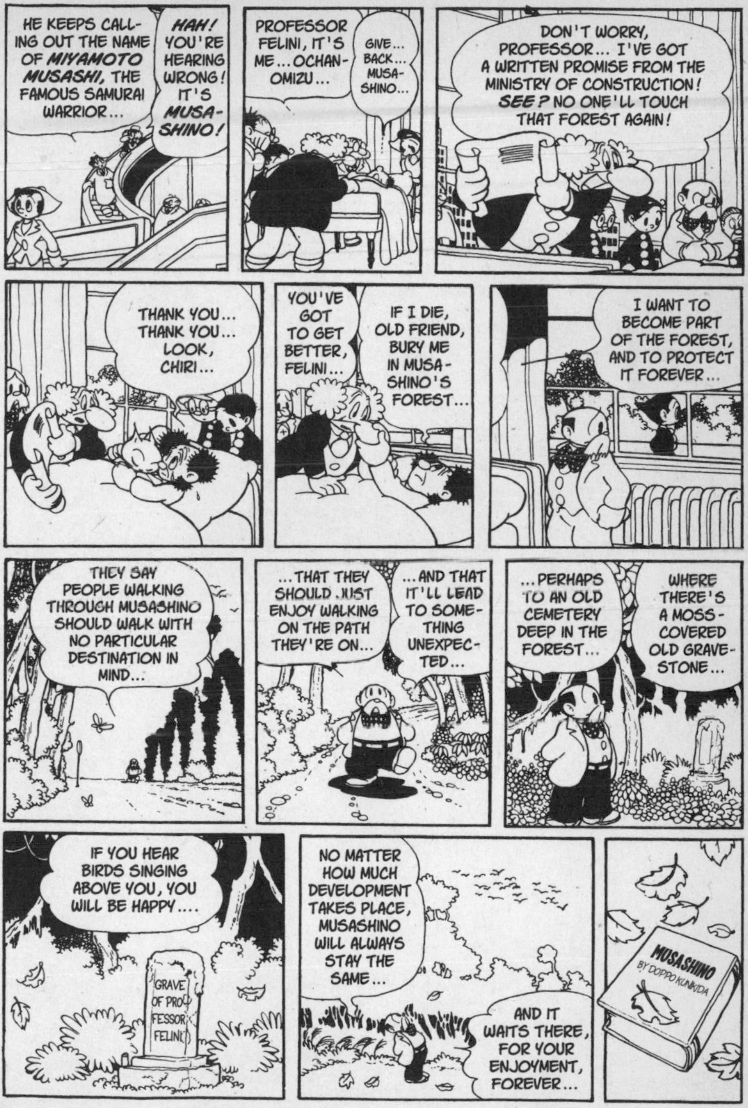

HE KEEPS CALLING OUT THE NAME OF *MIYAMOTO MUSASHI,* THE FAMOUS SAMURAI WARRIOR...
HAH! YOU'RE HEARING WRONG! IT'S *MUSASHINO!*
PROFESSOR FELINI, IT'S ME... OCHANOMIZU...
GIVE... BACK... MUSASHINO...
DON'T WORRY, PROFESSOR... I'VE GOT A WRITTEN PROMISE FROM THE MINISTRY OF CONSTRUCTION! *SEE?* NO ONE'LL TOUCH THAT FOREST AGAIN!
THANK YOU... THANK YOU... LOOK, CHIRI...
YOU'VE GOT TO GET BETTER, FELINI...
IF I DIE, OLD FRIEND, BURY ME IN MUSASHINO'S FOREST...
I WANT TO BECOME PART OF THE FOREST, AND TO PROTECT IT FOREVER...
THEY SAY PEOPLE WALKING THROUGH MUSASHINO SHOULD WALK WITH NO PARTICULAR DESTINATION IN MIND...
...THAT THEY SHOULD JUST ENJOY WALKING ON THE PATH THEY'RE ON...
...AND THAT IT'LL LEAD TO SOMETHING UNEXPECTED...
...PERHAPS TO AN OLD CEMETERY DEEP IN THE FOREST...
WHERE THERE'S A MOSS-COVERED OLD GRAVESTONE...
IF YOU HEAR BIRDS SINGING ABOVE YOU, YOU WILL BE HAPPY....
GRAVE OF PROFESSOR FELINI
NO MATTER HOW MUCH DEVELOPMENT TAKES PLACE, MUSASHINO WILL ALWAYS STAY THE SAME...
AND IT WAITS THERE, FOR YOUR ENJOYMENT, FOREVER...
MUSASHINO
BY DOPPO KUNIKIDA

THE MIDORO SWAMP

First serialized from August to November 1956
in *Shonen* magazine.

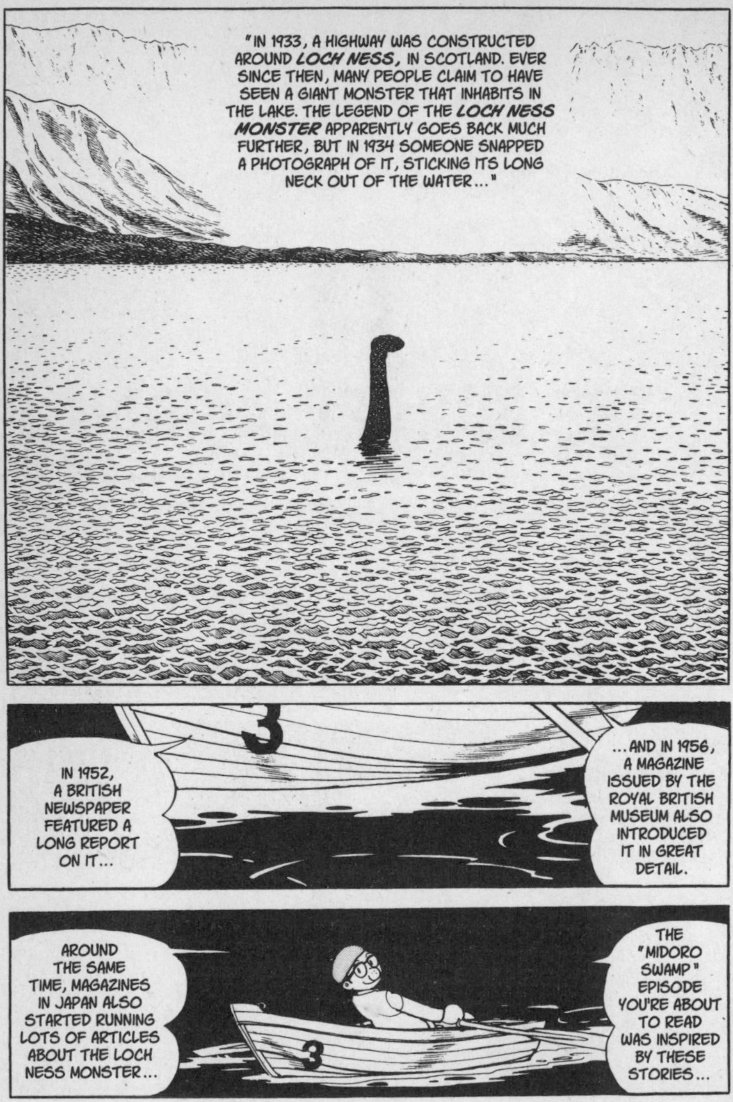
"IN 1933, A HIGHWAY WAS CONSTRUCTED AROUND LOCH NESS, IN SCOTLAND. EVER SINCE THEN, MANY PEOPLE CLAIM TO HAVE SEEN A GIANT MONSTER THAT INHABITS IN THE LAKE. THE LEGEND OF THE LOCH NESS MONSTER APPARENTLY GOES BACK MUCH FURTHER, BUT IN 1934 SOMEONE SNAPPED A PHOTOGRAPH OF IT, STICKING ITS LONG NECK OUT OF THE WATER..."
IN 1952, A BRITISH NEWSPAPER FEATURED A LONG REPORT ON IT...
...AND IN 1956, A MAGAZINE ISSUED BY THE ROYAL BRITISH MUSEUM ALSO INTRODUCED IT IN GREAT DETAIL.
AROUND THE SAME TIME, MAGAZINES IN JAPAN ALSO STARTED RUNNING LOTS OF ARTICLES ABOUT THE LOCH NESS MONSTER...
THE "MIDORO SWAMP" EPISODE YOU'RE ABOUT TO READ WAS INSPIRED BY THESE STORIES...

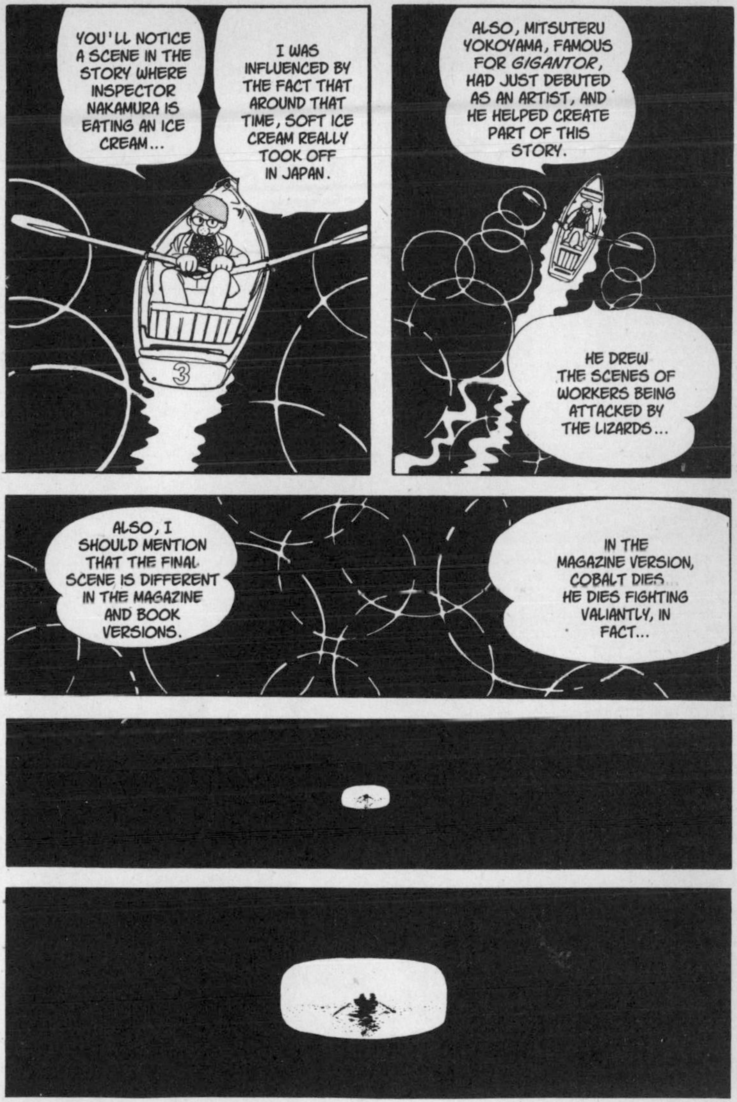
YOU'LL NOTICE A SCENE IN THE STORY WHERE INSPECTOR NAKAMURA IS EATING AN ICE CREAM...
I WAS INFLUENCED BY THE FACT THAT AROUND THAT TIME, SOFT ICE CREAM REALLY TOOK OFF IN JAPAN.
ALSO, MITSUTERU YOKOYAMA, FAMOUS FOR *GIGANTOR*, HAD JUST DEBUTED AS AN ARTIST, AND HE HELPED CREATE PART OF THIS STORY.
HE DREW THE SCENES OF WORKERS BEING ATTACKED BY THE LIZARDS...
ALSO, I SHOULD MENTION THAT THE FINAL SCENE IS DIFFERENT IN THE MAGAZINE AND BOOK VERSIONS.
IN THE MAGAZINE VERSION, COBALT DIES... HE DIES FIGHTING VALIANTLY, IN FACT...
3

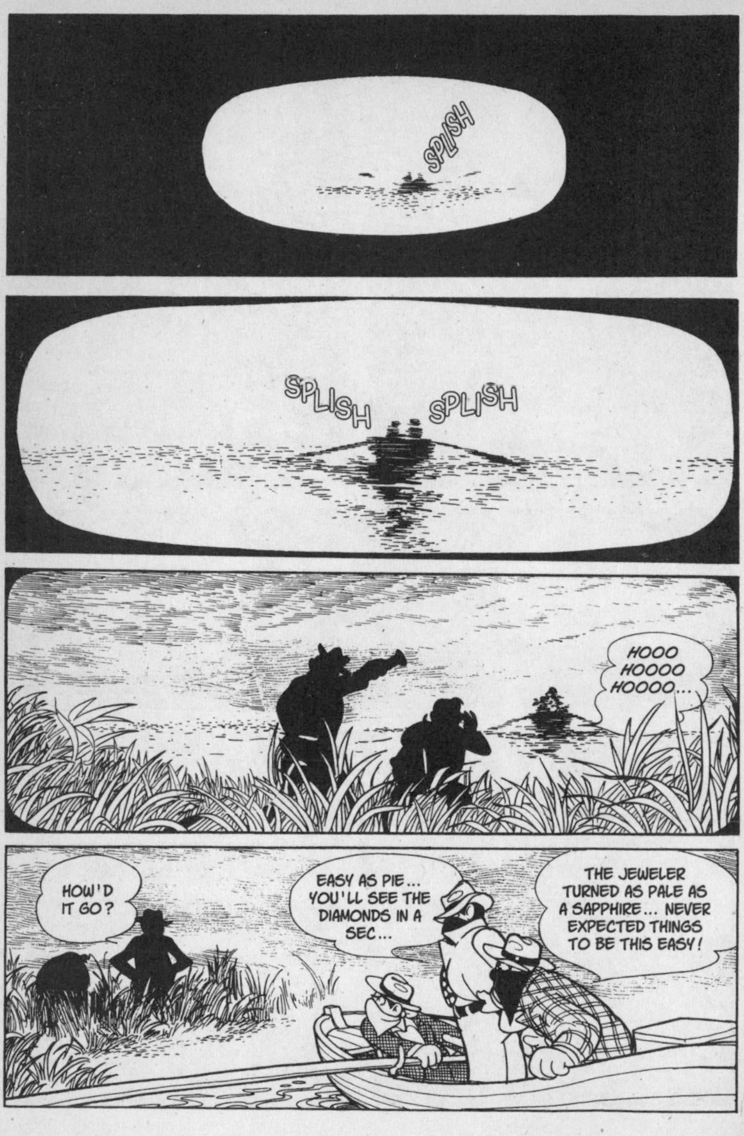
SPLISH
SPLISH
SPLISH
HOOO HOOOO HOOOO...
HOW'D IT GO?
EASY AS PIE... YOU'LL SEE THE DIAMONDS IN A SEC...
THE JEWELER TURNED AS PALE AS A SAPPHIRE... NEVER EXPECTED THINGS TO BE THIS EASY!

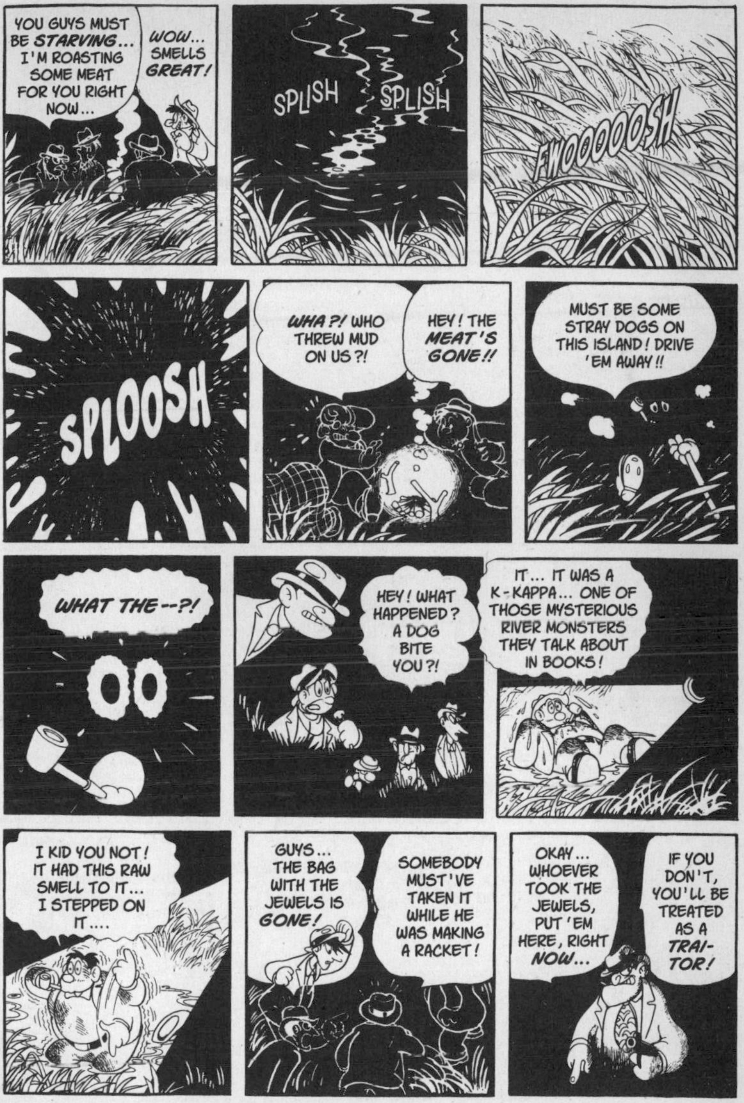
YOU GUYS MUST BE STARVING... I'M ROASTING SOME MEAT FOR YOU RIGHT NOW...
WOW... SMELLS GREAT!
SPLISH SPLISH
FWOOOOOSH
SPLOOSH
WHA?! WHO THREW MUD ON US?!
HEY! THE MEAT'S GONE!!
MUST BE SOME STRAY DOGS ON THIS ISLAND! DRIVE 'EM AWAY!!
WHAT THE--?!
HEY! WHAT HAPPENED? A DOG BITE YOU?!
IT... IT WAS A K-KAPPA... ONE OF THOSE MYSTERIOUS RIVER MONSTERS THEY TALK ABOUT IN BOOKS!
I KID YOU NOT! IT HAD THIS RAW SMELL TO IT... I STEPPED ON IT....
GUYS... THE BAG WITH THE JEWELS IS GONE!
SOMEBODY MUST'VE TAKEN IT WHILE HE WAS MAKING A RACKET!
OKAY... WHOEVER TOOK THE JEWELS, PUT 'EM HERE, RIGHT NOW...
IF YOU DON'T, YOU'LL BE TREATED AS A TRAI-TOR!

IT WASN'T ME, I *SWEAR!*

HAALP!

BLAM

BLAM

BLAM

YOU READ THE ARTICLE ABOUT THE TRAGEDY AT MIDORO SWAMP LAST NIGHT, INSPECTOR? ABOUT THE FIVE JEWELRY THIEVES...?

THE ONE ABOUT THE FIVE MEN, ALL FOUND HORRIBLY *MURDERED?* YUP, I READ IT ALL RIGHT. A MOST *BIZARRE* CASE...

IT SEEMS CRAZY, BUT PEOPLE DO SAY THERE'S SOMETHING AWFULLY *WEIRD* OUT THERE IN THAT SWAMP...

IN THE SUBURBS OF MODERN TOKYO? COME ON, YOU'VE GOTTA BE *KIDDING!*

HOTEL MIDORO

MAN, AM I EVER BEAT...

I NEED SOME REAL ENERGY... COULD YOU COOK ME UP A LEG OF BEEF?

THAT'S A PRO BOXER FOR YA... A HUGE APPETITE, EVEN IN THE SUMMER!

YOU'RE GOING EAT THAT ALL *YOURSELF,* SIR?

SURE AM... GOSH, THIS MEAT'S *TOUGH...*

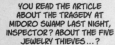

60

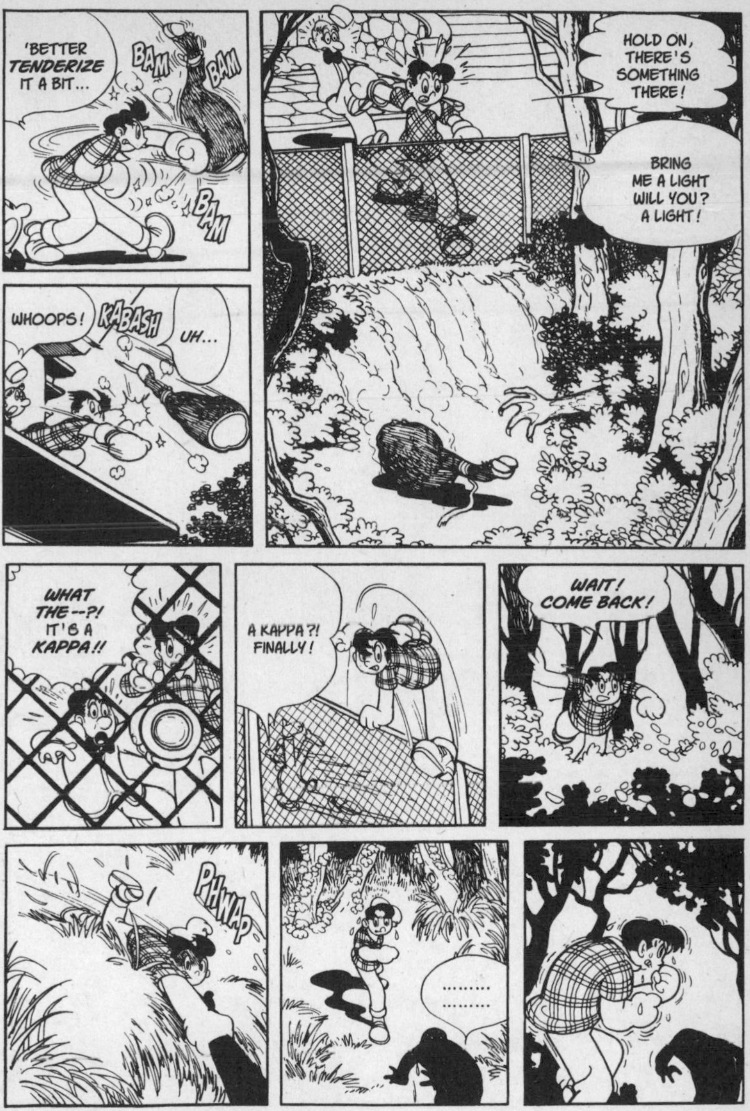
'BETTER *TENDERIZE* IT A BIT...
BAM
BAM
BAM
HOLD ON, THERE'S SOMETHING THERE!
BRING ME A LIGHT WILL YOU? A LIGHT!
WHOOPS!
KABASH
UH...
WHAT THE--?! IT'S A *KAPPA!!*
A KAPPA?! FINALLY!
WAIT! COME BACK!
PHWAP
....
....

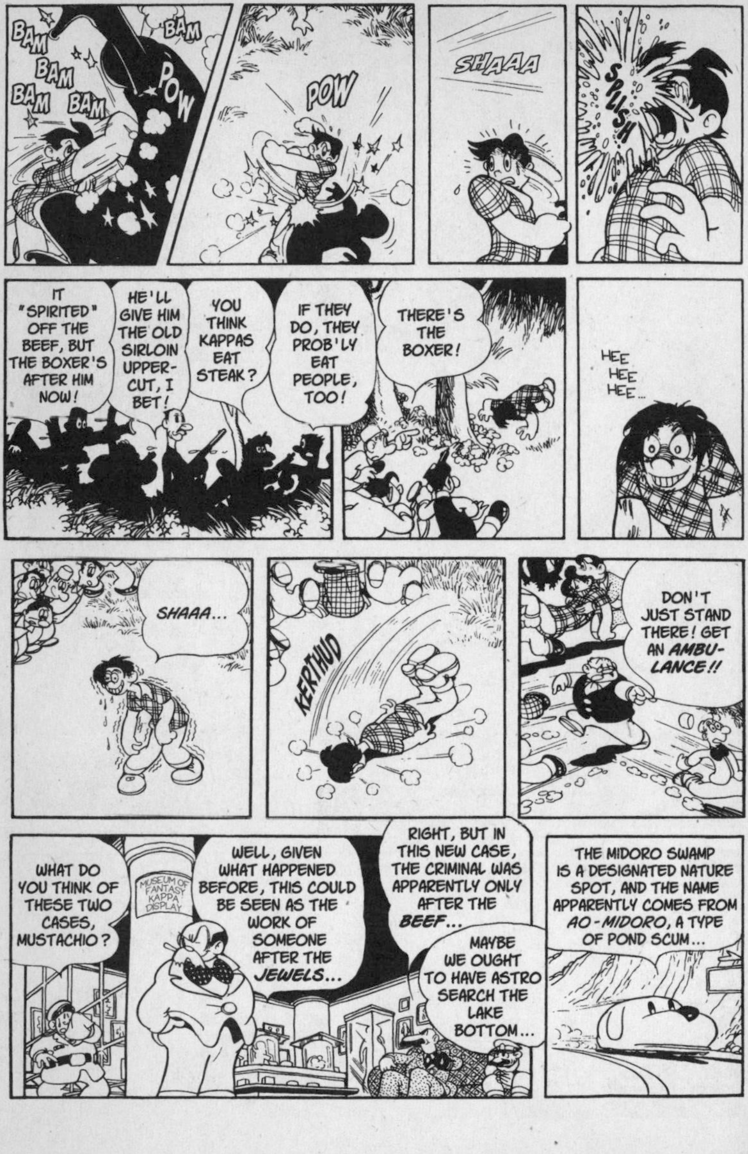
BAM
BAM
BAM
BAM
BAM
POW
POW
SHAAA
SPLISH
IT "SPIRITED" OFF THE BEEF, BUT THE BOXER'S AFTER HIM NOW!
HE'LL GIVE HIM THE OLD SIRLOIN UPPER-CUT, I BET!
YOU THINK KAPPAS EAT STEAK?
IF THEY DO, THEY PROB'LY EAT PEOPLE, TOO!
THERE'S THE BOXER!
HEE HEE HEE...
SHAAA...
KERTHUD
DON'T JUST STAND THERE! GET AN AMBU-LANCE!!
WHAT DO YOU THINK OF THESE TWO CASES, MUSTACHIO?
MUSEUM OF FANTASY KAPPA DISPLAY
WELL, GIVEN WHAT HAPPENED BEFORE, THIS COULD BE SEEN AS THE WORK OF SOMEONE AFTER THE JEWELS...
RIGHT, BUT IN THIS NEW CASE, THE CRIMINAL WAS APPARENTLY ONLY AFTER THE BEEF...
MAYBE WE OUGHT TO HAVE ASTRO SEARCH THE LAKE BOTTOM...
THE MIDORO SWAMP IS A DESIGNATED NATURE SPOT, AND THE NAME APPARENTLY COMES FROM AO-MIDORO, A TYPE OF POND SCUM...

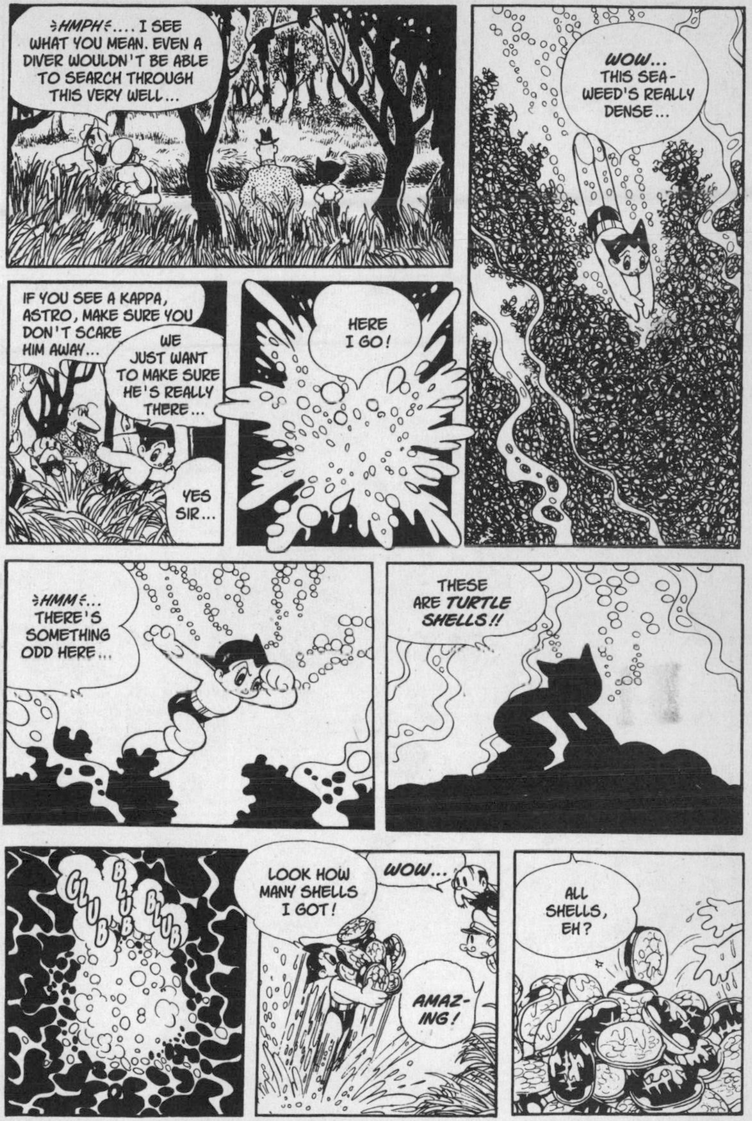

HMPH.... I SEE WHAT YOU MEAN. EVEN A DIVER WOULDN'T BE ABLE TO SEARCH THROUGH THIS VERY WELL...
IF YOU SEE A KAPPA, ASTRO, MAKE SURE YOU DON'T SCARE HIM AWAY...
WE JUST WANT TO MAKE SURE HE'S REALLY THERE...
YES SIR...
HERE I GO!
WOW... THIS SEA-WEED'S REALLY DENSE...
HMM... THERE'S SOMETHING ODD HERE...
THESE ARE TURTLE SHELLS!!
GLUB BLUB BLUB
LOOK HOW MANY SHELLS I GOT!
WOW...
AMAZ-ING!
ALL SHELLS, EH?

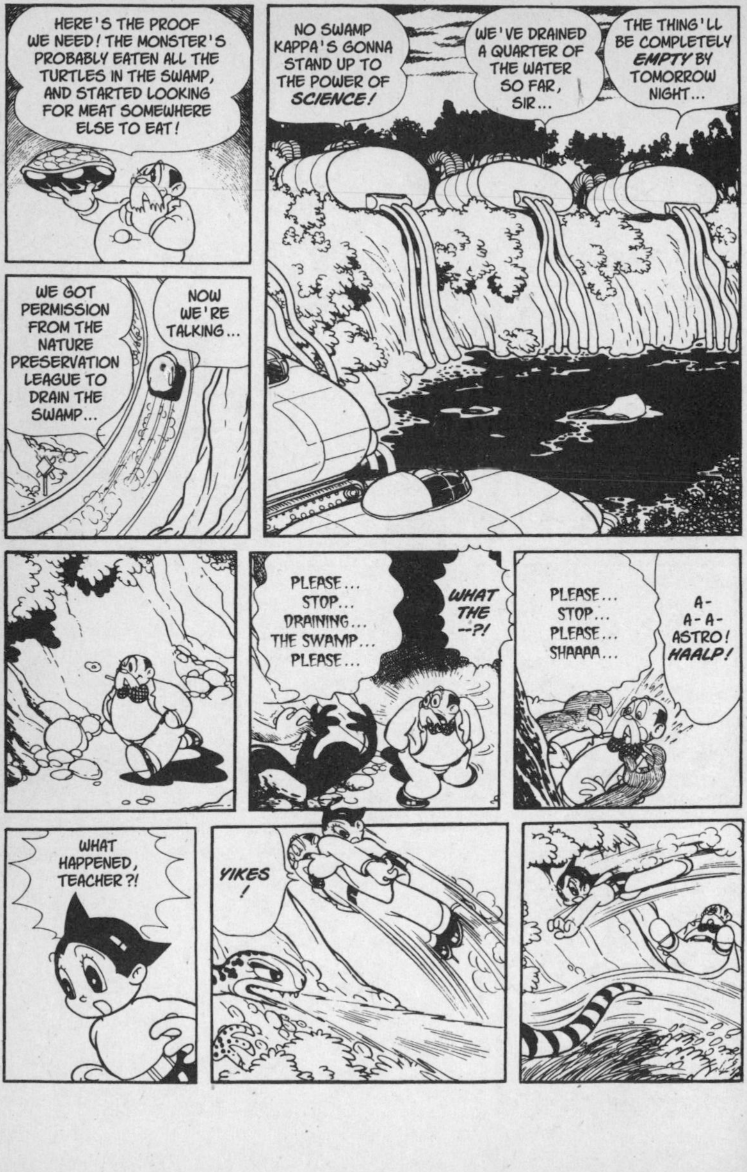

HERE'S THE PROOF WE NEED! THE MONSTER'S PROBABLY EATEN ALL THE TURTLES IN THE SWAMP, AND STARTED LOOKING FOR MEAT SOMEWHERE ELSE TO EAT!
NO SWAMP KAPPA'S GONNA STAND UP TO THE POWER OF *SCIENCE!*
WE'VE DRAINED A QUARTER OF THE WATER SO FAR, SIR...
THE THING'LL BE COMPLETELY *EMPTY* BY TOMORROW NIGHT...
WE GOT PERMISSION FROM THE NATURE PRESERVATION LEAGUE TO DRAIN THE SWAMP...
NOW WE'RE TALKING...
PLEASE... STOP... DRAINING... THE SWAMP... PLEASE...
WHAT THE --?!
PLEASE... STOP... PLEASE... SHAAAA...
A- A- A- ASTRO! *HAALP!*
WHAT HAPPENED, TEACHER?!
YIKES!

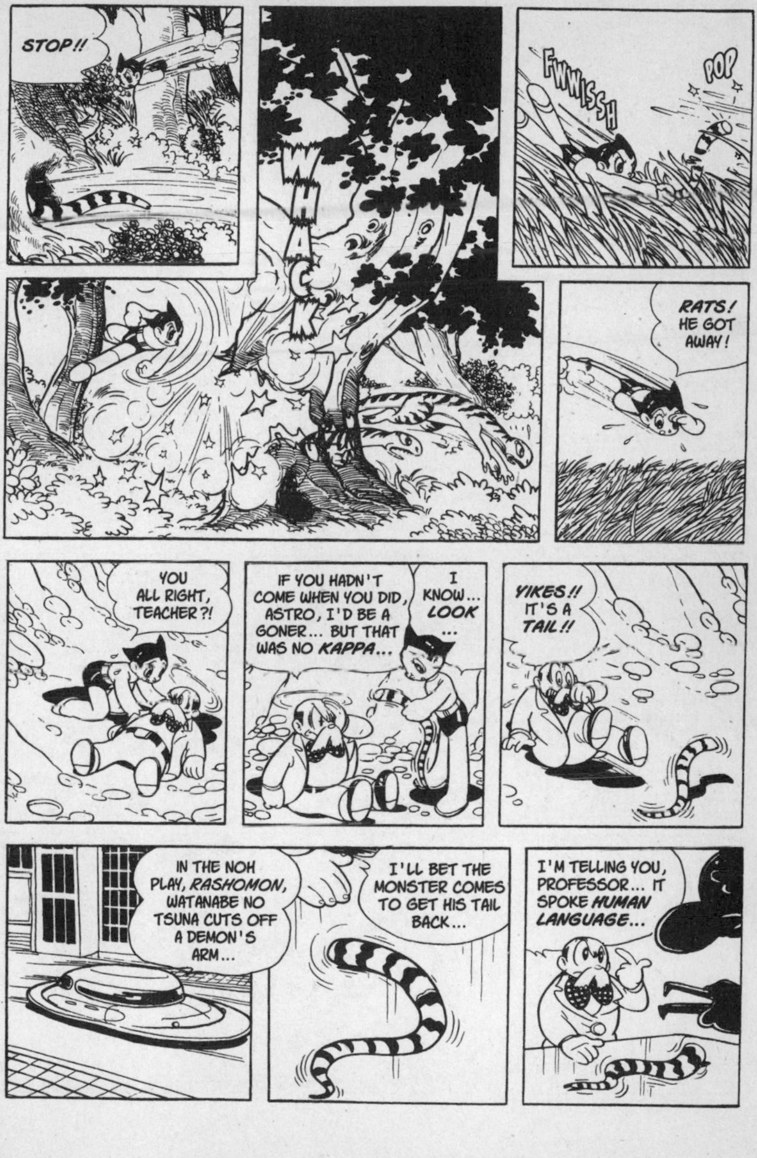
STOP!!
WHACK
FWWISSH
POP
RATS! HE GOT AWAY!
YOU ALL RIGHT, TEACHER?!
IF YOU HADN'T COME WHEN YOU DID, ASTRO, I'D BE A GONER... BUT THAT WAS NO KAPPA...
I KNOW... LOOK ...
YIKES!! IT'S A TAIL!!
IN THE NOH PLAY, RASHOMON, WATANABE NO TSUNA CUTS OFF A DEMON'S ARM...
I'LL BET THE MONSTER COMES TO GET HIS TAIL BACK...
I'M TELLING YOU, PROFESSOR... IT SPOKE HUMAN LANGUAGE...

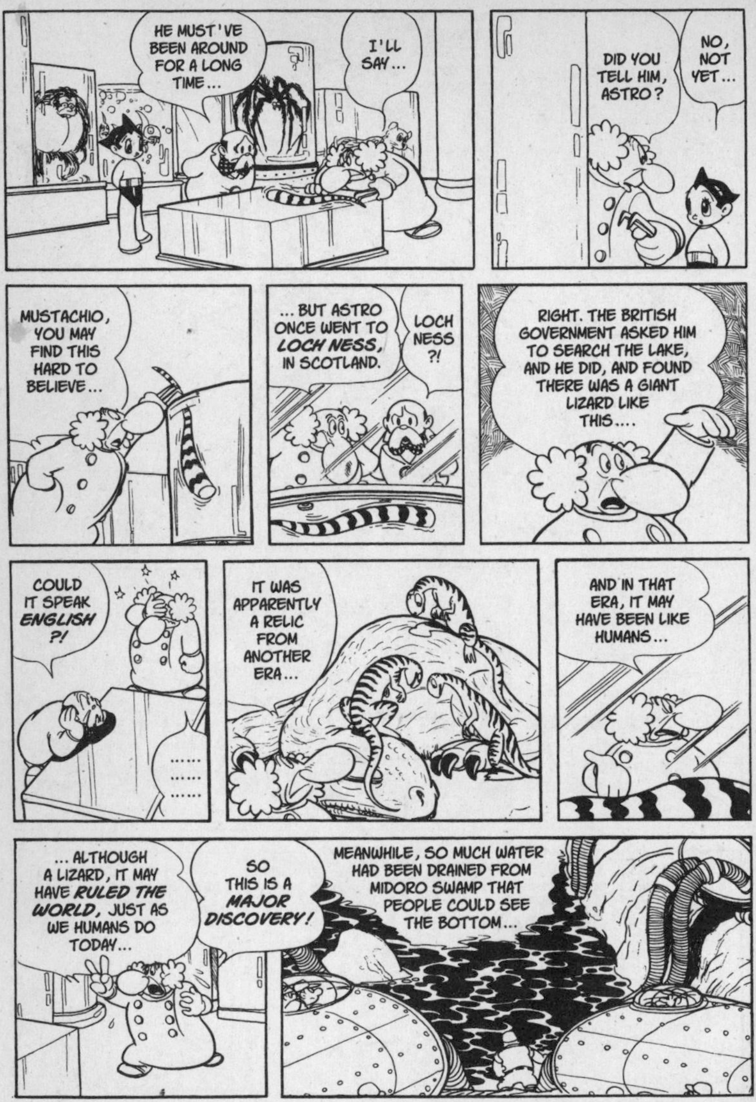
HE MUST'VE BEEN AROUND FOR A LONG TIME...
I'LL SAY...
DID YOU TELL HIM, ASTRO?
NO, NOT YET...
MUSTACHIO, YOU MAY FIND THIS HARD TO BELIEVE...
... BUT ASTRO ONCE WENT TO LOCH NESS, IN SCOTLAND.
LOCH NESS ?!
RIGHT. THE BRITISH GOVERNMENT ASKED HIM TO SEARCH THE LAKE, AND HE DID, AND FOUND THERE WAS A GIANT LIZARD LIKE THIS....
COULD IT SPEAK ENGLISH ?!
....
IT WAS APPARENTLY A RELIC FROM ANOTHER ERA...
AND IN THAT ERA, IT MAY HAVE BEEN LIKE HUMANS...
... ALTHOUGH A LIZARD, IT MAY HAVE RULED THE WORLD, JUST AS WE HUMANS DO TODAY...
SO THIS IS A MAJOR DISCOVERY!
MEANWHILE, SO MUCH WATER HAD BEEN DRAINED FROM MIDORO SWAMP THAT PEOPLE COULD SEE THE BOTTOM...

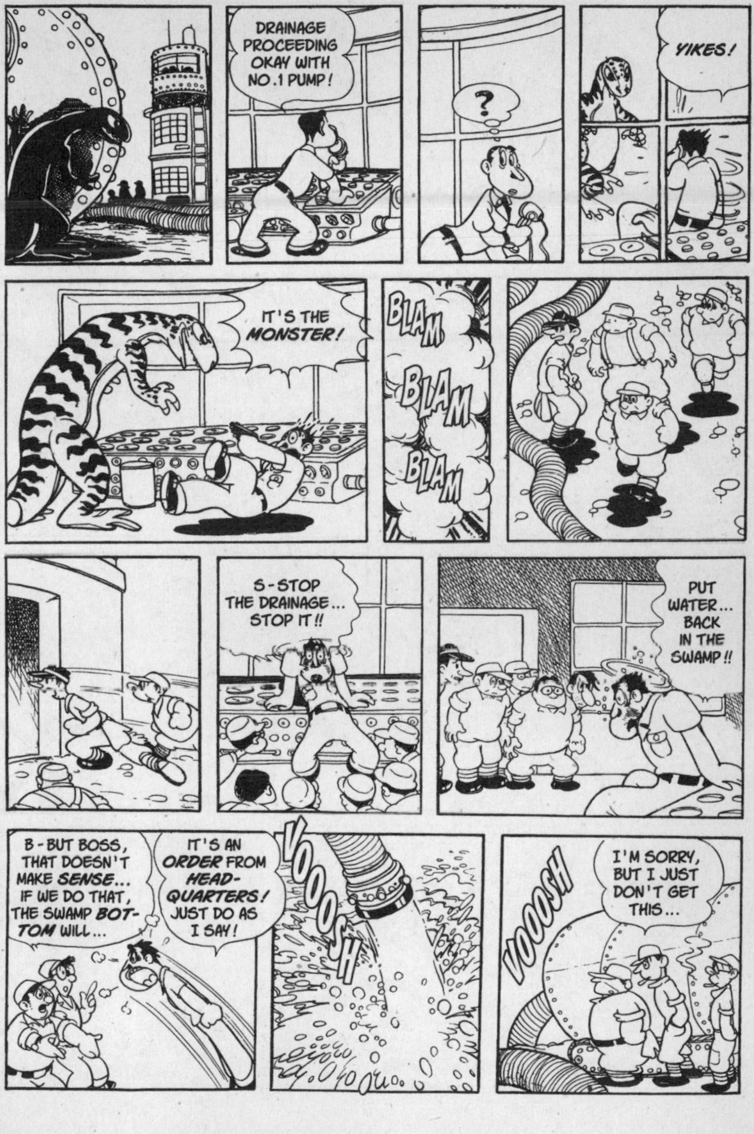
DRAINAGE PROCEEDING OKAY WITH NO.1 PUMP!
?
YIKES!
IT'S THE MONSTER!
BLAM
BLAM
BLAM
S-STOP THE DRAINAGE... STOP IT!!
PUT WATER... BACK IN THE SWAMP!!
B-BUT BOSS, THAT DOESN'T MAKE SENSE... IF WE DO THAT, THE SWAMP BOTTOM WILL...
IT'S AN ORDER FROM HEADQUARTERS! JUST DO AS I SAY!
VOOOSH
VOOOSH
I'M SORRY, BUT I JUST DON'T GET THIS...

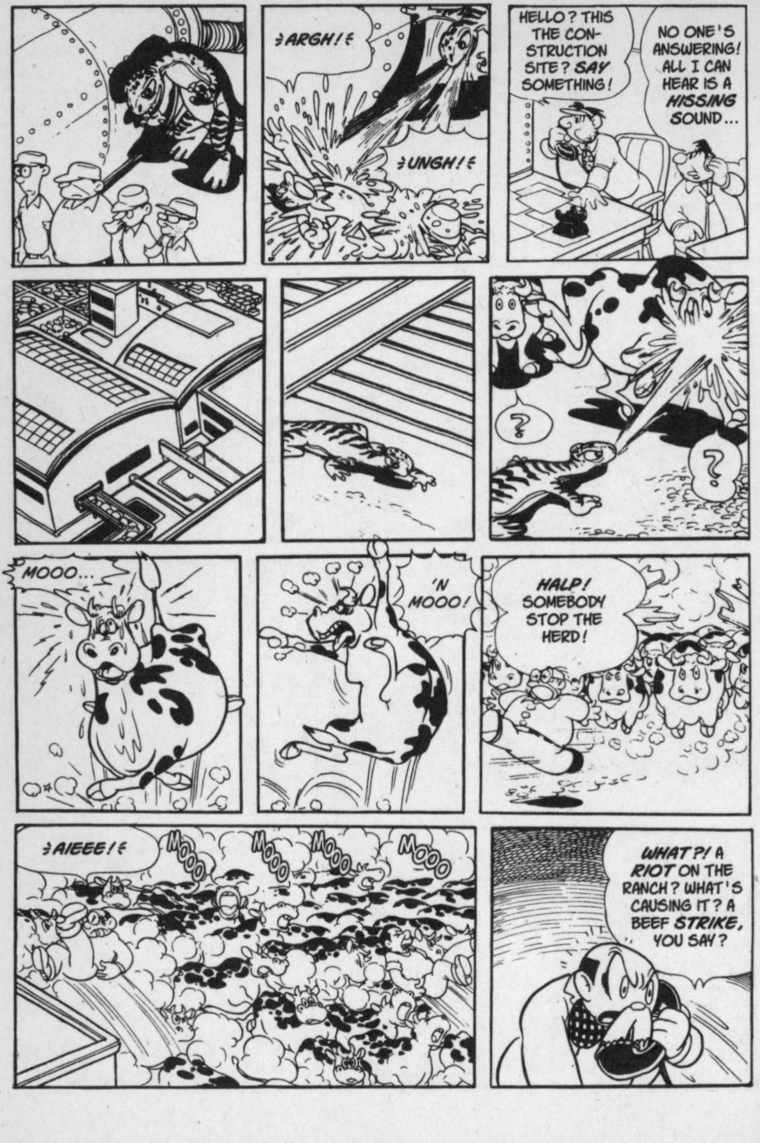
ARGH!
UNGH!
HELLO? THIS THE CON-STRUCTION SITE? SAY SOMETHING!
NO ONE'S ANSWERING! ALL I CAN HEAR IS A HISSING SOUND...
?
?
MOOO...
'N MOOO!
HALP! SOMEBODY STOP THE HERD!
AIEEE!
MOOO
MOOO
MOOO
MOOO
WHAT?! A RIOT ON THE RANCH? WHAT'S CAUSING IT? A BEEF STRIKE, YOU SAY?

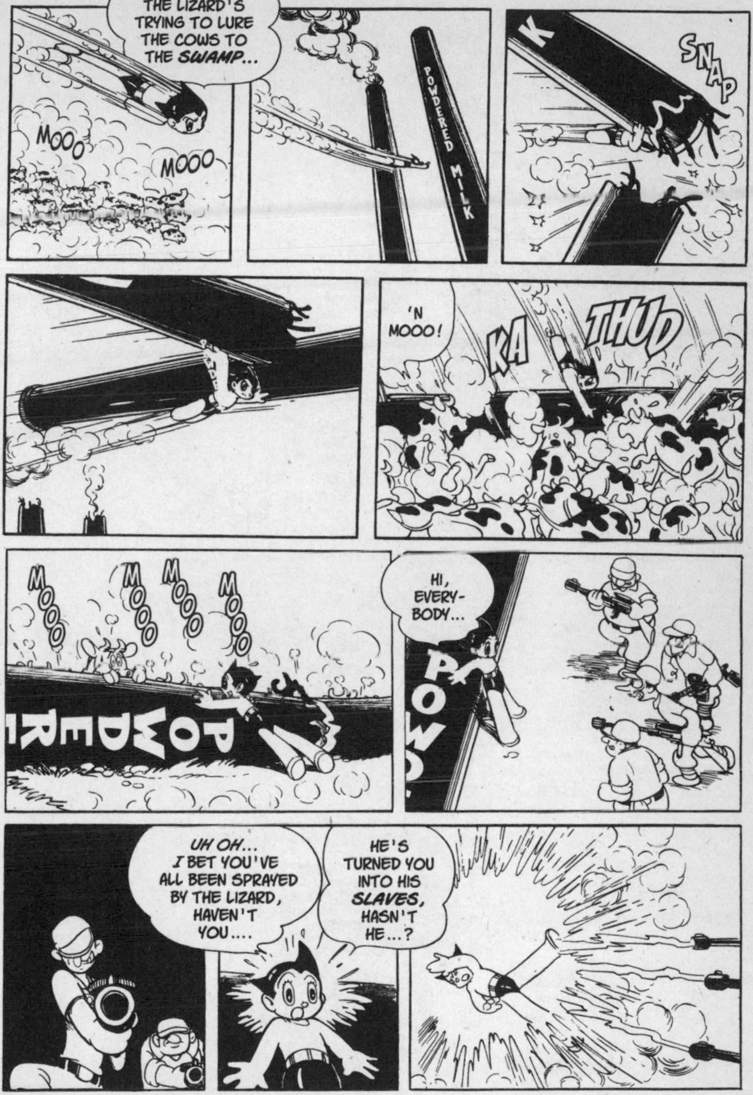
I GET IT... THE LIZARD'S TRYING TO LURE THE COWS TO THE *SWAMP*...
MOOO
MOOO
POWDERED MILK
K
SNAP
'N MOOO!
KA
THUD
MOOO
MOOO
MOOO
MOOO
POWDE
HI, EVERY-BODY...
POWD
UH OH... *I* BET YOU'VE ALL BEEN SPRAYED BY THE LIZARD, HAVEN'T YOU....
HE'S TURNED YOU INTO HIS *SLAVES,* HASN'T HE...?

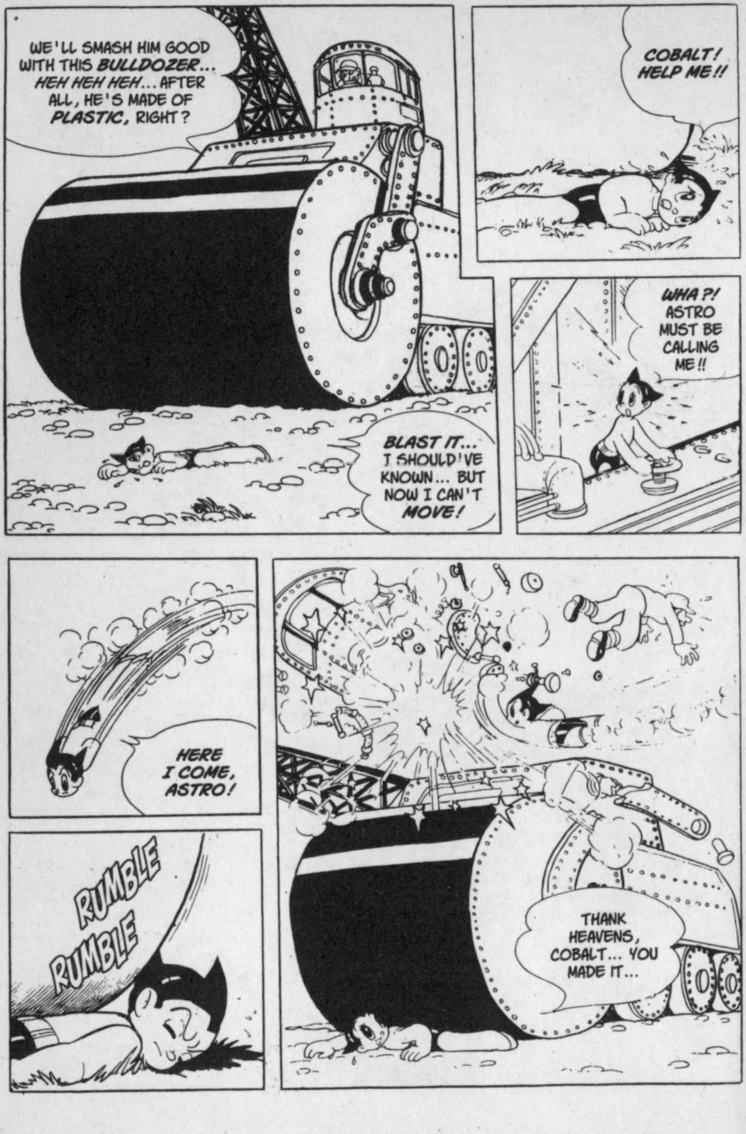
WE'LL SMASH HIM GOOD WITH THIS BULLDOZER... HEH HEH HEH... AFTER ALL, HE'S MADE OF PLASTIC, RIGHT?
BLAST IT... I SHOULD'VE KNOWN... BUT NOW I CAN'T MOVE!
COBALT! HELP ME!!
WHA?! ASTRO MUST BE CALLING ME!!
HERE I COME, ASTRO!
RUMBLE RUMBLE
THANK HEAVENS, COBALT... YOU MADE IT...

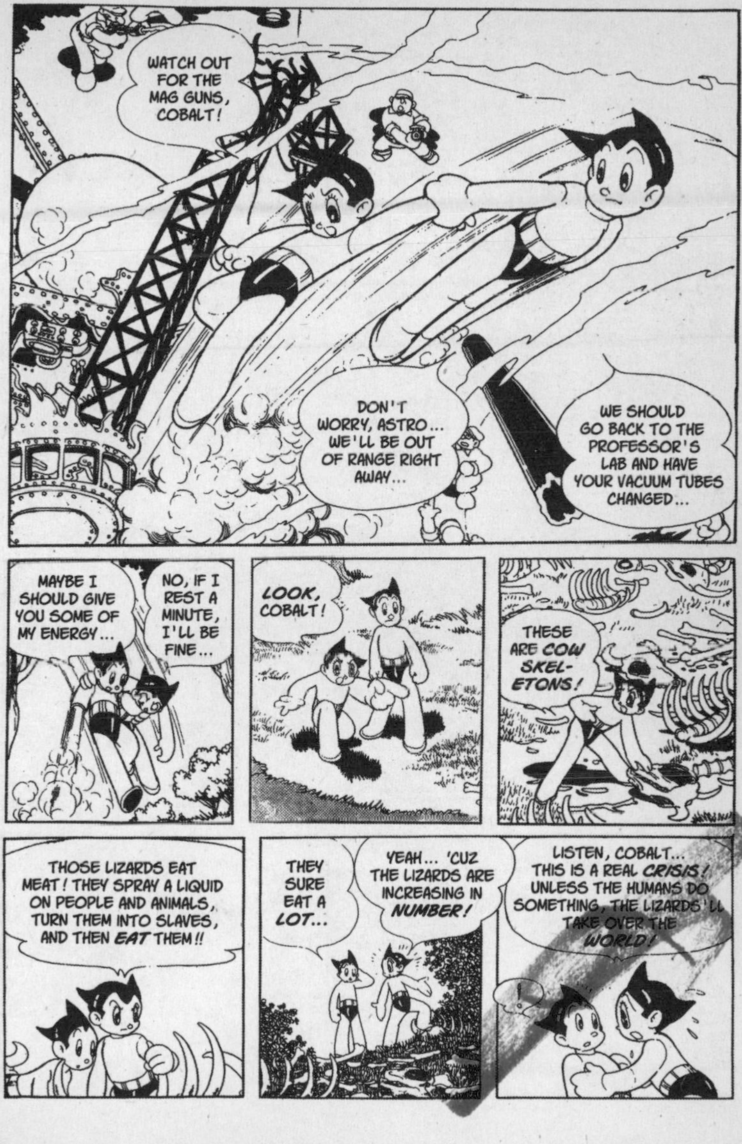
WATCH OUT FOR THE MAG GUNS, COBALT!
DON'T WORRY, ASTRO... WE'LL BE OUT OF RANGE RIGHT AWAY...
WE SHOULD GO BACK TO THE PROFESSOR'S LAB AND HAVE YOUR VACUUM TUBES CHANGED...
MAYBE I SHOULD GIVE YOU SOME OF MY ENERGY...
NO, IF I REST A MINUTE, I'LL BE FINE...
LOOK, COBALT!
THESE ARE COW SKEL-ETONS!
THOSE LIZARDS EAT MEAT! THEY SPRAY A LIQUID ON PEOPLE AND ANIMALS, TURN THEM INTO SLAVES, AND THEN EAT THEM!!
THEY SURE EAT A LOT...
YEAH... 'CUZ THE LIZARDS ARE INCREASING IN NUMBER!
LISTEN, COBALT... THIS IS A REAL CRISIS! UNLESS THE HUMANS DO SOMETHING, THE LIZARDS'LL TAKE OVER THE WORLD!
!

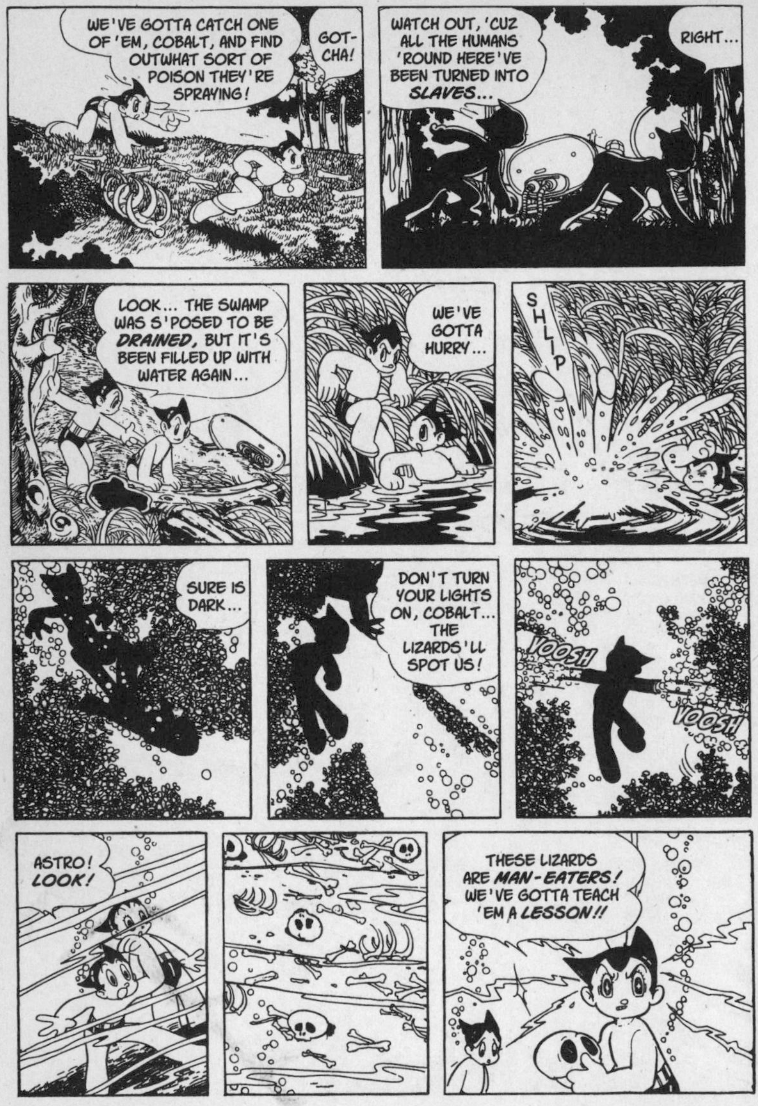
WE'VE GOTTA CATCH ONE OF 'EM, COBALT, AND FIND OUTWHAT SORT OF POISON THEY'RE SPRAYING!
GOT-CHA!
WATCH OUT, 'CUZ ALL THE HUMANS 'ROUND HERE'VE BEEN TURNED INTO SLAVES...
RIGHT...
LOOK... THE SWAMP WAS S'POSED TO BE DRAINED, BUT IT'S BEEN FILLED UP WITH WATER AGAIN...
WE'VE GOTTA HURRY...
SHLIP
SURE IS DARK...
DON'T TURN YOUR LIGHTS ON, COBALT... THE LIZARDS'LL SPOT US!
VOOSH
VOOSH
ASTRO! LOOK!
THESE LIZARDS ARE MAN-EATERS! WE'VE GOTTA TEACH 'EM A LESSON!!

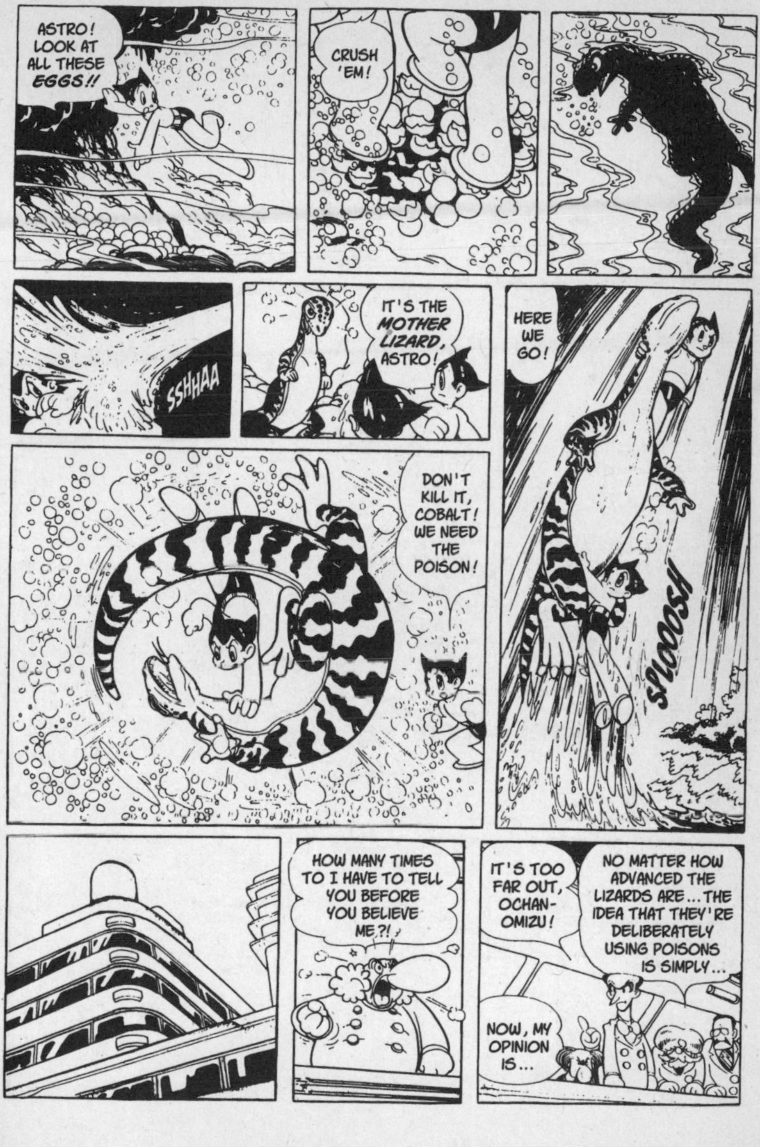
ASTRO! LOOK AT ALL THESE EGGS!!
CRUSH 'EM!
SSHHAA
IT'S THE MOTHER LIZARD, ASTRO!
DON'T KILL IT, COBALT! WE NEED THE POISON!
HERE WE GO!
SPLOOOSH
HOW MANY TIMES TO I HAVE TO TELL YOU BEFORE YOU BELIEVE ME?!
IT'S TOO FAR OUT, OCHAN-OMIZU!
NO MATTER HOW ADVANCED THE LIZARDS ARE... THE IDEA THAT THEY'RE DELIBERATELY USING POISONS IS SIMPLY...
NOW, MY OPINION IS...

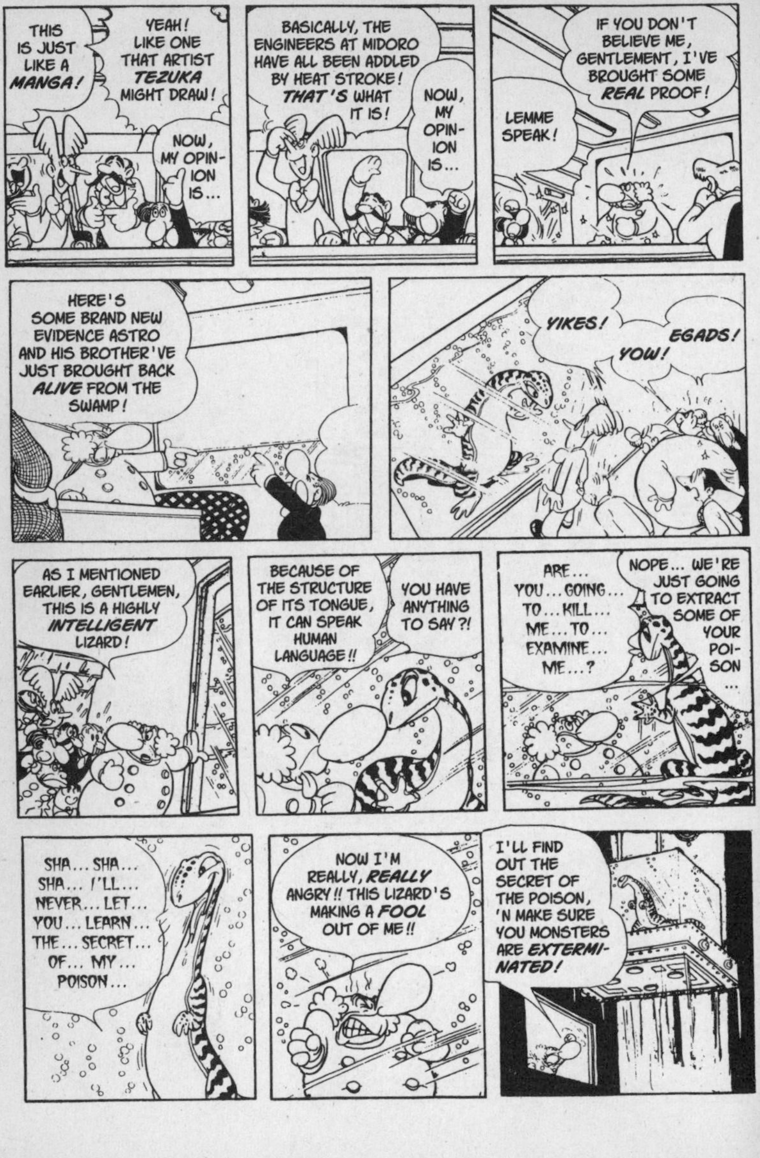
THIS IS JUST LIKE A MANGA!
YEAH! LIKE ONE THAT ARTIST TEZUKA MIGHT DRAW!
NOW, MY OPINION IS...
BASICALLY, THE ENGINEERS AT MIDORO HAVE ALL BEEN ADDLED BY HEAT STROKE! THAT'S WHAT IT IS!
NOW, MY OPINION IS...
IF YOU DON'T BELIEVE ME, GENTLEMENT, I'VE BROUGHT SOME REAL PROOF!
LEMME SPEAK!
HERE'S SOME BRAND NEW EVIDENCE ASTRO AND HIS BROTHER'VE JUST BROUGHT BACK ALIVE FROM THE SWAMP!
YIKES!
YOW!
EGADS!
AS I MENTIONED EARLIER, GENTLEMEN, THIS IS A HIGHLY INTELLIGENT LIZARD!
BECAUSE OF THE STRUCTURE OF ITS TONGUE, IT CAN SPEAK HUMAN LANGUAGE!!
YOU HAVE ANYTHING TO SAY?!
ARE... YOU... GOING... TO... KILL... ME... TO... EXAMINE... ME...?
NOPE... WE'RE JUST GOING TO EXTRACT SOME OF YOUR POISON...
SHA... SHA... SHA... I'LL... NEVER... LET... YOU... LEARN... THE... SECRET... OF... MY... POISON...
NOW I'M REALLY, REALLY ANGRY!! THIS LIZARD'S MAKING A FOOL OUT OF ME!!
I'LL FIND OUT THE SECRET OF THE POISON, 'N MAKE SURE YOU MONSTERS ARE EXTERMINATED!

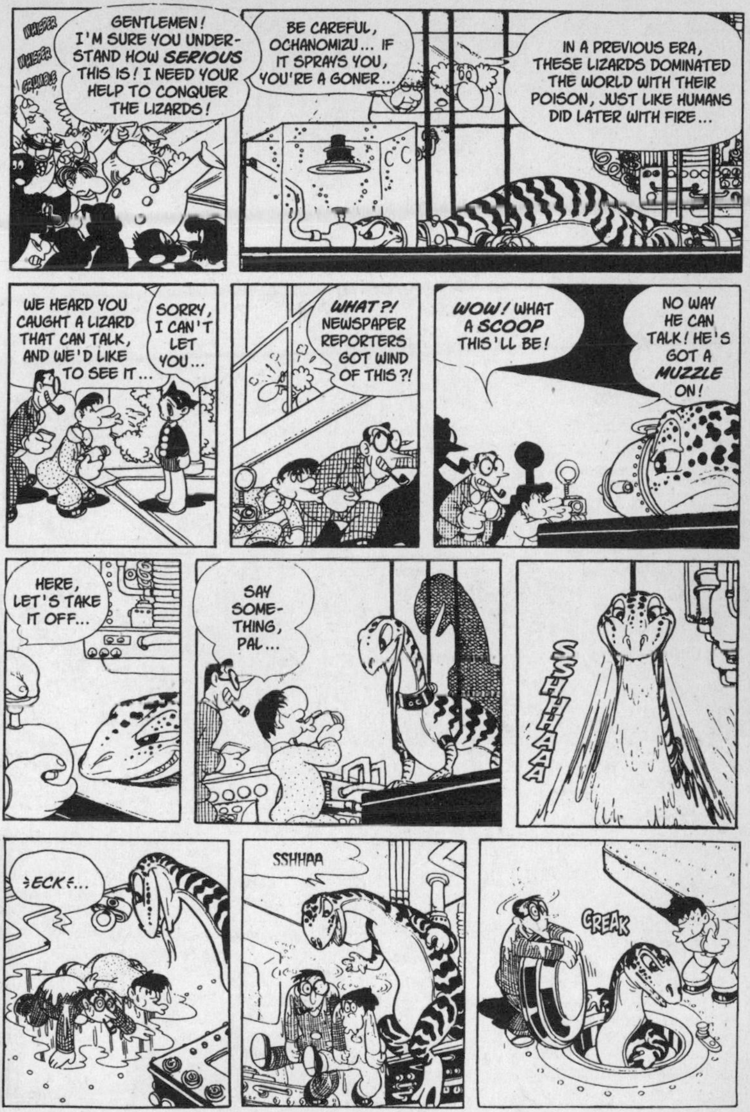
WHISPER
WHISPER
GRUMBLE
GENTLEMEN! I'M SURE YOU UNDERSTAND HOW SERIOUS THIS IS! I NEED YOUR HELP TO CONQUER THE LIZARDS!
BE CAREFUL, OCHANOMIZU... IF IT SPRAYS YOU, YOU'RE A GONER...
IN A PREVIOUS ERA, THESE LIZARDS DOMINATED THE WORLD WITH THEIR POISON, JUST LIKE HUMANS DID LATER WITH FIRE...
WE HEARD YOU CAUGHT A LIZARD THAT CAN TALK, AND WE'D LIKE TO SEE IT...
SORRY, I CAN'T LET YOU...
WHAT?! NEWSPAPER REPORTERS GOT WIND OF THIS?!
WOW! WHAT A SCOOP THIS'LL BE!
NO WAY HE CAN TALK! HE'S GOT A MUZZLE ON!
HERE, LET'S TAKE IT OFF...
SAY SOMETHING, PAL...
SSHHAAA
ECK...
SSHHAA
CREAK

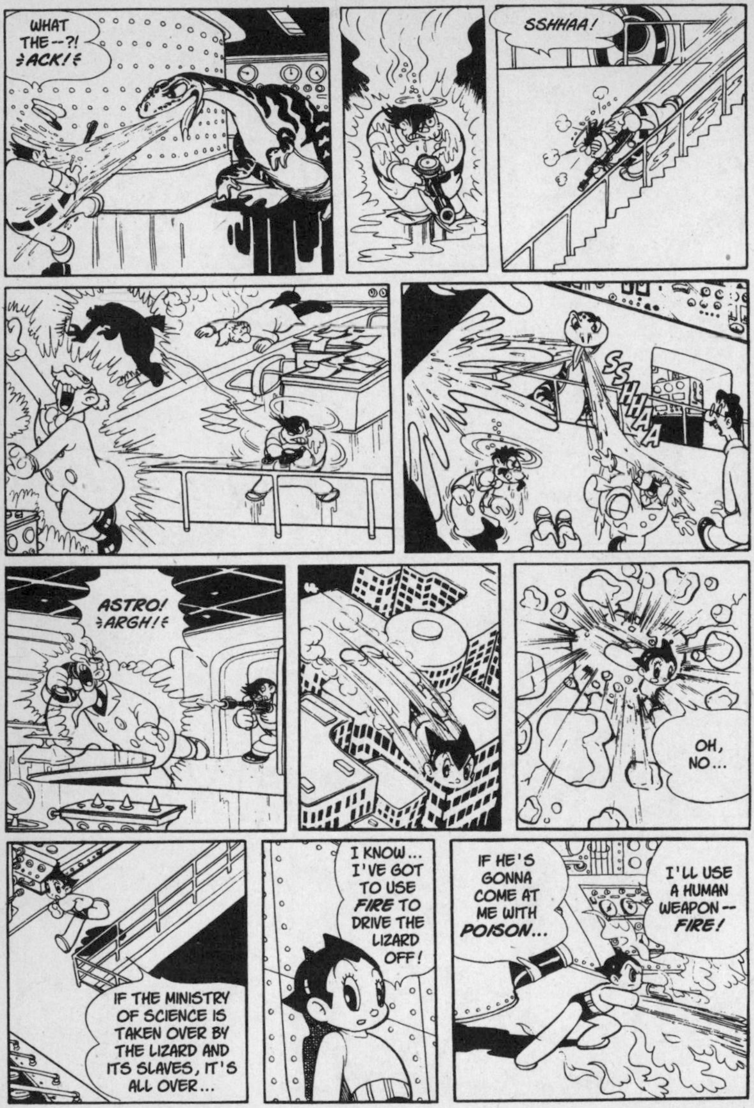
WHAT THE--?! ACK!
SSHHAA!
SSHHAA
ASTRO! ARGH!
OH, NO...
IF THE MINISTRY OF SCIENCE IS TAKEN OVER BY THE LIZARD AND ITS SLAVES, IT'S ALL OVER...
I KNOW... I'VE GOT TO USE FIRE TO DRIVE THE LIZARD OFF!
IF HE'S GONNA COME AT ME WITH POISON...
I'LL USE A HUMAN WEAPON-- FIRE!

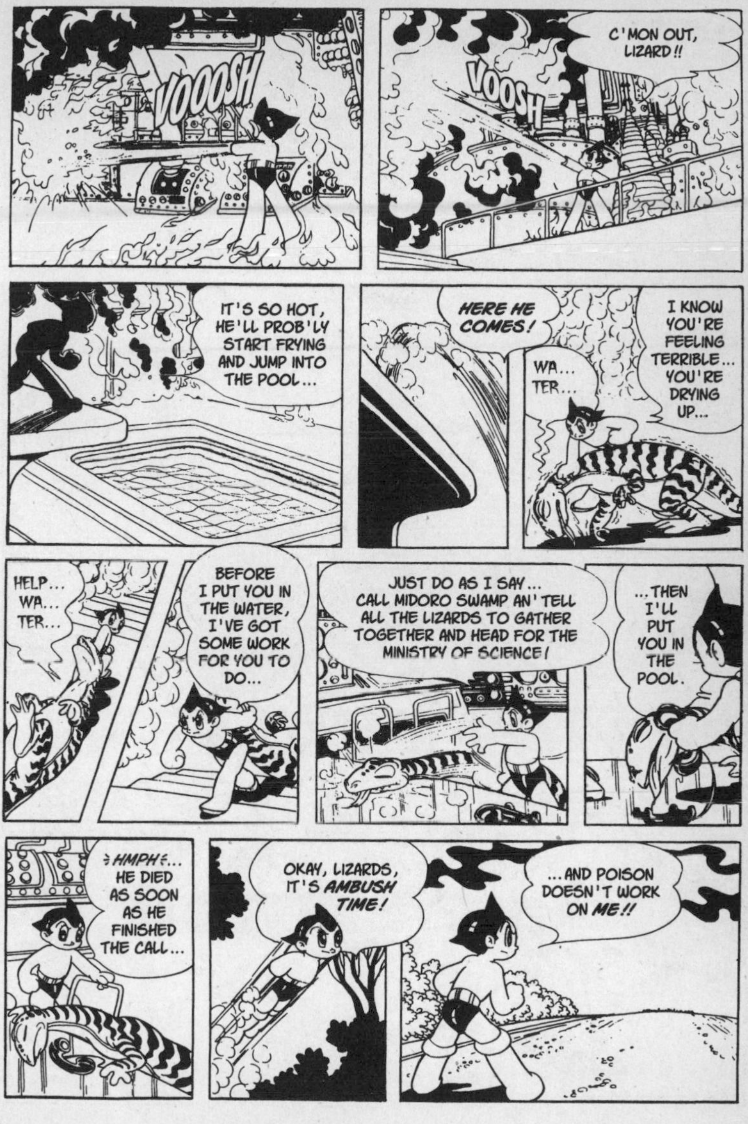
VOOOSH
VOOSH
C'MON OUT, LIZARD!!
IT'S SO HOT, HE'LL PROB'LY START FRYING AND JUMP INTO THE POOL...
HERE HE COMES!
WA... TER...
I KNOW YOU'RE FEELING TERRIBLE... YOU'RE DRYING UP...
HELP... WA... TER...
BEFORE I PUT YOU IN THE WATER, I'VE GOT SOME WORK FOR YOU TO DO...
JUST DO AS I SAY... CALL MIDORO SWAMP AN' TELL ALL THE LIZARDS TO GATHER TOGETHER AND HEAD FOR THE MINISTRY OF SCIENCE!
...THEN I'LL PUT YOU IN THE POOL.
≡HMPH≡... HE DIED AS SOON AS HE FINISHED THE CALL...
OKAY, LIZARDS, IT'S AMBUSH TIME!
...AND POISON DOESN'T WORK ON ME!!

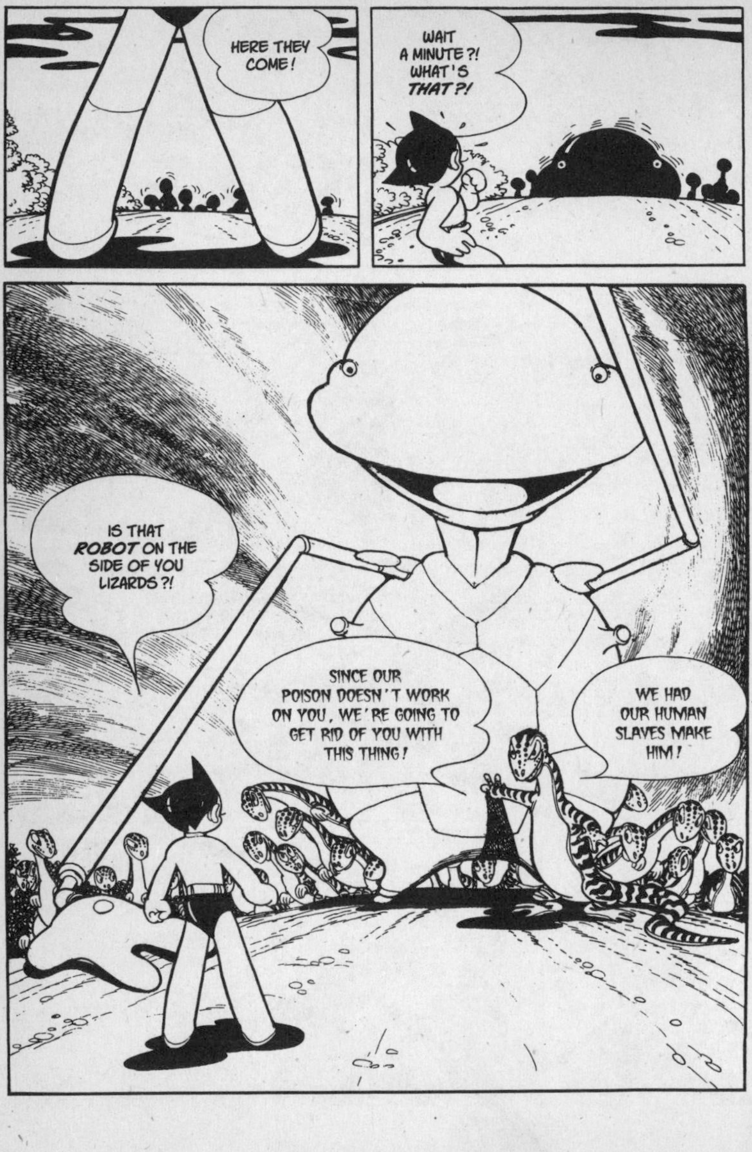
HERE THEY COME!
WAIT A MINUTE?! WHAT'S *THAT*?!
IS THAT *ROBOT* ON THE SIDE OF YOU LIZARDS?!
SINCE OUR POISON DOESN'T WORK ON YOU, WE'RE GOING TO GET RID OF YOU WITH THIS THING!
WE HAD OUR HUMAN SLAVES MAKE HIM!

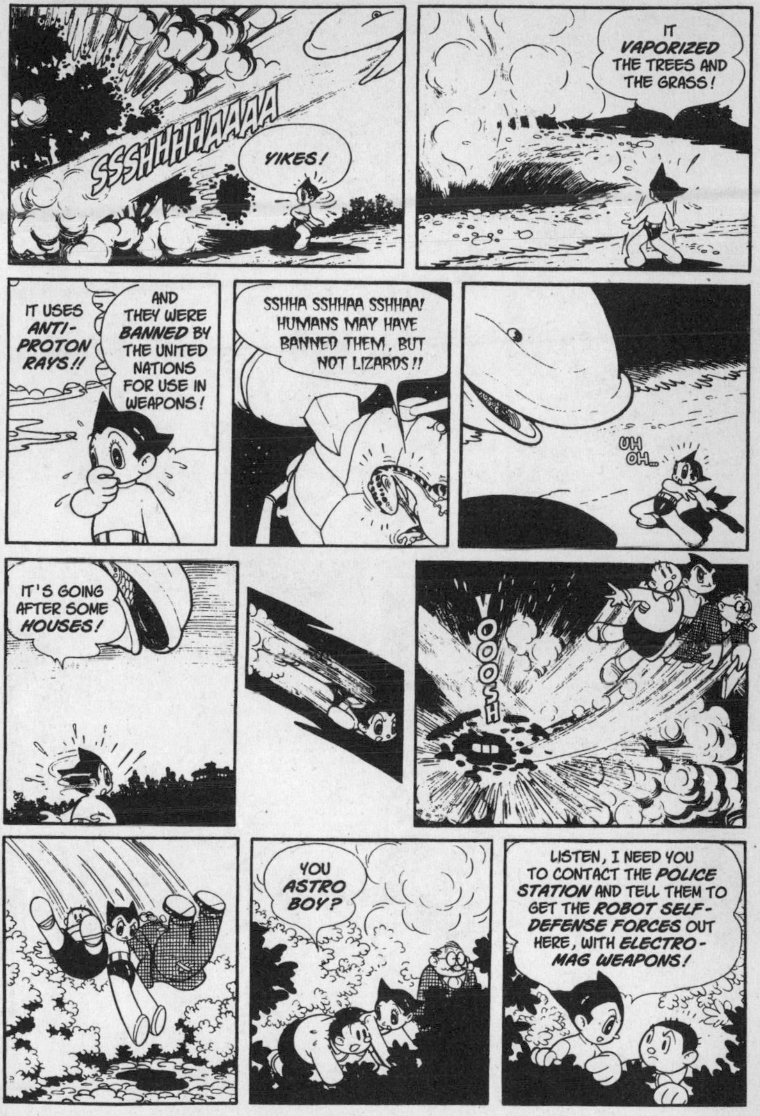
SSSHHHAAAA
YIKES!
IT VAPORIZED THE TREES AND THE GRASS!
IT USES ANTI-PROTON RAYS!!
AND THEY WERE BANNED BY THE UNITED NATIONS FOR USE IN WEAPONS!
SSHHA SSHHAA SSHHAA! HUMANS MAY HAVE BANNED THEM, BUT NOT LIZARDS!!
UH OH...
IT'S GOING AFTER SOME HOUSES!
VOOOOSH
YOU ASTRO BOY?
LISTEN, I NEED YOU TO CONTACT THE POLICE STATION AND TELL THEM TO GET THE ROBOT SELF-DEFENSE FORCES OUT HERE, WITH ELECTRO-MAG WEAPONS!

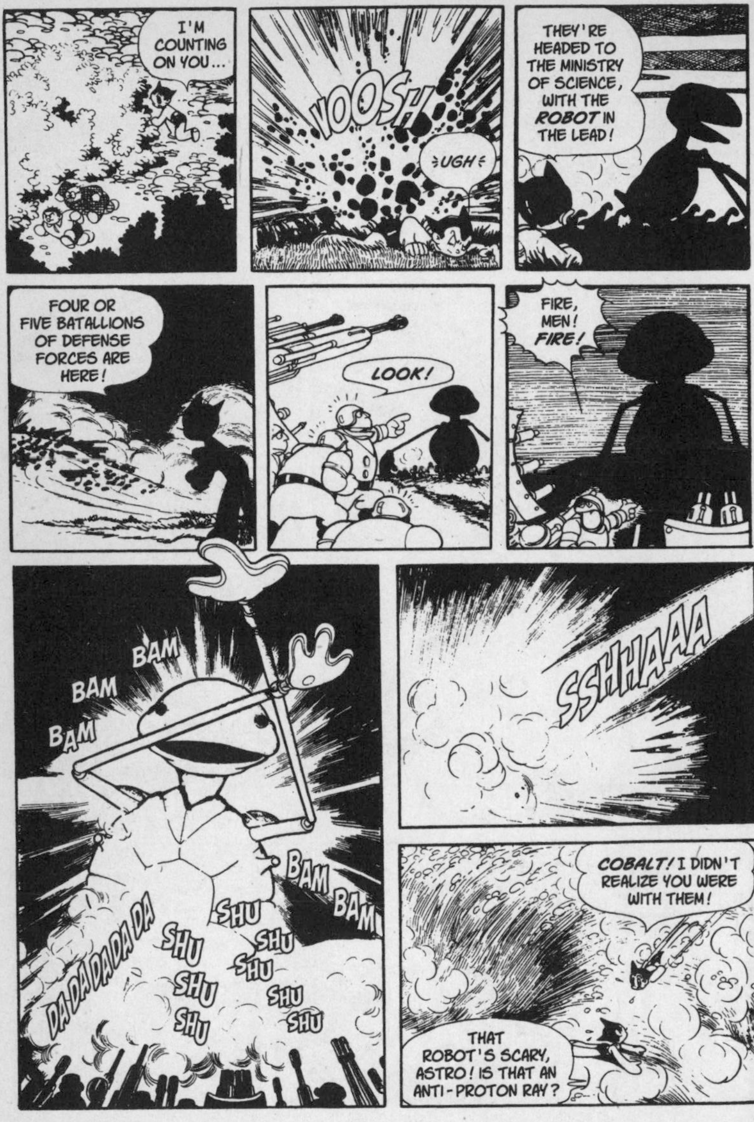
I'M COUNTING ON YOU...
VOOSH
UGH
THEY'RE HEADED TO THE MINISTRY OF SCIENCE, WITH THE ROBOT IN THE LEAD!
FOUR OR FIVE BATALLIONS OF DEFENSE FORCES ARE HERE!
LOOK!
FIRE, MEN! FIRE!
BAM
BAM
BAM
BAM
BAM
DA DA DA DA DA
SHU
SHU
SHU
SHU
SHU
SHU
SHU
SHU
SSHHAAA
COBALT! I DIDN'T REALIZE YOU WERE WITH THEM!
THAT ROBOT'S SCARY, ASTRO! IS THAT AN ANTI-PROTON RAY?

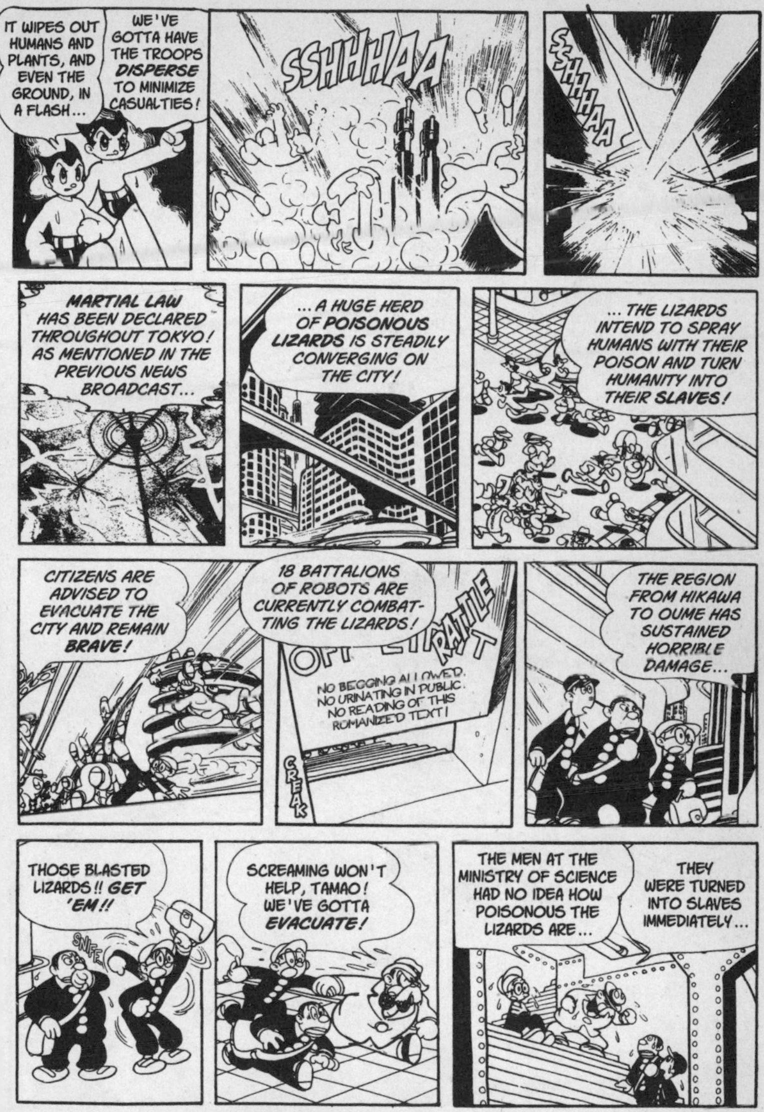
IT WIPES OUT HUMANS AND PLANTS, AND EVEN THE GROUND, IN A FLASH...
WE'VE GOTTA HAVE THE TROOPS DISPERSE TO MINIMIZE CASUALTIES!
SSHHHAA
SSHHHAA
MARTIAL LAW HAS BEEN DECLARED THROUGHOUT TOKYO! AS MENTIONED IN THE PREVIOUS NEWS BROADCAST...
...A HUGE HERD OF POISONOUS LIZARDS IS STEADILY CONVERGING ON THE CITY!
...THE LIZARDS INTEND TO SPRAY HUMANS WITH THEIR POISON AND TURN HUMANITY INTO THEIR SLAVES!
CITIZENS ARE ADVISED TO EVACUATE THE CITY AND REMAIN BRAVE!
18 BATTALIONS OF ROBOTS ARE CURRENTLY COMBAT-TING THE LIZARDS!
RATTLE
NO BEGGING ALLOWED. NO URINATING IN PUBLIC. NO READING OF THIS ROMANIZED TEXT!
CREAK
THE REGION FROM HIKAWA TO OUME HAS SUSTAINED HORRIBLE DAMAGE...
THOSE BLASTED LIZARDS!! GET 'EM!!
SNIFF
SCREAMING WON'T HELP, TAMAO! WE'VE GOTTA EVACUATE!
THE MEN AT THE MINISTRY OF SCIENCE HAD NO IDEA HOW POISONOUS THE LIZARDS ARE...
THEY WERE TURNED INTO SLAVES IMMEDIATELY...

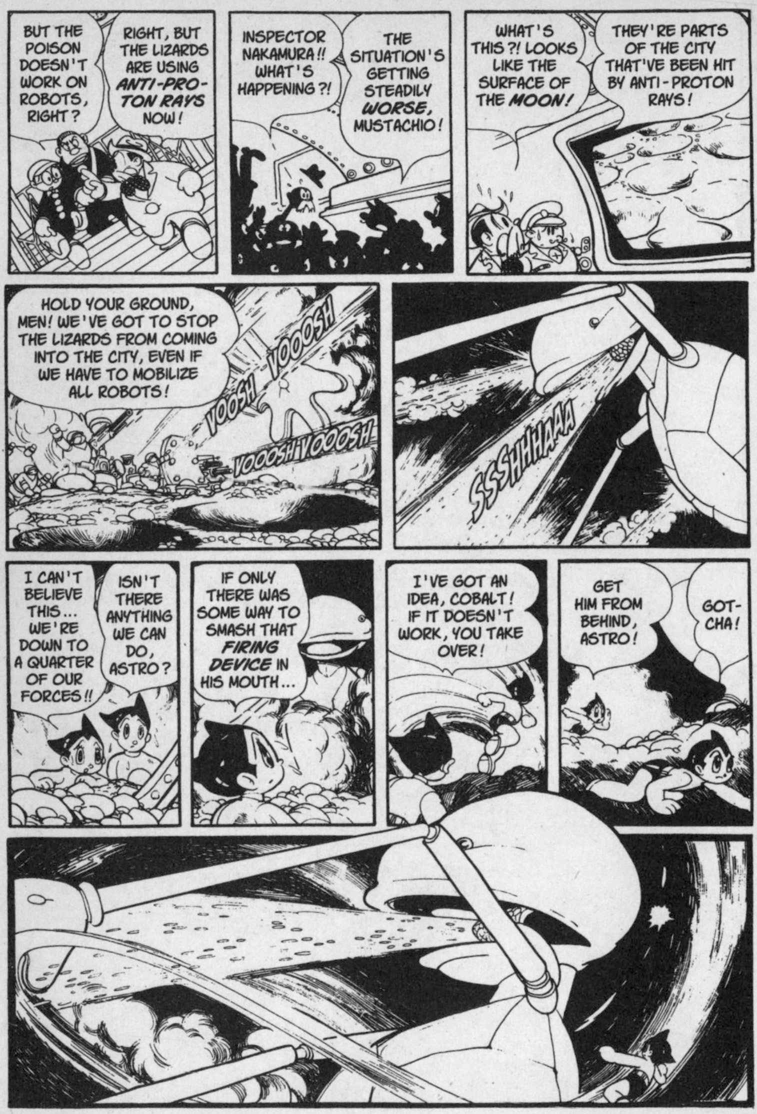
BUT THE POISON DOESN'T WORK ON ROBOTS, RIGHT?
RIGHT, BUT THE LIZARDS ARE USING ANTI-PROTON RAYS NOW!
INSPECTOR NAKAMURA!! WHAT'S HAPPENING?!
THE SITUATION'S GETTING STEADILY WORSE, MUSTACHIO!
WHAT'S THIS?! LOOKS LIKE THE SURFACE OF THE MOON!
THEY'RE PARTS OF THE CITY THAT'VE BEEN HIT BY ANTI-PROTON RAYS!
HOLD YOUR GROUND, MEN! WE'VE GOT TO STOP THE LIZARDS FROM COMING INTO THE CITY, EVEN IF WE HAVE TO MOBILIZE ALL ROBOTS!
VOOSH VOOOSH
VOOOSH VOOOSH
SSSHHHAAA
I CAN'T BELIEVE THIS... WE'RE DOWN TO A QUARTER OF OUR FORCES!!
ISN'T THERE ANYTHING WE CAN DO, ASTRO?
IF ONLY THERE WAS SOME WAY TO SMASH THAT FIRING DEVICE IN HIS MOUTH...
I'VE GOT AN IDEA, COBALT! IF IT DOESN'T WORK, YOU TAKE OVER!
GET HIM FROM BEHIND, ASTRO!
GOT-CHA!

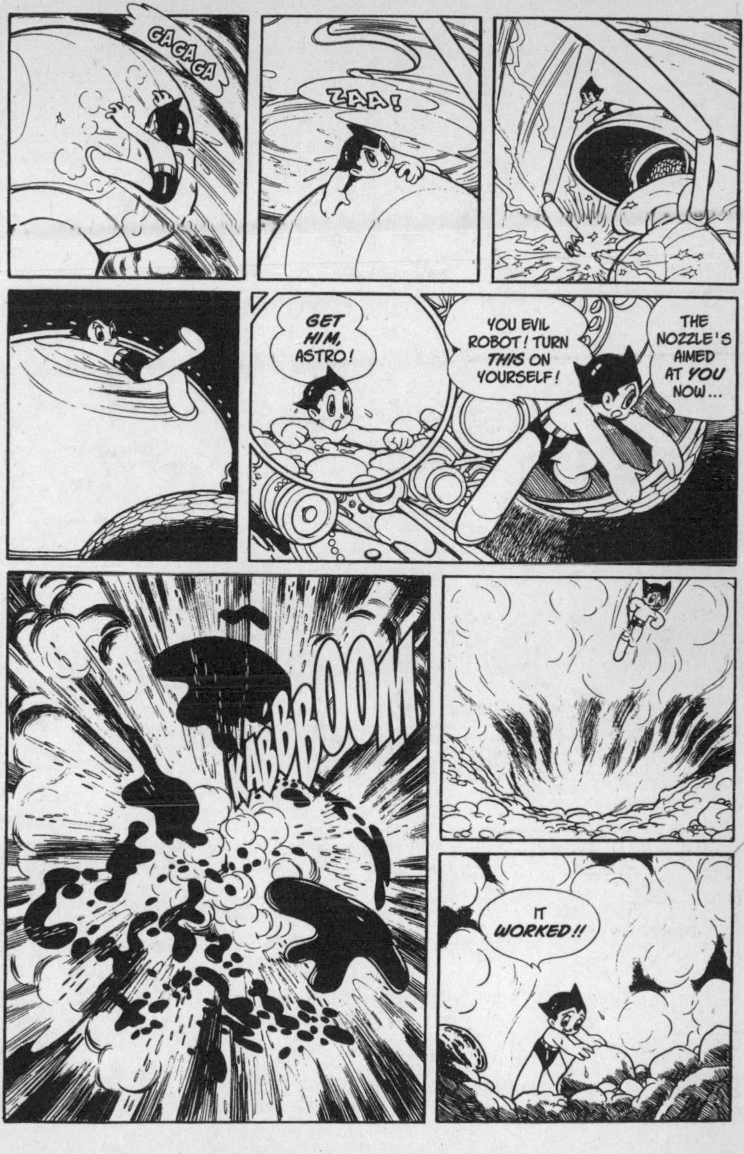
GAGAGA
ZAA!
GET HIM, ASTRO!
YOU EVIL ROBOT! TURN THIS ON YOURSELF!
THE NOZZLE'S AIMED AT YOU NOW...
KABBBOOM
IT WORKED!!

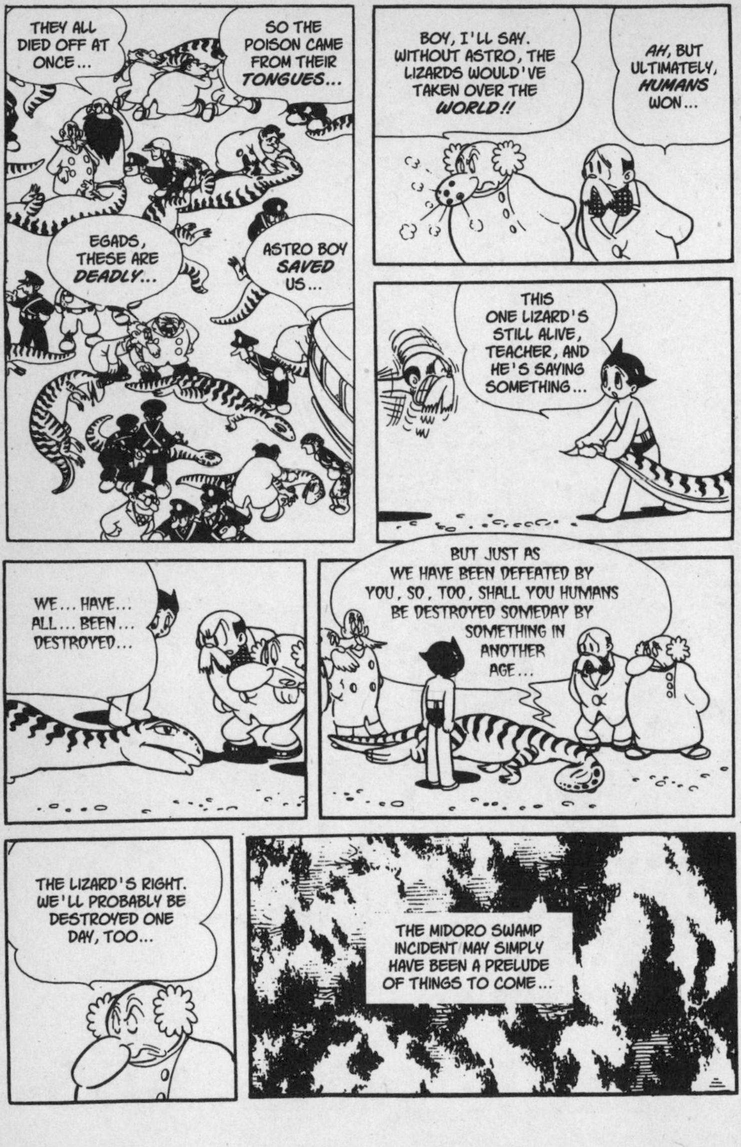
THEY ALL DIED OFF AT ONCE...
SO THE POISON CAME FROM THEIR *TONGUES...*
EGADS, THESE ARE *DEADLY...*
ASTRO BOY *SAVED* US...
BOY, I'LL SAY. WITHOUT ASTRO, THE LIZARDS WOULD'VE TAKEN OVER THE *WORLD!!*
AH, BUT ULTIMATELY, *HUMANS* WON...
THIS ONE LIZARD'S STILL ALIVE, TEACHER, AND HE'S SAYING SOMETHING...
WE... HAVE... ALL... BEEN... DESTROYED...
BUT JUST AS WE HAVE BEEN DEFEATED BY YOU, SO, TOO, SHALL YOU HUMANS BE DESTROYED SOMEDAY BY SOMETHING IN ANOTHER AGE...
THE LIZARD'S RIGHT. WE'LL PROBABLY BE DESTROYED ONE DAY, TOO...
THE MIDORO SWAMP INCIDENT MAY SIMPLY HAVE BEEN A PRELUDE OF THINGS TO COME...

ROBIO AND ROBIETTE

First serialized from May to September 1965
in *Shonen* magazine.

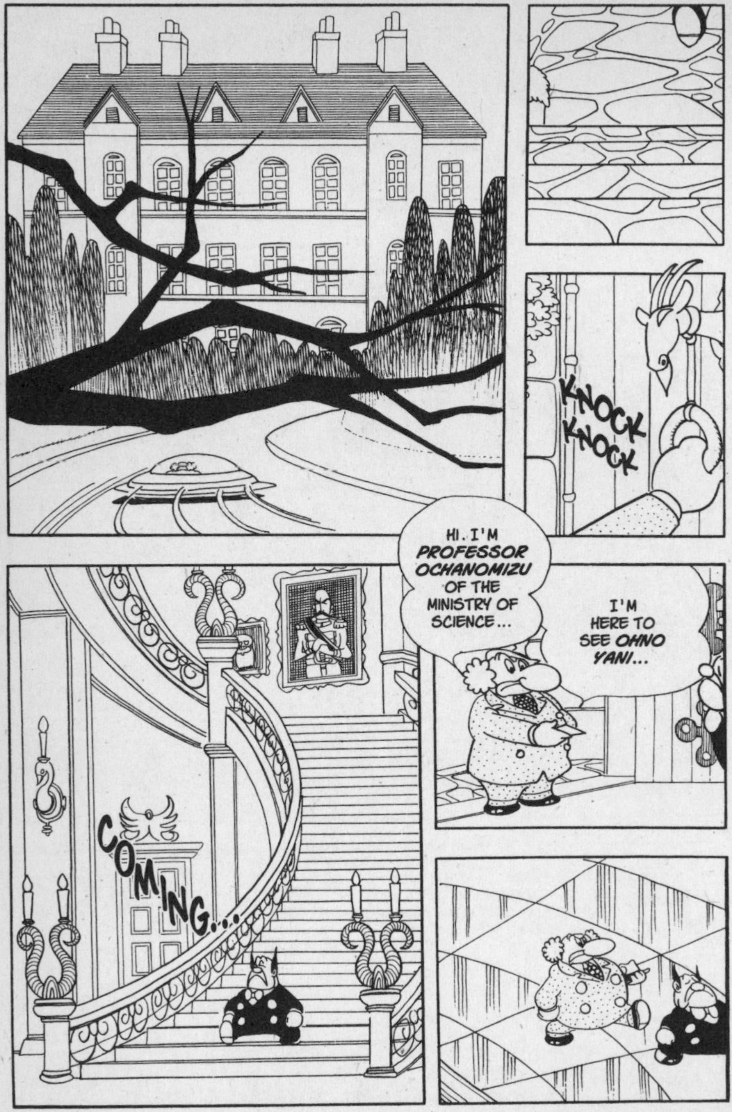
KNOCK KNOCK
HI. I'M PROFESSOR OCHANOMIZU OF THE MINISTRY OF SCIENCE...
COMING...
I'M HERE TO SEE OHNO YANI...

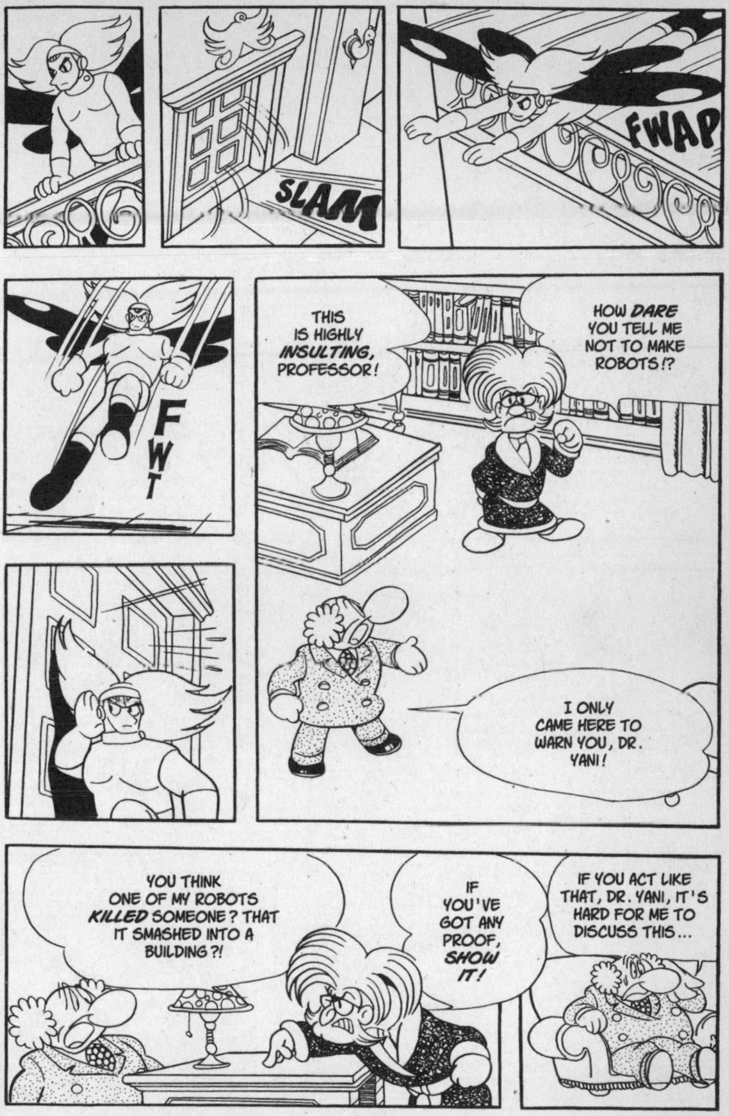
SLAM
FWAP
FWT
THIS IS HIGHLY *INSULTING*, PROFESSOR!
HOW *DARE* YOU TELL ME NOT TO MAKE ROBOTS!?
I ONLY CAME HERE TO WARN YOU, DR. YANI!
YOU THINK ONE OF MY ROBOTS *KILLED* SOMEONE? THAT IT SMASHED INTO A BUILDING?!
IF YOU'VE GOT ANY PROOF, *SHOW IT*!
IF YOU ACT LIKE THAT, DR. YANI, IT'S HARD FOR ME TO DISCUSS THIS...

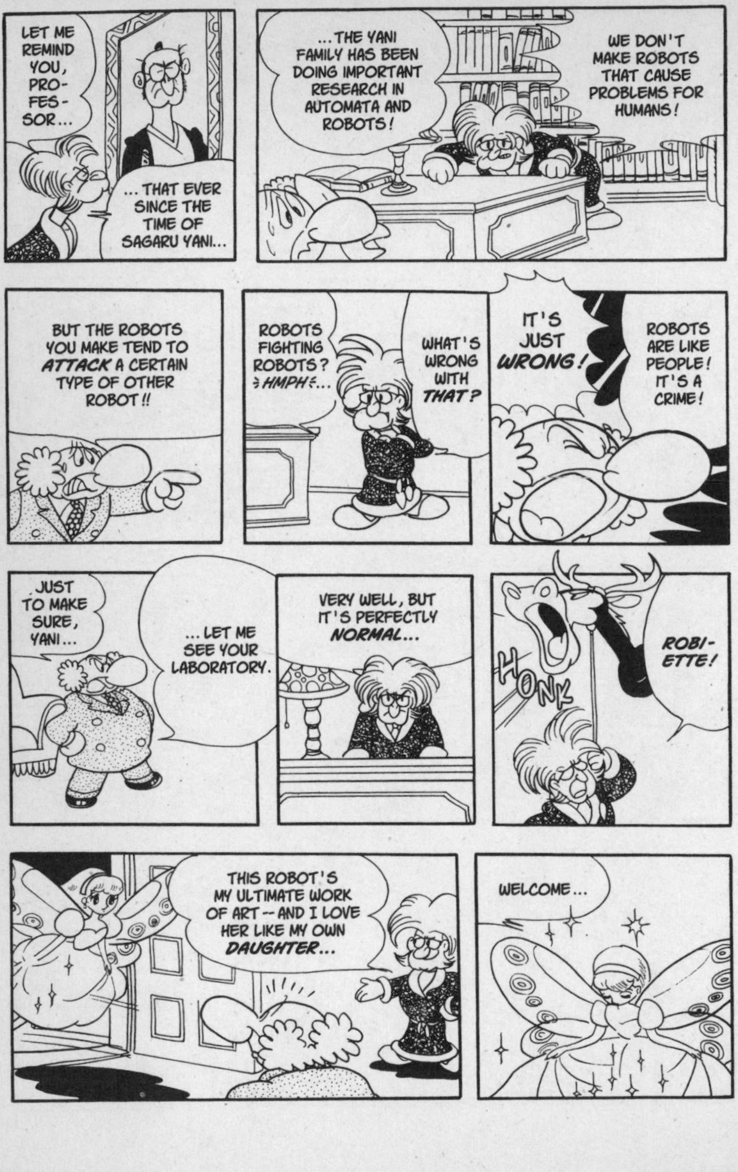
LET ME REMIND YOU, PRO-FES-SOR...
... THAT EVER SINCE THE TIME OF SAGARU YANI...
... THE YANI FAMILY HAS BEEN DOING IMPORTANT RESEARCH IN AUTOMATA AND ROBOTS!
WE DON'T MAKE ROBOTS THAT CAUSE PROBLEMS FOR HUMANS!
BUT THE ROBOTS YOU MAKE TEND TO ATTACK A CERTAIN TYPE OF OTHER ROBOT!!
ROBOTS FIGHTING ROBOTS? HMPH...
WHAT'S WRONG WITH THAT?
IT'S JUST WRONG!
ROBOTS ARE LIKE PEOPLE! IT'S A CRIME!
JUST TO MAKE SURE, YANI...
... LET ME SEE YOUR LABORATORY.
VERY WELL, BUT IT'S PERFECTLY NORMAL...
HONK
ROBI-ETTE!
THIS ROBOT'S MY ULTIMATE WORK OF ART -- AND I LOVE HER LIKE MY OWN DAUGHTER...
WELCOME...

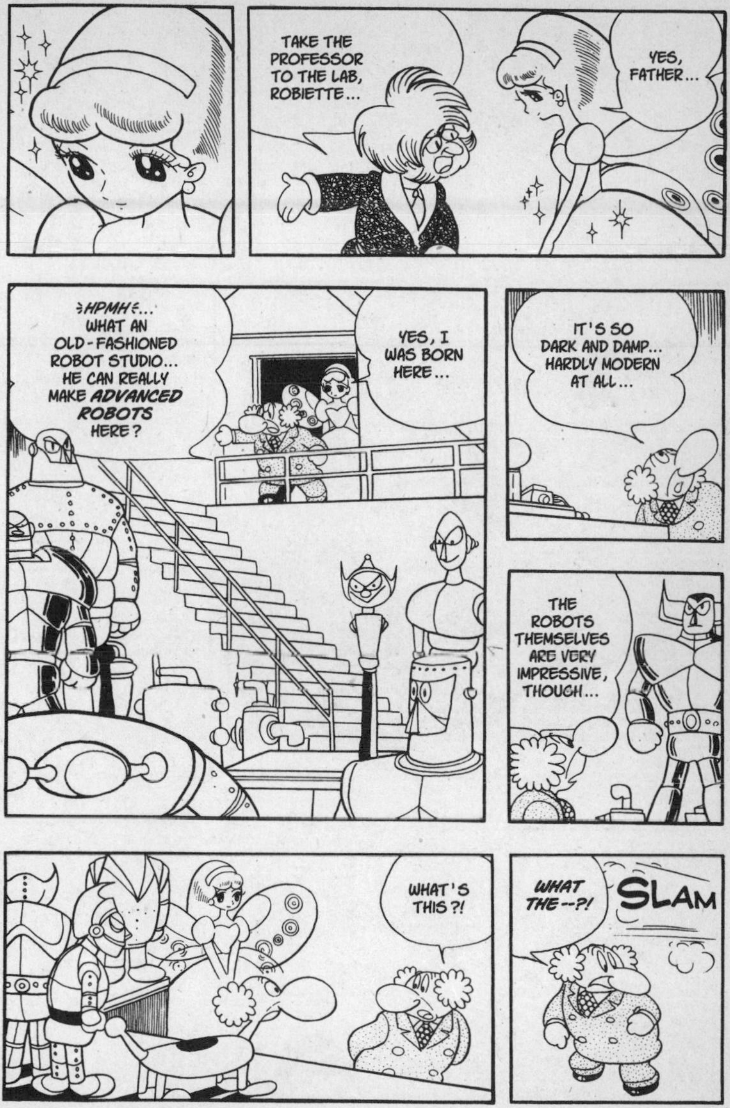

TAKE THE PROFESSOR TO THE LAB, ROBIETTE...
YES, FATHER...
≑HPMH≑... WHAT AN OLD-FASHIONED ROBOT STUDIO... HE CAN REALLY MAKE ADVANCED ROBOTS HERE?
YES, I WAS BORN HERE...
IT'S SO DARK AND DAMP... HARDLY MODERN AT ALL...
THE ROBOTS THEMSELVES ARE VERY IMPRESSIVE, THOUGH...
WHAT'S THIS?!
WHAT THE--?!
SLAM

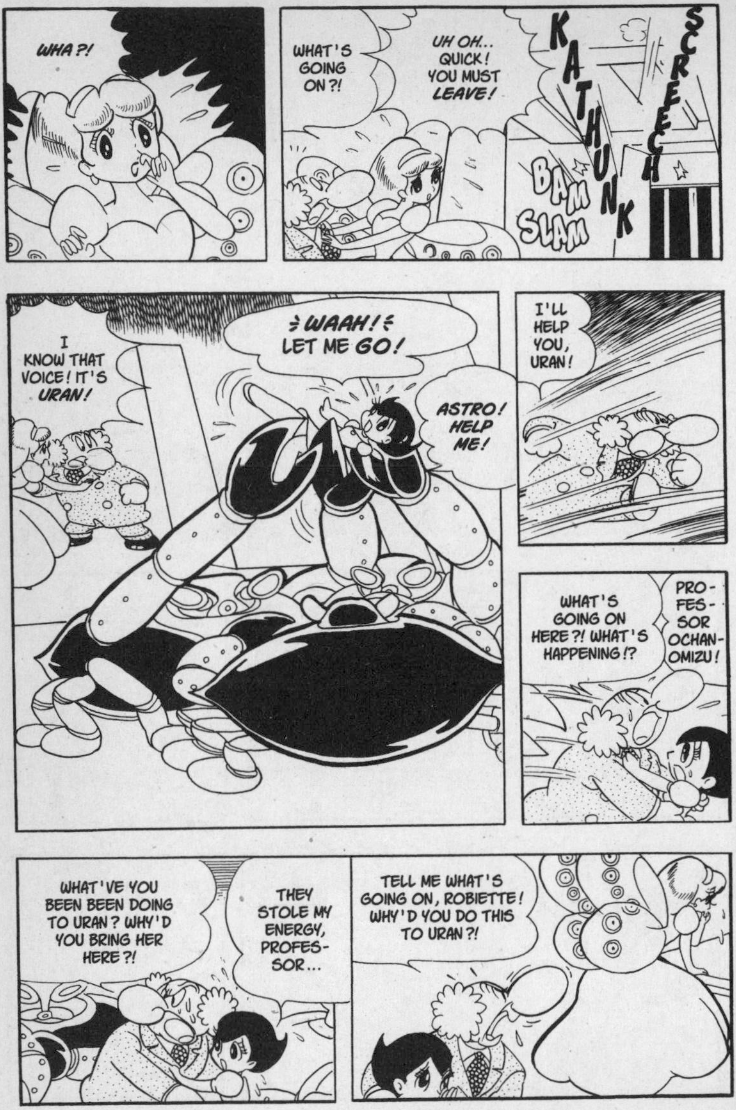
WHA?!
WHAT'S GOING ON?!
UH OH... QUICK! YOU MUST LEAVE!
KATHUNK
SCREECH
BAM
SLAM
I KNOW THAT VOICE! IT'S URAN!
WAAH! LET ME GO!
ASTRO! HELP ME!
I'LL HELP YOU, URAN!
WHAT'S GOING ON HERE?! WHAT'S HAPPENING!?
PRO-FES-SOR OCHAN-OMIZU!
WHAT'VE YOU BEEN BEEN DOING TO URAN? WHY'D YOU BRING HER HERE?!
THEY STOLE MY ENERGY, PROFES-SOR...
TELL ME WHAT'S GOING ON, ROBIETTE! WHY'D YOU DO THIS TO URAN?!

THIS SORT OF VIOLENCE WON'T STAND, ROBIETTE! AND IF IT DOESN'T STOP, I'LL TELL THE *POLICE!!* I'LL...

... I'LL HAVE YOU ARRESTED UNDER THE ANTI-VIOLENCE LAWS! WELL, WHAT DO YOU SAY?

WHAT'S GOING ON?! THAT ROBOT'S SUPPOSED TO BE SMASHED!

UH OH... ANOTHER WEIRDO...

GET THEM!

YIKES!

STOP!!

91

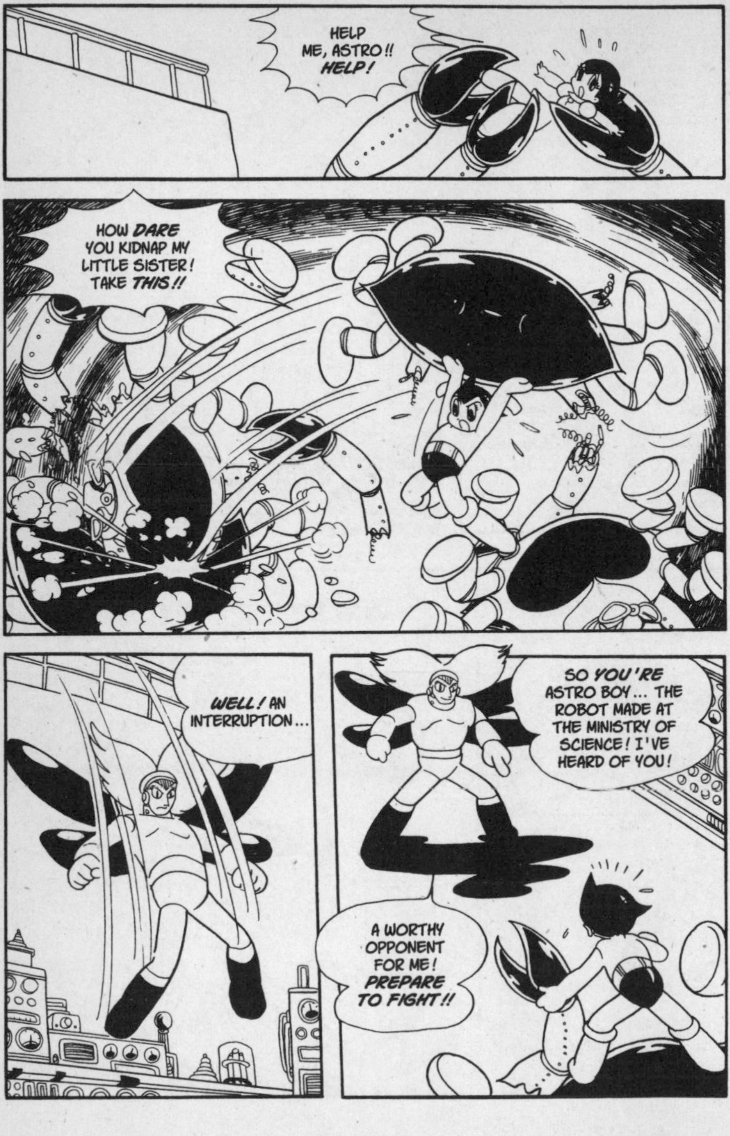
HELP ME, ASTRO!! HELP!
HOW DARE YOU KIDNAP MY LITTLE SISTER! TAKE THIS!!
WELL! AN INTERRUPTION...
SO YOU'RE ASTRO BOY... THE ROBOT MADE AT THE MINISTRY OF SCIENCE! I'VE HEARD OF YOU!
A WORTHY OPPONENT FOR ME! PREPARE TO FIGHT!!

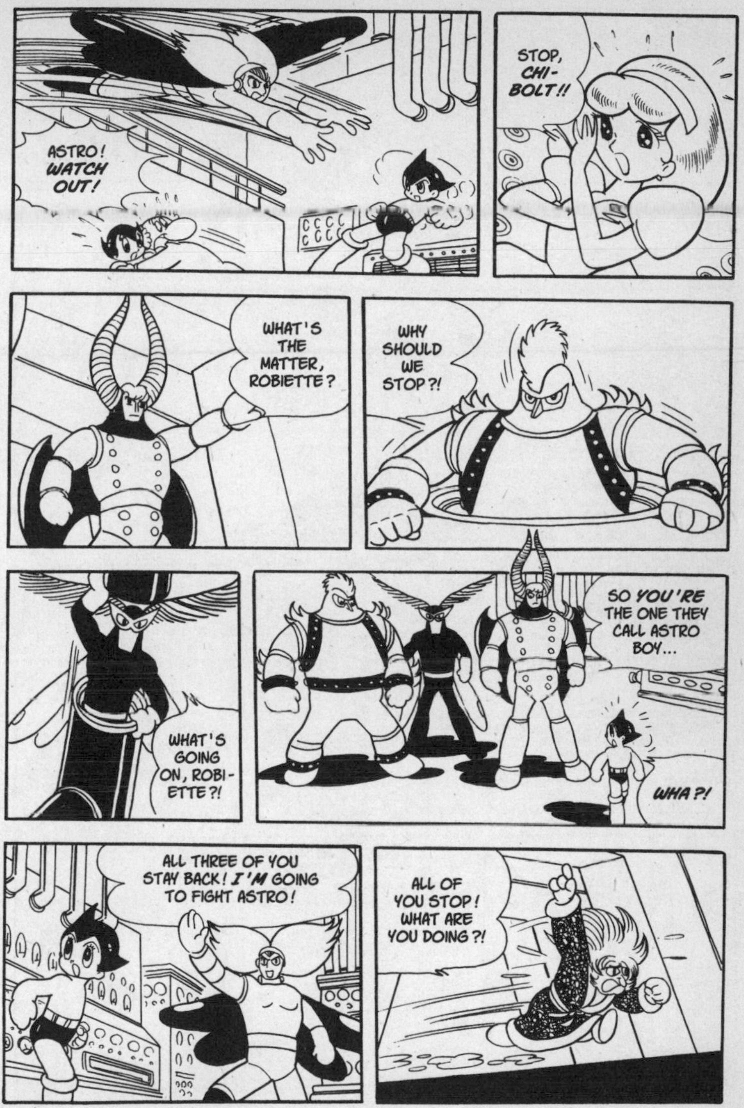
ASTRO! WATCH OUT!
STOP, CHI-BOLT!!
WHAT'S THE MATTER, ROBIETTE?
WHY SHOULD WE STOP?!
WHAT'S GOING ON, ROBI-ETTE?!
SO YOU'RE THE ONE THEY CALL ASTRO BOY...
WHA?!
ALL THREE OF YOU STAY BACK! I'M GOING TO FIGHT ASTRO!
ALL OF YOU STOP! WHAT ARE YOU DOING?!

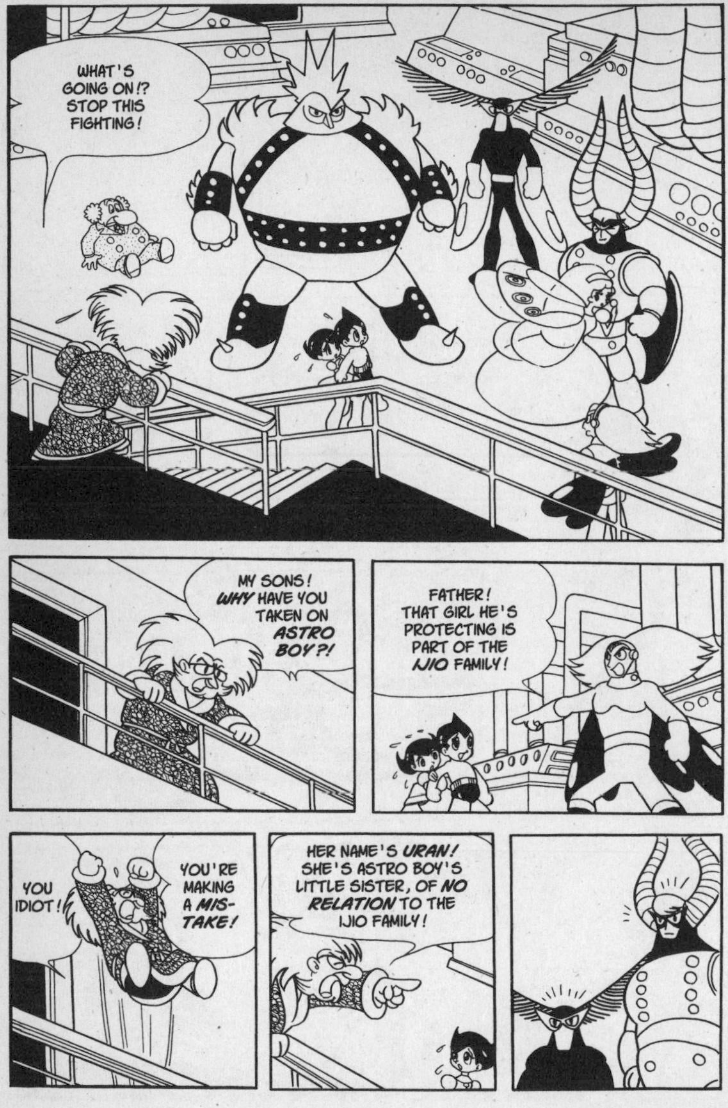
WHAT'S GOING ON!? STOP THIS FIGHTING!
MY SONS! WHY HAVE YOU TAKEN ON ASTRO BOY?!
FATHER! THAT GIRL HE'S PROTECTING IS PART OF THE IJIO FAMILY!
YOU IDIOT!
YOU'RE MAKING A MIS-TAKE!
HER NAME'S URAN! SHE'S ASTRO BOY'S LITTLE SISTER, OF NO RELATION TO THE IJIO FAMILY!

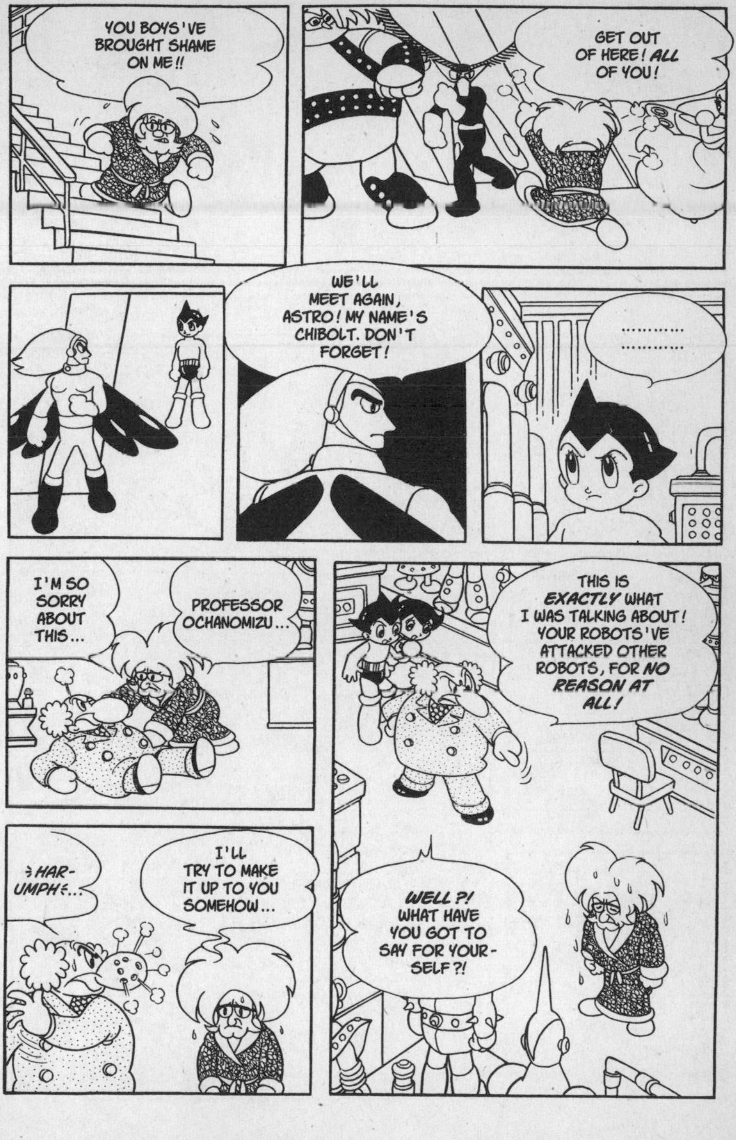
YOU BOYS'VE BROUGHT SHAME ON ME!!
GET OUT OF HERE! ALL OF YOU!
WE'LL MEET AGAIN, ASTRO! MY NAME'S CHIBOLT. DON'T FORGET!
....
....
I'M SO SORRY ABOUT THIS...
PROFESSOR OCHANOMIZU...
THIS IS EXACTLY WHAT I WAS TALKING ABOUT! YOUR ROBOTS'VE ATTACKED OTHER ROBOTS, FOR NO REASON AT ALL!
≠HAR-UMPH≠...
I'LL TRY TO MAKE IT UP TO YOU SOMEHOW...
WELL?! WHAT HAVE YOU GOT TO SAY FOR YOURSELF?!

OKAY, URAN... TELL US HOW YOU WERE KIDNAPPED!

IT WAS RIGHT AFTER DINNER... I WAS INVITED SOME-PLACE, 'N THEN THAT BIG CRAB GUY CAME ALONG...

SEE, YANI? YOUR ROBOTS MISTOOK URAN FOR A MEMBER OF THE IJIO FAMILY AND *KIDNAPPED* HER!

WELL, YANI? WHAT DO YOU HAVE TO SAY?

....

....

I KNOW YOU HATE MR. IJIO. BUT YOUR FEELINGS HAVE TRANSFERRED TO YOUR ROBOTS. THEY'RE CAUSING TROUBLE AS A RESULT!

ASTRO, TAKE YOUR SISTER HOME, OKAY...?

SURE, BUT...

I'VE GOT SOMETHING TO TALK ABOUT WITH DR. YANI...

OKAY...

WAIT!

WHA?! WHO'S CALLING ME?!

96

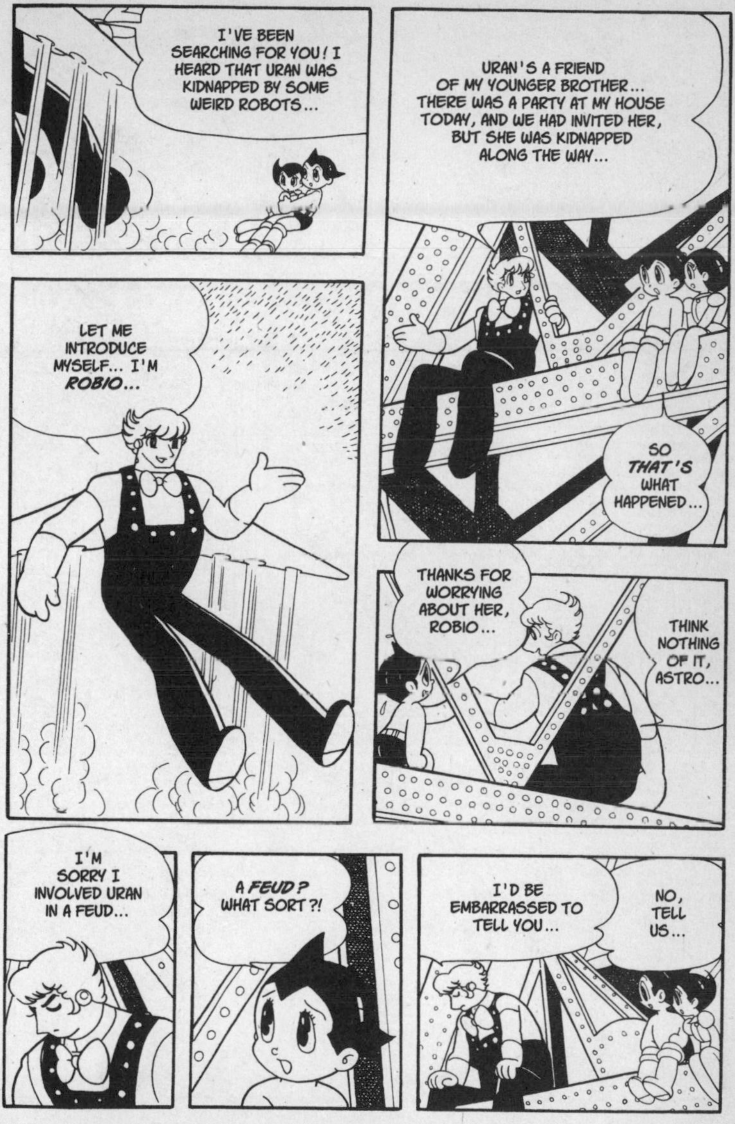
I'VE BEEN SEARCHING FOR YOU! I HEARD THAT URAN WAS KIDNAPPED BY SOME WEIRD ROBOTS...
LET ME INTRODUCE MYSELF... I'M *ROBIO*...
URAN'S A FRIEND OF MY YOUNGER BROTHER... THERE WAS A PARTY AT MY HOUSE TODAY, AND WE HAD INVITED HER, BUT SHE WAS KIDNAPPED ALONG THE WAY...
SO *THAT'S* WHAT HAPPENED...
THANKS FOR WORRYING ABOUT HER, ROBIO...
THINK NOTHING OF IT, ASTRO...
I'M SORRY I INVOLVED URAN IN A FEUD...
A *FEUD?* WHAT SORT?!
I'D BE EMBARRASSED TO TELL YOU...
NO, TELL US...

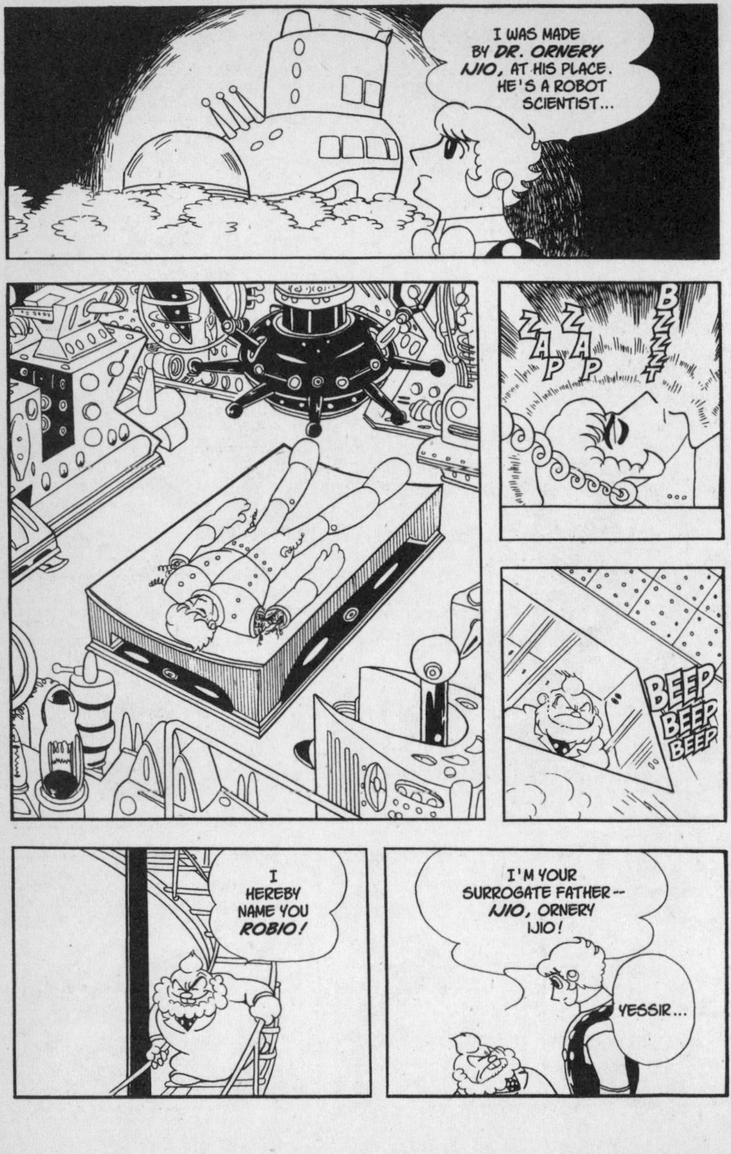
I WAS MADE BY DR. ORNERY IJIO, AT HIS PLACE. HE'S A ROBOT SCIENTIST...
ZAP ZAP
BZZZT
...
BEEP BEEP BEEP
I HEREBY NAME YOU ROBIO!
I'M YOUR SURROGATE FATHER-- IJIO, ORNERY IJIO!
YESSIR...

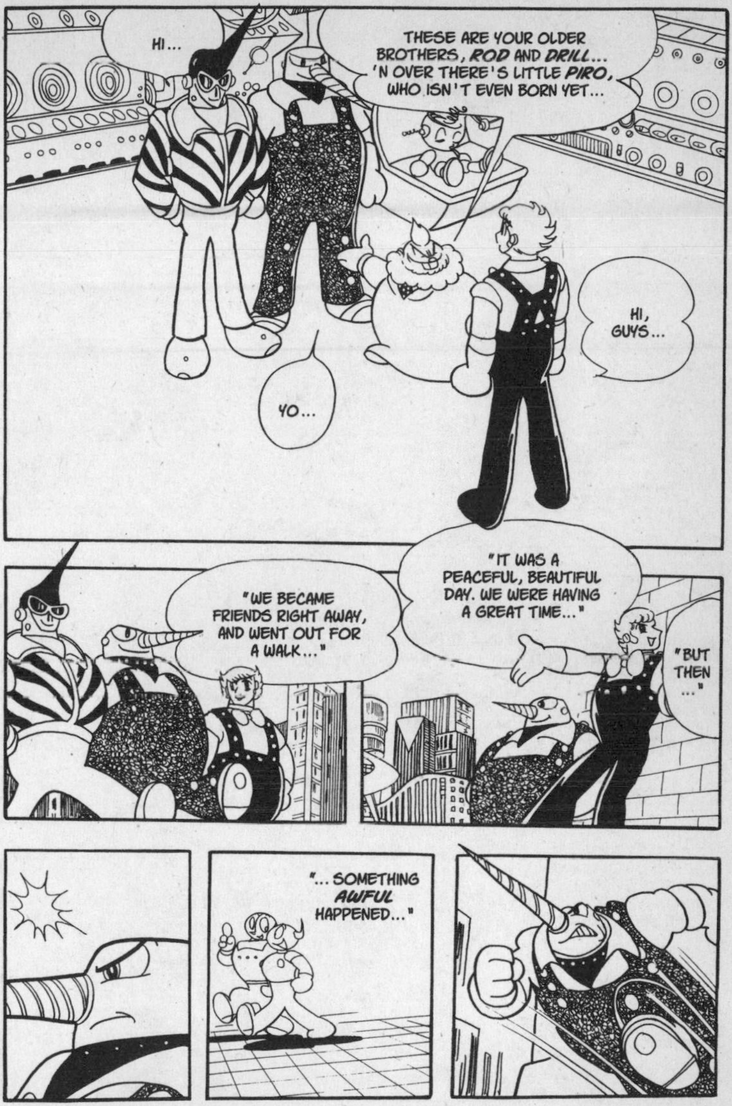
HI...
THESE ARE YOUR OLDER BROTHERS, ROD AND DRILL... 'N OVER THERE'S LITTLE PIRO, WHO ISN'T EVEN BORN YET...
YO...
HI, GUYS...
"WE BECAME FRIENDS RIGHT AWAY, AND WENT OUT FOR A WALK..."
"IT WAS A PEACEFUL, BEAUTIFUL DAY. WE WERE HAVING A GREAT TIME..."
"BUT THEN ..."
"... SOMETHING AWFUL HAPPENED..."

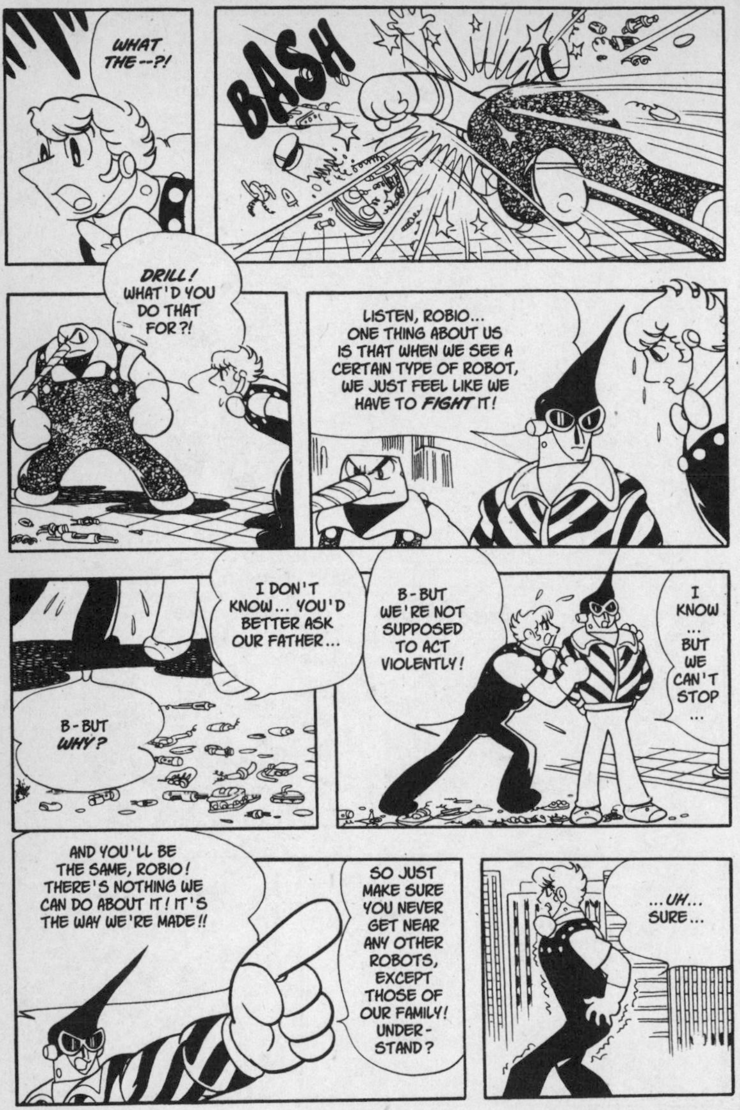
WHAT THE--?!
BASH
DRILL! WHAT'D YOU DO THAT FOR?!
LISTEN, ROBIO... ONE THING ABOUT US IS THAT WHEN WE SEE A CERTAIN TYPE OF ROBOT, WE JUST FEEL LIKE WE HAVE TO *FIGHT* IT!
B-BUT *WHY*?
I DON'T KNOW... YOU'D BETTER ASK OUR FATHER...
B-BUT WE'RE NOT SUPPOSED TO ACT VIOLENTLY!
I KNOW ... BUT WE CAN'T STOP ...
AND YOU'LL BE THE SAME, ROBIO! THERE'S NOTHING WE CAN DO ABOUT IT! IT'S THE WAY WE'RE MADE!!
SO JUST MAKE SURE YOU NEVER GET NEAR ANY OTHER ROBOTS, EXCEPT THOSE OF OUR FAMILY! UNDER-STAND?
...UH... SURE...

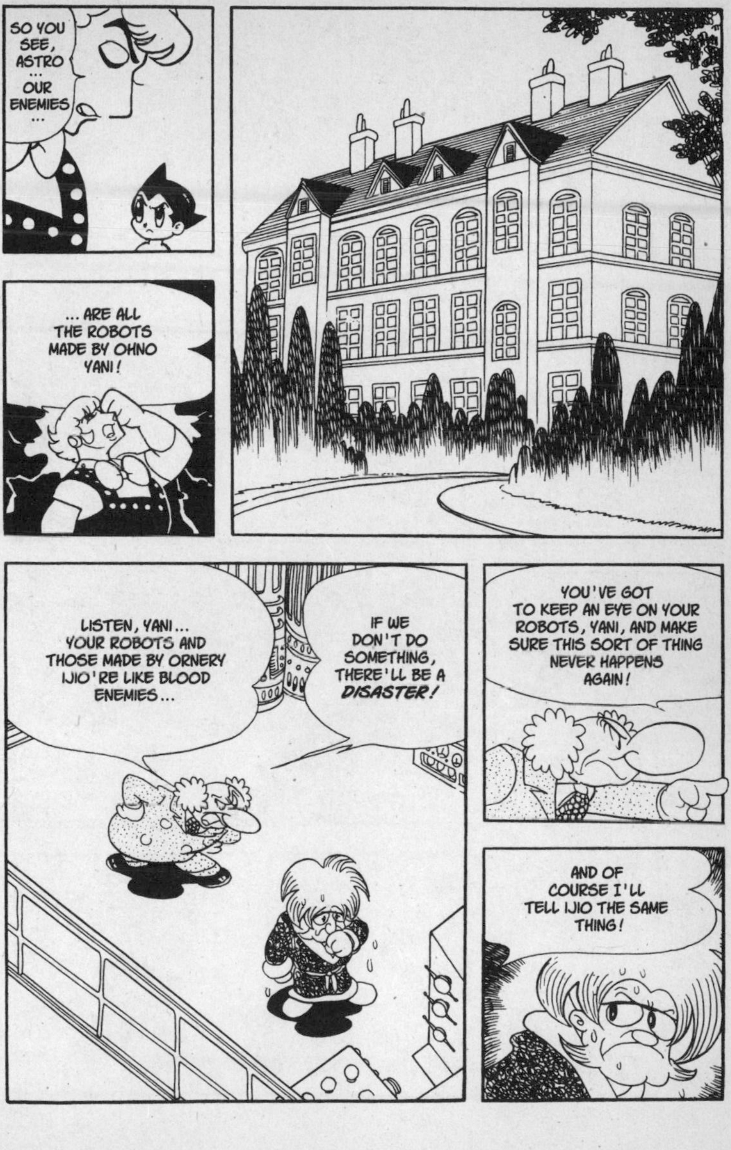
SO YOU SEE, ASTRO ... OUR ENEMIES ...
... ARE ALL THE ROBOTS MADE BY OHNO YANI!
LISTEN, YANI... YOUR ROBOTS AND THOSE MADE BY ORNERY IJIO'RE LIKE BLOOD ENEMIES...
IF WE DON'T DO SOMETHING, THERE'LL BE A *DISASTER!*
YOU'VE GOT TO KEEP AN EYE ON YOUR ROBOTS, YANI, AND MAKE SURE THIS SORT OF THING NEVER HAPPENS AGAIN!
AND OF COURSE I'LL TELL IJIO THE SAME THING!

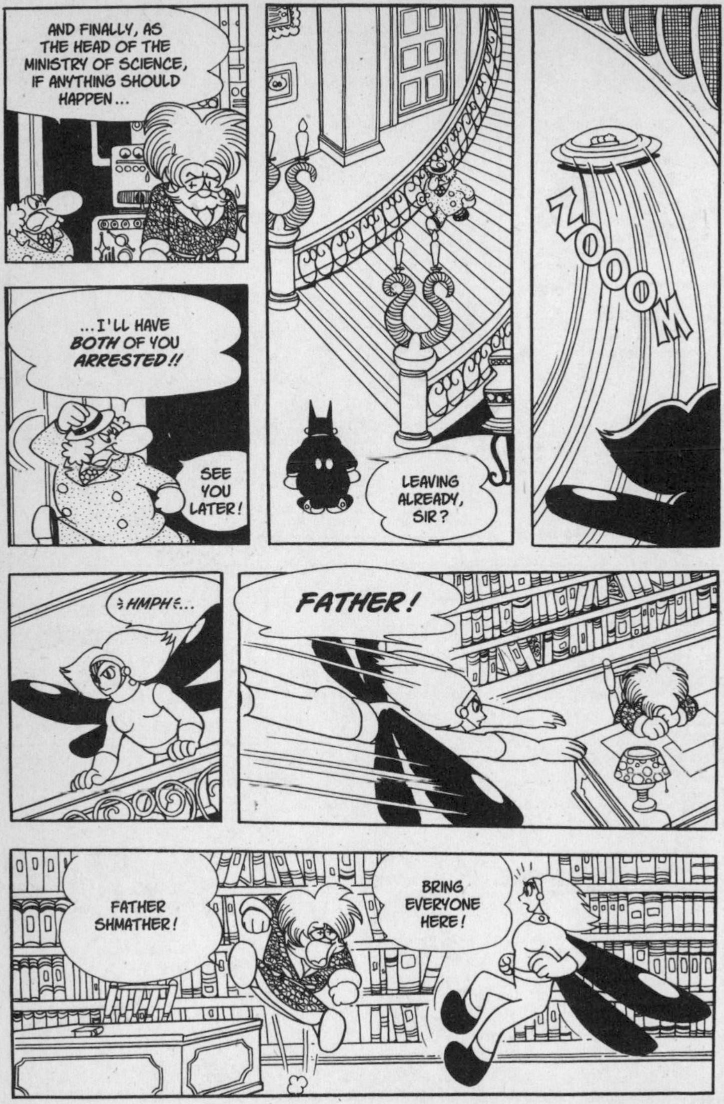
AND FINALLY, AS THE HEAD OF THE MINISTRY OF SCIENCE, IF ANYTHING SHOULD HAPPEN ...
...I'LL HAVE *BOTH* OF YOU *ARRESTED!!*
SEE YOU LATER!
LEAVING ALREADY, SIR?
ZOOOM
HMPH...
FATHER!
FATHER SHMATHER!
BRING EVERYONE HERE!

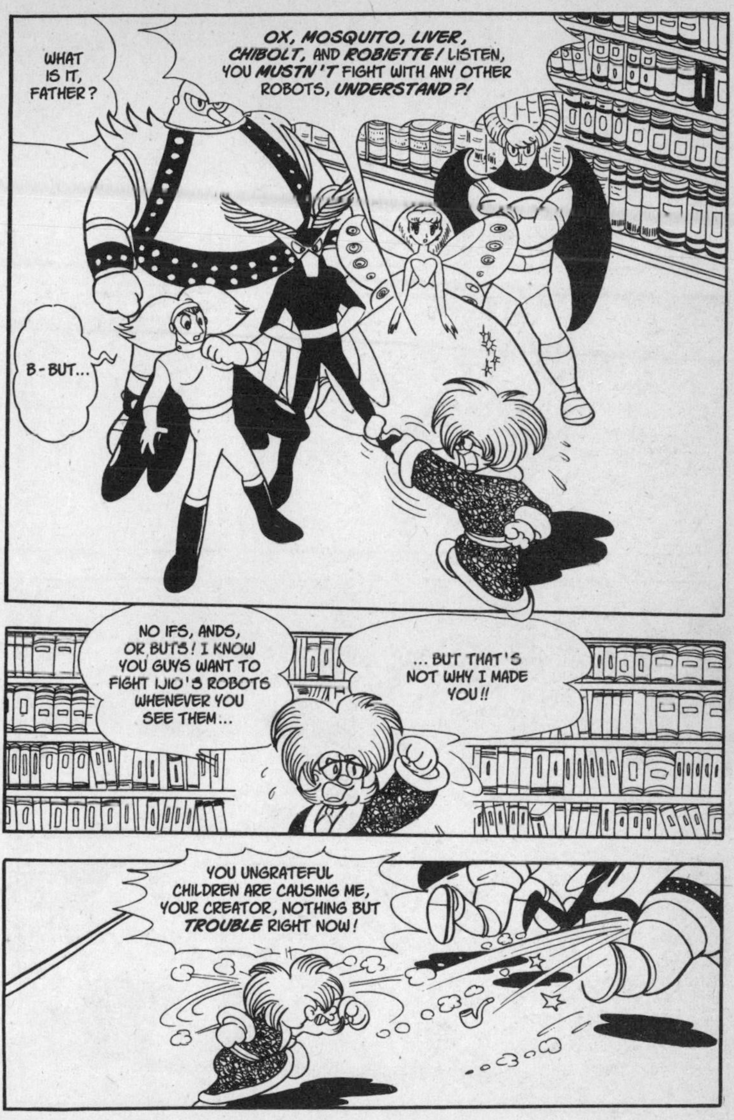
WHAT IS IT, FATHER?
OX, MOSQUITO, LIVER, CHIBOLT, AND ROBIETTE! LISTEN, YOU MUSTN'T FIGHT WITH ANY OTHER ROBOTS, UNDERSTAND?!
B-BUT...
NO IFS, ANDS, OR BUTS! I KNOW YOU GUYS WANT TO FIGHT IJIO'S ROBOTS WHENEVER YOU SEE THEM...
... BUT THAT'S NOT WHY I MADE YOU!!
YOU UNGRATEFUL CHILDREN ARE CAUSING ME, YOUR CREATOR, NOTHING BUT TROUBLE RIGHT NOW!

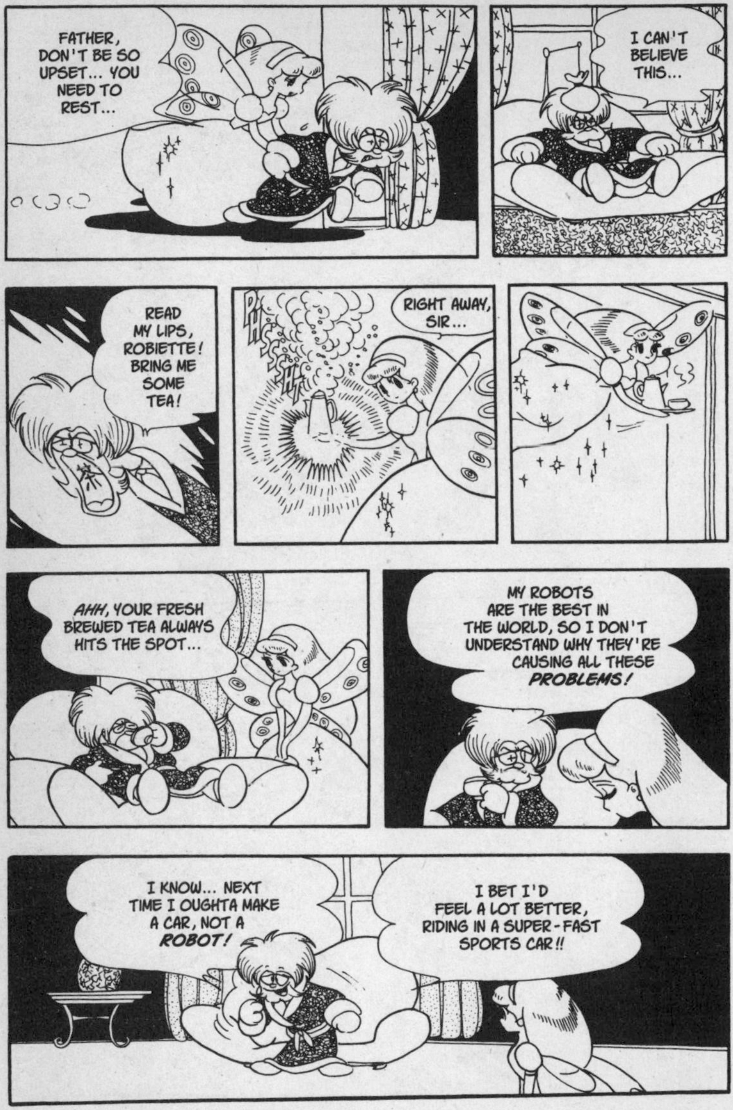
FATHER, DON'T BE SO UPSET... YOU NEED TO REST...
I CAN'T BELIEVE THIS...
READ MY LIPS, ROBIETTE! BRING ME SOME TEA!
PHSSH
RIGHT AWAY, SIR...
AHH, YOUR FRESH BREWED TEA ALWAYS HITS THE SPOT...
MY ROBOTS ARE THE BEST IN THE WORLD, SO I DON'T UNDERSTAND WHY THEY'RE CAUSING ALL THESE PROBLEMS!
I KNOW... NEXT TIME I OUGHTA MAKE A CAR, NOT A ROBOT!
I BET I'D FEEL A LOT BETTER, RIDING IN A SUPER-FAST SPORTS CAR!!

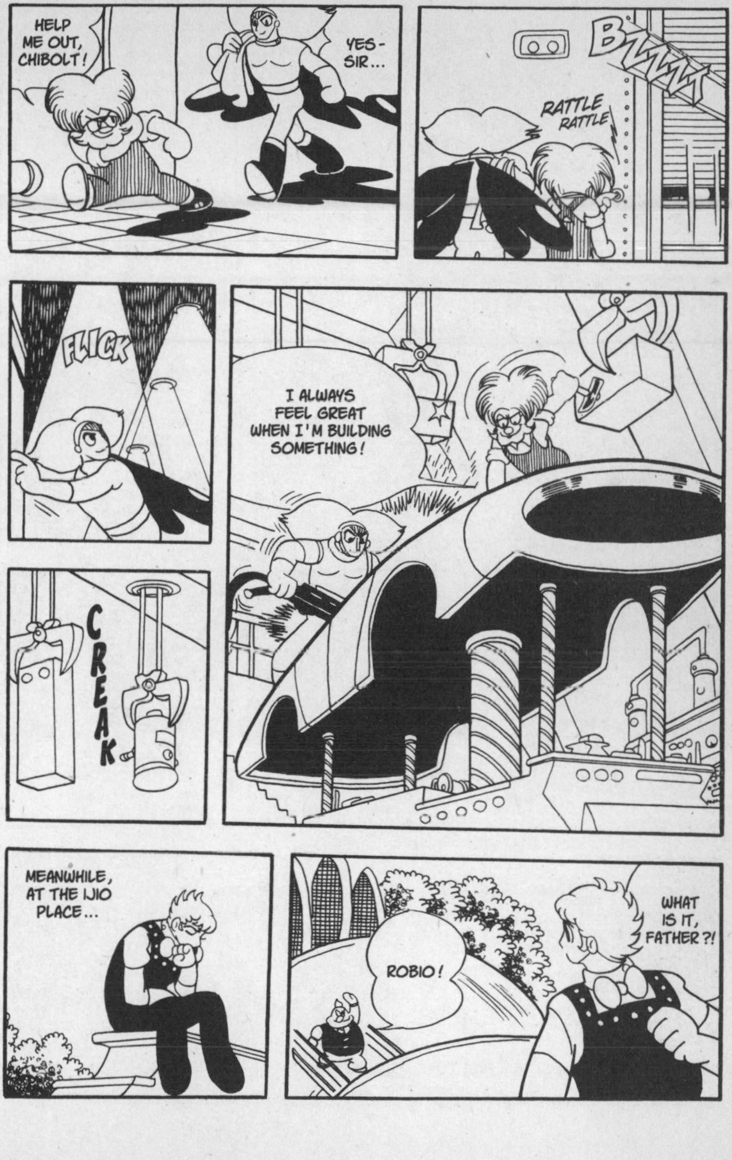
HELP ME OUT, CHIBOLT!
YES-SIR...
BZZZT
RATTLE RATTLE
FLICK
I ALWAYS FEEL GREAT WHEN I'M BUILDING SOMETHING!
CREAK
MEANWHILE, AT THE IJIO PLACE...
ROBIO!
WHAT IS IT, FATHER?!

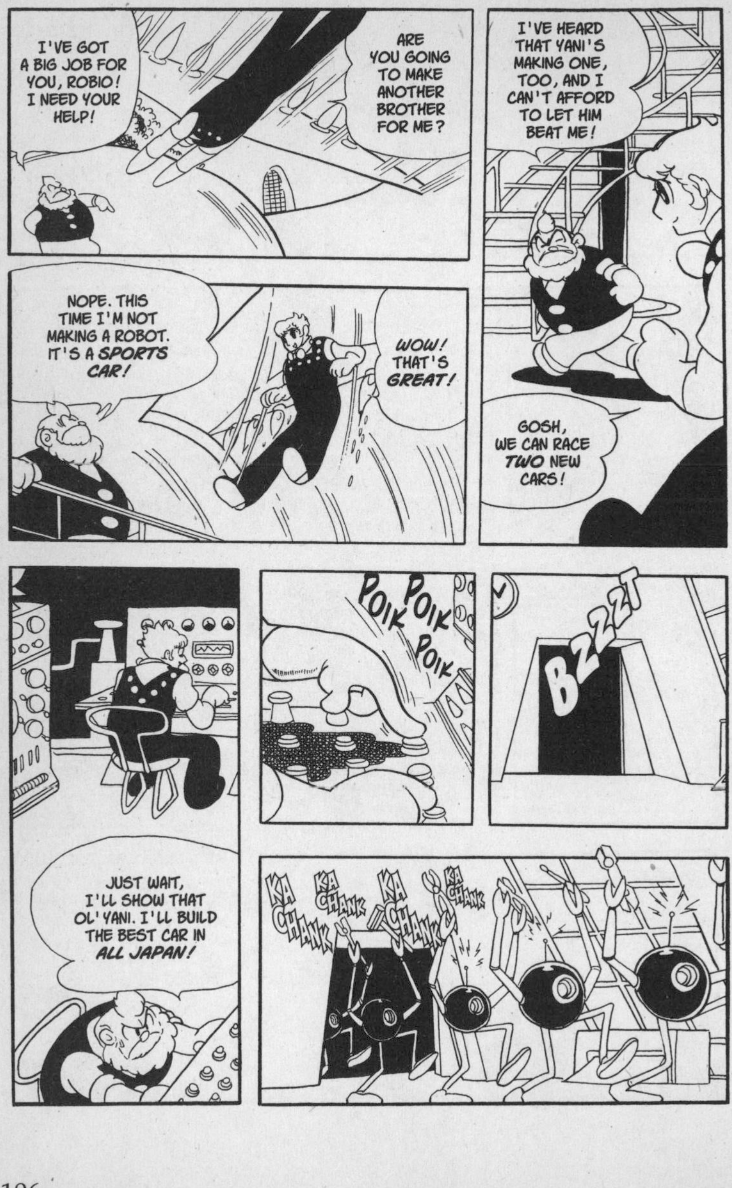
I'VE GOT A BIG JOB FOR YOU, ROBIO! I NEED YOUR HELP!
ARE YOU GOING TO MAKE ANOTHER BROTHER FOR ME?
NOPE. THIS TIME I'M NOT MAKING A ROBOT. IT'S A *SPORTS CAR!*
WOW! THAT'S *GREAT!*
I'VE HEARD THAT YANI'S MAKING ONE, TOO, AND I CAN'T AFFORD TO LET HIM BEAT ME!
GOSH, WE CAN RACE *TWO* NEW CARS!
JUST WAIT, I'LL SHOW THAT OL' YANI. I'LL BUILD THE BEST CAR IN *ALL JAPAN!*
POIK POIK POIK POIK
BZZZZT
KA CHANK
KA CHANK
KA CHANK
KA CHANK

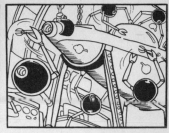

'ELLO...
IJIO HERE...

WHAT?!
YANI? WHAT
THE --?!

I MEAN, GOSH, SURE IS NICE
WEATHER... TOMORROW, TOO,
HUH... DUNNO 'BOUT THE DAY
AFTER TOMORROW,
THOUGH...

DID OCHANOMIZU
VISIT YOUR PLACE, TOO,
DR. YANI? REALLY? WELL,
HE CAME HERE, TOO...

HE SAID WE WERE
SWORN ENEMIES...
EVER HEAR OF SUCH
NONSENSE?!

BY
THE WAY,
I'VE HEARD
YOU'RE MAKING
A *SPORTS
CAR*...

SO YOU'VE
HEARD ALREADY, *EH*?
WELL, IT'S TRUE. I
AM MAKING ONE, THE
BEST IN *ALL
JAPAN*!

107

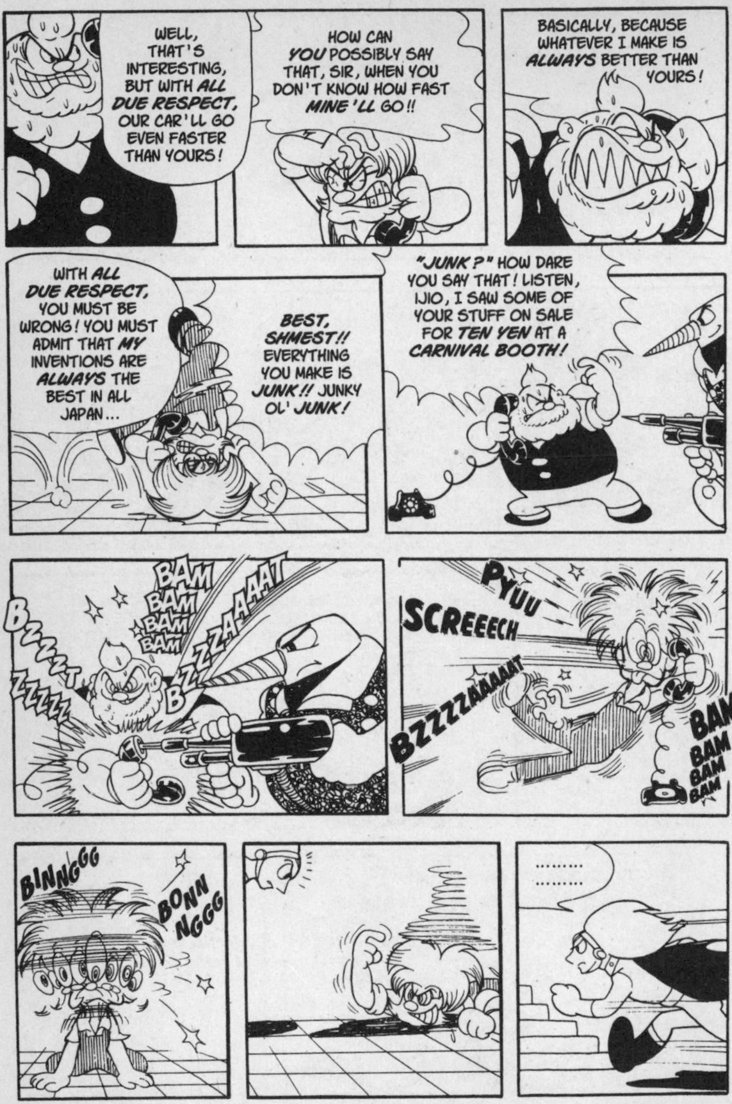
WELL, THAT'S INTERESTING, BUT WITH ALL DUE RESPECT, OUR CAR'LL GO EVEN FASTER THAN YOURS!
HOW CAN YOU POSSIBLY SAY THAT, SIR, WHEN YOU DON'T KNOW HOW FAST MINE'LL GO!!
BASICALLY, BECAUSE WHATEVER I MAKE IS ALWAYS BETTER THAN YOURS!
WITH ALL DUE RESPECT, YOU MUST BE WRONG! YOU MUST ADMIT THAT MY INVENTIONS ARE ALWAYS THE BEST IN ALL JAPAN...
BEST, SHMEST!! EVERYTHING YOU MAKE IS JUNK!! JUNKY OL' JUNK!
"JUNK?" HOW DARE YOU SAY THAT! LISTEN, IJIO, I SAW SOME OF YOUR STUFF ON SALE FOR TEN YEN AT A CARNIVAL BOOTH!
BZZZZT
ZZZZZ
BAM
BAM
BAM
BAM
BZZZZAAAAT
PYUU
SCREEECH
BZZZZAAAAAT
BAM
BAM
BAM
BAM
BINNGGG
BONNNGGG
....
....

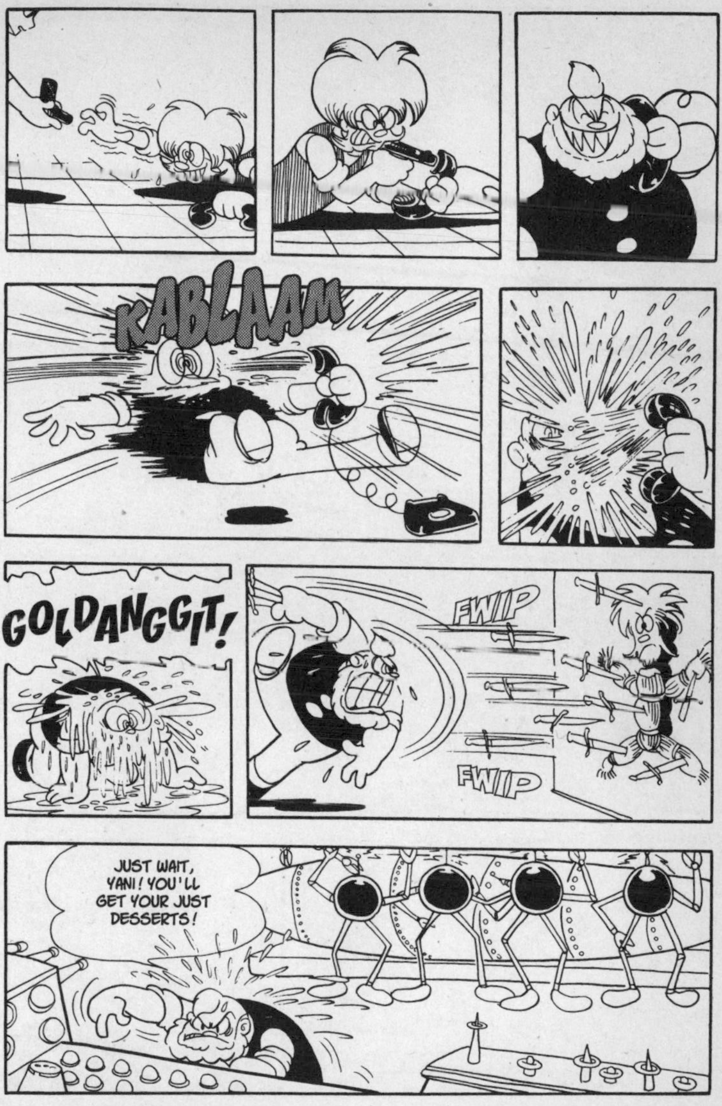
KABLAAM
GOLDANGGIT!
FWIP
FWIP
JUST WAIT, YANI! YOU'LL GET YOUR JUST DESSERTS!

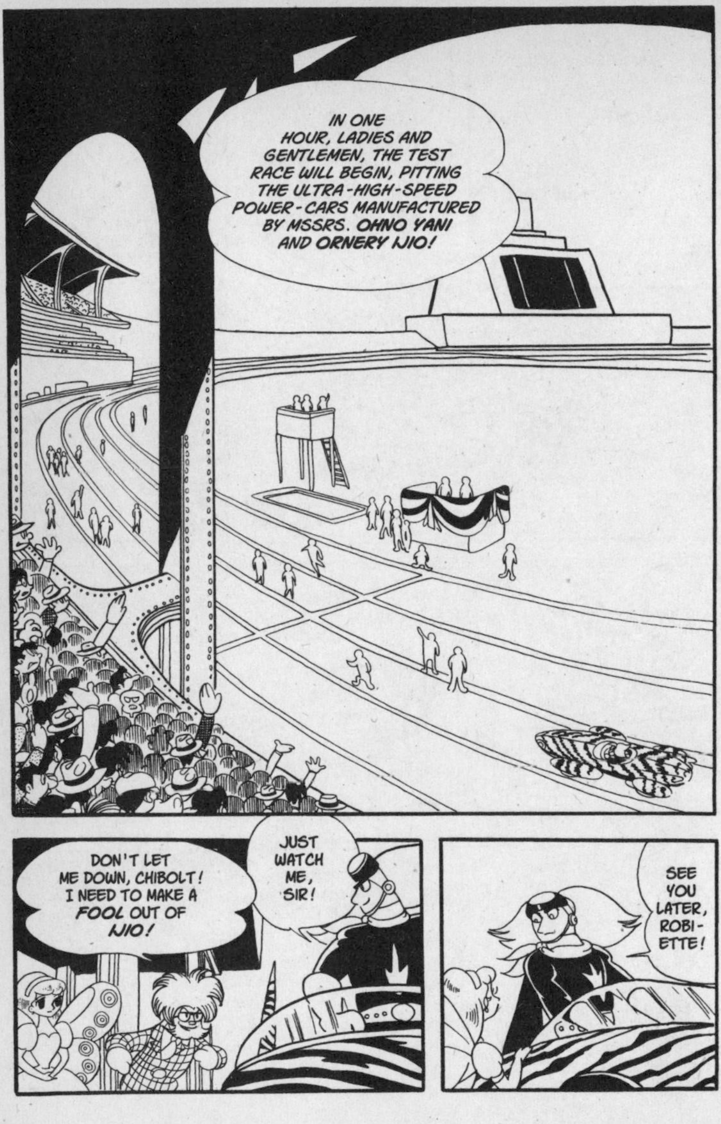
IN ONE HOUR, LADIES AND GENTLEMEN, THE TEST RACE WILL BEGIN, PITTING THE ULTRA-HIGH-SPEED POWER-CARS MANUFACTURED BY MSSRS. OHNO YANI AND ORNERY IJIO!
DON'T LET ME DOWN, CHIBOLT! I NEED TO MAKE A FOOL OUT OF IJIO!
JUST WATCH ME, SIR!
SEE YOU LATER, ROBI-ETTE!

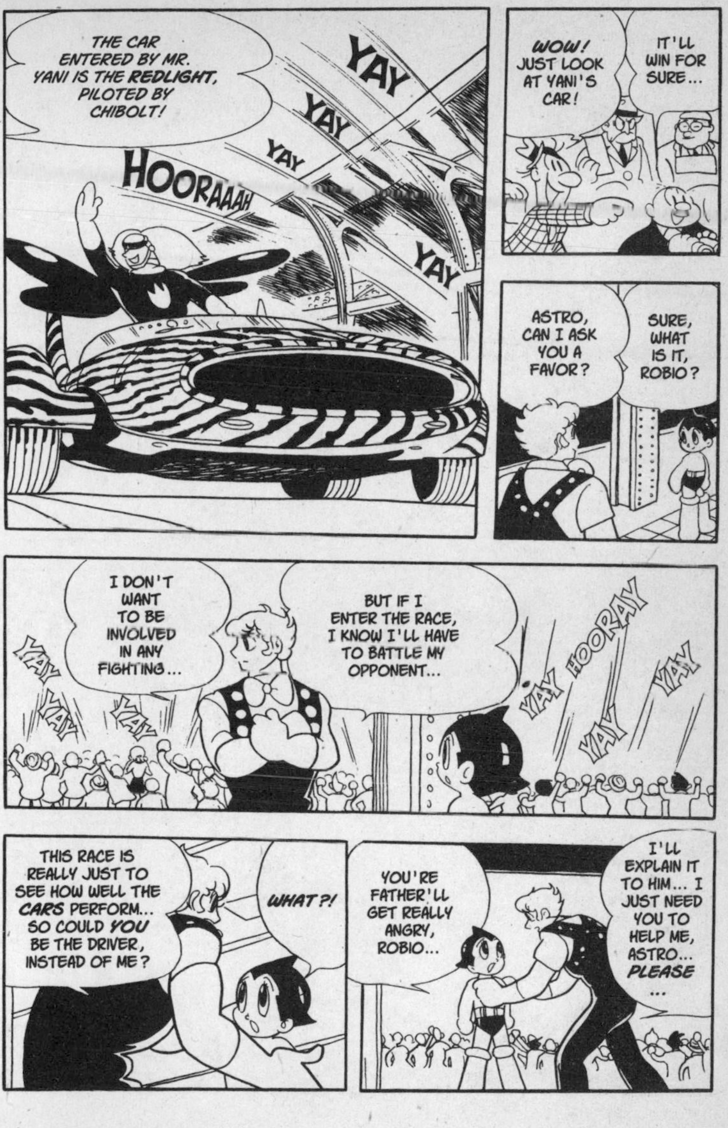
THE CAR ENTERED BY MR. YANI IS THE **REDLIGHT**, PILOTED BY CHIBOLT!
YAY
YAY
YAY
HOORAAAH
YAY
WOW! JUST LOOK AT YANI'S CAR!
IT'LL WIN FOR SURE...
ASTRO, CAN I ASK YOU A FAVOR?
SURE, WHAT IS IT, ROBIO?
I DON'T WANT TO BE INVOLVED IN ANY FIGHTING...
BUT IF I ENTER THE RACE, I KNOW I'LL HAVE TO BATTLE MY OPPONENT...
YAY
YAY
YAY
YAY
HOORAY
YAY
YAY
THIS RACE IS REALLY JUST TO SEE HOW WELL THE ***CARS*** PERFORM... SO COULD ***YOU*** BE THE DRIVER, INSTEAD OF ME?
WHAT?!
YOU'RE FATHER'LL GET REALLY ANGRY, ROBIO...
I'LL EXPLAIN IT TO HIM... I JUST NEED YOU TO HELP ME, ASTRO... ***PLEASE***...

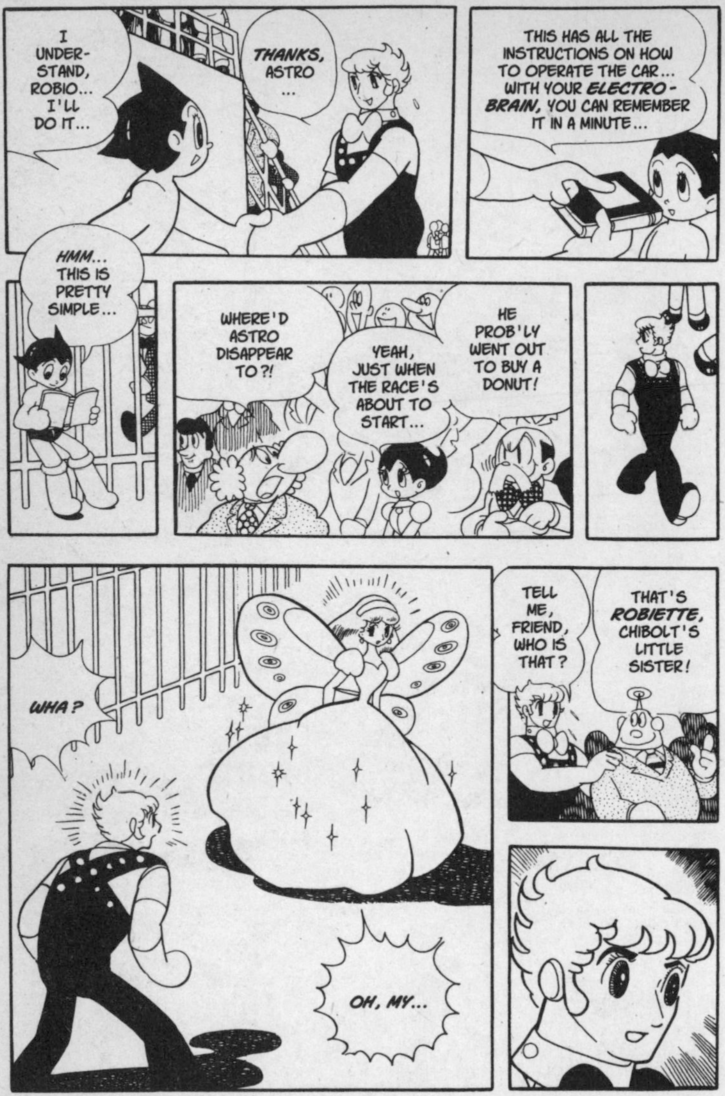
I UNDER-STAND, ROBIO... I'LL DO IT...
THANKS, ASTRO...
THIS HAS ALL THE INSTRUCTIONS ON HOW TO OPERATE THE CAR... WITH YOUR ELECTRO-BRAIN, YOU CAN REMEMBER IT IN A MINUTE...
HMM... THIS IS PRETTY SIMPLE...
WHERE'D ASTRO DISAPPEAR TO?!
YEAH, JUST WHEN THE RACE'S ABOUT TO START...
HE PROB'LY WENT OUT TO BUY A DONUT!
WHA?
OH, MY...
TELL ME, FRIEND, WHO IS THAT?
THAT'S ROBIETTE, CHIBOLT'S LITTLE SISTER!

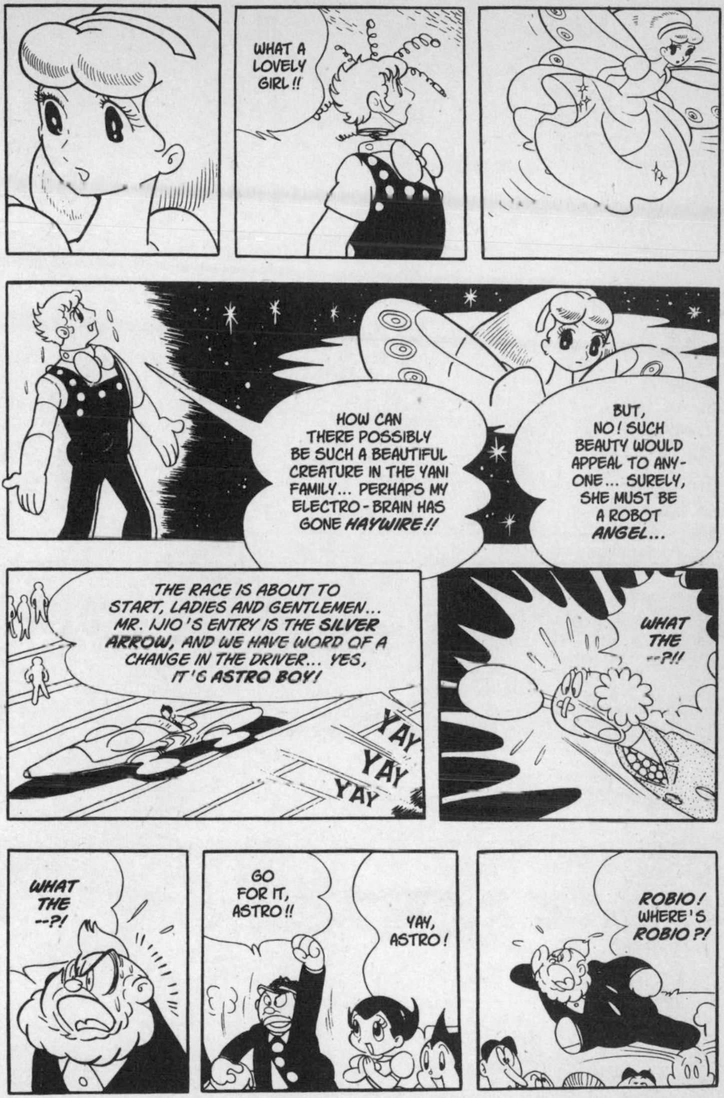
WHAT A LOVELY GIRL !!
HOW CAN THERE POSSIBLY BE SUCH A BEAUTIFUL CREATURE IN THE YANI FAMILY... PERHAPS MY ELECTRO-BRAIN HAS GONE HAYWIRE !!
BUT, NO! SUCH BEAUTY WOULD APPEAL TO ANY-ONE... SURELY, SHE MUST BE A ROBOT ANGEL...
THE RACE IS ABOUT TO START, LADIES AND GENTLEMEN... MR. IJIO'S ENTRY IS THE SILVER ARROW, AND WE HAVE WORD OF A CHANGE IN THE DRIVER... YES, IT'S ASTRO BOY!
YAY
YAY
YAY
WHAT THE --?!!
WHAT THE --?!
GO FOR IT, ASTRO !!
YAY, ASTRO!
ROBIO! WHERE'S ROBIO ?!

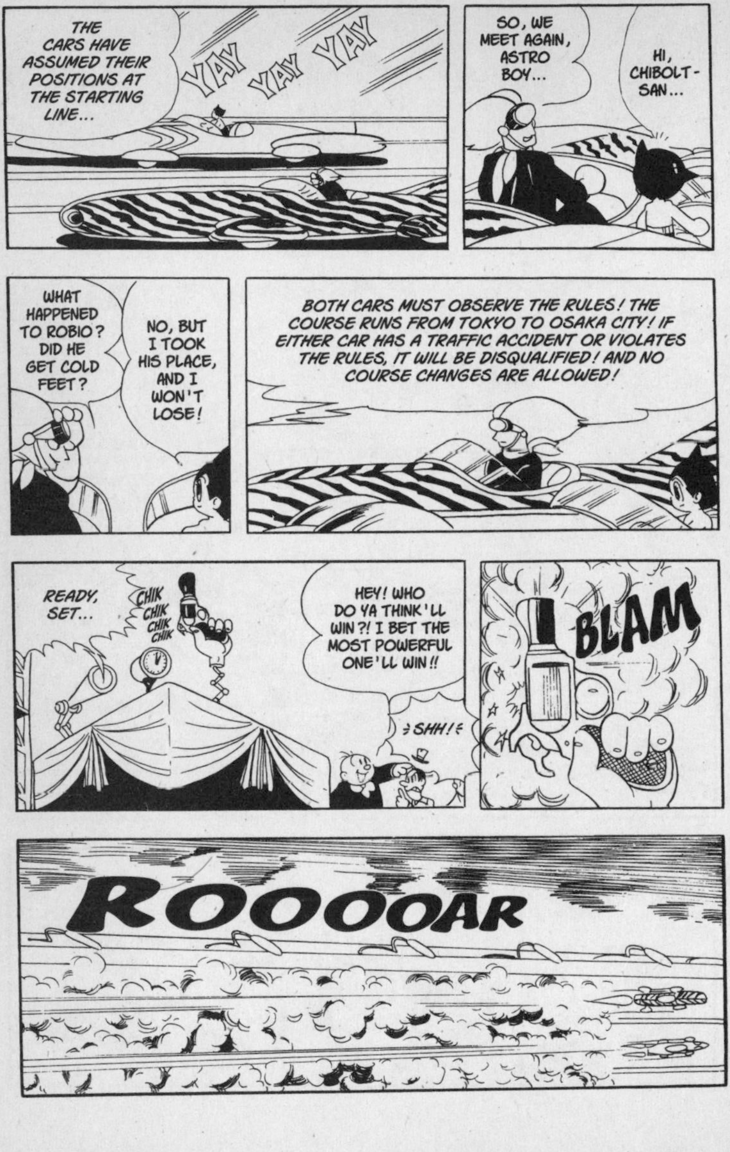
THE CARS HAVE ASSUMED THEIR POSITIONS AT THE STARTING LINE...
YAY YAY YAY
SO, WE MEET AGAIN, ASTRO BOY...
HI, CHIBOLT-SAN...
WHAT HAPPENED TO ROBIO? DID HE GET COLD FEET?
NO, BUT I TOOK HIS PLACE, AND I WON'T LOSE!
BOTH CARS MUST OBSERVE THE RULES! THE COURSE RUNS FROM TOKYO TO OSAKA CITY! IF EITHER CAR HAS A TRAFFIC ACCIDENT OR VIOLATES THE RULES, IT WILL BE DISQUALIFIED! AND NO COURSE CHANGES ARE ALLOWED!
READY, SET...
CHIK CHIK CHIK CHIK
HEY! WHO DO YA THINK'LL WIN?! I BET THE MOST POWERFUL ONE'LL WIN!!
SHH!
BLAM
ROOOOAR

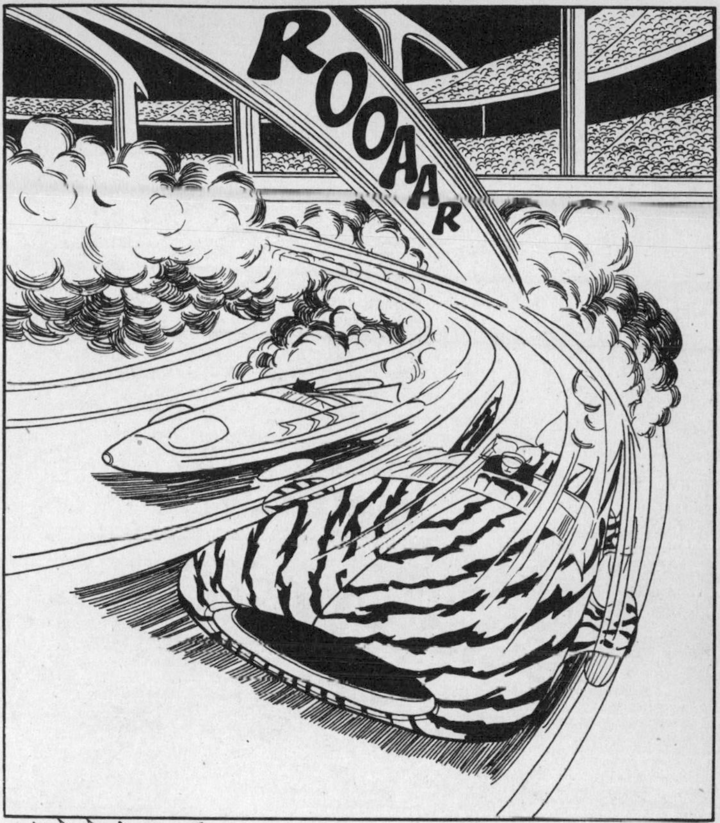
ROOAAAR

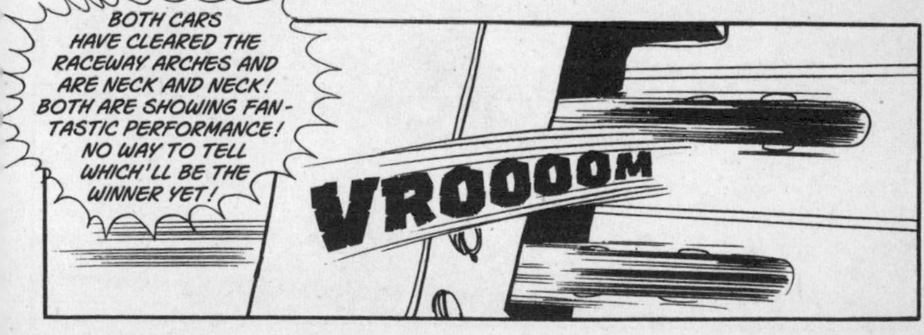
BOTH CARS HAVE CLEARED THE RACEWAY ARCHES AND ARE NECK AND NECK! BOTH ARE SHOWING FAN-TASTIC PERFORMANCE! NO WAY TO TELL WHICH'LL BE THE WINNER YET!
VROOOOM

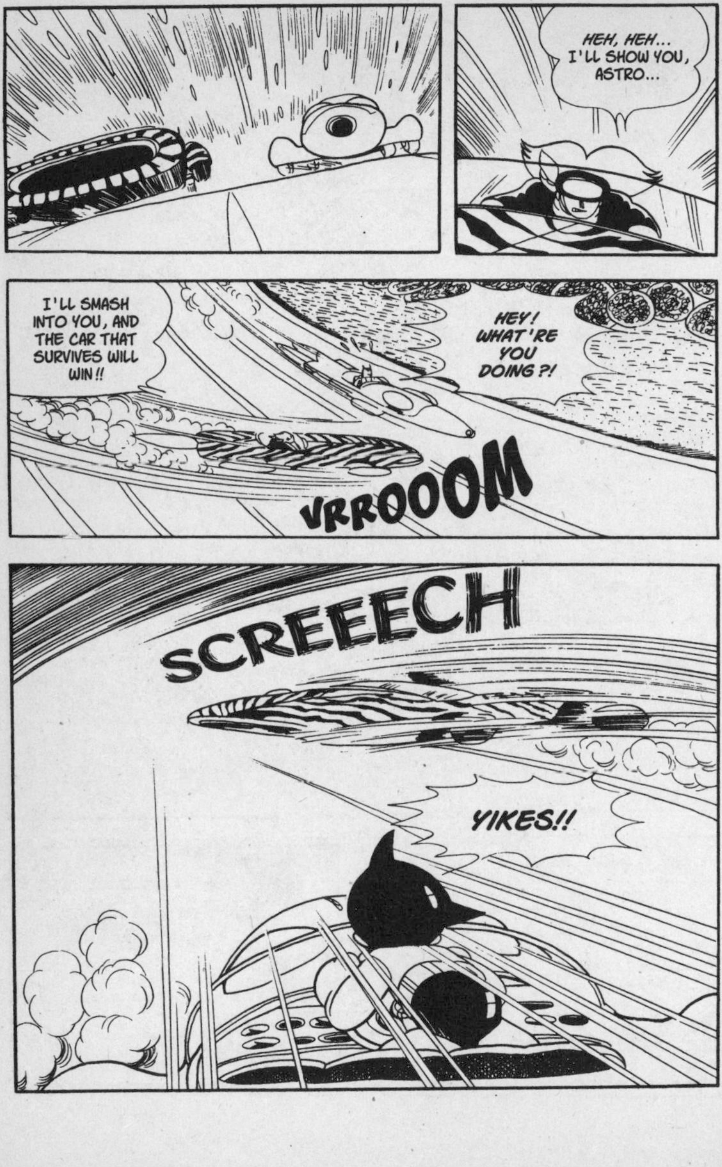
HEH, HEH...
I'LL SHOW YOU, ASTRO...
I'LL SMASH INTO YOU, AND THE CAR THAT SURVIVES WILL WIN!!
HEY! WHAT'RE YOU DOING?!
VRROOOM
SCREEECH
YIKES!!

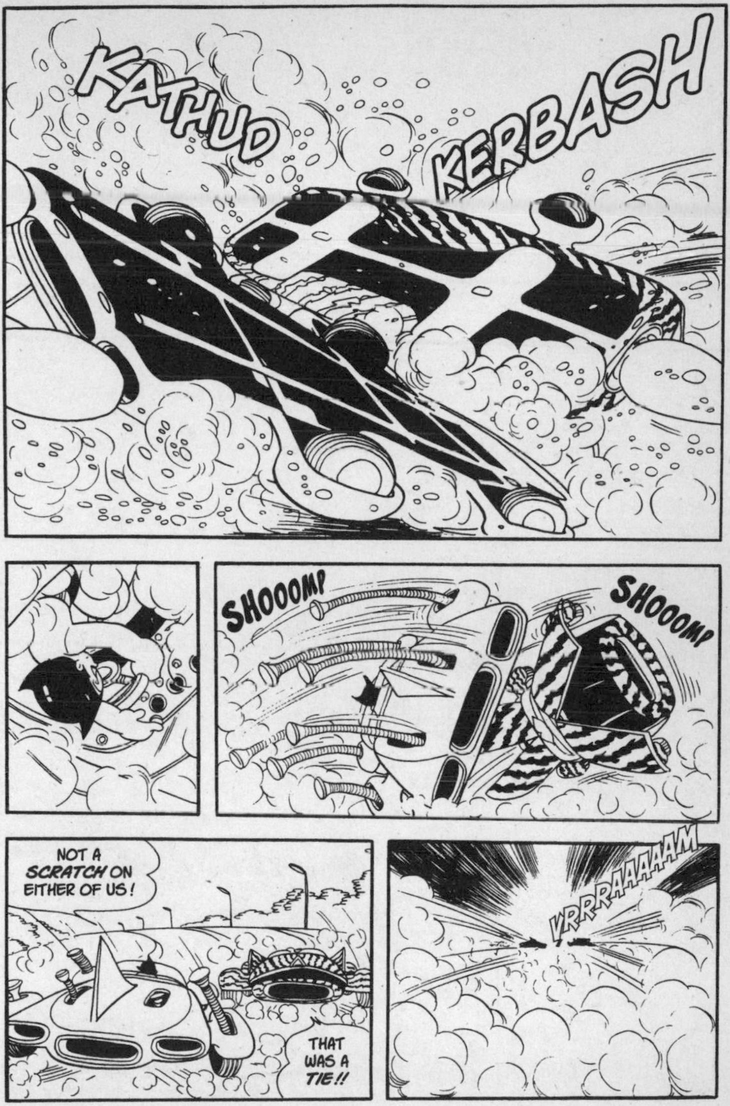
KATHUD
KERBASH
SHOOOM!
SHOOOM!
NOT A SCRATCH ON EITHER OF US!
THAT WAS A TIE!!
VRRRAAAAAM

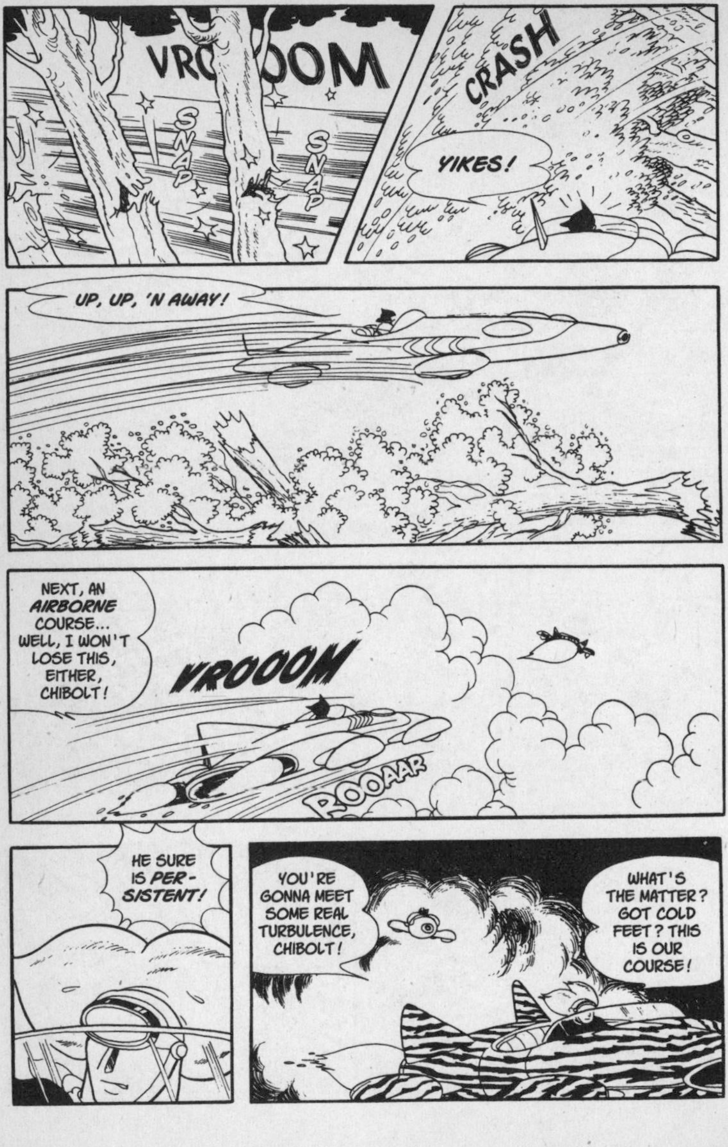
VROOOOM
SNAP
SNAP
CRASH
YIKES!
UP, UP, 'N AWAY!
NEXT, AN AIRBORNE COURSE... WELL, I WON'T LOSE THIS, EITHER, CHIBOLT!
VROOOM
ROOAAR
HE SURE IS PERSISTENT!
YOU'RE GONNA MEET SOME REAL TURBULENCE, CHIBOLT!
WHAT'S THE MATTER? GOT COLD FEET? THIS IS OUR COURSE!

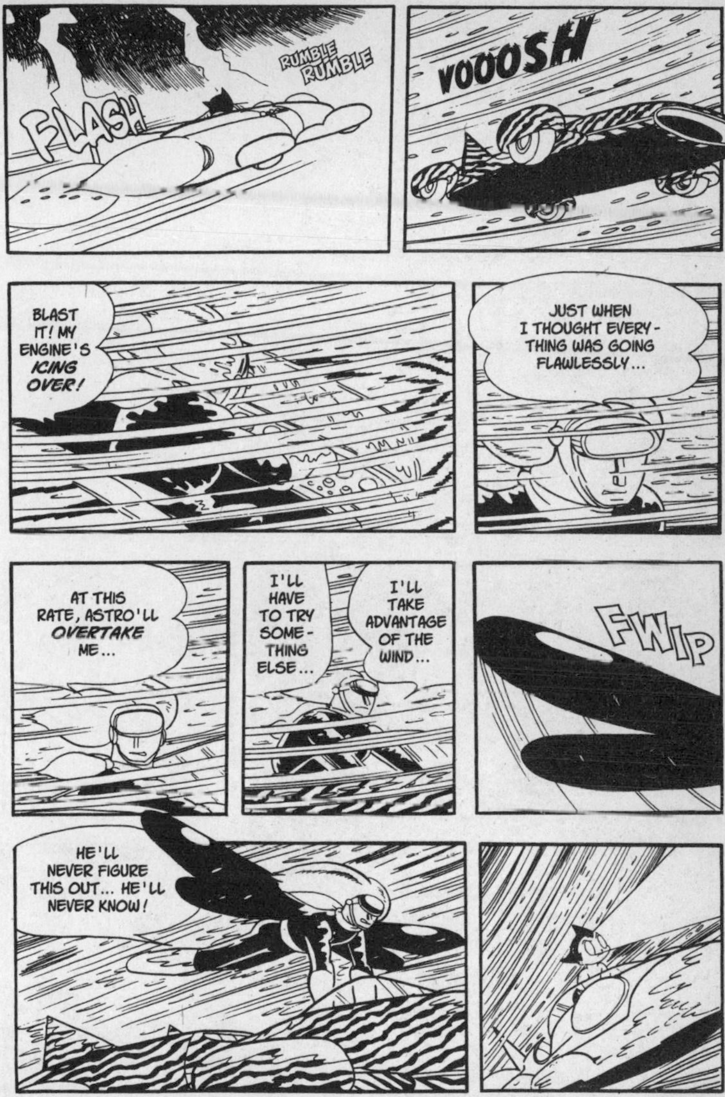
RUMBLE RUMBLE
FLASH
VOOOSH
BLAST IT! MY ENGINE'S *ICING OVER!*
JUST WHEN I THOUGHT EVERY-THING WAS GOING FLAWLESSLY...
AT THIS RATE, ASTRO'LL *OVERTAKE* ME...
I'LL HAVE TO TRY SOME-THING ELSE...
I'LL TAKE ADVANTAGE OF THE WIND...
FWIP
HE'LL NEVER FIGURE THIS OUT... HE'LL NEVER KNOW!

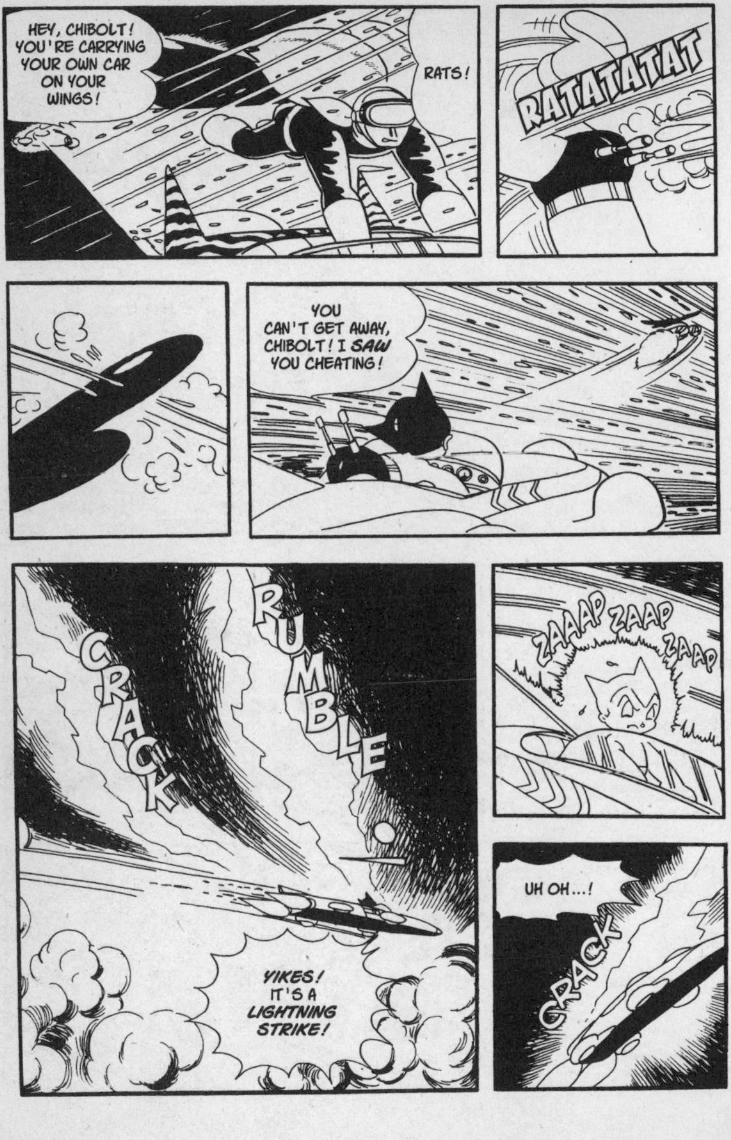
HEY, CHIBOLT! YOU'RE CARRYING YOUR OWN CAR ON YOUR WINGS!
RATS!
RATATATAT
YOU CAN'T GET AWAY, CHIBOLT! I *SAW* YOU CHEATING!
CRACK
RUMBLE
YIKES! IT'S A *LIGHTNING STRIKE!*
ZAAAP ZAAP ZAAAP
UH OH...!
CRACK

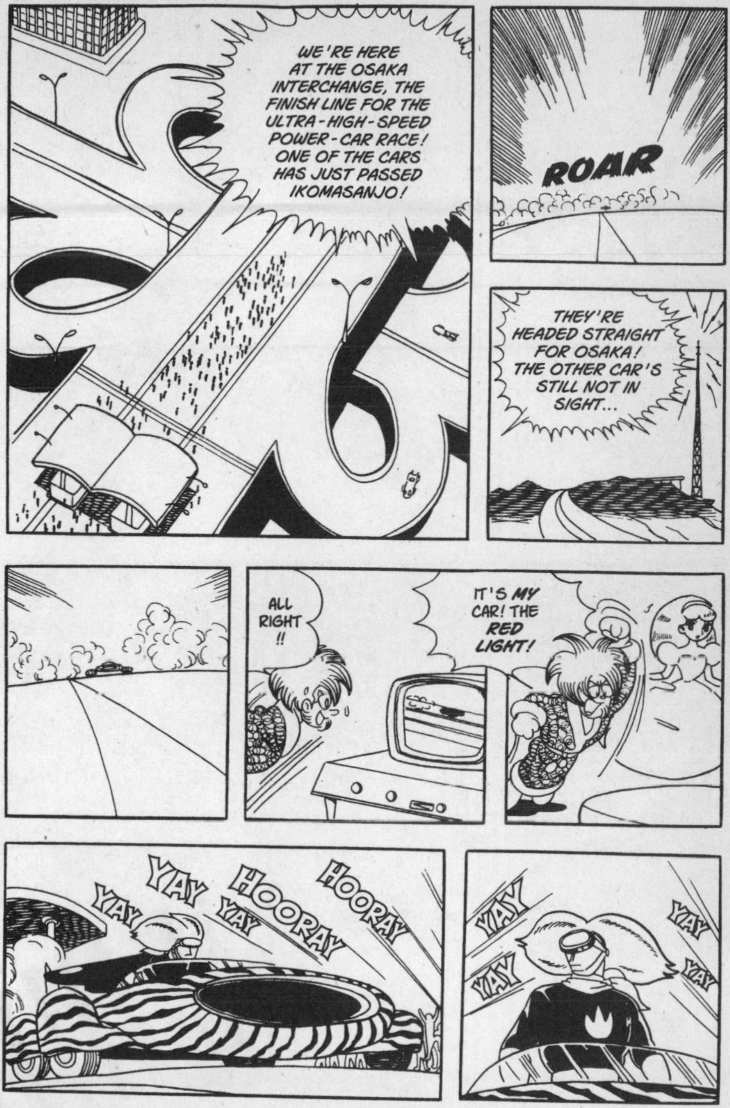
WE'RE HERE AT THE OSAKA INTERCHANGE, THE FINISH LINE FOR THE ULTRA-HIGH-SPEED POWER-CAR RACE! ONE OF THE CARS HAS JUST PASSED IKOMASANJO!
ROAR
THEY'RE HEADED STRAIGHT FOR OSAKA! THE OTHER CAR'S STILL NOT IN SIGHT...
ALL RIGHT !!
IT'S MY CAR! THE RED LIGHT!
YAY
YAY
HOORAY
YAY
HOORAY
YAY
YAY
YAY
YAY

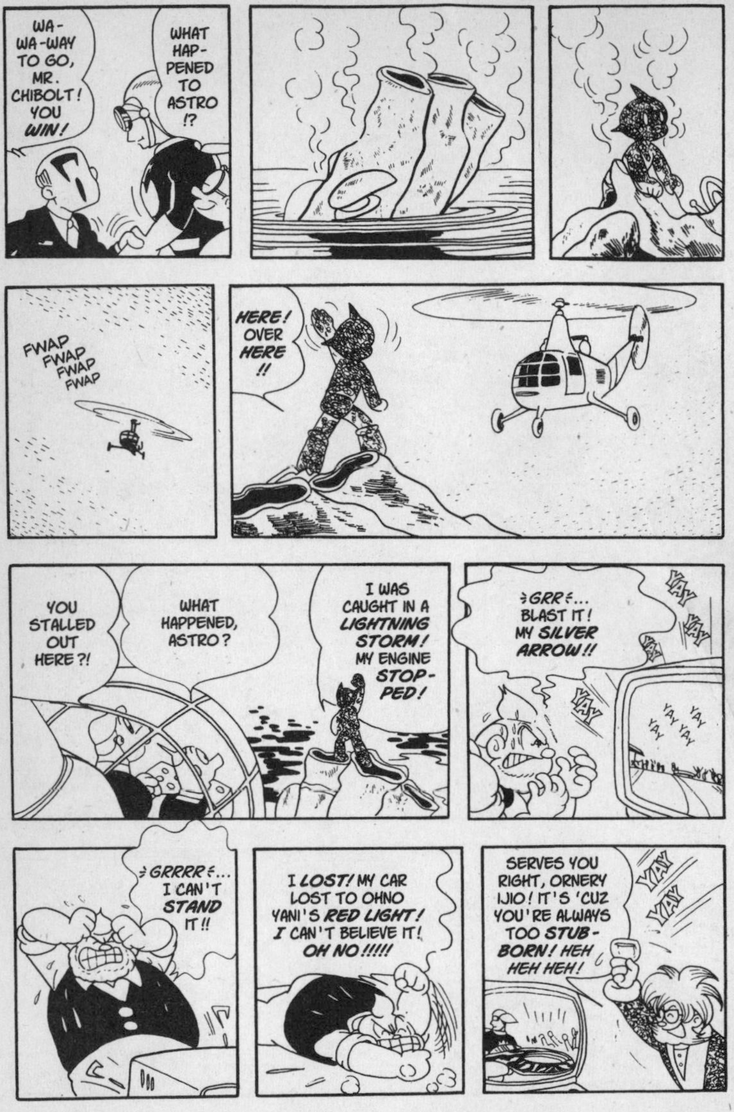
WA-WA-WAY TO GO, MR. CHIBOLT! YOU WIN!
WHAT HAPPENED TO ASTRO!?
FWAP FWAP FWAP FWAP
HERE! OVER HERE!!
YOU STALLED OUT HERE?!
WHAT HAPPENED, ASTRO?
I WAS CAUGHT IN A LIGHTNING STORM! MY ENGINE STOPPED!
GRR... BLAST IT! MY SILVER ARROW!!
YAY YAY YAY
YAY YAY YAY YAY
GRRRR... I CAN'T STAND IT!!
I LOST! MY CAR LOST TO OHNO YANI'S RED LIGHT! I CAN'T BELIEVE IT! OH NO!!!!!
SERVES YOU RIGHT, ORNERY IJIO! IT'S 'CUZ YOU'RE ALWAYS TOO STUBBORN! HEH HEH HEH HEH!
YAY YAY

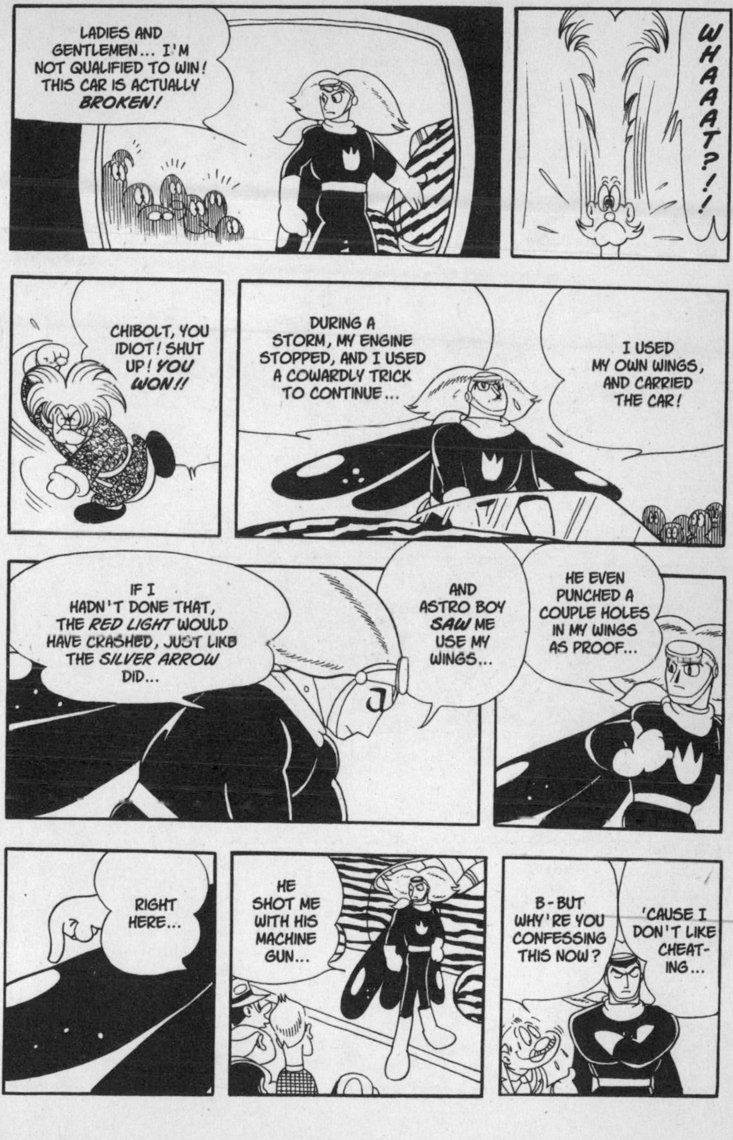
LADIES AND GENTLEMEN... I'M NOT QUALIFIED TO WIN! THIS CAR IS ACTUALLY BROKEN!
WHAAAAT?!!
CHIBOLT, YOU IDIOT! SHUT UP! YOU WON!!
DURING A STORM, MY ENGINE STOPPED, AND I USED A COWARDLY TRICK TO CONTINUE...
I USED MY OWN WINGS, AND CARRIED THE CAR!
IF I HADN'T DONE THAT, THE RED LIGHT WOULD HAVE CRASHED, JUST LIKE THE SILVER ARROW DID...
AND ASTRO BOY SAW ME USE MY WINGS...
HE EVEN PUNCHED A COUPLE HOLES IN MY WINGS AS PROOF...
RIGHT HERE...
HE SHOT ME WITH HIS MACHINE GUN...
B-BUT WHY'RE YOU CONFESSING THIS NOW?
'CAUSE I DON'T LIKE CHEAT-ING...

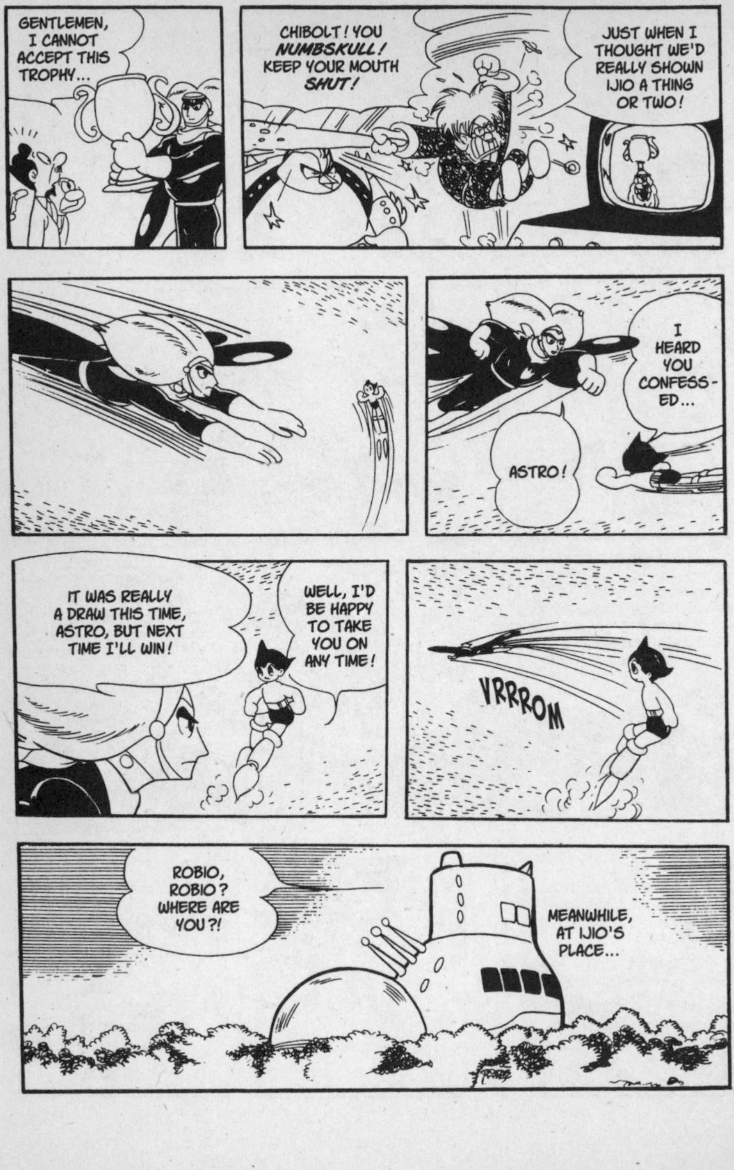
GENTLEMEN, I CANNOT ACCEPT THIS TROPHY...
CHIBOLT! YOU NUMBSKULL! KEEP YOUR MOUTH SHUT!
JUST WHEN I THOUGHT WE'D REALLY SHOWN IJIO A THING OR TWO!
I HEARD YOU CONFESS-ED...
ASTRO!
IT WAS REALLY A DRAW THIS TIME, ASTRO, BUT NEXT TIME I'LL WIN!
WELL, I'D BE HAPPY TO TAKE YOU ON ANY TIME!
VRRROM
ROBIO, ROBIO? WHERE ARE YOU?!
MEANWHILE, AT IJIO'S PLACE...

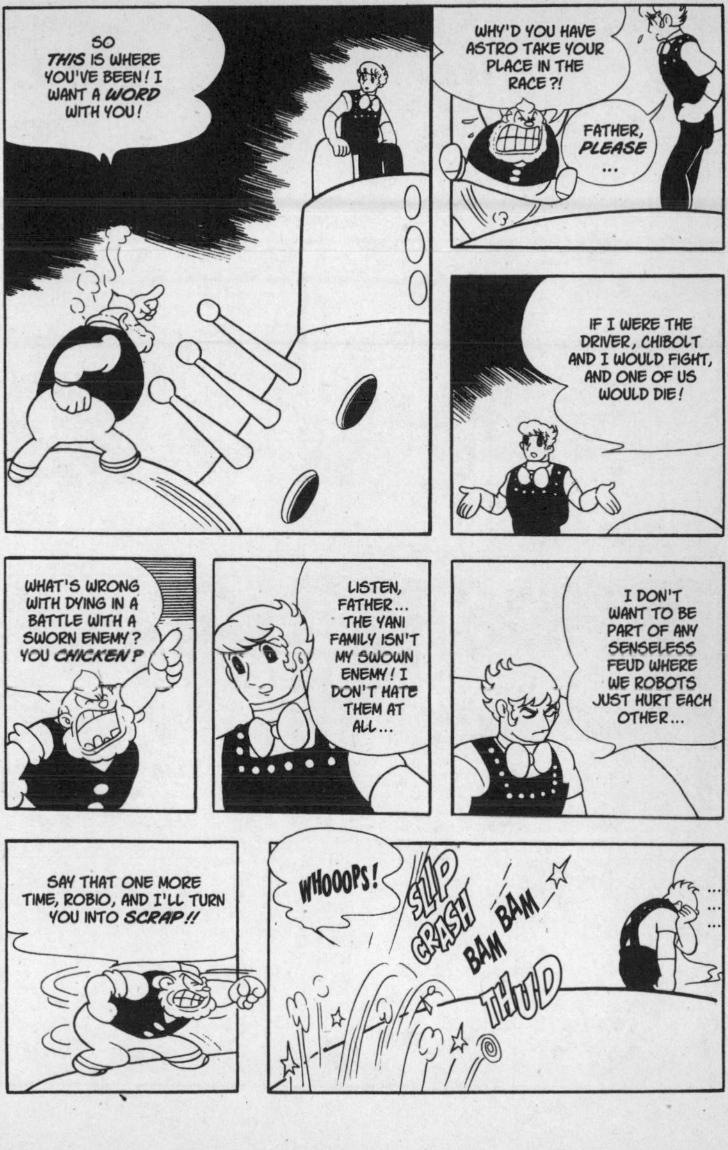
SO *THIS* IS WHERE YOU'VE BEEN! I WANT A *WORD* WITH YOU!
WHY'D YOU HAVE ASTRO TAKE YOUR PLACE IN THE RACE?!
FATHER, *PLEASE* ...
IF I WERE THE DRIVER, CHIBOLT AND I WOULD FIGHT, AND ONE OF US WOULD DIE!
WHAT'S WRONG WITH DYING IN A BATTLE WITH A SWORN ENEMY? YOU *CHICKEN*?
LISTEN, FATHER... THE YANI FAMILY ISN'T MY SWOWN ENEMY! I DON'T HATE THEM AT ALL...
I DON'T WANT TO BE PART OF ANY SENSELESS FEUD WHERE WE ROBOTS JUST HURT EACH OTHER...
SAY THAT ONE MORE TIME, ROBIO, AND I'LL TURN YOU INTO *SCRAP*!!
WHOOOPS!
SLIP
CRASH
BAM BAM
BAM
THUD
...
...
...

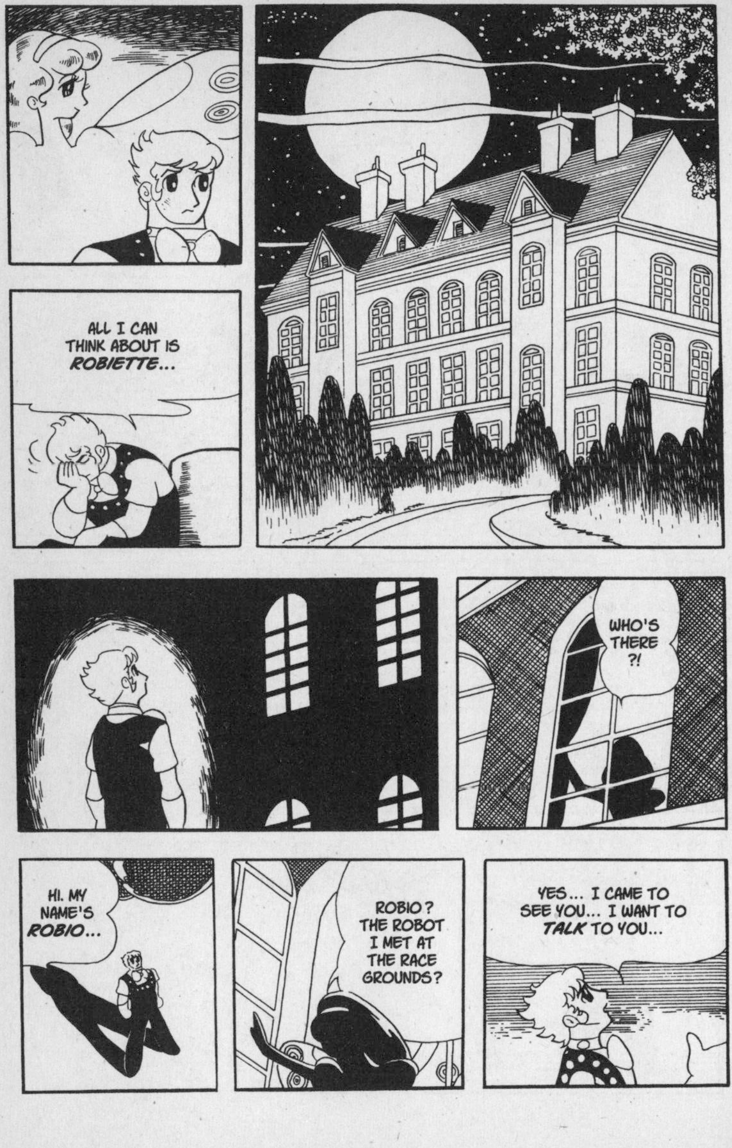
ALL I CAN THINK ABOUT IS *ROBIETTE*...
WHO'S THERE ?!
HI. MY NAME'S *ROBIO*...
ROBIO ? THE ROBOT I MET AT THE RACE GROUNDS?
YES... I CAME TO SEE YOU... I WANT TO *TALK* TO YOU...

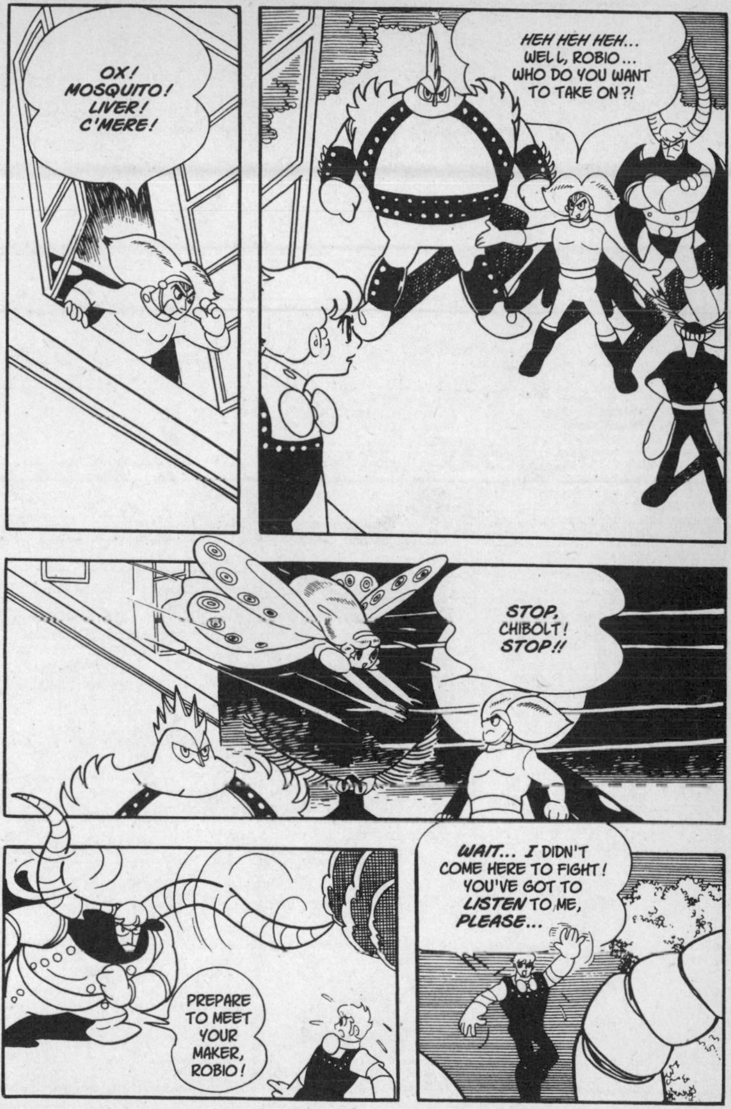
OX! MOSQUITO! LIVER! C'MERE!
HEH HEH HEH... WELL, ROBIO... WHO DO YOU WANT TO TAKE ON?!
STOP, CHIBOLT! STOP!!
PREPARE TO MEET YOUR MAKER, ROBIO!
WAIT... I DIDN'T COME HERE TO FIGHT! YOU'VE GOT TO LISTEN TO ME, PLEASE...

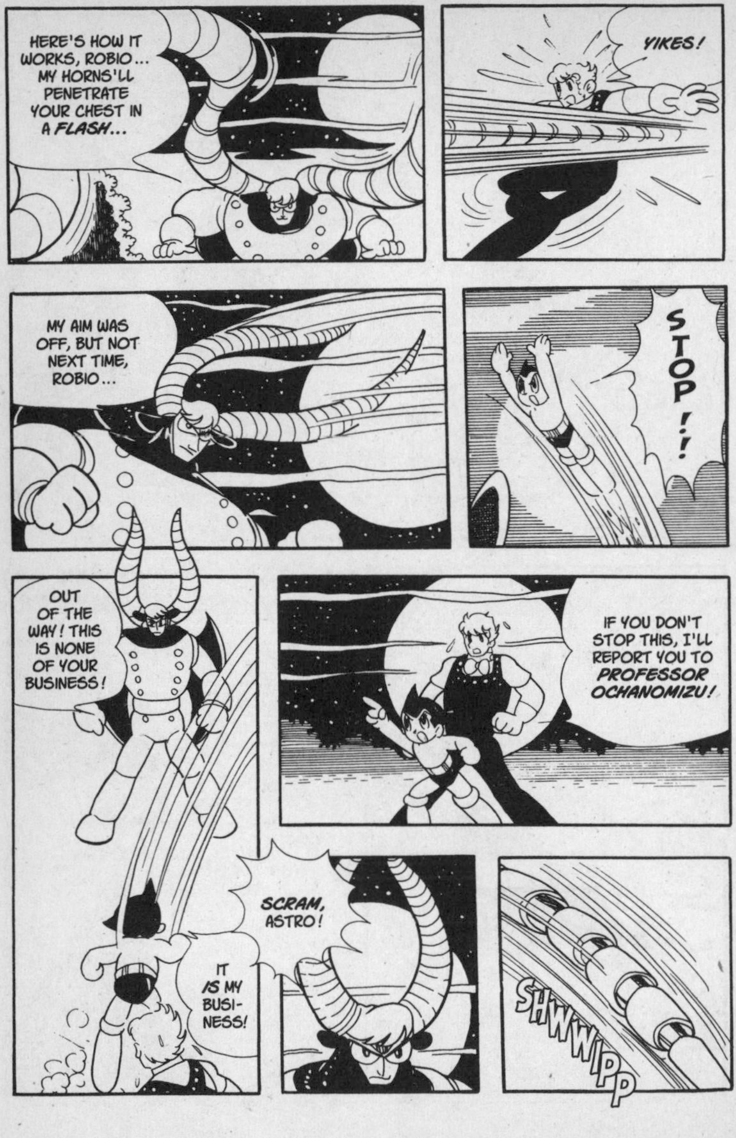
HERE'S HOW IT WORKS, ROBIO... MY HORNS'LL PENETRATE YOUR CHEST IN A *FLASH*...
YIKES!
MY AIM WAS OFF, BUT NOT NEXT TIME, ROBIO...
STOP!!
OUT OF THE WAY! THIS IS NONE OF YOUR BUSINESS!
IF YOU DON'T STOP THIS, I'LL REPORT YOU TO *PROFESSOR OCHANOMIZU*!
IT *IS* MY BUSI-NESS!
SCRAM, ASTRO!
SHWWIPP

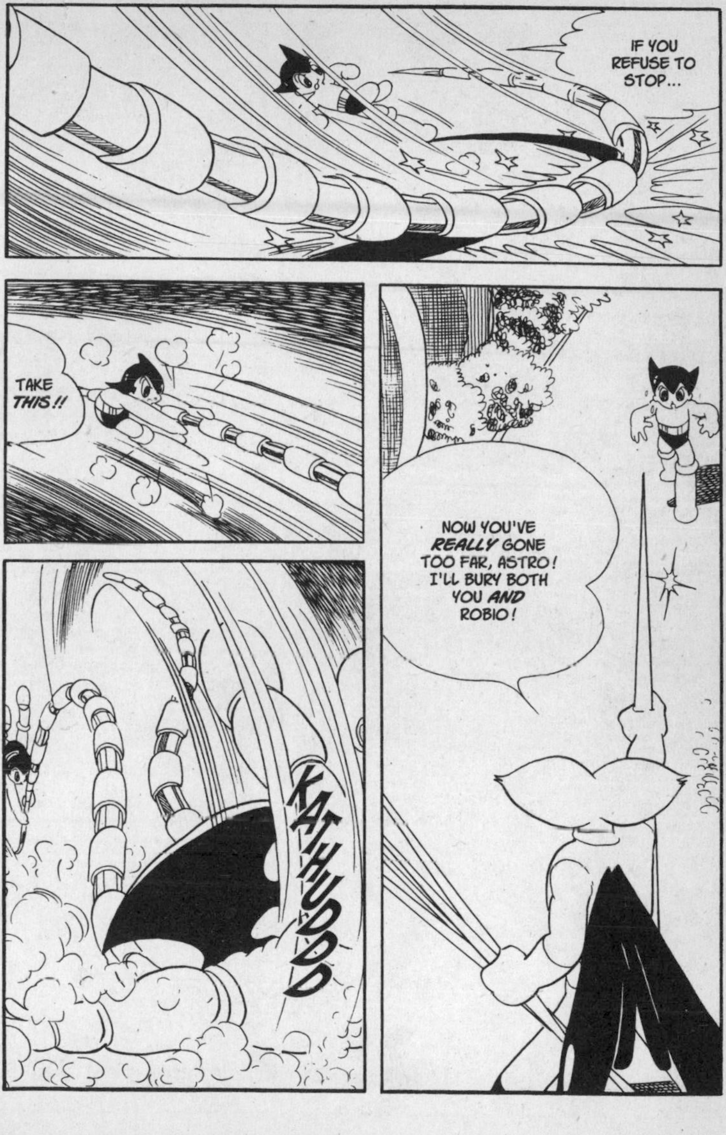
IF YOU REFUSE TO STOP...
TAKE THIS!!
KATHUDDD
NOW YOU'VE REALLY GONE TOO FAR, ASTRO! I'LL BURY BOTH YOU AND ROBIO!

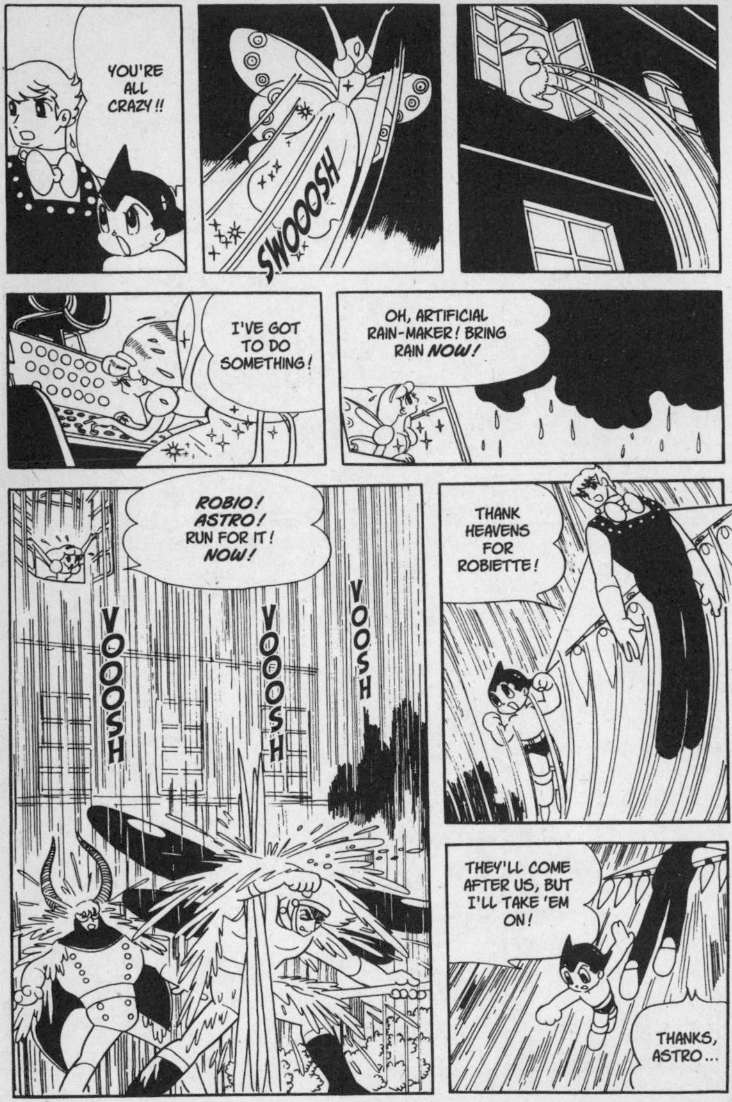
YOU'RE ALL CRAZY!!
SWOOOSH
I'VE GOT TO DO SOMETHING!
OH, ARTIFICIAL RAIN-MAKER! BRING RAIN NOW!
ROBIO! ASTRO! RUN FOR IT! NOW!
VOOOSH
VOOOSH
VOOSH
THANK HEAVENS FOR ROBIETTE!
THEY'LL COME AFTER US, BUT I'LL TAKE 'EM ON!
THANKS, ASTRO...

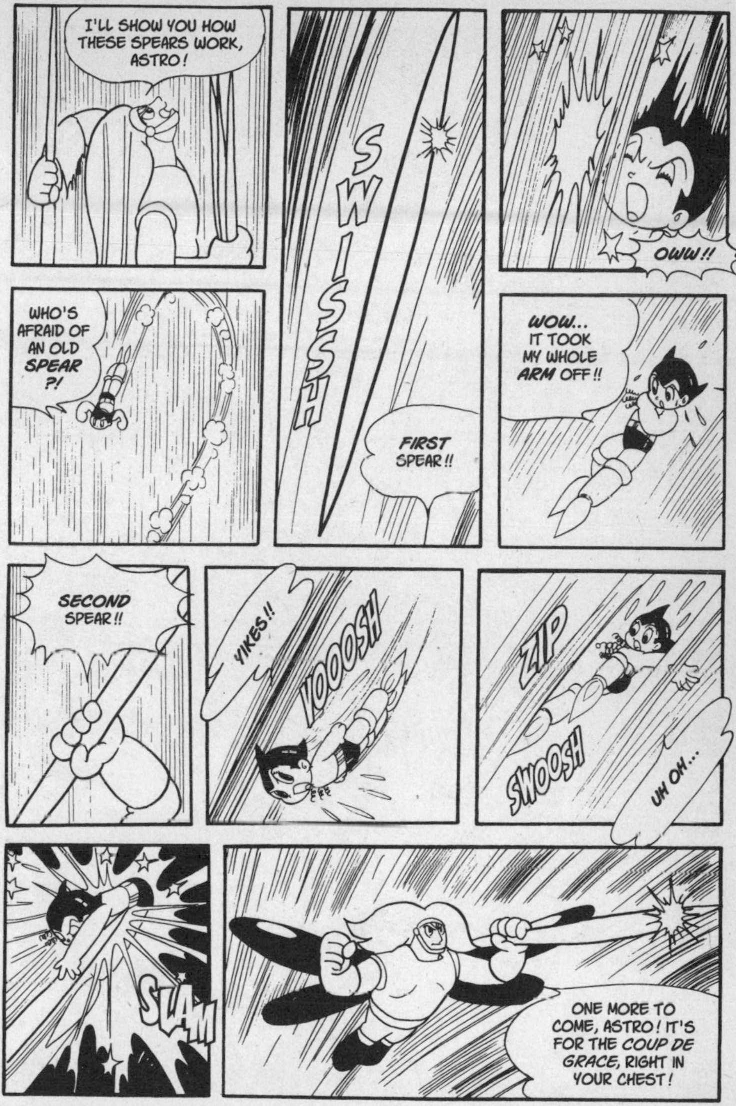
I'LL SHOW YOU HOW THESE SPEARS WORK, ASTRO!
WHO'S AFRAID OF AN OLD SPEAR ?!
SWISSH
FIRST SPEAR!!
OWW!!
WOW... IT TOOK MY WHOLE ARM OFF!!
SECOND SPEAR!!
YIKES!!
VOOOSH
ZIP
SWOOSH
UH OH...
SLAM
ONE MORE TO COME, ASTRO! IT'S FOR THE COUP DE GRACE, RIGHT IN YOUR CHEST!

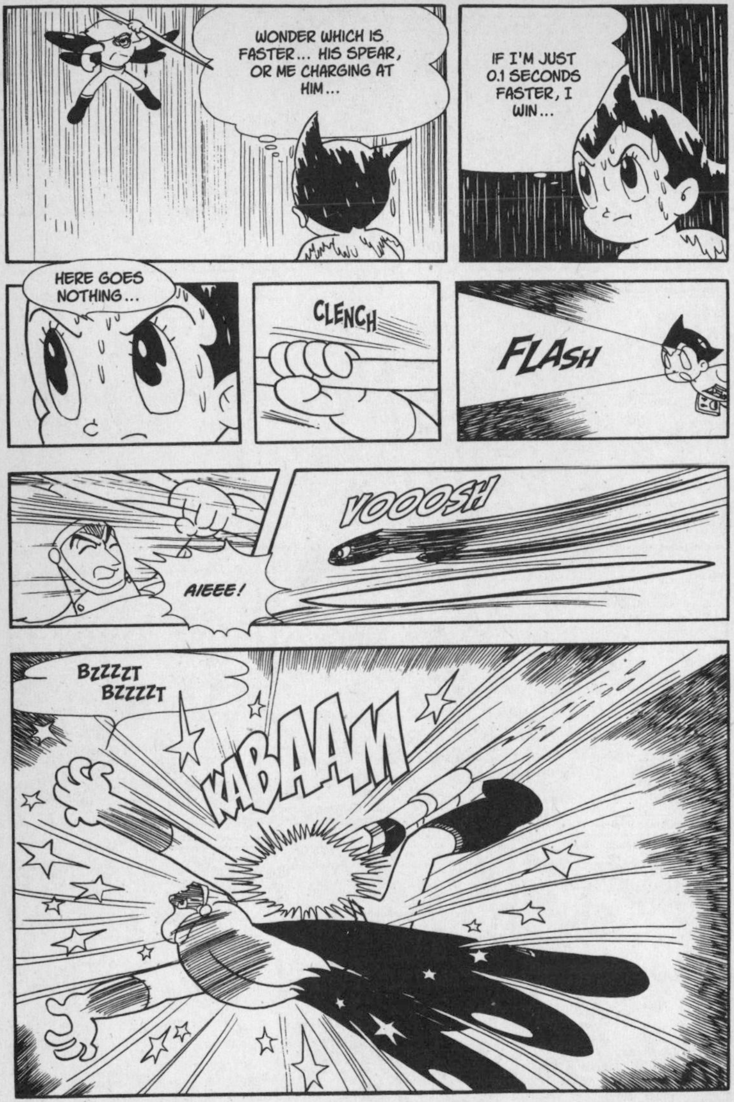
WONDER WHICH IS FASTER... HIS SPEAR, OR ME CHARGING AT HIM...
IF I'M JUST 0.1 SECONDS FASTER, I WIN...
HERE GOES NOTHING...
CLENCH
FLASH
AIEEE!
VOOOSH
BZZZZT BZZZZT
KABAAM

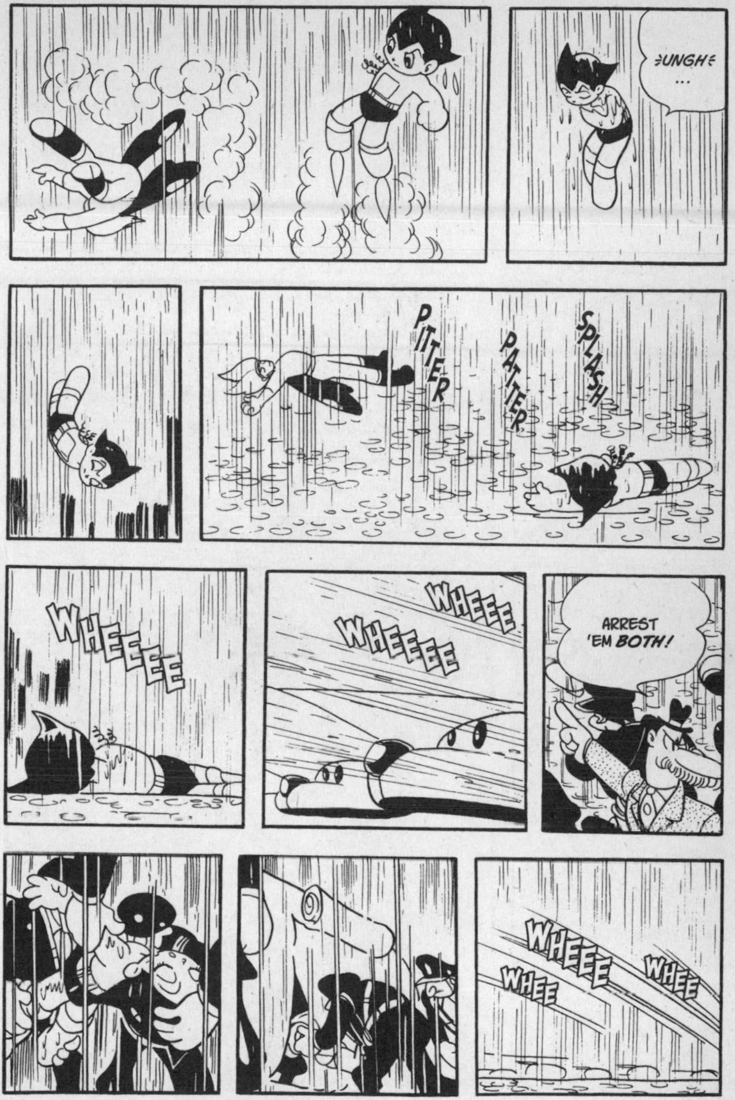

UNGH
...
PITTER
PATTER
SPLASH
WHEEEE
WHEEEE
WHEEE
ARREST 'EM BOTH!
WHEEE
WHEE
WHEE

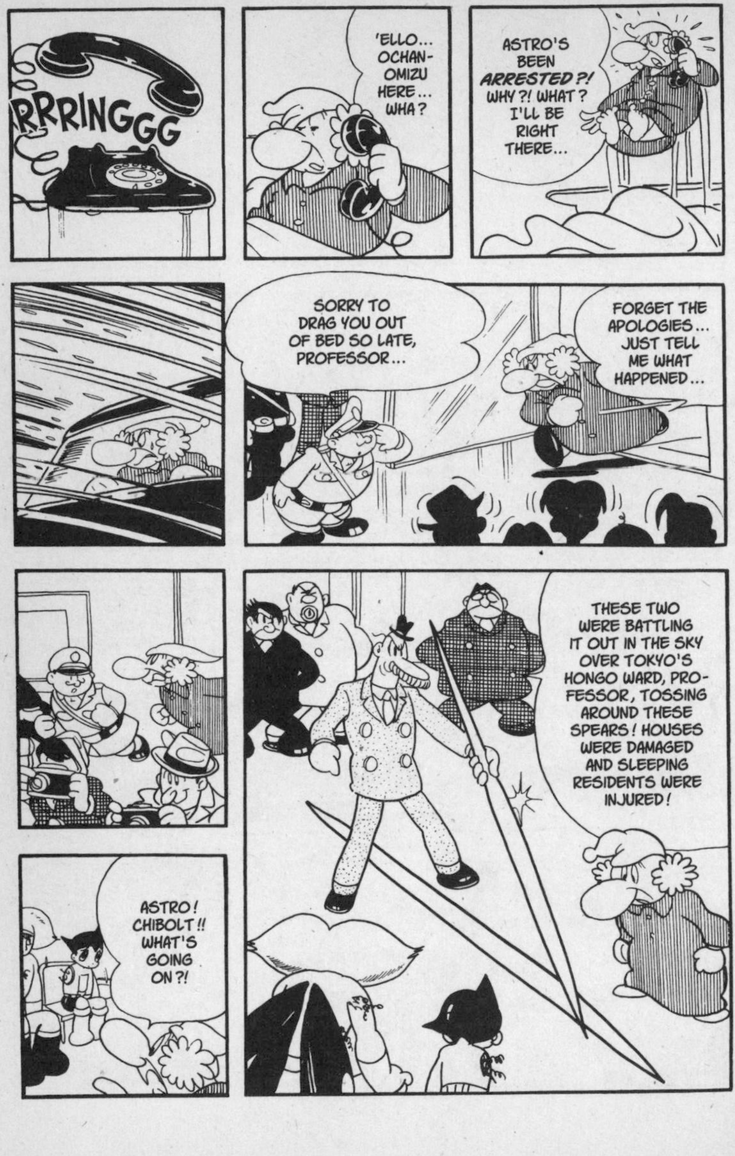
RRRINGGG
'ELLO... OCHAN-OMIZU HERE... WHA?
ASTRO'S BEEN ARRESTED?! WHY?! WHAT? I'LL BE RIGHT THERE...
SORRY TO DRAG YOU OUT OF BED SO LATE, PROFESSOR...
FORGET THE APOLOGIES... JUST TELL ME WHAT HAPPENED...
THESE TWO WERE BATTLING IT OUT IN THE SKY OVER TOKYO'S HONGO WARD, PRO-FESSOR, TOSSING AROUND THESE SPEARS! HOUSES WERE DAMAGED AND SLEEPING RESIDENTS WERE INJURED!
ASTRO! CHIBOLT!! WHAT'S GOING ON?!

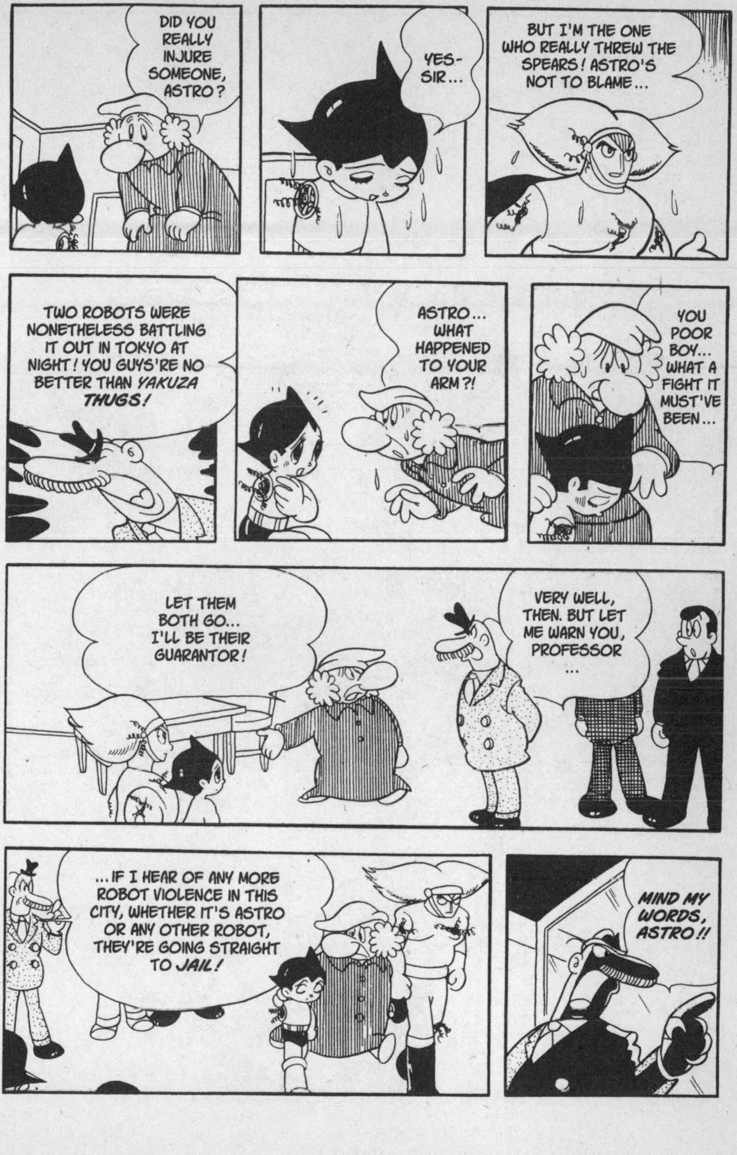
DID YOU REALLY INJURE SOMEONE, ASTRO?
YES-SIR...
BUT I'M THE ONE WHO REALLY THREW THE SPEARS! ASTRO'S NOT TO BLAME...
TWO ROBOTS WERE NONETHELESS BATTLING IT OUT IN TOKYO AT NIGHT! YOU GUYS'RE NO BETTER THAN *YAKUZA* ***THUGS!***
ASTRO... WHAT HAPPENED TO YOUR ARM?!
YOU POOR BOY... WHAT A FIGHT IT MUST'VE BEEN...
LET THEM BOTH GO... I'LL BE THEIR GUARANTOR!
VERY WELL, THEN. BUT LET ME WARN YOU, PROFESSOR ...
...IF I HEAR OF ANY MORE ROBOT VIOLENCE IN THIS CITY, WHETHER IT'S ASTRO OR ANY OTHER ROBOT, THEY'RE GOING STRAIGHT TO *JAIL!*
MIND MY WORDS, ASTRO!!

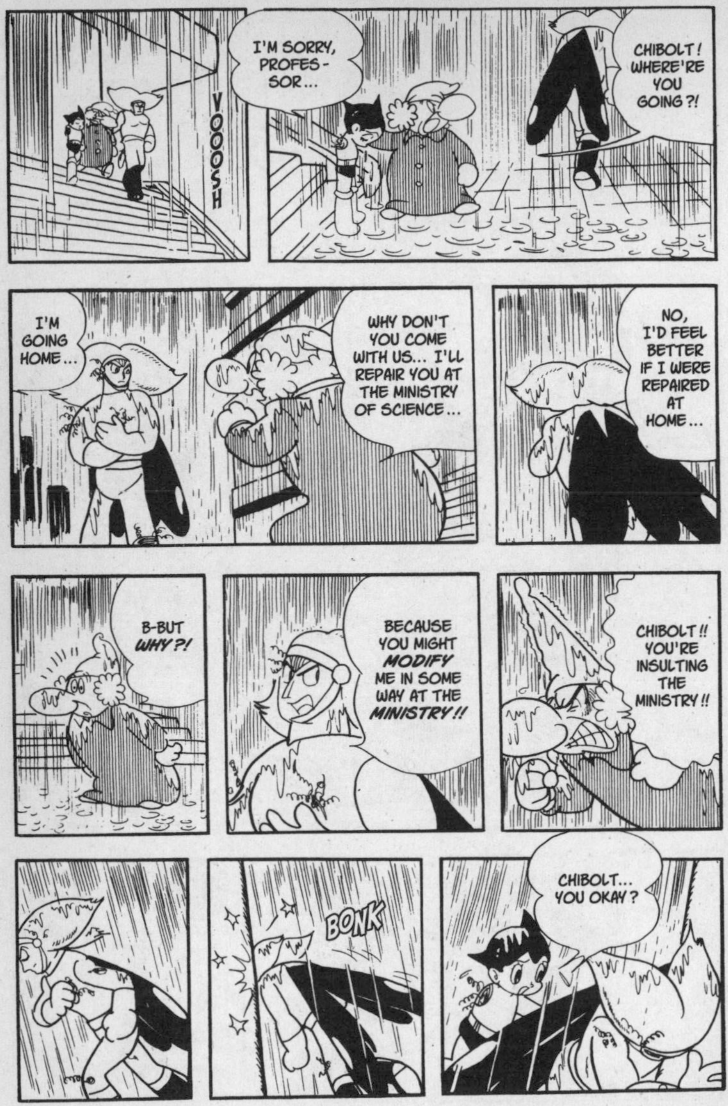
VOOOSH
I'M SORRY, PROFES-SOR...
CHIBOLT! WHERE'RE YOU GOING?!
I'M GOING HOME...
WHY DON'T YOU COME WITH US... I'LL REPAIR YOU AT THE MINISTRY OF SCIENCE...
NO, I'D FEEL BETTER IF I WERE REPAIRED AT HOME...
B-BUT *WHY?!*
BECAUSE YOU MIGHT *MODIFY* ME IN SOME WAY AT THE *MINISTRY!!*
CHIBOLT!! YOU'RE INSULTING THE MINISTRY!!
BONK
CHIBOLT... YOU OKAY?

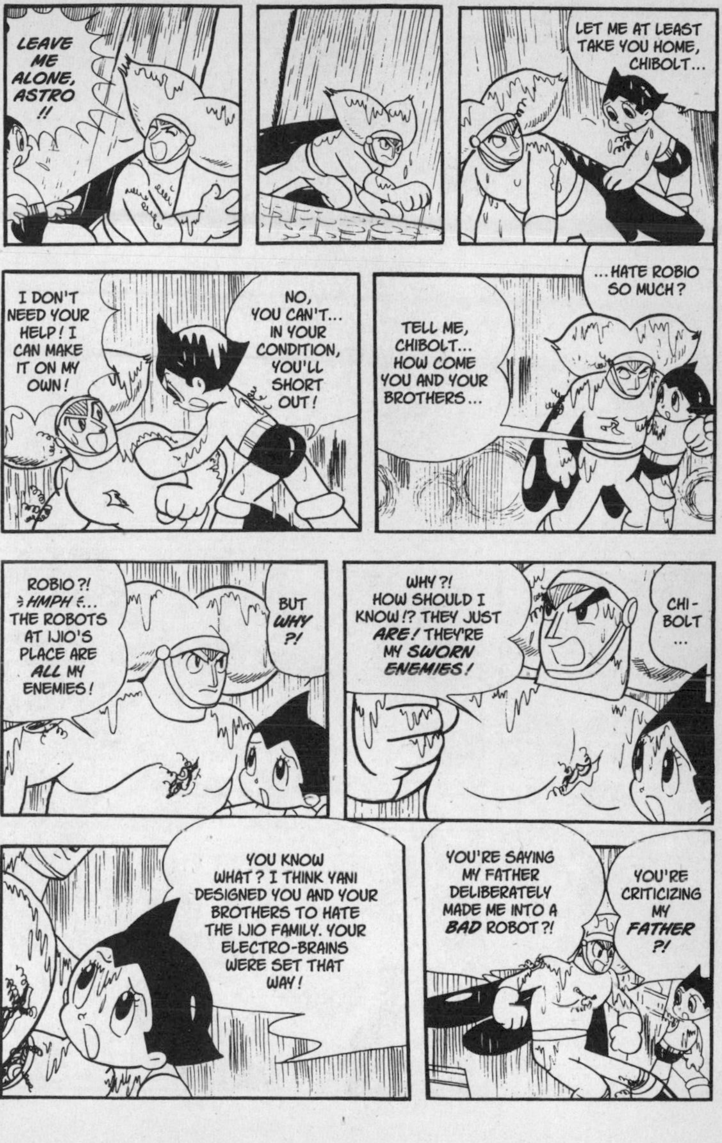
LEAVE ME ALONE, ASTRO !!
LET ME AT LEAST TAKE YOU HOME, CHIBOLT...
I DON'T NEED YOUR HELP! I CAN MAKE IT ON MY OWN!
NO, YOU CAN'T... IN YOUR CONDITION, YOU'LL SHORT OUT!
TELL ME, CHIBOLT... HOW COME YOU AND YOUR BROTHERS...
...HATE ROBIO SO MUCH?
ROBIO?! HMPH... THE ROBOTS AT IJIO'S PLACE ARE ALL MY ENEMIES!
BUT WHY?!
WHY?! HOW SHOULD I KNOW!? THEY JUST ARE! THEY'RE MY SWORN ENEMIES!
CHI-BOLT...
YOU KNOW WHAT? I THINK YANI DESIGNED YOU AND YOUR BROTHERS TO HATE THE IJIO FAMILY. YOUR ELECTRO-BRAINS WERE SET THAT WAY!
YOU'RE SAYING MY FATHER DELIBERATELY MADE ME INTO A BAD ROBOT?!
YOU'RE CRITICIZING MY FATHER?!

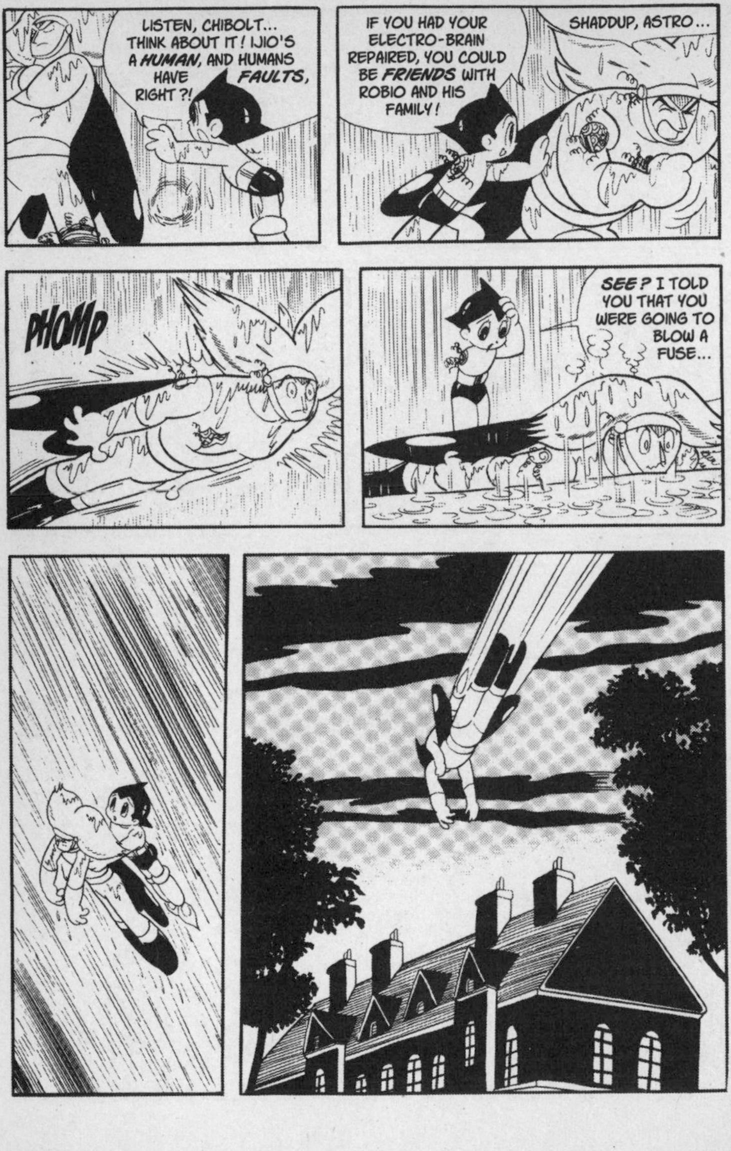
LISTEN, CHIBOLT... THINK ABOUT IT! IJIO'S A HUMAN, AND HUMANS HAVE FAULTS, RIGHT?!
IF YOU HAD YOUR ELECTRO-BRAIN REPAIRED, YOU COULD BE FRIENDS WITH ROBIO AND HIS FAMILY!
SHADDUP, ASTRO...
PHOMP
SEE? I TOLD YOU THAT YOU WERE GOING TO BLOW A FUSE...

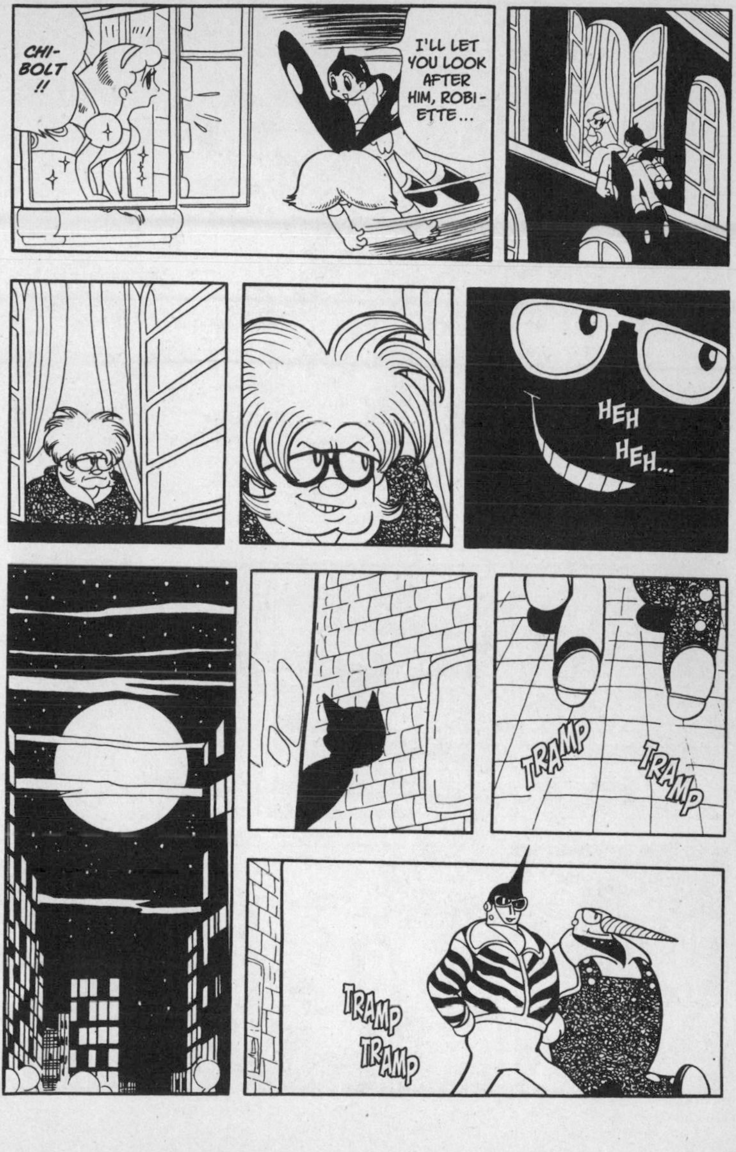
CHI-BOLT !!
I'LL LET YOU LOOK AFTER HIM, ROBI-ETTE...
HEH HEH...
TRAMP TRAMP
TRAMP TRAMP

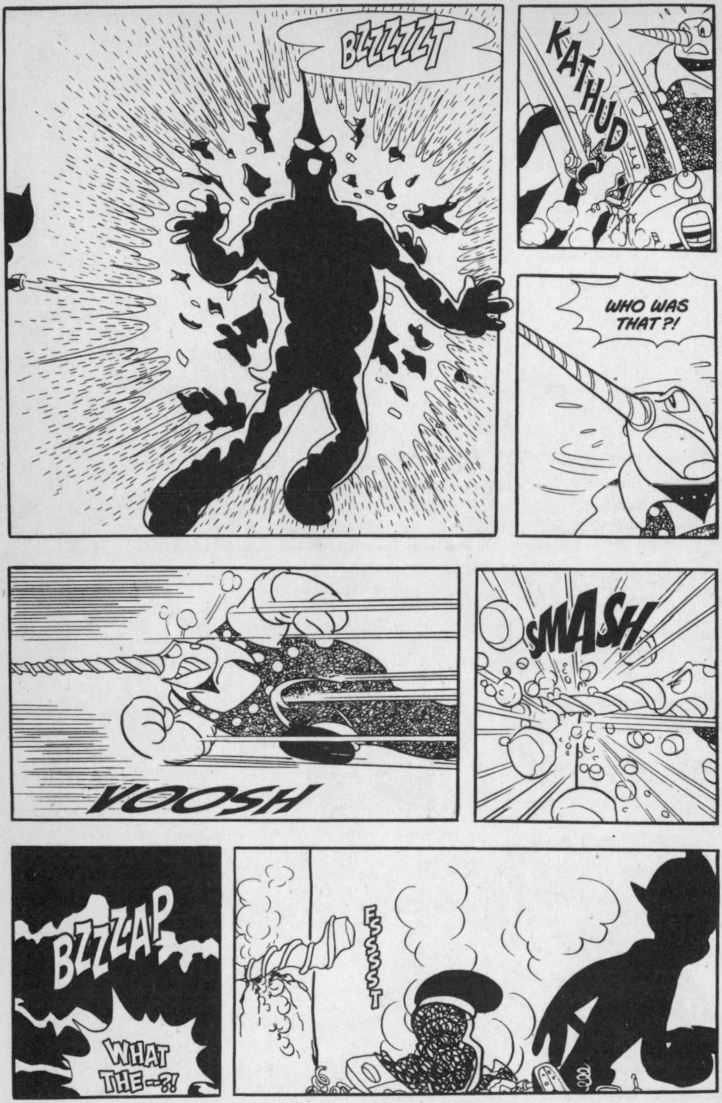
BZZZZZT
KATHUD
WHO WAS THAT?!
VOOSH
SMASH
BZZZAP
WHAT THE--?!
FSSSST

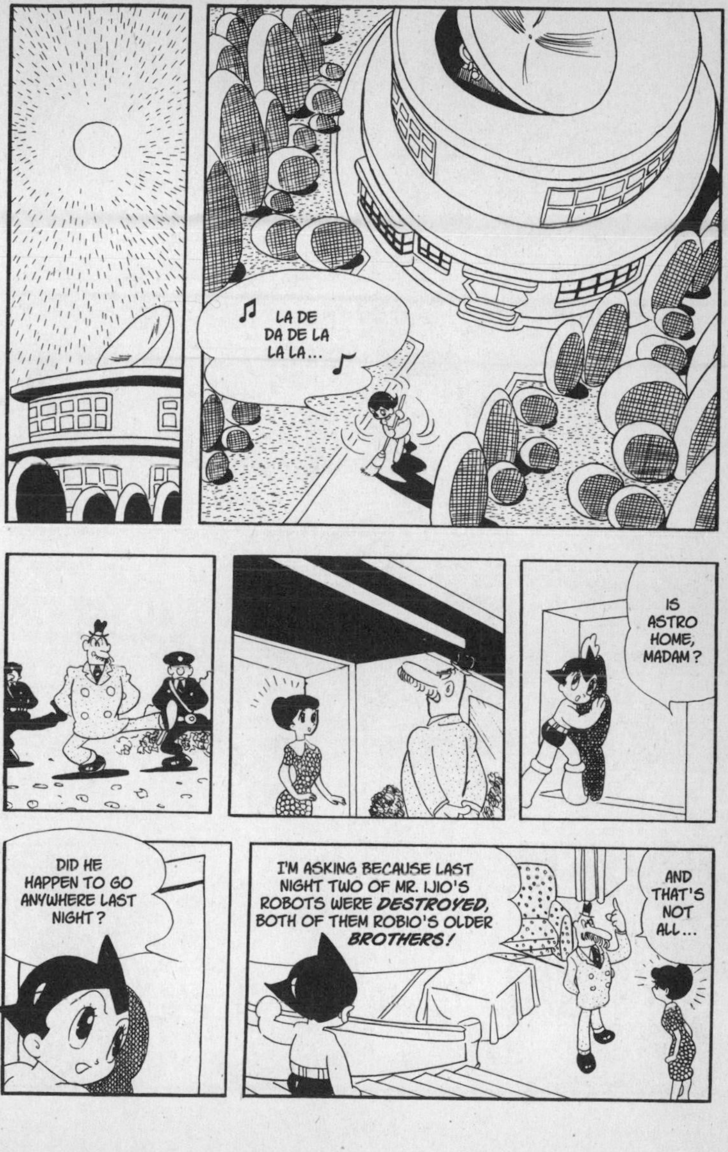
♪ LA DE DA DE LA LA LA... ♪
IS ASTRO HOME, MADAM?
DID HE HAPPEN TO GO ANYWHERE LAST NIGHT?
I'M ASKING BECAUSE LAST NIGHT TWO OF MR. IJIO'S ROBOTS WERE *DESTROYED*, BOTH OF THEM ROBIO'S OLDER *BROTHERS!*
AND THAT'S NOT ALL...

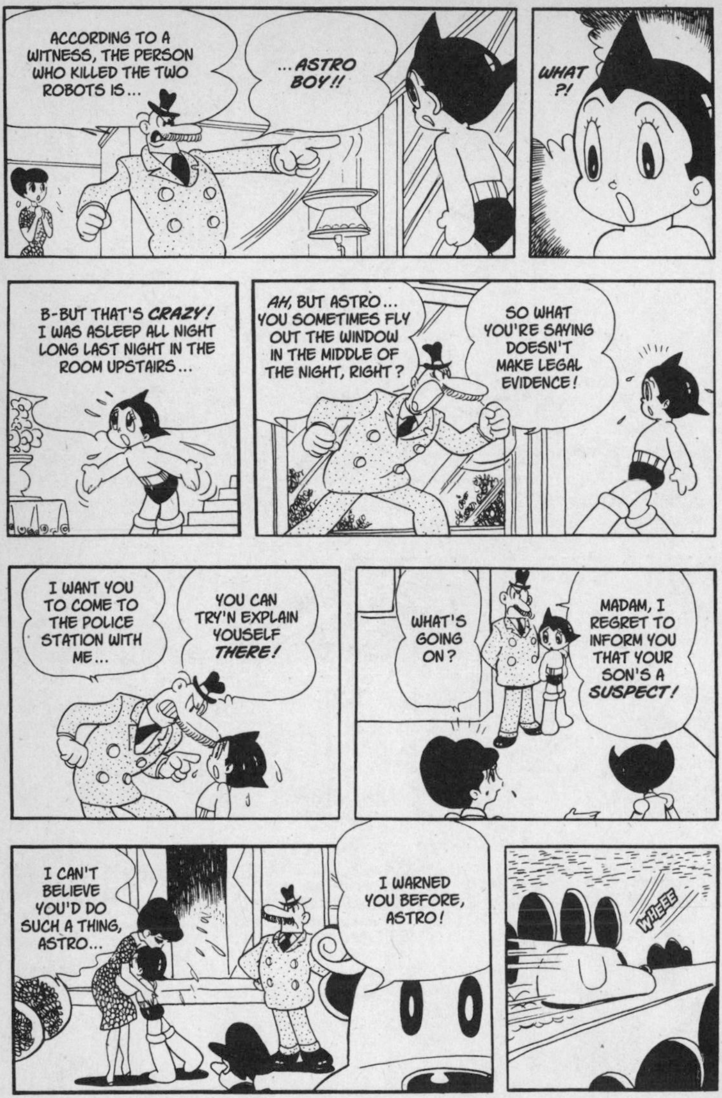

ACCORDING TO A WITNESS, THE PERSON WHO KILLED THE TWO ROBOTS IS...
...ASTRO BOY!!
WHAT?!
B-BUT THAT'S CRAZY! I WAS ASLEEP ALL NIGHT LONG LAST NIGHT IN THE ROOM UPSTAIRS...
AH, BUT ASTRO... YOU SOMETIMES FLY OUT THE WINDOW IN THE MIDDLE OF THE NIGHT, RIGHT?
SO WHAT YOU'RE SAYING DOESN'T MAKE LEGAL EVIDENCE!
I WANT YOU TO COME TO THE POLICE STATION WITH ME...
YOU CAN TRY'N EXPLAIN YOUSELF THERE!
WHAT'S GOING ON?
MADAM, I REGRET TO INFORM YOU THAT YOUR SON'S A SUSPECT!
I CAN'T BELIEVE YOU'D DO SUCH A THING, ASTRO...
I WARNED YOU BEFORE, ASTRO!
WHEEE

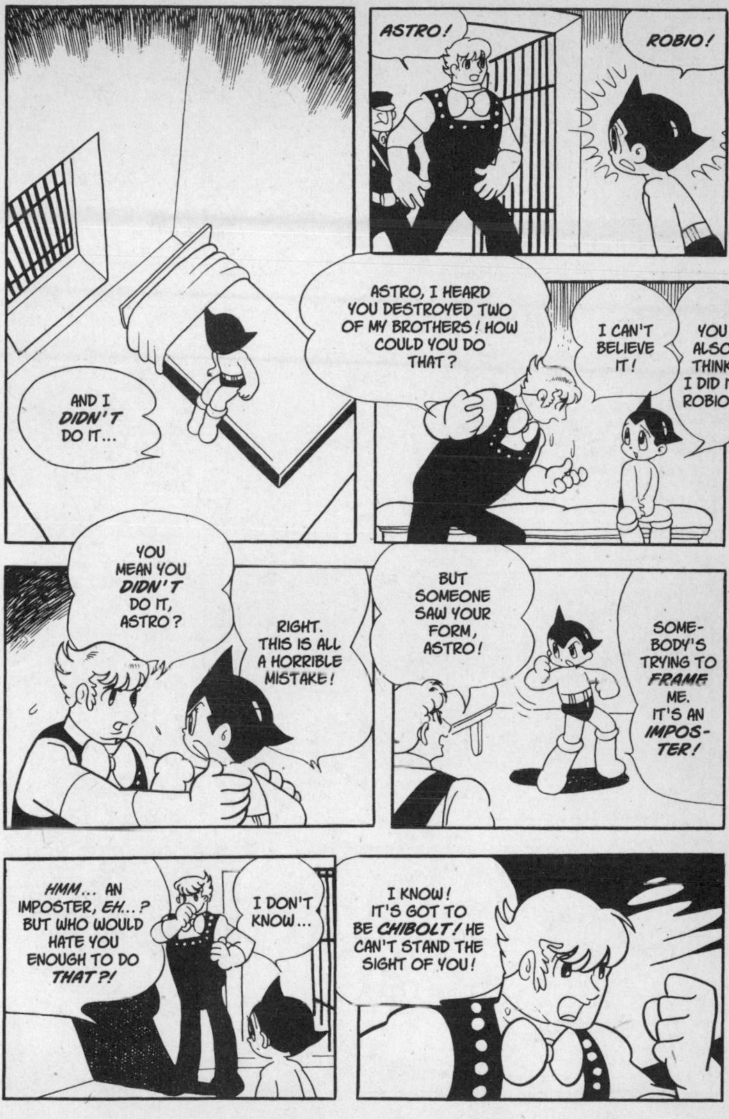
AND I *DIDN'T* DO IT...
ASTRO!
ROBIO!
ASTRO, I HEARD YOU DESTROYED TWO OF MY BROTHERS! HOW COULD YOU DO THAT?
I CAN'T BELIEVE IT!
YOU ALSO THINK I DID IT, ROBIO?
YOU MEAN YOU *DIDN'T* DO IT, ASTRO?
RIGHT. THIS IS ALL A HORRIBLE MISTAKE!
BUT SOMEONE SAW YOUR FORM, ASTRO!
SOMEBODY'S TRYING TO *FRAME* ME. IT'S AN *IMPOSTER!*
HMM... AN IMPOSTER, *EH*...? BUT WHO WOULD HATE YOU ENOUGH TO DO *THAT?!*
I DON'T KNOW...
I KNOW! IT'S GOT TO BE *CHIBOLT!* HE CAN'T STAND THE SIGHT OF YOU!

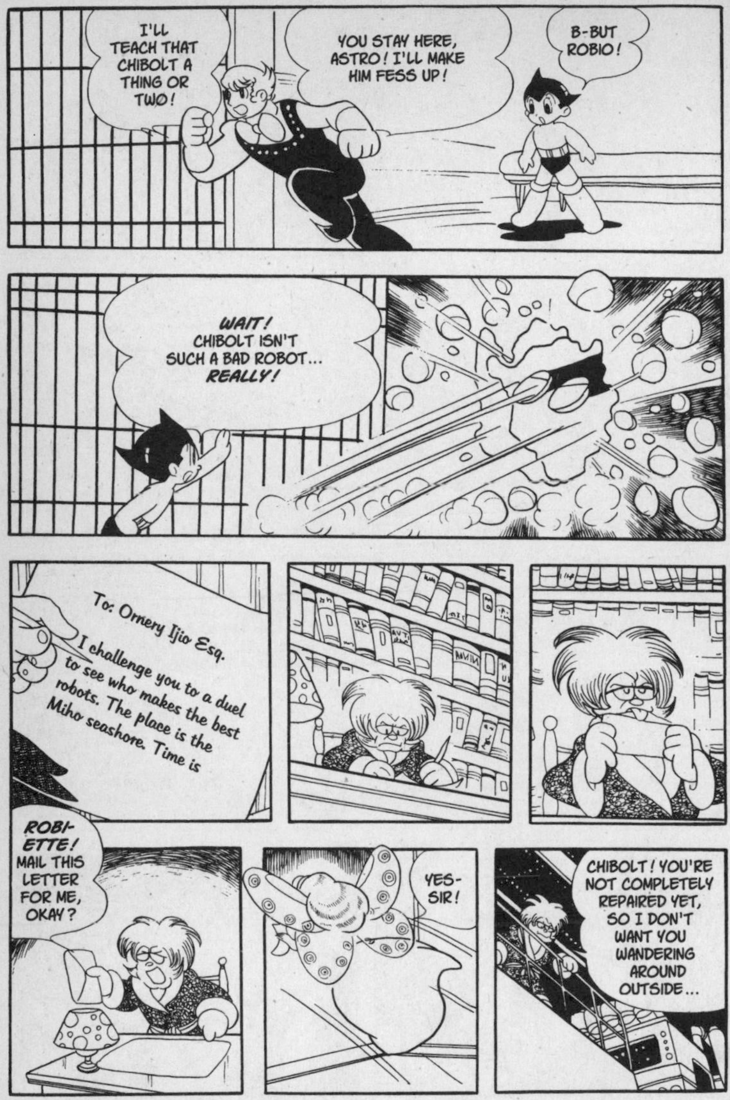
I'LL TEACH THAT CHIBOLT A THING OR TWO!
YOU STAY HERE, ASTRO! I'LL MAKE HIM FESS UP!
B-BUT ROBIO!
WAIT! CHIBOLT ISN'T SUCH A BAD ROBOT... REALLY!
To: Ornery Ijio Esq.
I challenge you to a duel to see who makes the best robots. The place is the Miho seashore. Time is
ROBI-ETTE! MAIL THIS LETTER FOR ME, OKAY?
YES-SIR!
CHIBOLT! YOU'RE NOT COMPLETELY REPAIRED YET, SO I DON'T WANT YOU WANDERING AROUND OUTSIDE...

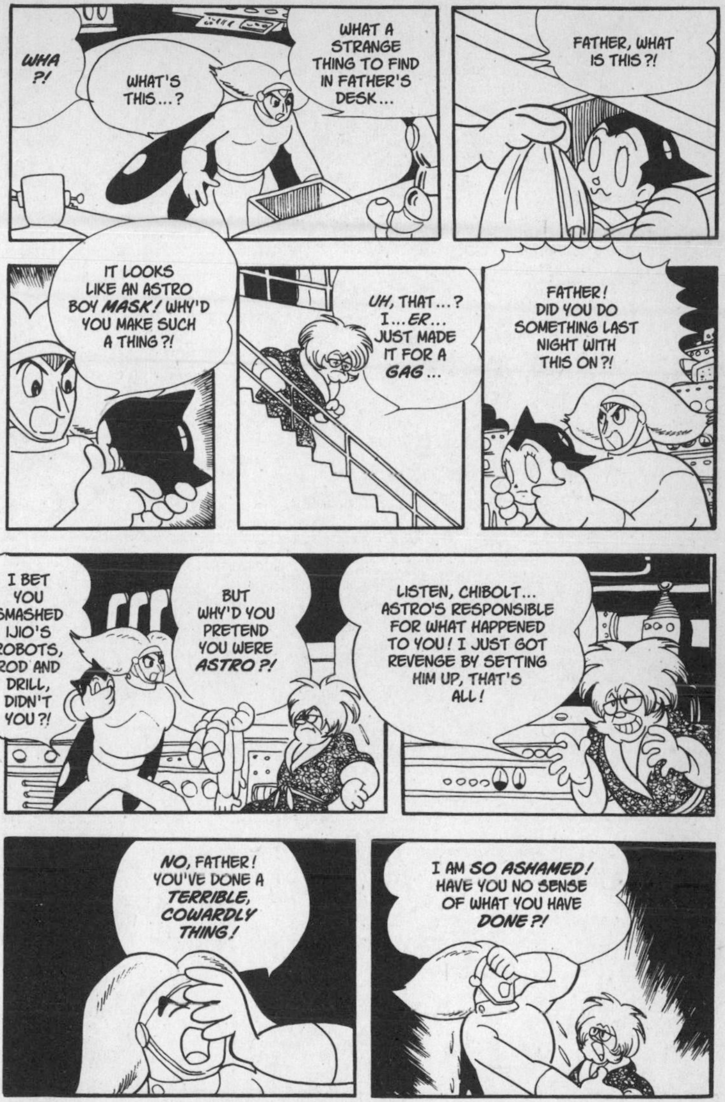
WHA ?!
WHAT'S THIS...?
WHAT A STRANGE THING TO FIND IN FATHER'S DESK...
FATHER, WHAT IS THIS ?!
IT LOOKS LIKE AN ASTRO BOY MASK! WHY'D YOU MAKE SUCH A THING ?!
UH, THAT...? I...ER... JUST MADE IT FOR A GAG...
FATHER! DID YOU DO SOMETHING LAST NIGHT WITH THIS ON ?!
I BET YOU SMASHED IJIO'S ROBOTS, ROD AND DRILL, DIDN'T YOU ?!
BUT WHY'D YOU PRETEND YOU WERE ASTRO ?!
LISTEN, CHIBOLT... ASTRO'S RESPONSIBLE FOR WHAT HAPPENED TO YOU! I JUST GOT REVENGE BY SETTING HIM UP, THAT'S ALL!
NO, FATHER! YOU'VE DONE A TERRIBLE, COWARDLY THING!
I AM SO ASHAMED! HAVE YOU NO SENSE OF WHAT YOU HAVE DONE ?!

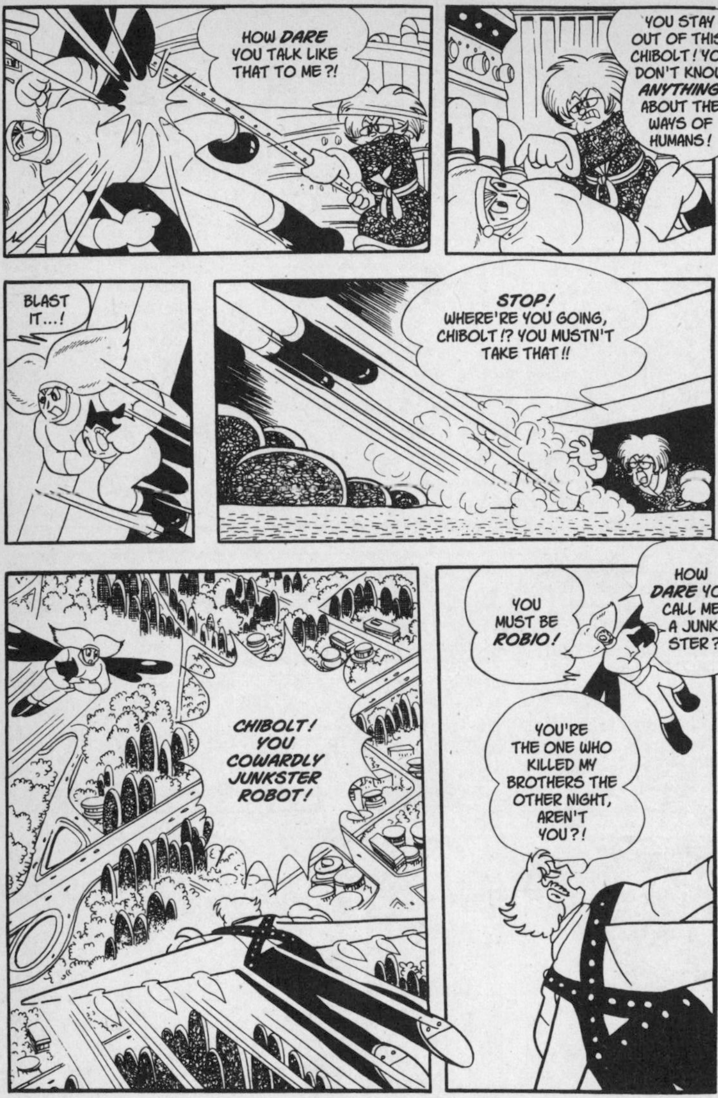
HOW DARE YOU TALK LIKE THAT TO ME?!
YOU STAY OUT OF THIS, CHIBOLT! YOU DON'T KNOW ANYTHING ABOUT THE WAYS OF HUMANS!
BLAST IT...!
STOP! WHERE'RE YOU GOING, CHIBOLT!? YOU MUSTN'T TAKE THAT!!
CHIBOLT! YOU COWARDLY JUNKSTER ROBOT!
YOU MUST BE ROBIO!
HOW DARE YOU CALL ME A JUNK-STER?!
YOU'RE THE ONE WHO KILLED MY BROTHERS THE OTHER NIGHT, AREN'T YOU?!

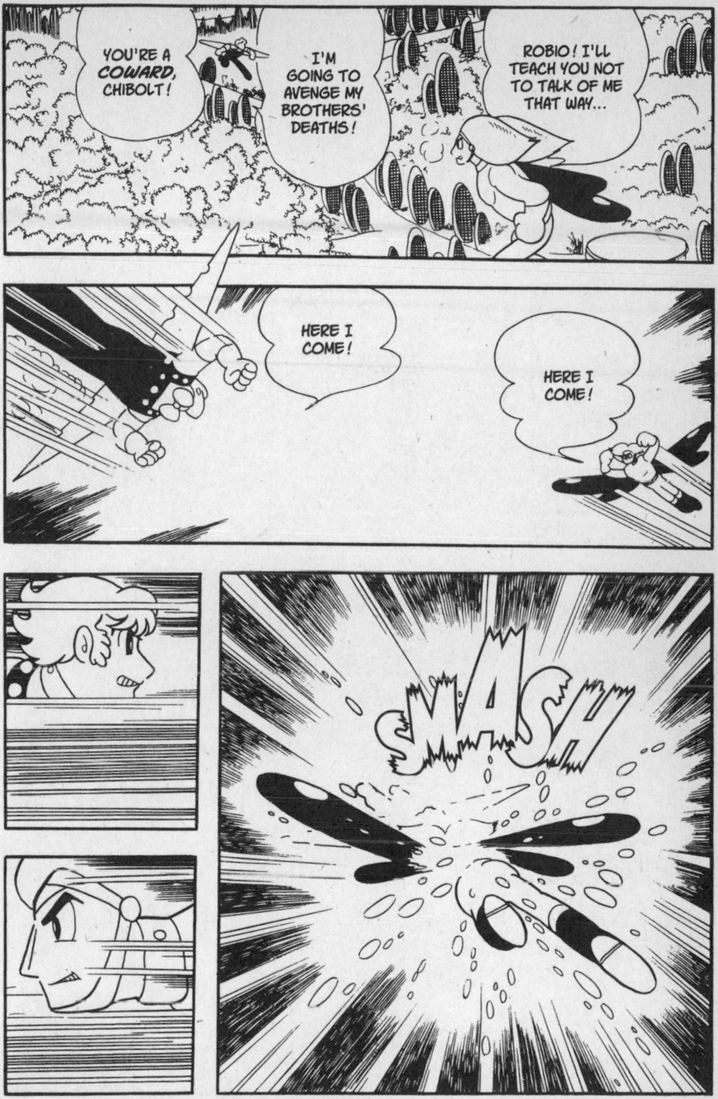
YOU'RE A *COWARD*, CHIBOLT!
I'M GOING TO AVENGE MY BROTHERS' DEATHS!
ROBIO! I'LL TEACH YOU NOT TO TALK OF ME THAT WAY...
HERE I COME!
HERE I COME!
SMASH

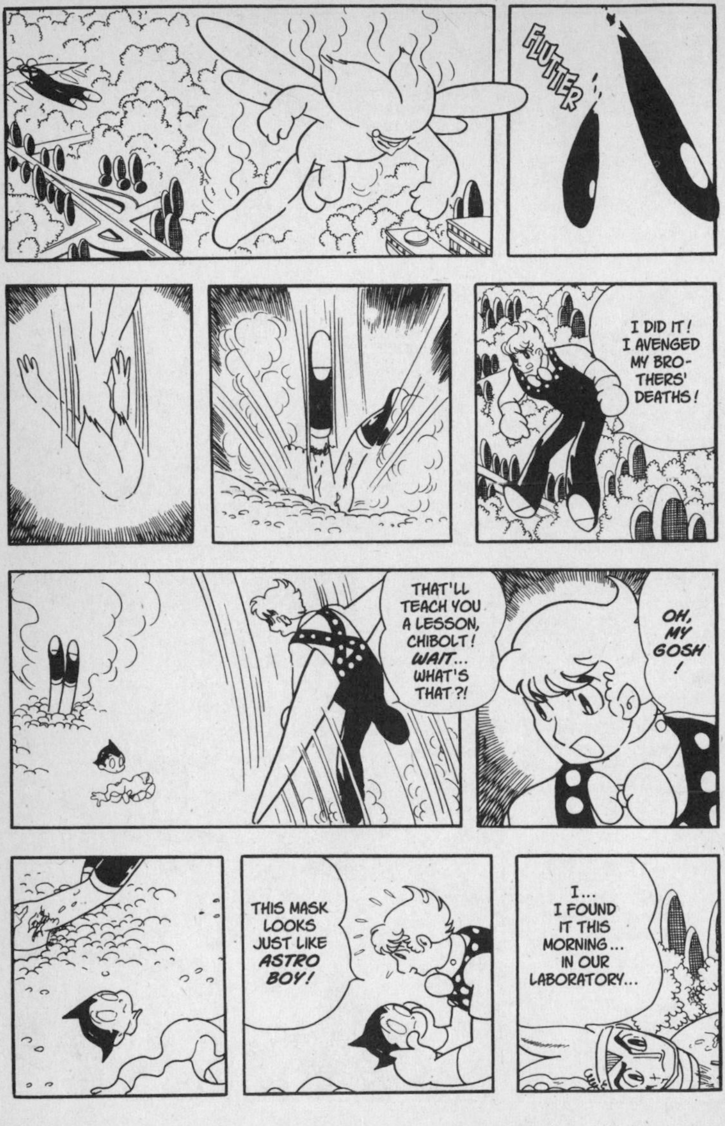
FLUTTER
I DID IT! I AVENGED MY BRO-THERS' DEATHS!
THAT'LL TEACH YOU A LESSON, CHIBOLT! *WAIT*... WHAT'S THAT?!
OH, MY GOSH!
THIS MASK LOOKS JUST LIKE *ASTRO BOY*!
I... I FOUND IT THIS MORNING... IN OUR LABORATORY...

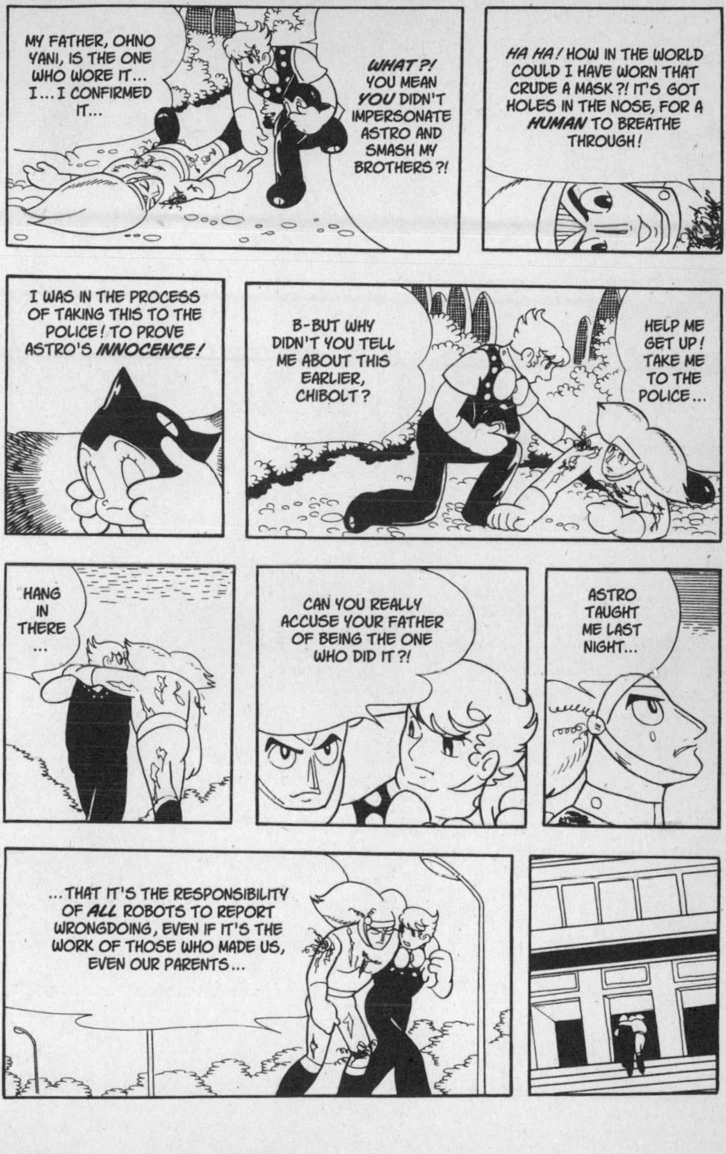
MY FATHER, OHNO YANI, IS THE ONE WHO WORE IT... I... I CONFIRMED IT...
WHAT?! YOU MEAN YOU DIDN'T IMPERSONATE ASTRO AND SMASH MY BROTHERS?!
HA HA! HOW IN THE WORLD COULD I HAVE WORN THAT CRUDE A MASK?! IT'S GOT HOLES IN THE NOSE, FOR A HUMAN TO BREATHE THROUGH!
I WAS IN THE PROCESS OF TAKING THIS TO THE POLICE! TO PROVE ASTRO'S INNOCENCE!
B-BUT WHY DIDN'T YOU TELL ME ABOUT THIS EARLIER, CHIBOLT?
HELP ME GET UP! TAKE ME TO THE POLICE...
HANG IN THERE ...
CAN YOU REALLY ACCUSE YOUR FATHER OF BEING THE ONE WHO DID IT?!
ASTRO TAUGHT ME LAST NIGHT...
...THAT IT'S THE RESPONSIBILITY OF ALL ROBOTS TO REPORT WRONGDOING, EVEN IF IT'S THE WORK OF THOSE WHO MADE US, EVEN OUR PARENTS...

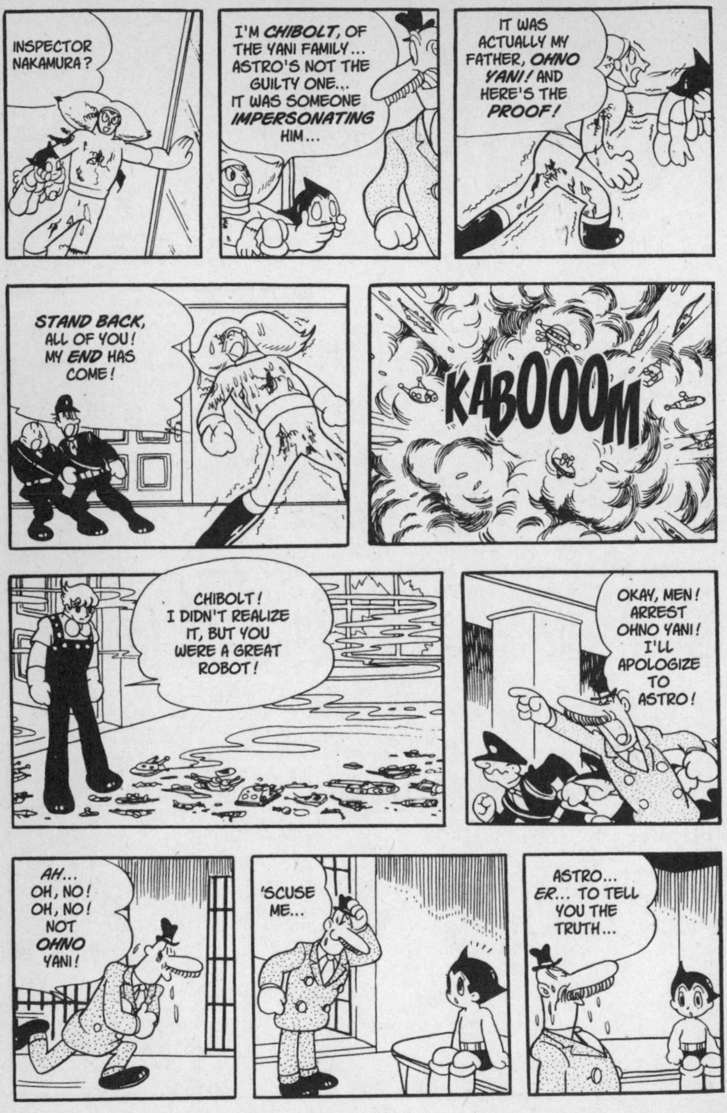
INSPECTOR NAKAMURA?
I'M CHIBOLT, OF THE YANI FAMILY... ASTRO'S NOT THE GUILTY ONE... IT WAS SOMEONE IMPERSONATING HIM...
IT WAS ACTUALLY MY FATHER, OHNO YANI! AND HERE'S THE PROOF!
STAND BACK, ALL OF YOU! MY END HAS COME!
KABOOOM
CHIBOLT! I DIDN'T REALIZE IT, BUT YOU WERE A GREAT ROBOT!
OKAY, MEN! ARREST OHNO YANI! I'LL APOLOGIZE TO ASTRO!
AH... OH, NO! OH, NO! NOT OHNO YANI!
'SCUSE ME...
ASTRO... ER... TO TELL YOU THE TRUTH...

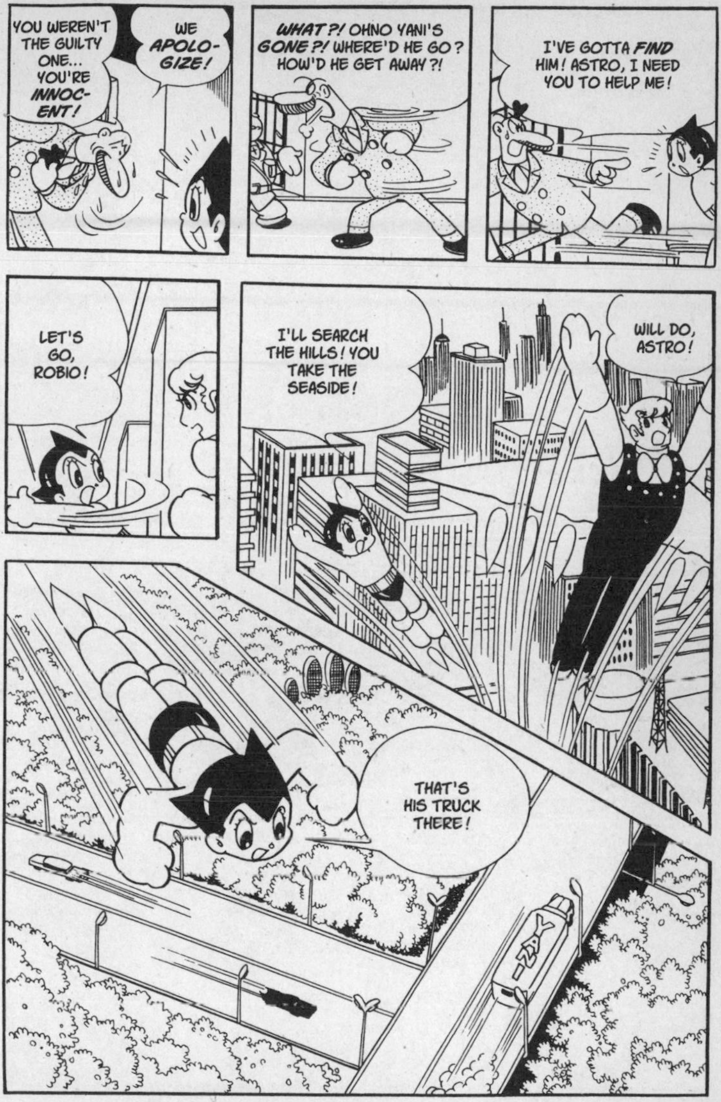
YOU WEREN'T THE GUILTY ONE... YOU'RE INNOCENT!
WE APOLOGIZE!
WHAT?! OHNO YANI'S GONE?! WHERE'D HE GO? HOW'D HE GET AWAY?!
I'VE GOTTA FIND HIM! ASTRO, I NEED YOU TO HELP ME!
LET'S GO, ROBIO!
I'LL SEARCH THE HILLS! YOU TAKE THE SEASIDE!
WILL DO, ASTRO!
THAT'S HIS TRUCK THERE!

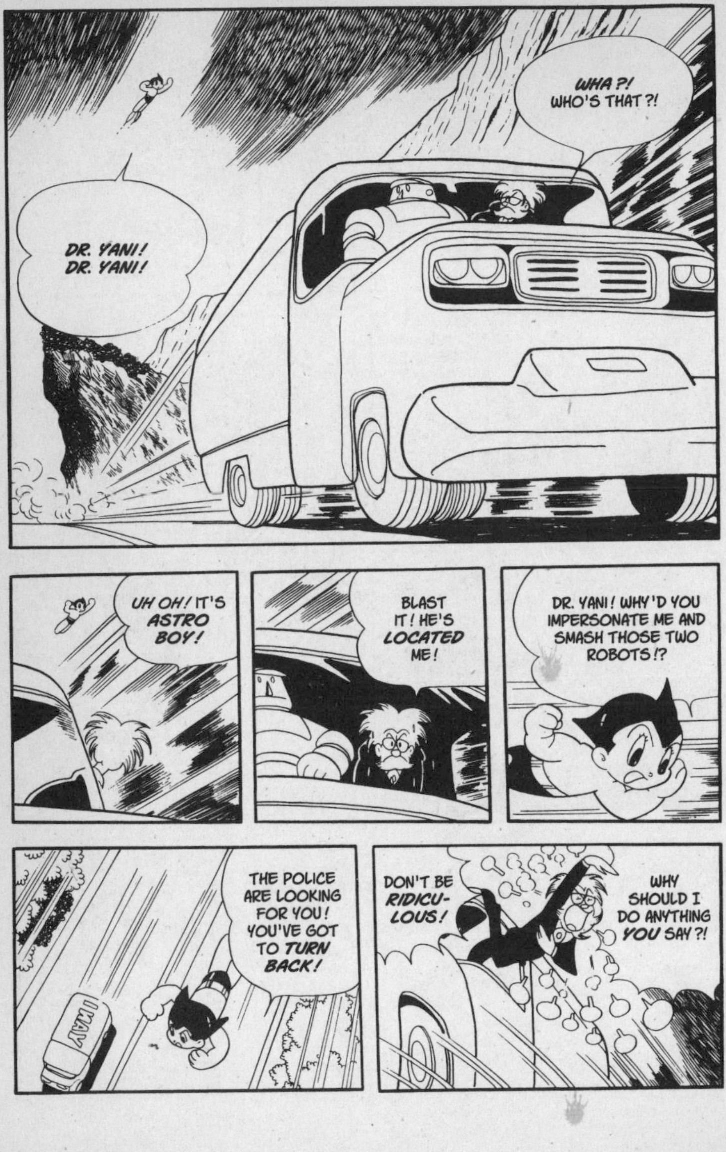
DR. YANI! DR. YANI!
WHA?! WHO'S THAT?!
UH OH! IT'S ASTRO BOY!
BLAST IT! HE'S LOCATED ME!
DR. YANI! WHY'D YOU IMPERSONATE ME AND SMASH THOSE TWO ROBOTS!?
THE POLICE ARE LOOKING FOR YOU! YOU'VE GOT TO TURN BACK!
DON'T BE RIDICULOUS!
WHY SHOULD I DO ANYTHING YOU SAY?!

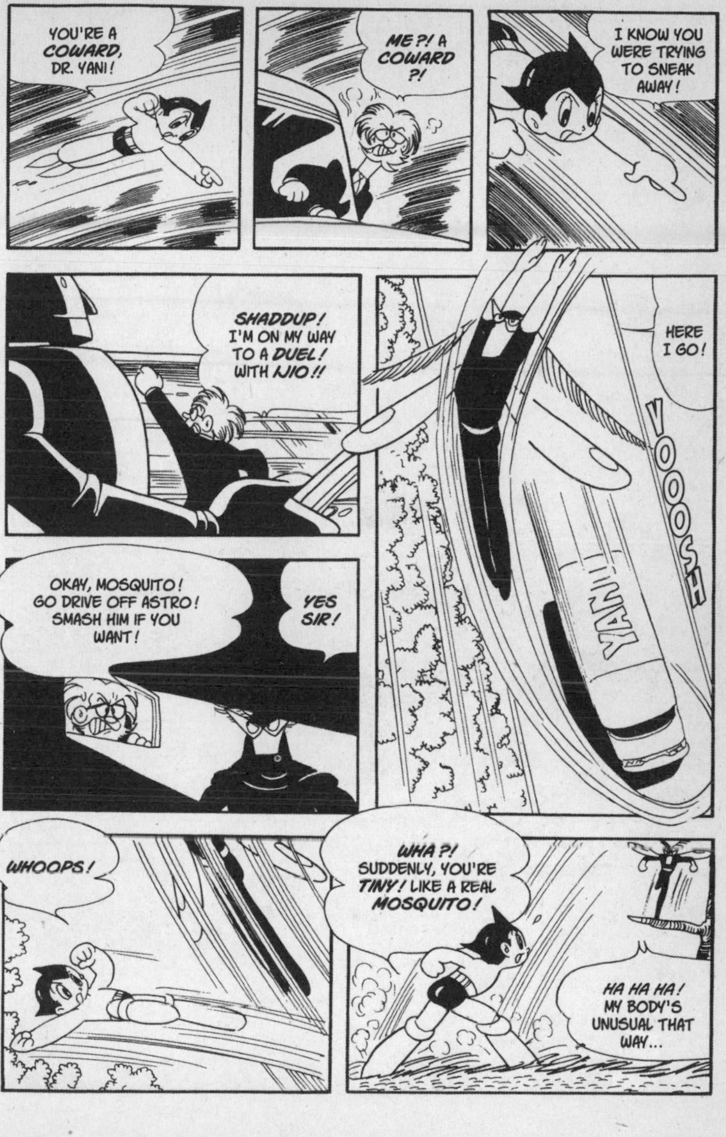
YOU'RE A COWARD, DR. YANI!
ME?! A COWARD ?!
I KNOW YOU WERE TRYING TO SNEAK AWAY!
SHADDUP! I'M ON MY WAY TO A DUEL! WITH IJIO!!
OKAY, MOSQUITO! GO DRIVE OFF ASTRO! SMASH HIM IF YOU WANT!
YES SIR!
HERE I GO!
VOOOOSH
YANI
WHOOPS!
WHA?! SUDDENLY, YOU'RE TINY! LIKE A REAL MOSQUITO!
HA HA HA! MY BODY'S UNUSUAL THAT WAY...

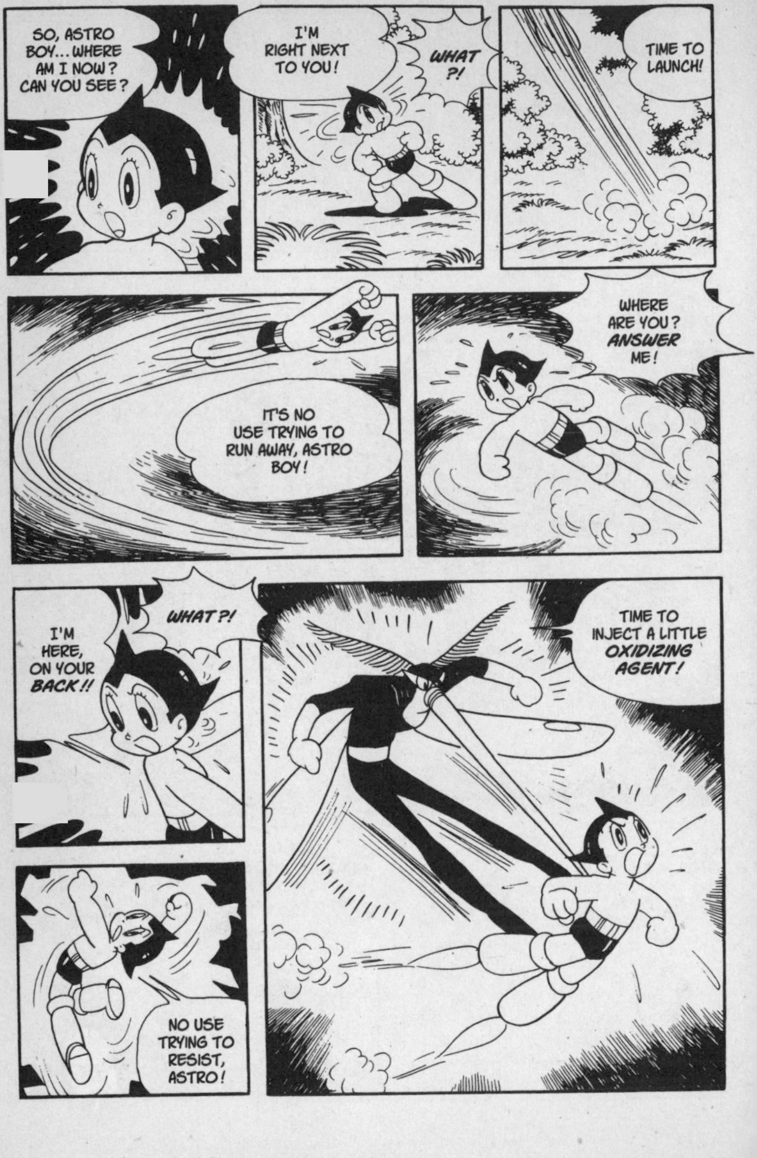
SO, ASTRO BOY... WHERE AM I NOW? CAN YOU SEE?
I'M RIGHT NEXT TO YOU!
WHAT ?!
TIME TO LAUNCH!
IT'S NO USE TRYING TO RUN AWAY, ASTRO BOY!
WHERE ARE YOU? ANSWER ME!
I'M HERE, ON YOUR BACK!!
WHAT?!
TIME TO INJECT A LITTLE OXIDIZING AGENT!
NO USE TRYING TO RESIST, ASTRO!

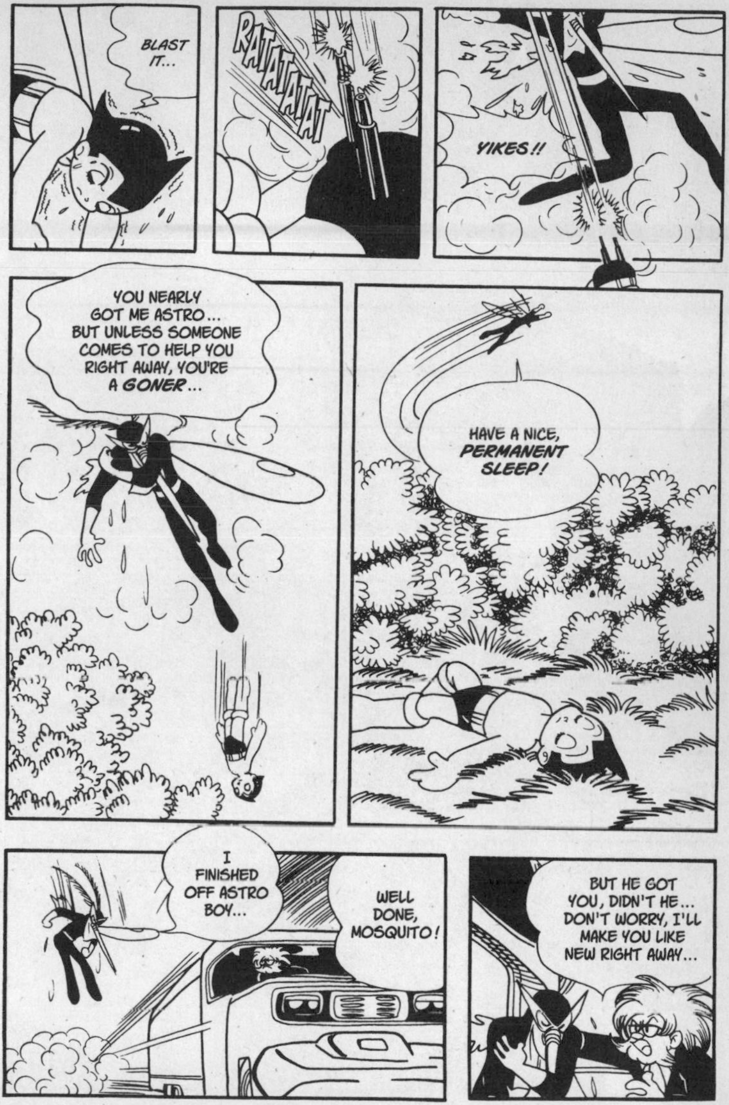
BLAST IT...
RATATATATAT
YIKES!!
YOU NEARLY GOT ME ASTRO... BUT UNLESS SOMEONE COMES TO HELP YOU RIGHT AWAY, YOU'RE A GONER...
HAVE A NICE, PERMANENT SLEEP!
I FINISHED OFF ASTRO BOY...
WELL DONE, MOSQUITO!
BUT HE GOT YOU, DIDN'T HE... DON'T WORRY, I'LL MAKE YOU LIKE NEW RIGHT AWAY...

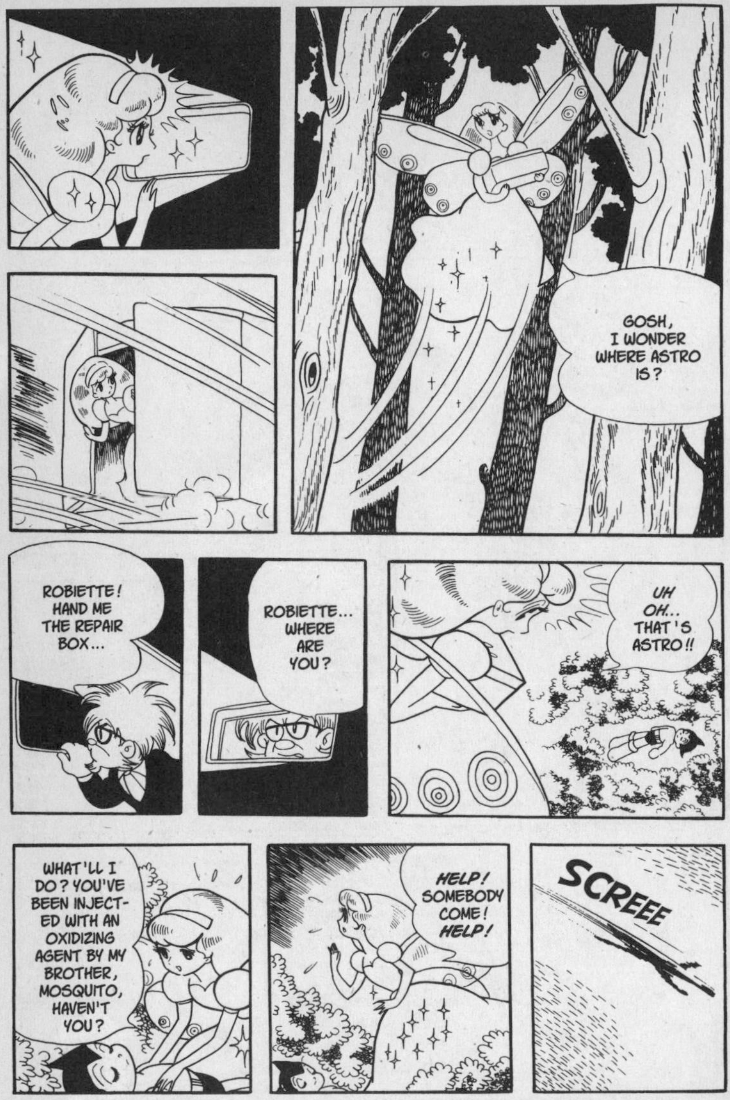
GOSH, I WONDER WHERE ASTRO IS?
ROBIETTE! HAND ME THE REPAIR BOX...
ROBIETTE... WHERE ARE YOU?
UH OH... THAT'S ASTRO!!
WHAT'LL I DO? YOU'VE BEEN INJECTED WITH AN OXIDIZING AGENT BY MY BROTHER, MOSQUITO, HAVEN'T YOU?
HELP! SOMEBODY COME! HELP!
SCREEE

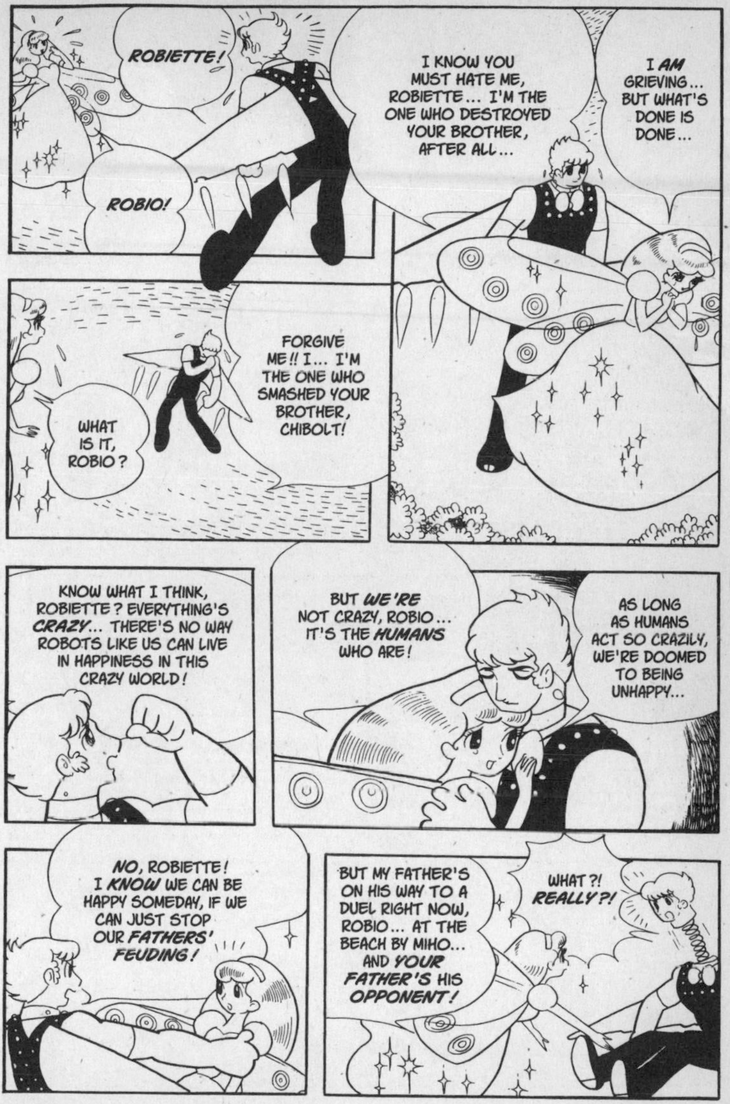
ROBIETTE!
ROBIO!
I KNOW YOU MUST HATE ME, ROBIETTE... I'M THE ONE WHO DESTROYED YOUR BROTHER, AFTER ALL...
I AM GRIEVING... BUT WHAT'S DONE IS DONE...
FORGIVE ME!! I... I'M THE ONE WHO SMASHED YOUR BROTHER, CHIBOLT!
WHAT IS IT, ROBIO?
KNOW WHAT I THINK, ROBIETTE? EVERYTHING'S CRAZY... THERE'S NO WAY ROBOTS LIKE US CAN LIVE IN HAPPINESS IN THIS CRAZY WORLD!
BUT WE'RE NOT CRAZY, ROBIO... IT'S THE HUMANS WHO ARE!
AS LONG AS HUMANS ACT SO CRAZILY, WE'RE DOOMED TO BEING UNHAPPY...
NO, ROBIETTE! I KNOW WE CAN BE HAPPY SOMEDAY, IF WE CAN JUST STOP OUR FATHERS' FEUDING!
BUT MY FATHER'S ON HIS WAY TO A DUEL RIGHT NOW, ROBIO... AT THE BEACH BY MIHO... AND YOUR FATHER'S HIS OPPONENT!
WHAT?! REALLY?!

WE'VE GOT TO HURRY AND STOP THEM, ROBIETTE!

THEY'RE BOTH SO STUBBORN, ROBIO...

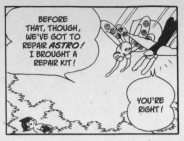

BEFORE THAT, THOUGH, WE'VE GOT TO REPAIR *ASTRO*! I BROUGHT A REPAIR KIT!

YOU'RE RIGHT!

THINK YOU CAN FIX HIM? HE'S BADLY HURT...

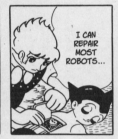

I CAN REPAIR MOST ROBOTS...

BLAST IT... ASTRO'S BODY DESIGN IS TOO *COMPLICATED!*

I NEED YOU TO TAKE ASTRO TO THE MINISTRY OF SCIENCE, ROBIETTE. I'LL GO TO THE SITE OF THE DUEL AT MIHO...

I'LL JOIN YOU LATER, ROBIO!

TAKE CARE OF ASTRO!

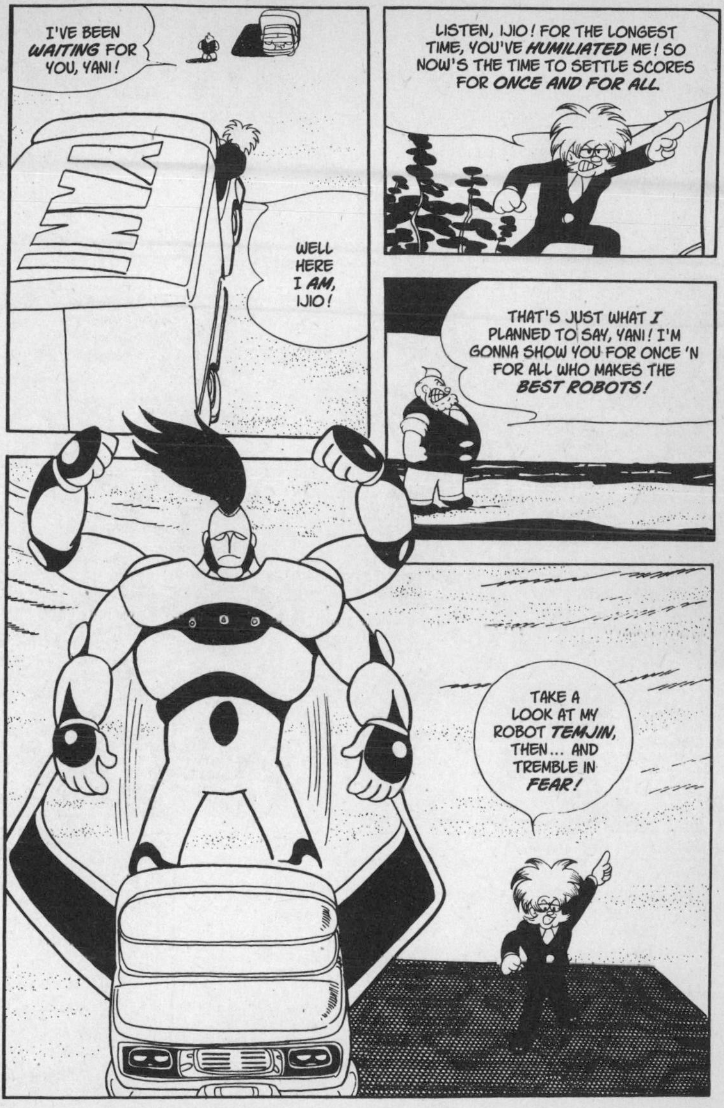

I'VE BEEN WAITING FOR YOU, YANI!
WELL HERE I AM, IJIO!
LISTEN, IJIO! FOR THE LONGEST TIME, YOU'VE HUMILIATED ME! SO NOW'S THE TIME TO SETTLE SCORES FOR ONCE AND FOR ALL.
THAT'S JUST WHAT I PLANNED TO SAY, YANI! I'M GONNA SHOW YOU FOR ONCE 'N FOR ALL WHO MAKES THE BEST ROBOTS!
TAKE A LOOK AT MY ROBOT TEMJIN, THEN... AND TREMBLE IN FEAR!

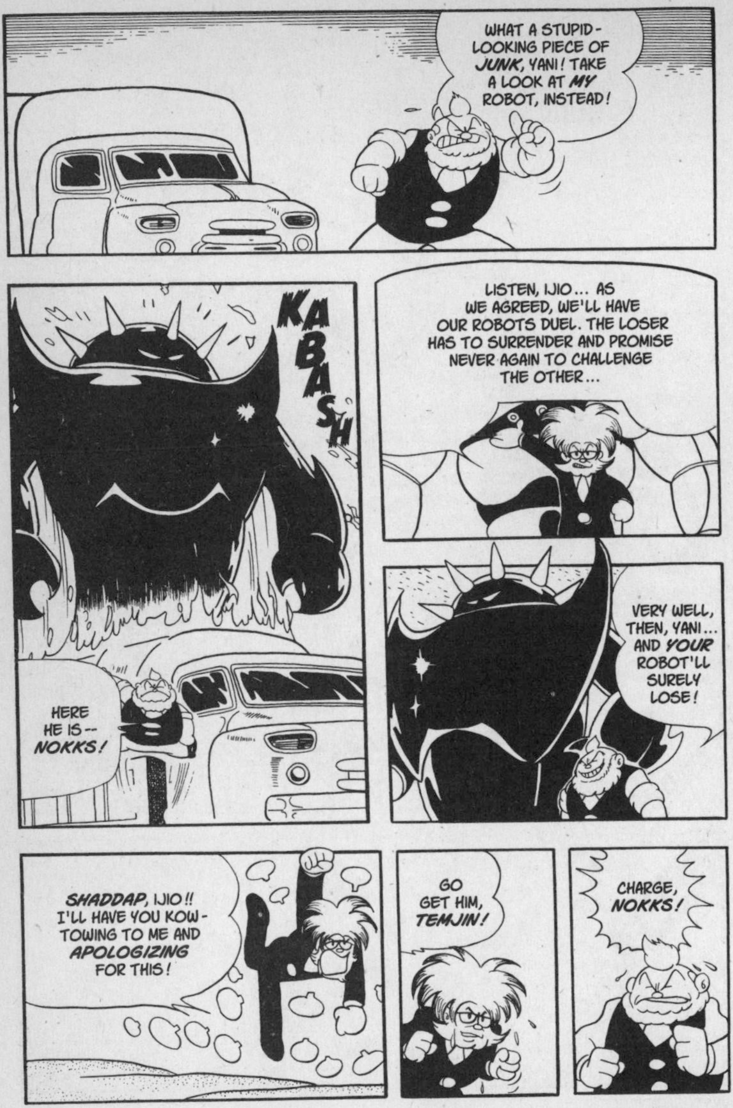
WHAT A STUPID-LOOKING PIECE OF JUNK, YANI! TAKE A LOOK AT MY ROBOT, INSTEAD!
KABASH
HERE HE IS -- NOKKS!
LISTEN, IJIO... AS WE AGREED, WE'LL HAVE OUR ROBOTS DUEL. THE LOSER HAS TO SURRENDER AND PROMISE NEVER AGAIN TO CHALLENGE THE OTHER...
VERY WELL, THEN, YANI... AND YOUR ROBOT'LL SURELY LOSE!
SHADDAP, IJIO!! I'LL HAVE YOU KOW-TOWING TO ME AND APOLOGIZING FOR THIS!
GO GET HIM, TEMJIN!
CHARGE, NOKKS!

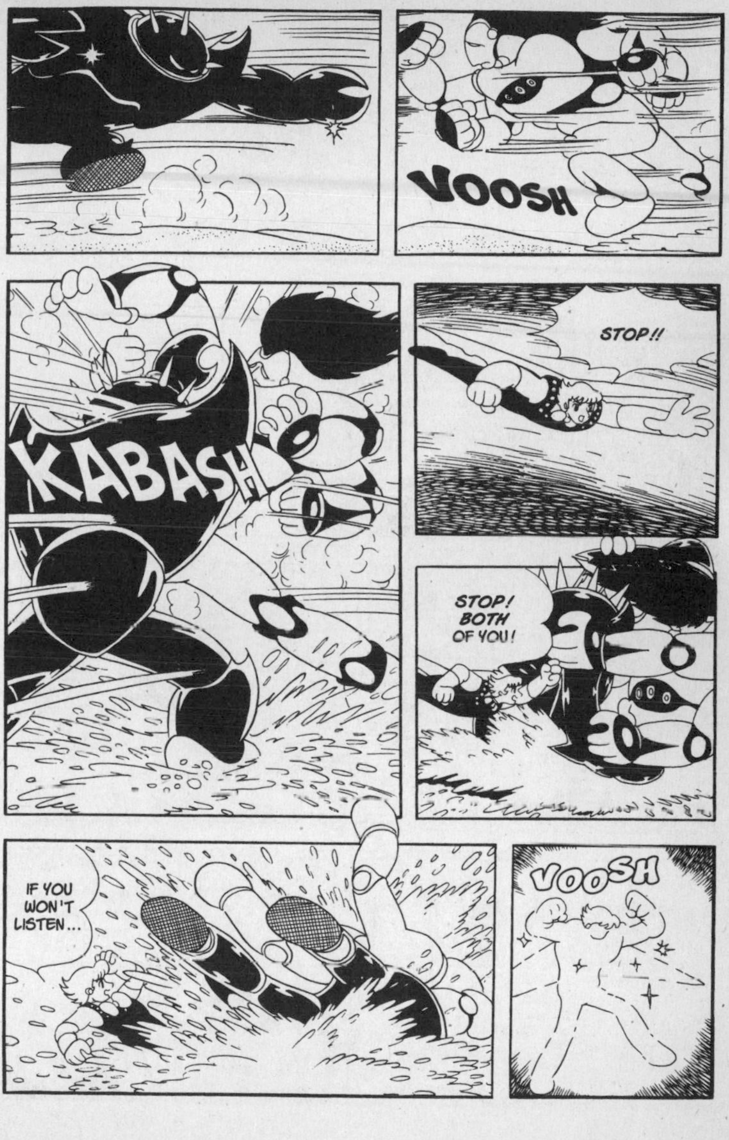
VOOSH
KABASH
STOP!!
STOP! BOTH OF YOU!
IF YOU WON'T LISTEN...
VOOSH

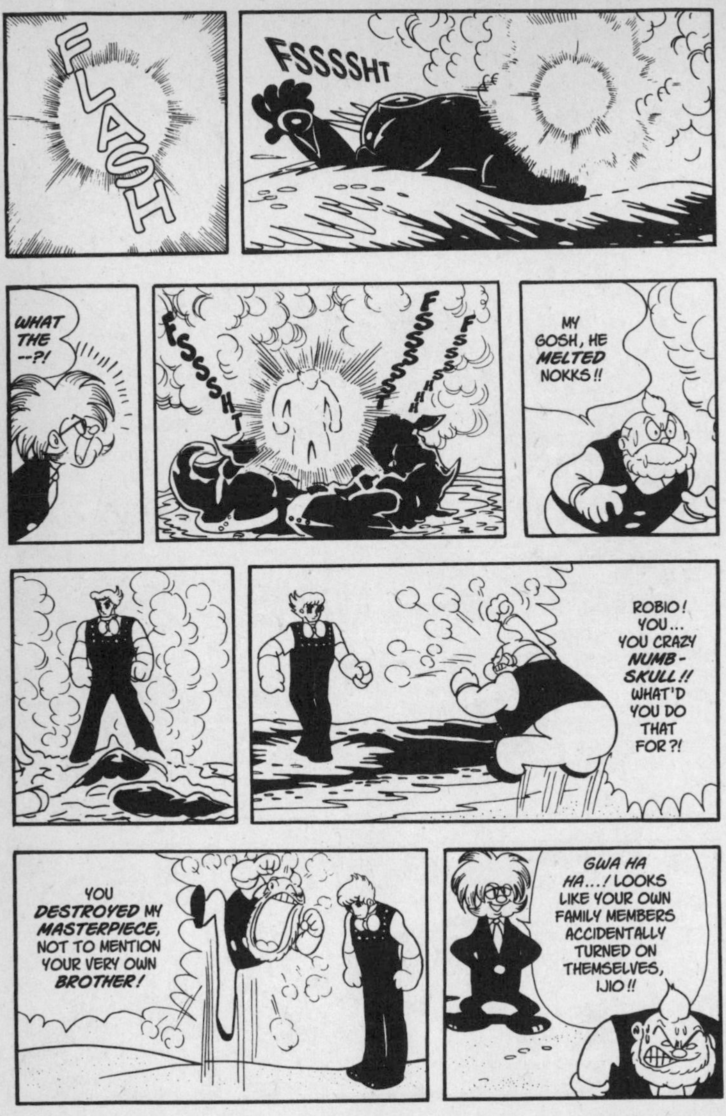
FLASH
FSSSSHT
WHAT THE --?!
FSSSSHT
FSSSSST
FSSSSHH
MY GOSH, HE MELTED NOKKS!!
ROBIO! YOU... YOU CRAZY NUMB-SKULL!! WHAT'D YOU DO THAT FOR?!
YOU DESTROYED MY MASTERPIECE, NOT TO MENTION YOUR VERY OWN BROTHER!
GWA HA HA...! LOOKS LIKE YOUR OWN FAMILY MEMBERS ACCIDENTALLY TURNED ON THEMSELVES, IJIO!!

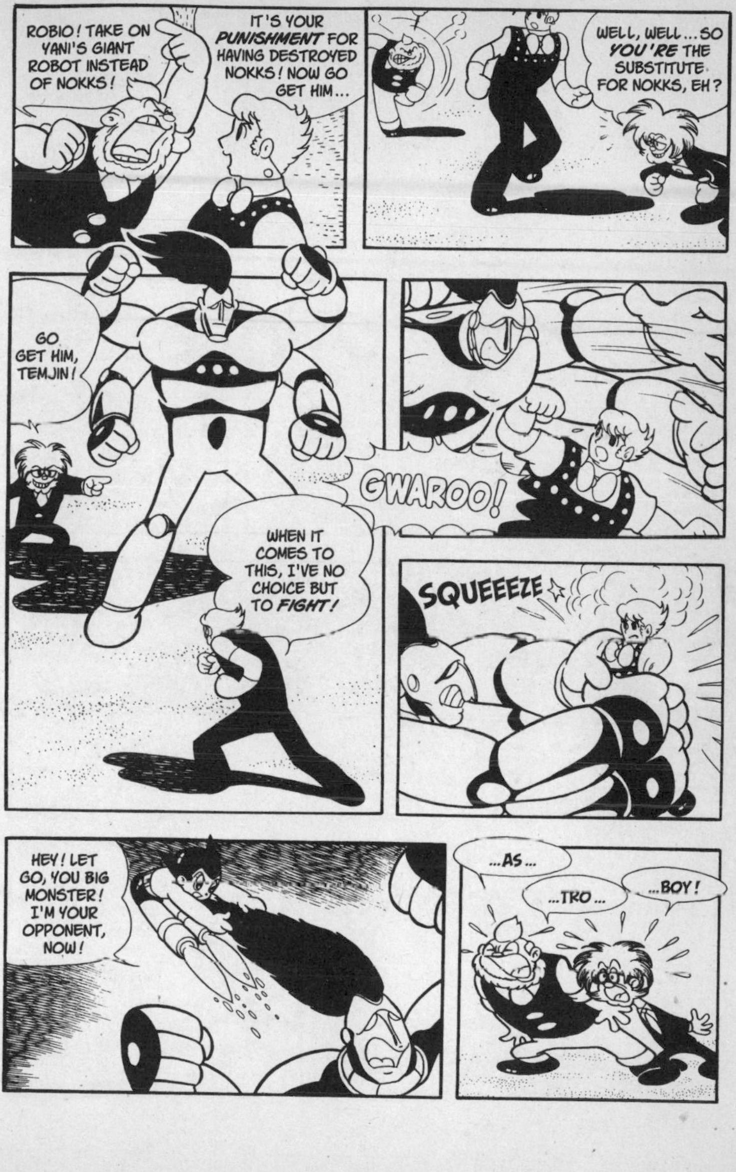
ROBIO! TAKE ON YANI'S GIANT ROBOT INSTEAD OF NOKKS!
IT'S YOUR PUNISHMENT FOR HAVING DESTROYED NOKKS! NOW GO GET HIM...
WELL, WELL... SO YOU'RE THE SUBSTITUTE FOR NOKKS, EH?
GO GET HIM, TEMJIN!
WHEN IT COMES TO THIS, I'VE NO CHOICE BUT TO FIGHT!
GWAROO!
SQUEEEZE
HEY! LET GO, YOU BIG MONSTER! I'M YOUR OPPONENT, NOW!
...AS...
...TRO...
...BOY!

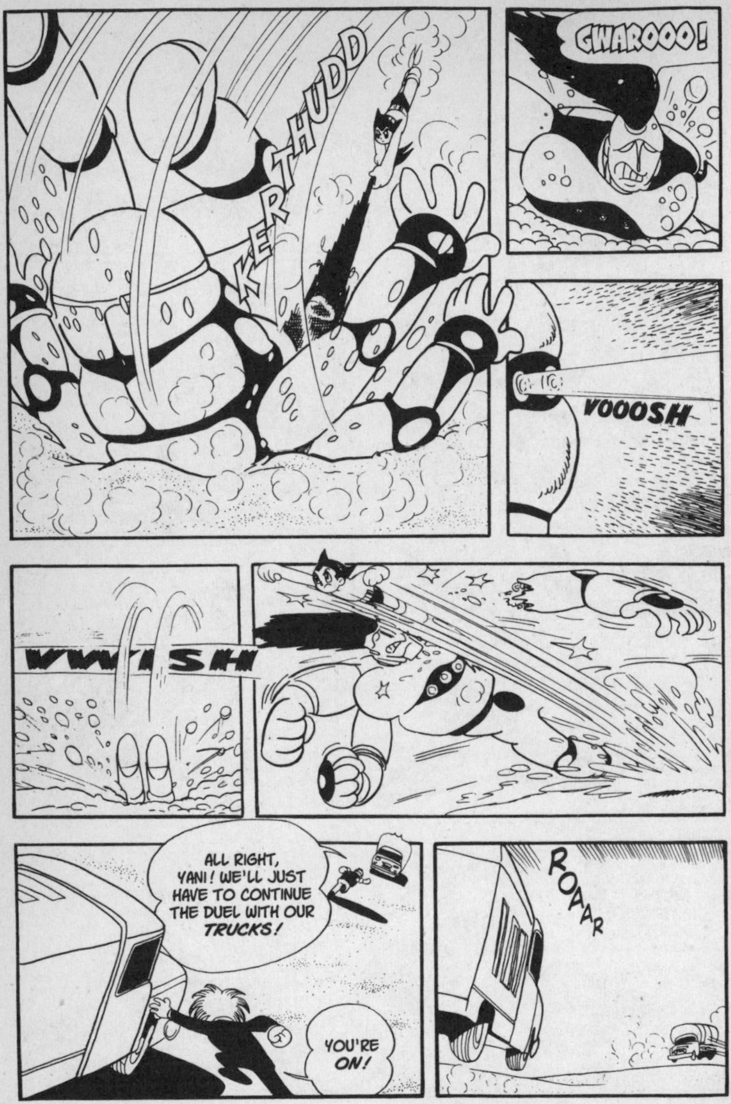
KERTHUDD
GWAROOO!
VOOOSH
WWISH
ALL RIGHT, YANI! WE'LL JUST HAVE TO CONTINUE THE DUEL WITH OUR TRUCKS!
YOU'RE ON!
ROAAAR

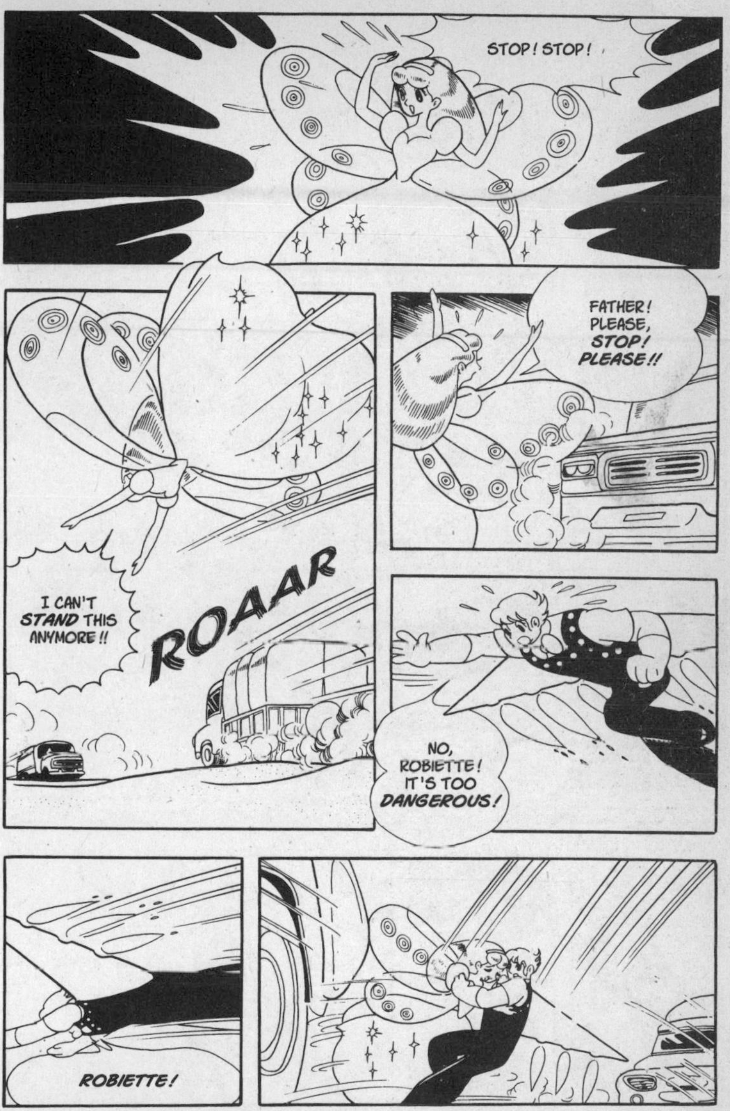
STOP! STOP!
I CAN'T STAND THIS ANYMORE!!
ROAAR
FATHER! PLEASE, STOP! PLEASE!!
NO, ROBIETTE! IT'S TOO DANGEROUS!
ROBIETTE!

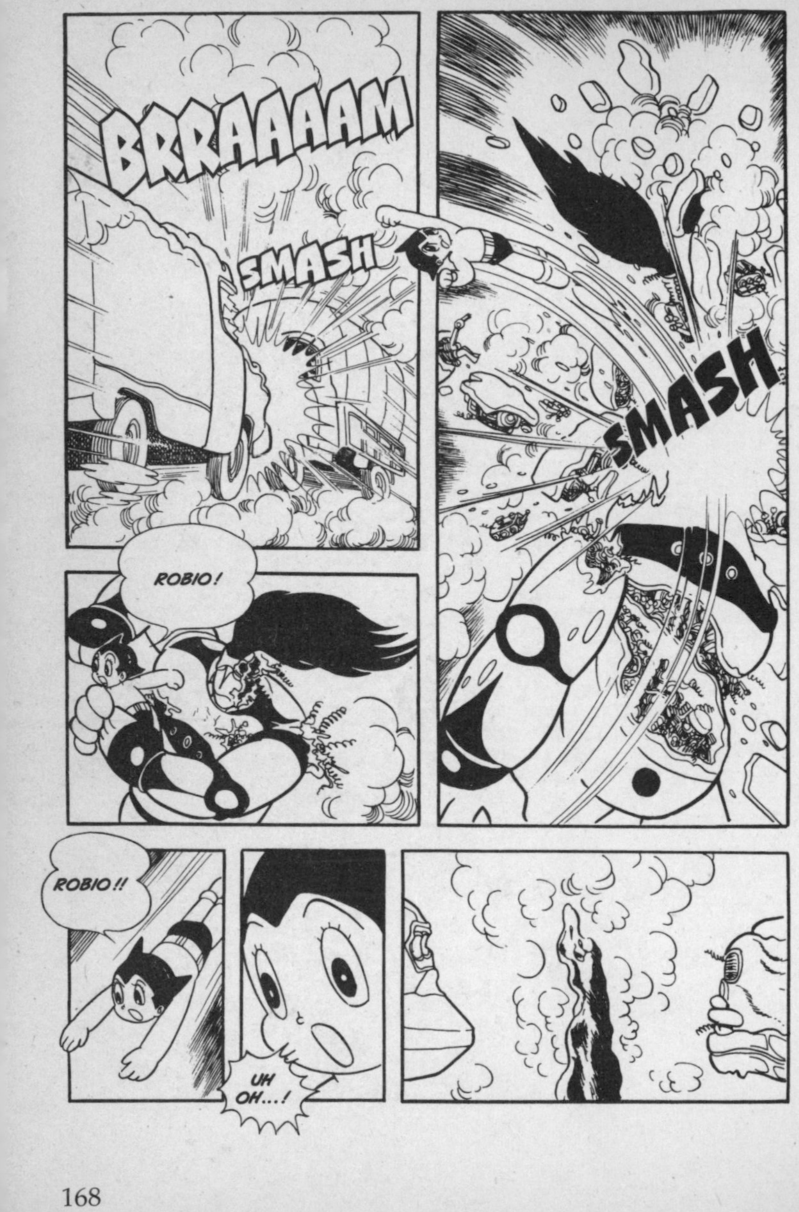
BRRAAAAM
SMASH
ROBIO!
SMASH
ROBIO!!
UH OH...!

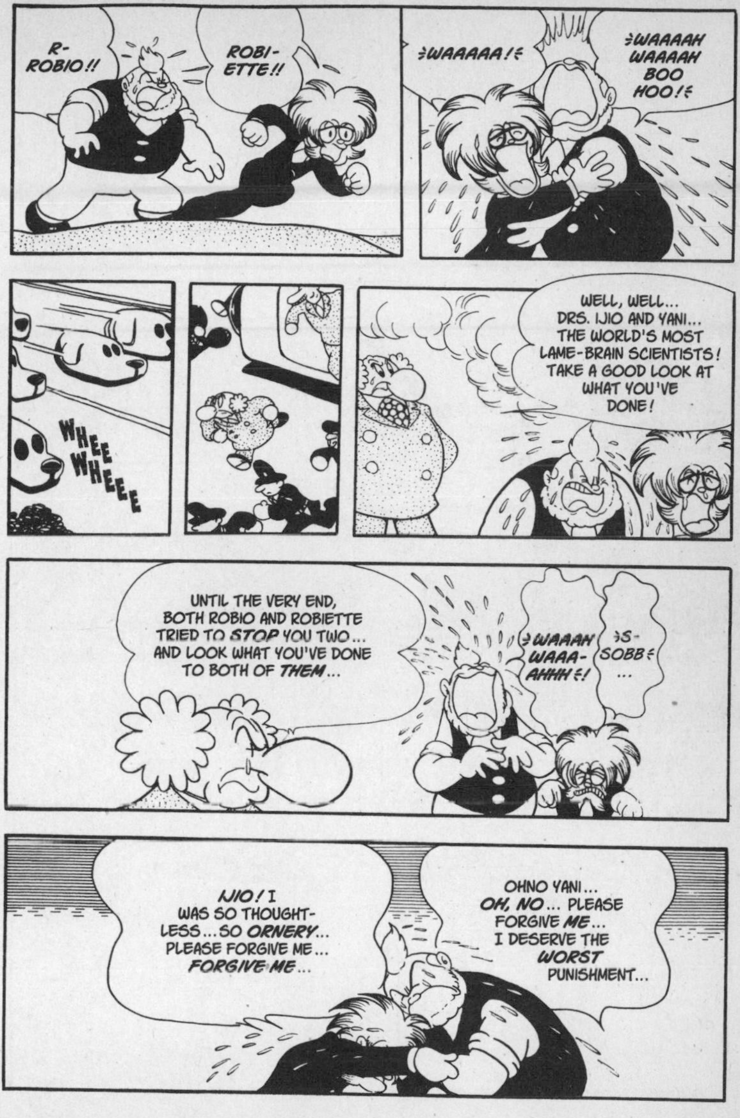
R-ROBIO!!
ROBIETTE!!
WAAAAA!
WAAAAH WAAAAH BOO HOO!
WHEE WHEEEE
WELL, WELL... DRS. IJIO AND YANI... THE WORLD'S MOST LAME-BRAIN SCIENTISTS! TAKE A GOOD LOOK AT WHAT YOU'VE DONE!
UNTIL THE VERY END, BOTH ROBIO AND ROBIETTE TRIED TO STOP YOU TWO... AND LOOK WHAT YOU'VE DONE TO BOTH OF THEM...
WAAAH WAAA-AHHH!
S-SOBB...
IJIO! I WAS SO THOUGHT-LESS... SO ORNERY... PLEASE FORGIVE ME... FORGIVE ME...
OHNO YANI... OH, NO... PLEASE FORGIVE ME... I DESERVE THE WORST PUNISHMENT...

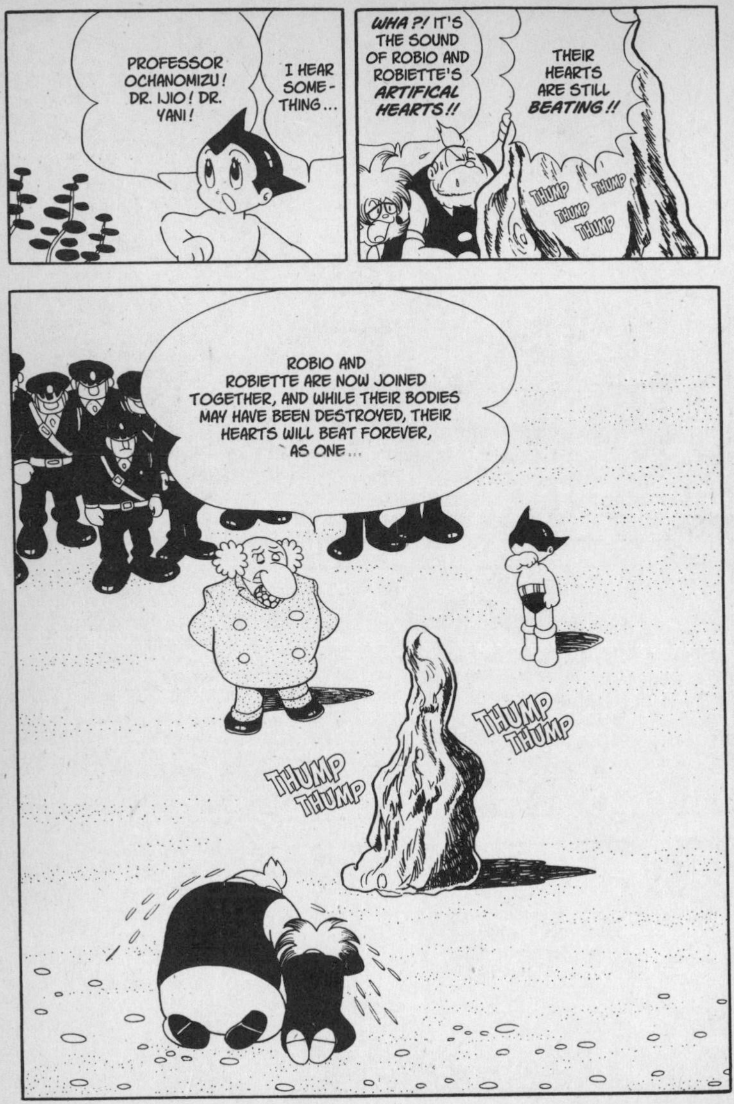
PROFESSOR OCHANOMIZU! DR. IJIO! DR. YANI!
I HEAR SOME-THING...
WHA?! IT'S THE SOUND OF ROBIO AND ROBIETTE'S ARTIFICAL HEARTS!!
THEIR HEARTS ARE STILL BEATING!!
THUMP THUMP THUMP THUMP
ROBIO AND ROBIETTE ARE NOW JOINED TOGETHER, AND WHILE THEIR BODIES MAY HAVE BEEN DESTROYED, THEIR HEARTS WILL BEAT FOREVER, AS ONE...
THUMP THUMP
THUMP THUMP

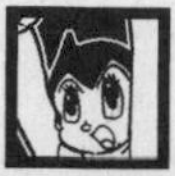

THE DEVIL'S BALLOONS

First serialized from December 1963 to February 1964 in the supplement editions of *Shonen* magazine.

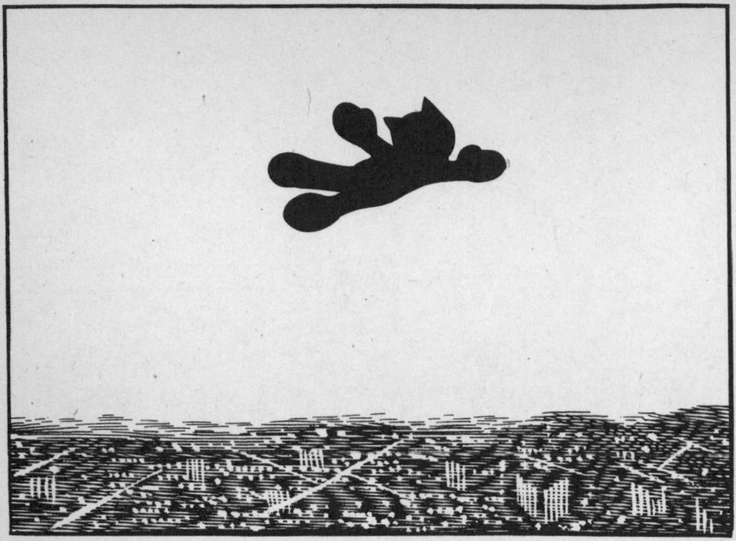

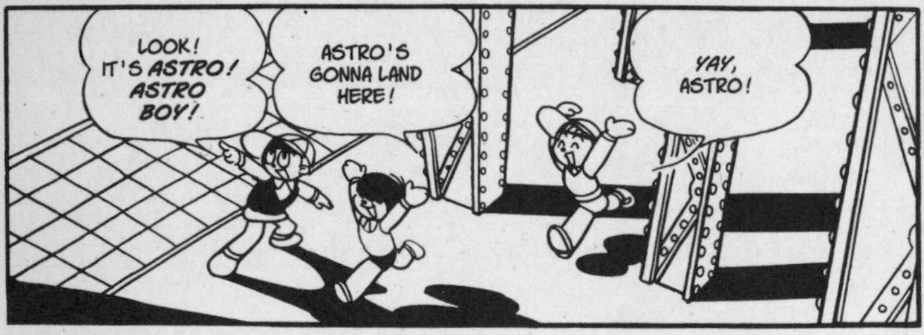
LOOK! IT'S ASTRO! ASTRO BOY!
ASTRO'S GONNA LAND HERE!
YAY, ASTRO!

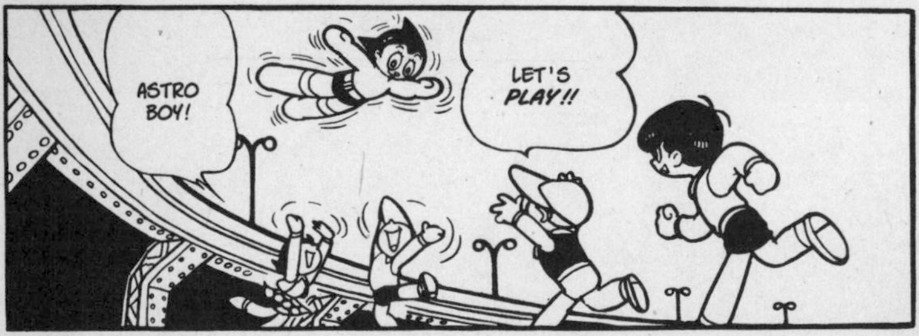
ASTRO BOY!
LET'S PLAY!!

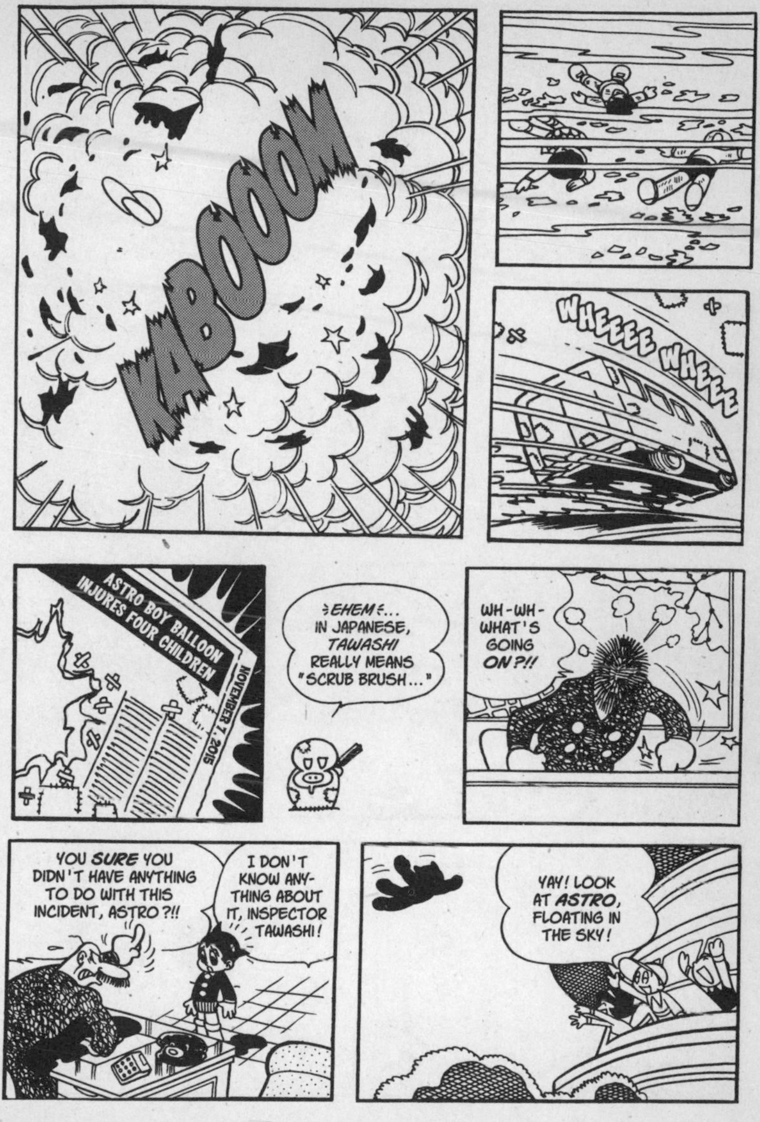
KABOOOM
WHEEEE WHEEEE
ASTRO BOY BALLOON INJURES FOUR CHILDREN
NOVEMBER 7, 2015
EHEM... IN JAPANESE, TAWASHI REALLY MEANS "SCRUB BRUSH..."
WH-WH-WHAT'S GOING ON?!!
YOU SURE YOU DIDN'T HAVE ANYTHING TO DO WITH THIS INCIDENT, ASTRO?!!
I DON'T KNOW ANYTHING ABOUT IT, INSPECTOR TAWASHI!
YAY! LOOK AT ASTRO, FLOATING IN THE SKY!

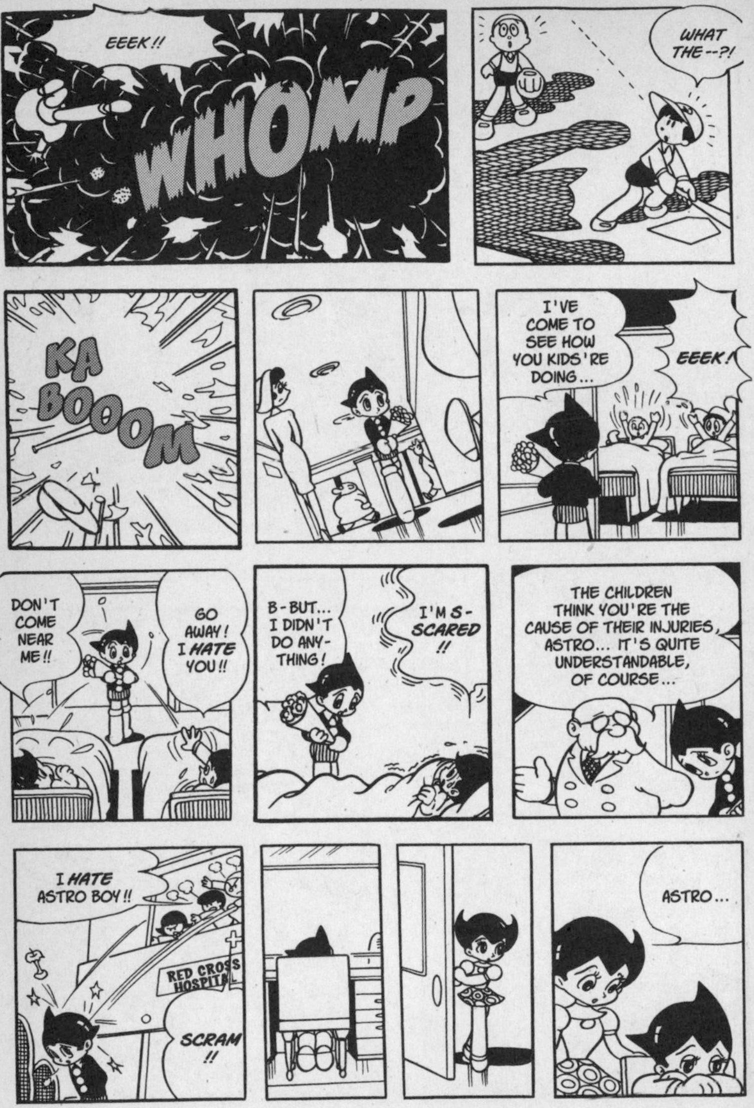
EEEK!!
WHOMP
WHAT THE--?!
KA BOOOOM
I'VE COME TO SEE HOW YOU KIDS'RE DOING...
EEEK!
DON'T COME NEAR ME!!
GO AWAY! I HATE YOU!!
B-BUT... I DIDN'T DO ANY-THING!
I'M S-SCARED!!
THE CHILDREN THINK YOU'RE THE CAUSE OF THEIR INJURIES, ASTRO... IT'S QUITE UNDERSTANDABLE, OF COURSE...
I HATE ASTRO BOY!!
RED CROSS HOSPITAL
SCRAM!!
ASTRO...

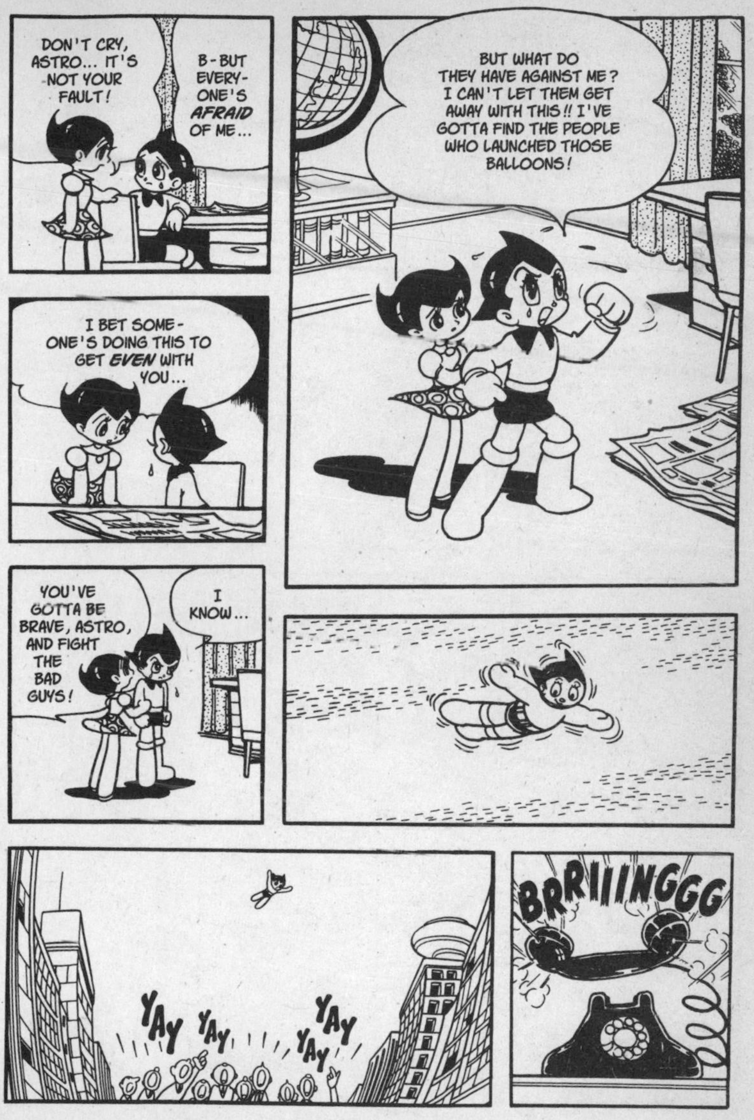
DON'T CRY, ASTRO... IT'S NOT YOUR FAULT!
B-BUT EVERY-ONE'S AFRAID OF ME...
BUT WHAT DO THEY HAVE AGAINST ME? I CAN'T LET THEM GET AWAY WITH THIS!! I'VE GOTTA FIND THE PEOPLE WHO LAUNCHED THOSE BALLOONS!
I BET SOME-ONE'S DOING THIS TO GET EVEN WITH YOU...
YOU'VE GOTTA BE BRAVE, ASTRO, AND FIGHT THE BAD GUYS!
I KNOW...
YAY YAY YAY YAY
BRRIIINGGG

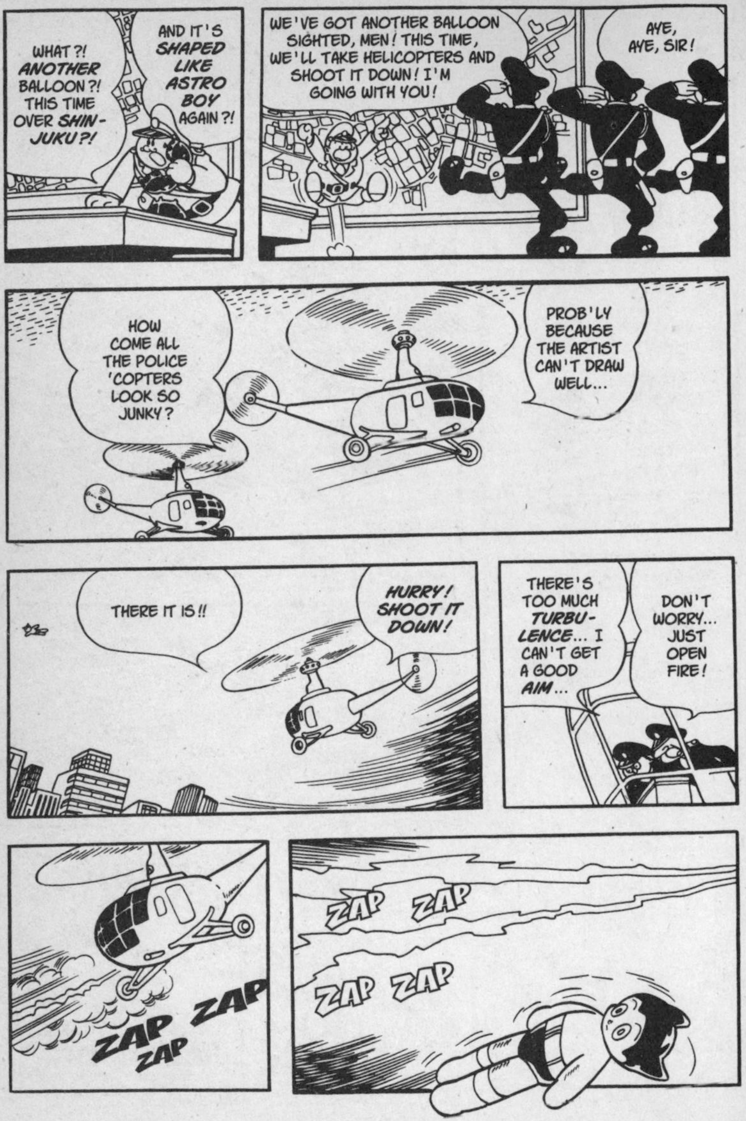
WHAT ?! ANOTHER BALLOON ?! THIS TIME OVER SHIN-JUKU ?!
AND IT'S SHAPED LIKE ASTRO BOY AGAIN ?!
WE'VE GOT ANOTHER BALLOON SIGHTED, MEN! THIS TIME, WE'LL TAKE HELICOPTERS AND SHOOT IT DOWN! I'M GOING WITH YOU!
AYE, AYE, SIR!
HOW COME ALL THE POLICE 'COPTERS LOOK SO JUNKY?
PROB'LY BECAUSE THE ARTIST CAN'T DRAW WELL...
THERE IT IS!!
HURRY! SHOOT IT DOWN!
THERE'S TOO MUCH TURBU-LENCE... I CAN'T GET A GOOD AIM...
DON'T WORRY... JUST OPEN FIRE!
ZAP ZAP
ZAP
ZAP ZAP
ZAP ZAP

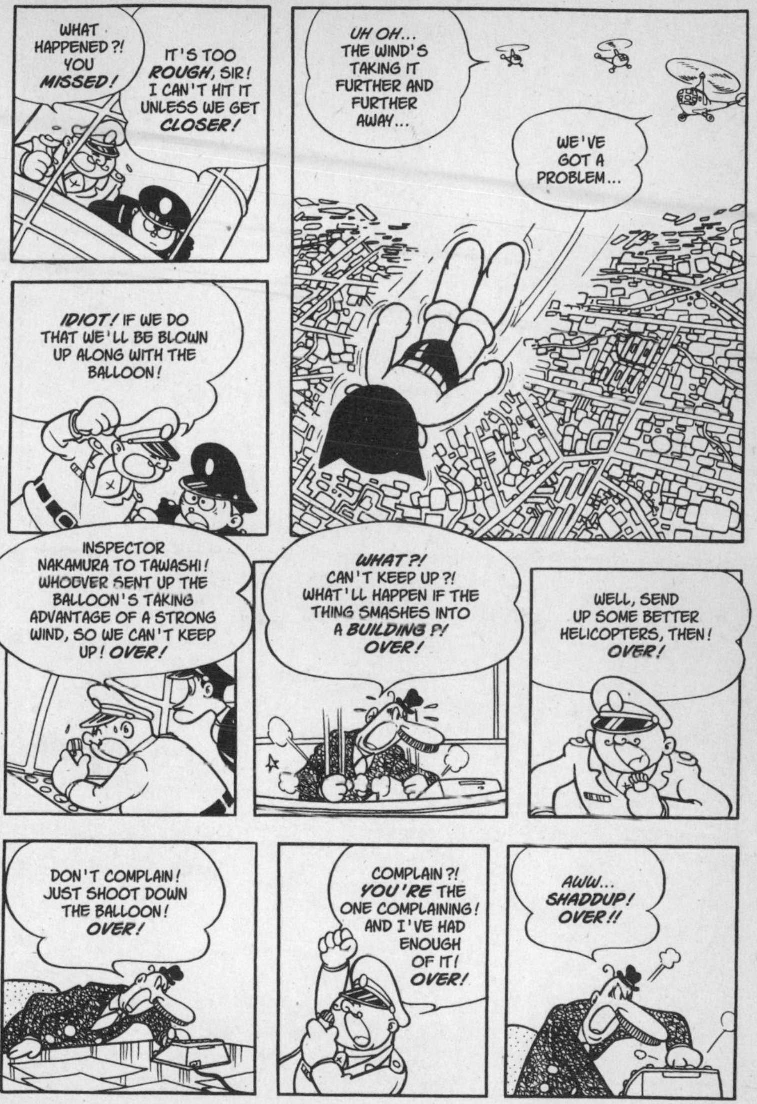
WHAT HAPPENED?! YOU MISSED!
IT'S TOO ROUGH, SIR! I CAN'T HIT IT UNLESS WE GET CLOSER!
UH OH... THE WIND'S TAKING IT FURTHER AND FURTHER AWAY...
WE'VE GOT A PROBLEM...
IDIOT! IF WE DO THAT WE'LL BE BLOWN UP ALONG WITH THE BALLOON!
INSPECTOR NAKAMURA TO TAWASHI! WHOEVER SENT UP THE BALLOON'S TAKING ADVANTAGE OF A STRONG WIND, SO WE CAN'T KEEP UP! OVER!
WHAT?! CAN'T KEEP UP?! WHAT'LL HAPPEN IF THE THING SMASHES INTO A BUILDING?! OVER!
WELL, SEND UP SOME BETTER HELICOPTERS, THEN! OVER!
DON'T COMPLAIN! JUST SHOOT DOWN THE BALLOON! OVER!
COMPLAIN?! YOU'RE THE ONE COMPLAINING! AND I'VE HAD ENOUGH OF IT! OVER!
AWW... SHADDUP! OVER!!

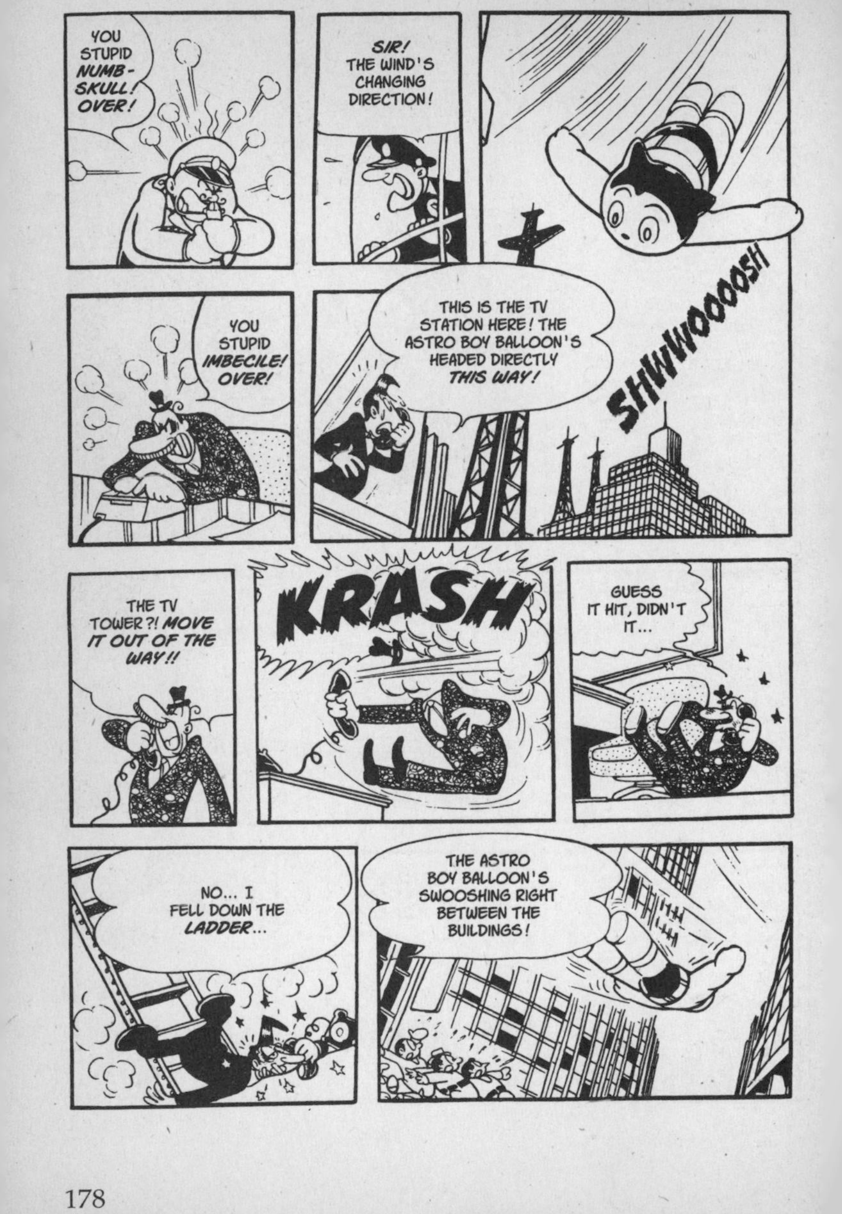
YOU STUPID NUMB-SKULL! OVER!
SIR! THE WIND'S CHANGING DIRECTION!
SHWWOOOSH
YOU STUPID IMBECILE! OVER!
THIS IS THE TV STATION HERE! THE ASTRO BOY BALLOON'S HEADED DIRECTLY THIS WAY!
THE TV TOWER?! MOVE IT OUT OF THE WAY!!
KRASH
GUESS IT HIT, DIDN'T IT...
NO... I FELL DOWN THE LADDER...
THE ASTRO BOY BALLOON'S SWOOSHING RIGHT BETWEEN THE BUILDINGS!

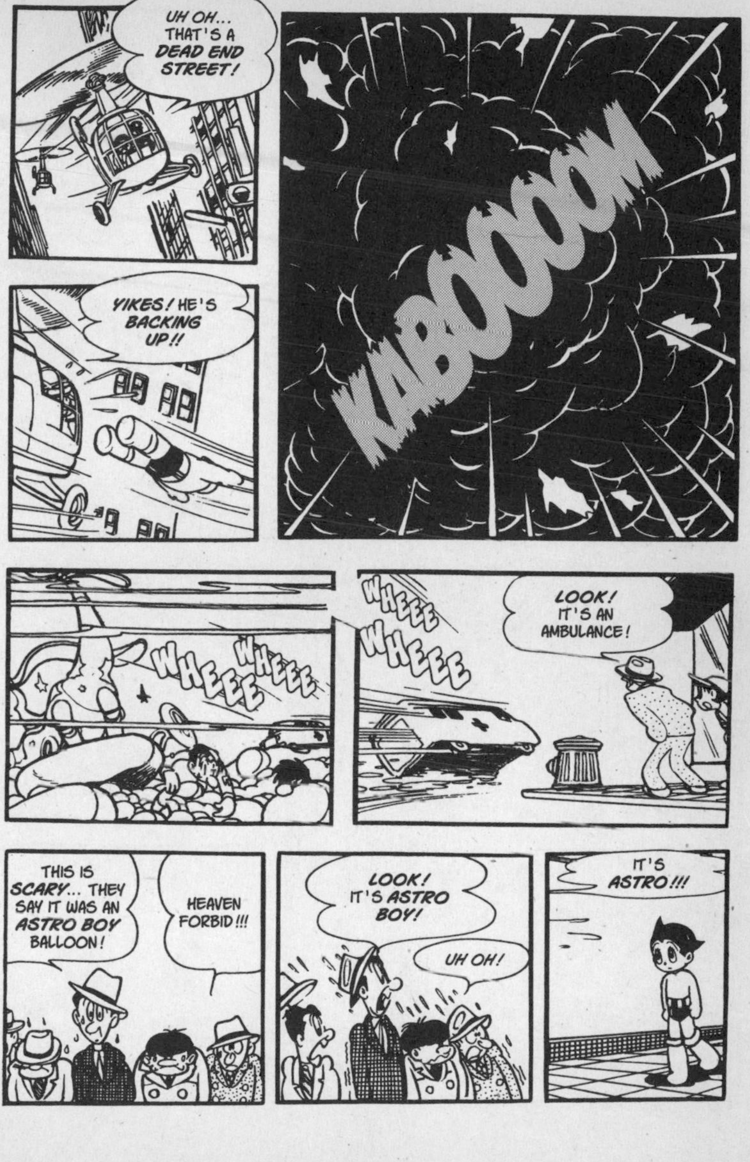
UH OH... THAT'S A DEAD END STREET!
YIKES! HE'S BACKING UP!!
KABOOOOM
WHEEE WHEEE
WHEEE WHEEE
LOOK! IT'S AN AMBULANCE!
THIS IS SCARY... THEY SAY IT WAS AN ASTRO BOY BALLOON!
HEAVEN FORBID!!!
LOOK! IT'S ASTRO BOY!
UH OH!
IT'S ASTRO!!!

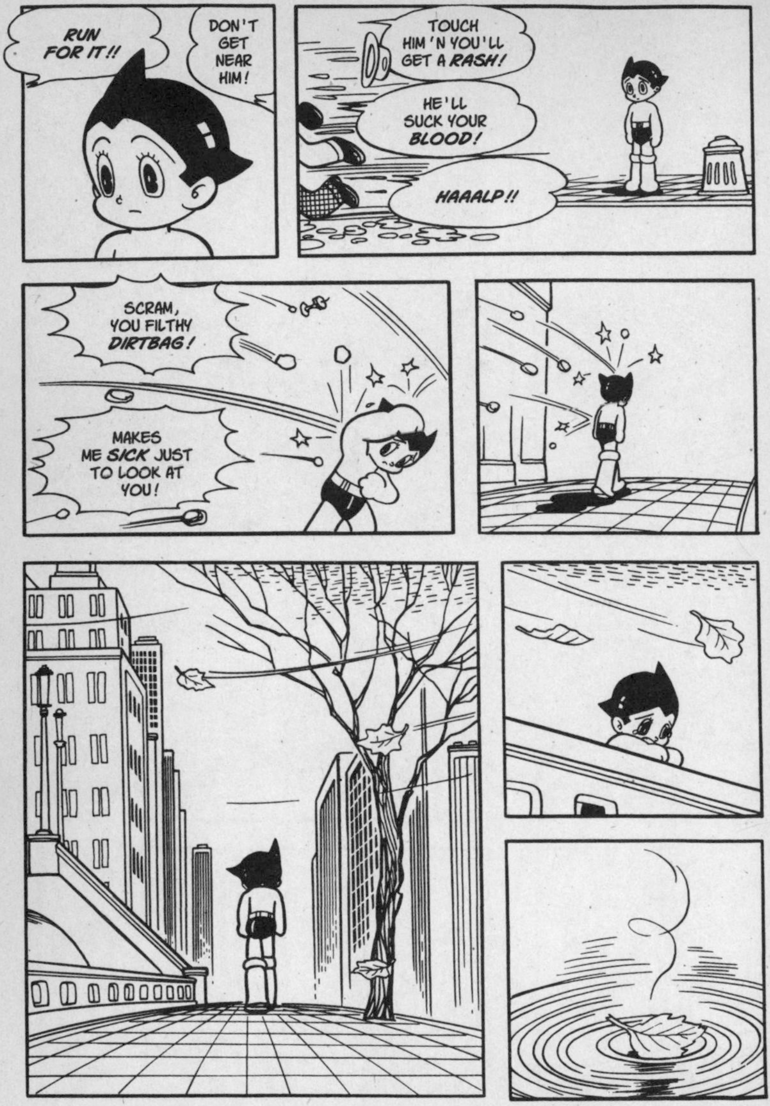
RUN FOR IT!!
DON'T GET NEAR HIM!
TOUCH HIM 'N YOU'LL GET A RASH!
HE'LL SUCK YOUR BLOOD!
HAAALP!!
SCRAM, YOU FILTHY DIRTBAG!
MAKES ME SICK JUST TO LOOK AT YOU!

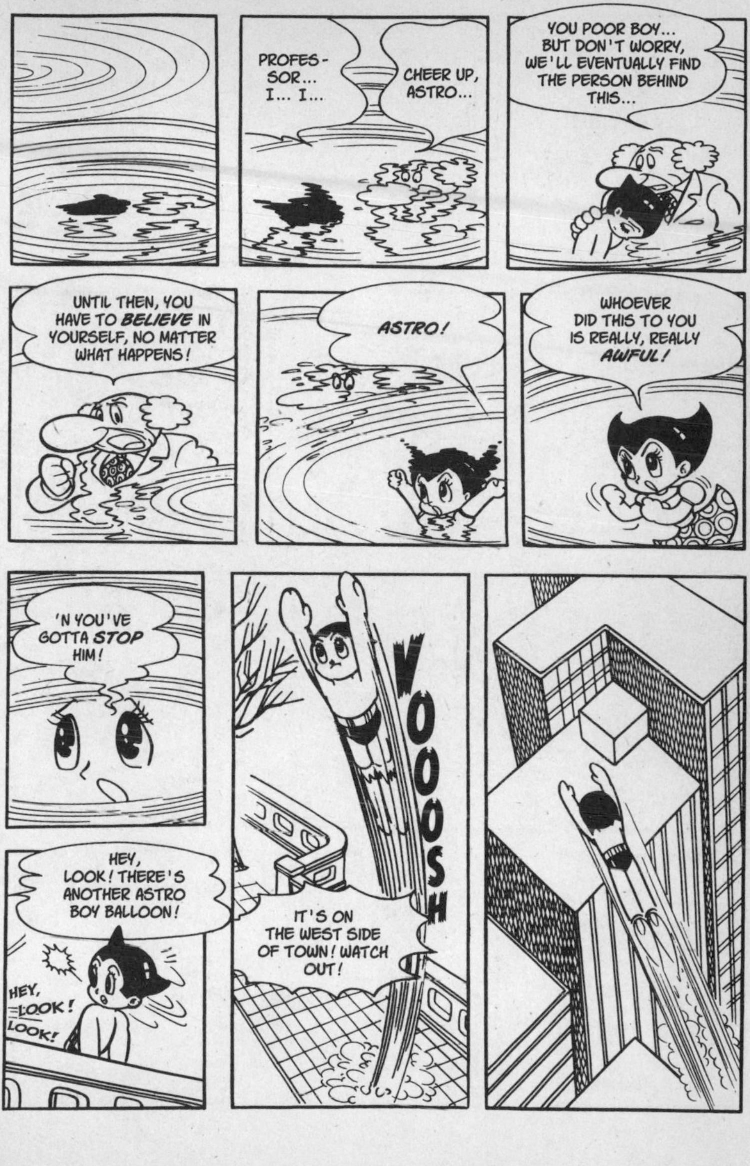
PROFES-SOR... I... I...
CHEER UP, ASTRO...
YOU POOR BOY... BUT DON'T WORRY, WE'LL EVENTUALLY FIND THE PERSON BEHIND THIS...
UNTIL THEN, YOU HAVE TO BELIEVE IN YOURSELF, NO MATTER WHAT HAPPENS!
ASTRO!
WHOEVER DID THIS TO YOU IS REALLY, REALLY AWFUL!
'N YOU'VE GOTTA STOP HIM!
HEY, LOOK! THERE'S ANOTHER ASTRO BOY BALLOON!
HEY, LOOK! LOOK!
VOOOOSH
IT'S ON THE WEST SIDE OF TOWN! WATCH OUT!

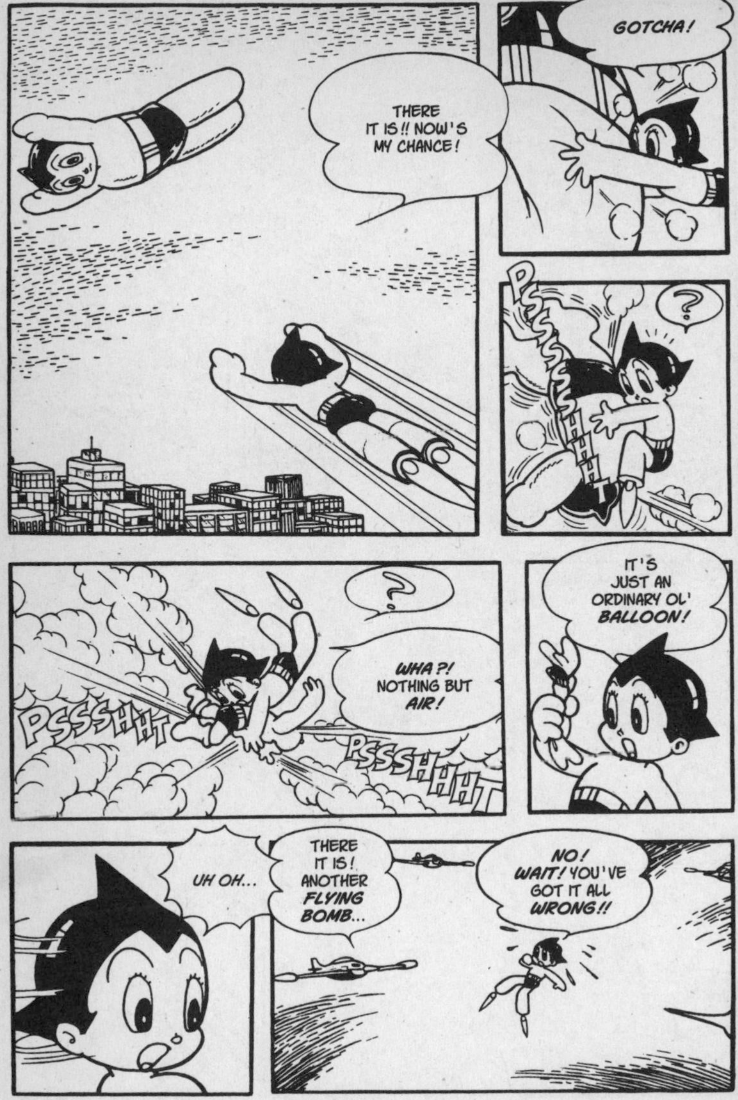
THERE IT IS!! NOW'S MY CHANCE!
GOTCHA!
PSSSSHHHT
?
?
PSSSHHT
WHA?! NOTHING BUT AIR!
PSSSHHHT
IT'S JUST AN ORDINARY OL' BALLOON!
UH OH...
THERE IT IS! ANOTHER FLYING BOMB...
NO! WAIT! YOU'VE GOT IT ALL WRONG!!

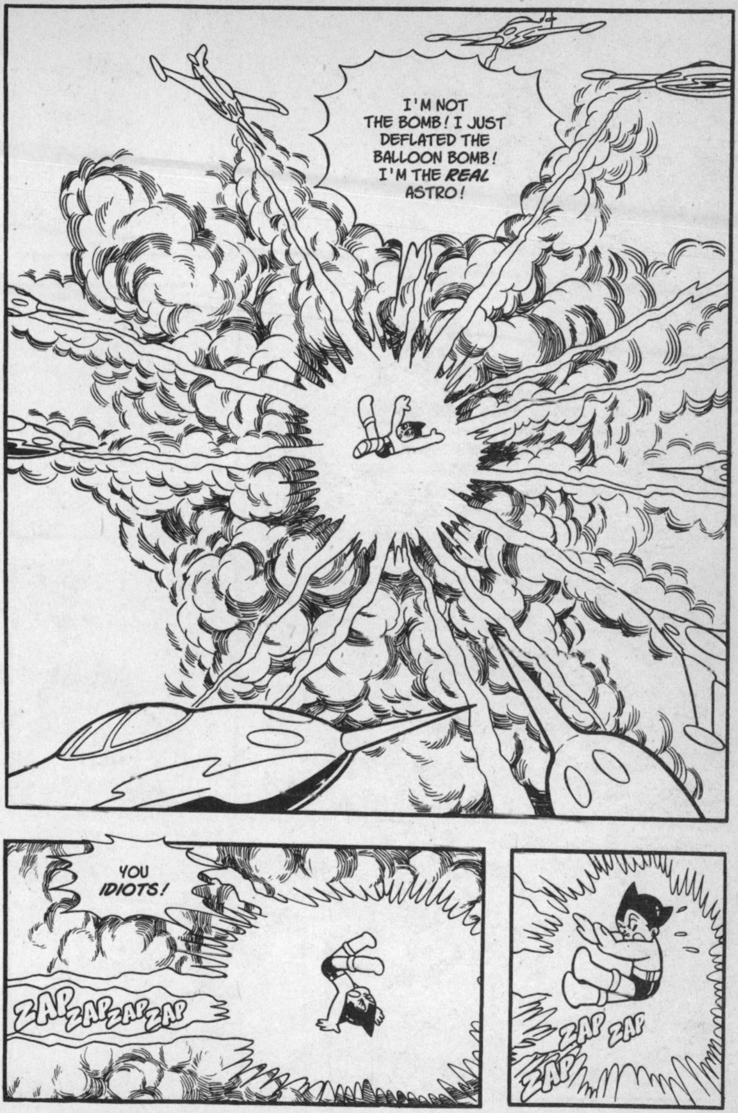
I'M NOT THE BOMB! I JUST DEFLATED THE BALLOON BOMB! I'M THE REAL ASTRO!
YOU IDIOTS!
ZAP ZAP ZAP ZAP
ZAP ZAP ZAP

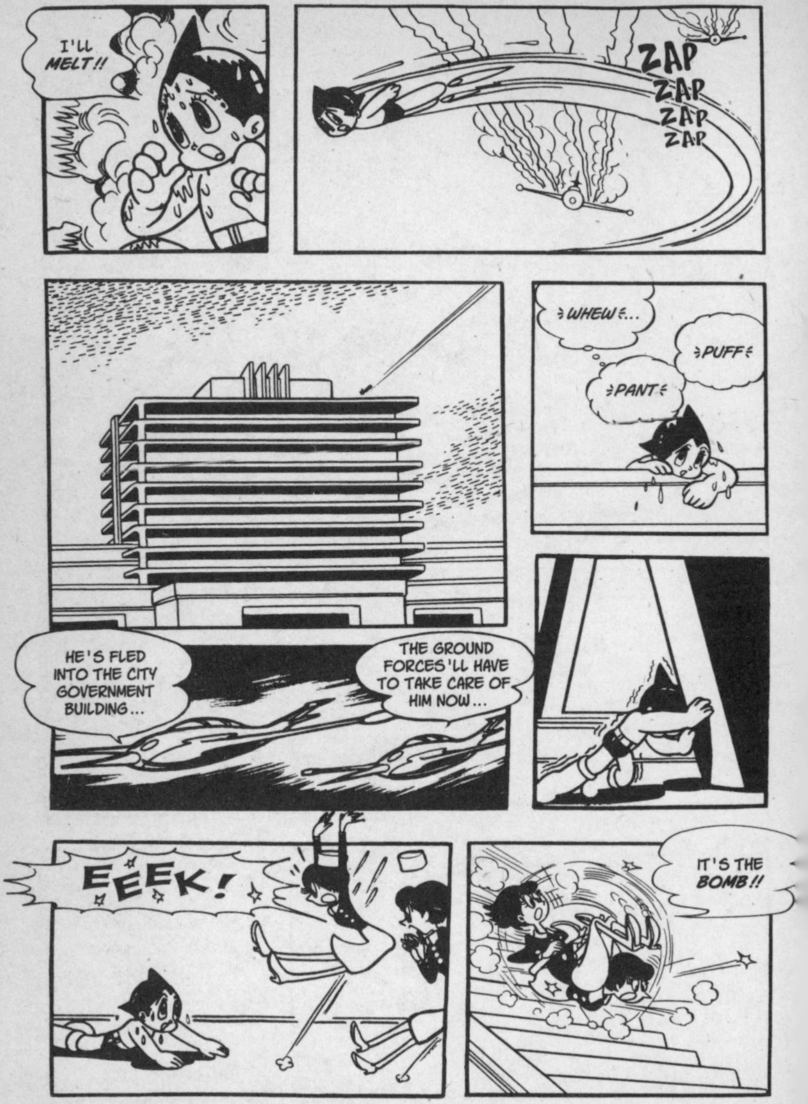
I'LL MELT!!
ZAP ZAP ZAP ZAP
WHEW...
PANT
PUFF
HE'S FLED INTO THE CITY GOVERNMENT BUILDING...
THE GROUND FORCES'LL HAVE TO TAKE CARE OF HIM NOW...
EEEK!
IT'S THE BOMB!!

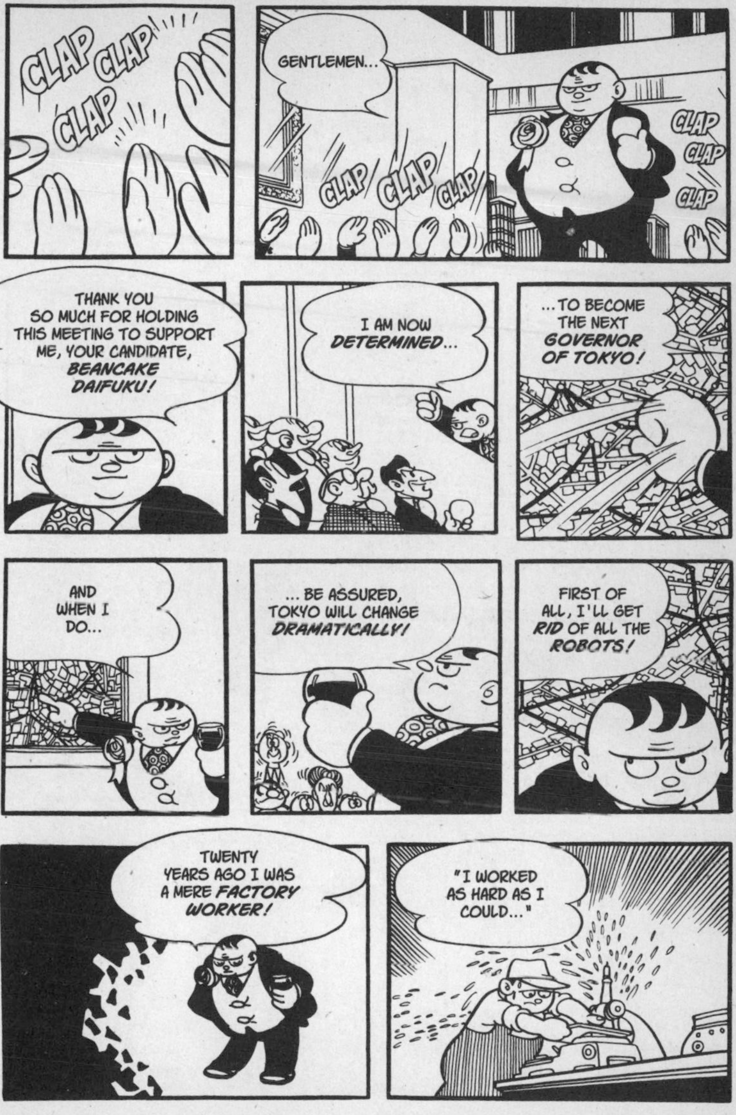
CLAP CLAP CLAP
GENTLEMEN...
CLAP CLAP CLAP
CLAP CLAP CLAP
THANK YOU SO MUCH FOR HOLDING THIS MEETING TO SUPPORT ME, YOUR CANDIDATE, BEANCAKE DAIFUKU!
I AM NOW DETERMINED...
...TO BECOME THE NEXT GOVERNOR OF TOKYO!
AND WHEN I DO...
... BE ASSURED, TOKYO WILL CHANGE DRAMATICALLY!
FIRST OF ALL, I'LL GET RID OF ALL THE ROBOTS!
TWENTY YEARS AGO I WAS A MERE FACTORY WORKER!
"I WORKED AS HARD AS I COULD..."

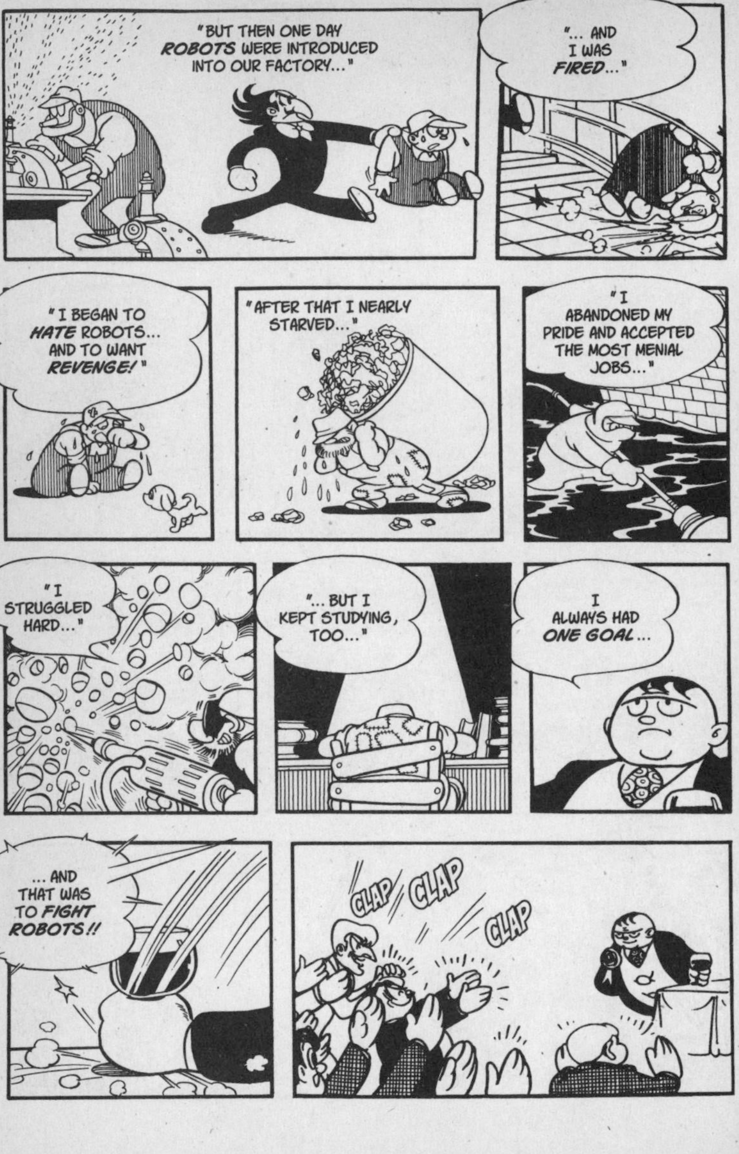
"BUT THEN ONE DAY ROBOTS WERE INTRODUCED INTO OUR FACTORY..."
"... AND I WAS FIRED..."
"I BEGAN TO HATE ROBOTS... AND TO WANT REVENGE!"
"AFTER THAT I NEARLY STARVED..."
"I ABANDONED MY PRIDE AND ACCEPTED THE MOST MENIAL JOBS..."
"I STRUGGLED HARD..."
"... BUT I KEPT STUDYING, TOO..."
I ALWAYS HAD ONE GOAL...
... AND THAT WAS TO FIGHT ROBOTS!!
CLAP
CLAP
CLAP

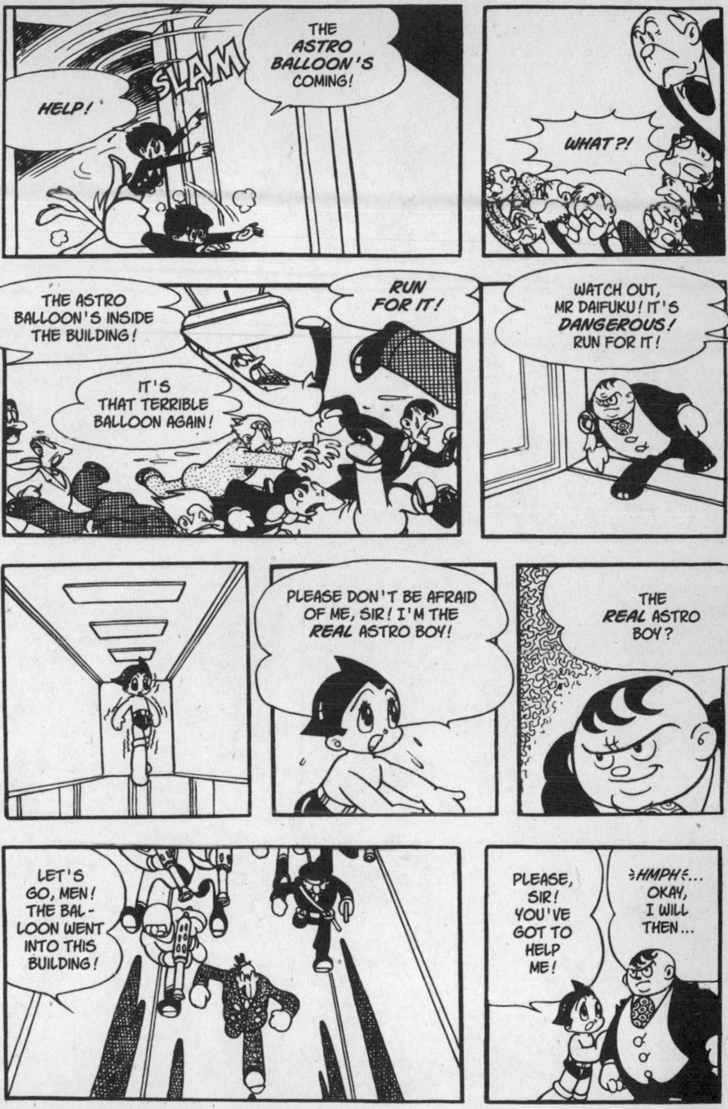
THE ASTRO BALLOON'S COMING!
SLAM
HELP!
WHAT?!
THE ASTRO BALLOON'S INSIDE THE BUILDING!
RUN FOR IT!
IT'S THAT TERRIBLE BALLOON AGAIN!
WATCH OUT, MR DAIFUKU! IT'S DANGEROUS! RUN FOR IT!
PLEASE DON'T BE AFRAID OF ME, SIR! I'M THE REAL ASTRO BOY!
THE REAL ASTRO BOY?
LET'S GO, MEN! THE BAL-LOON WENT INTO THIS BUILDING!
PLEASE, SIR! YOU'VE GOT TO HELP ME!
HMPH... OKAY, I WILL THEN...

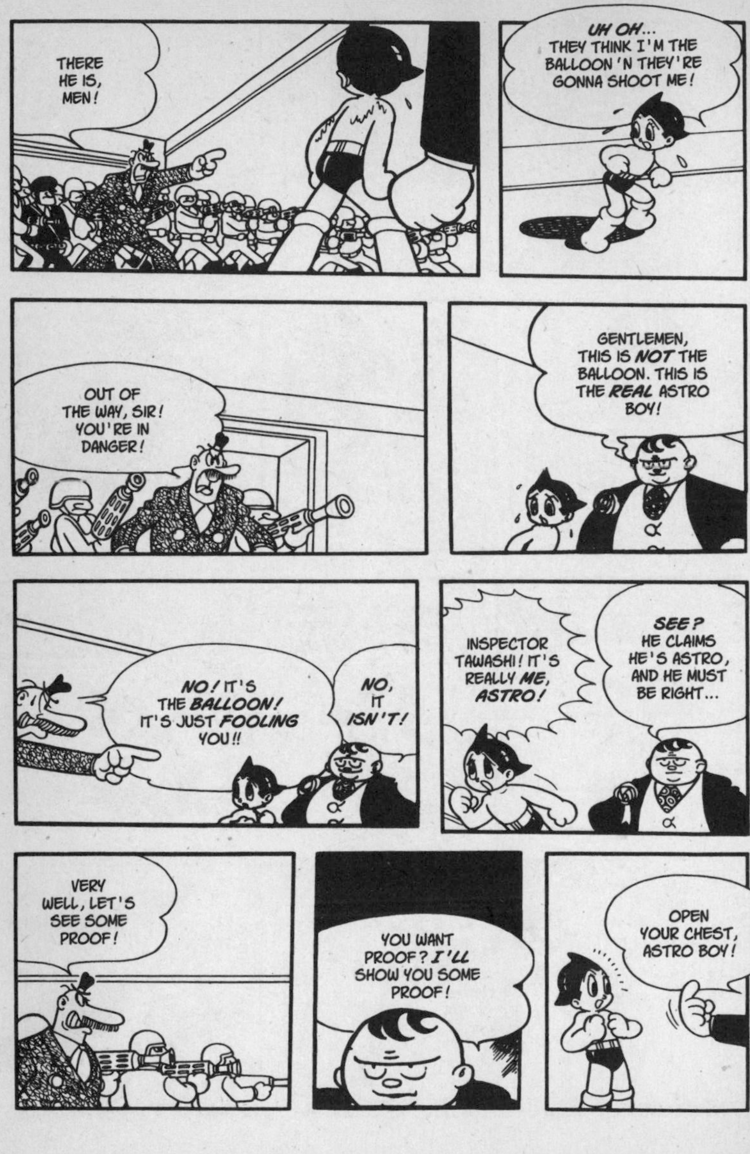
THERE HE IS, MEN!
UH OH... THEY THINK I'M THE BALLOON 'N THEY'RE GONNA SHOOT ME!
OUT OF THE WAY, SIR! YOU'RE IN DANGER!
GENTLEMEN, THIS IS NOT THE BALLOON. THIS IS THE REAL ASTRO BOY!
NO! IT'S THE BALLOON! IT'S JUST FOOLING YOU!!
NO, IT ISN'T!
INSPECTOR TAWASHI! IT'S REALLY ME, ASTRO!
SEE? HE CLAIMS HE'S ASTRO, AND HE MUST BE RIGHT...
VERY WELL, LET'S SEE SOME PROOF!
YOU WANT PROOF? I'LL SHOW YOU SOME PROOF!
OPEN YOUR CHEST, ASTRO BOY!

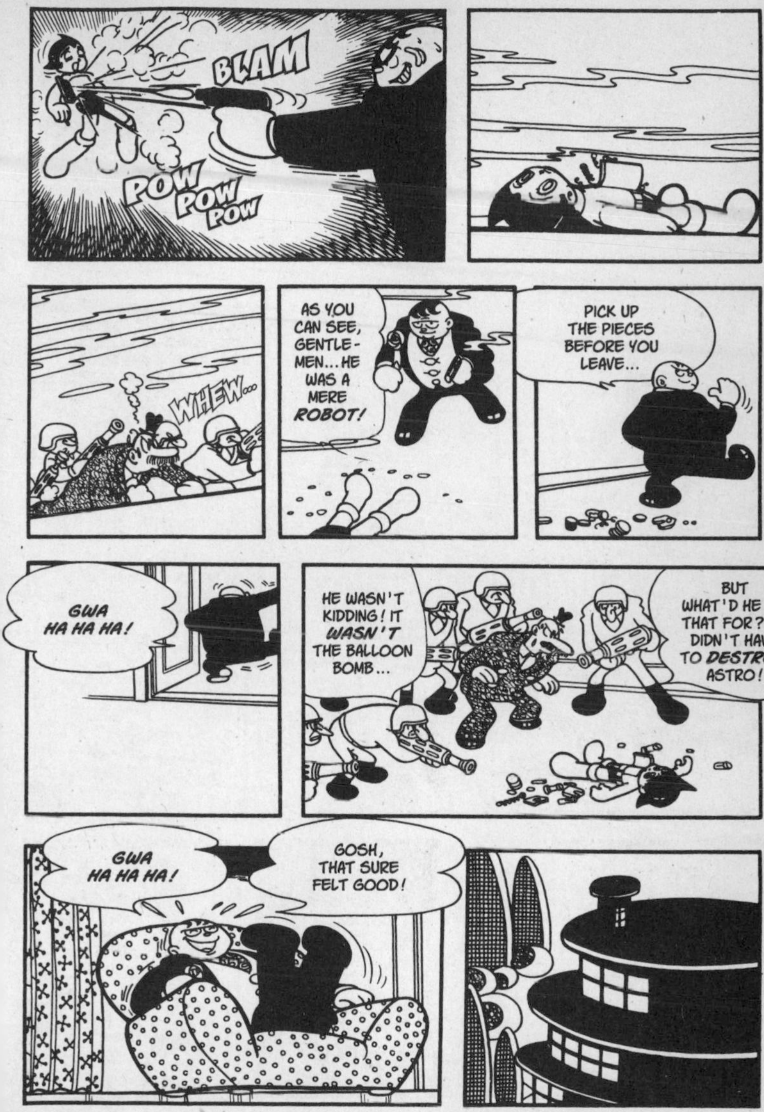
BLAM
POW
POW
POW
WHEW...
AS YOU CAN SEE, GENTLE-MEN... HE WAS A MERE ROBOT!
PICK UP THE PIECES BEFORE YOU LEAVE...
GWA HA HA HA!
HE WASN'T KIDDING! IT WASN'T THE BALLOON BOMB...
BUT WHAT'D HE DO THAT FOR? HE DIDN'T HAVE TO DESTROY ASTRO!
GWA HA HA HA!
GOSH, THAT SURE FELT GOOD!

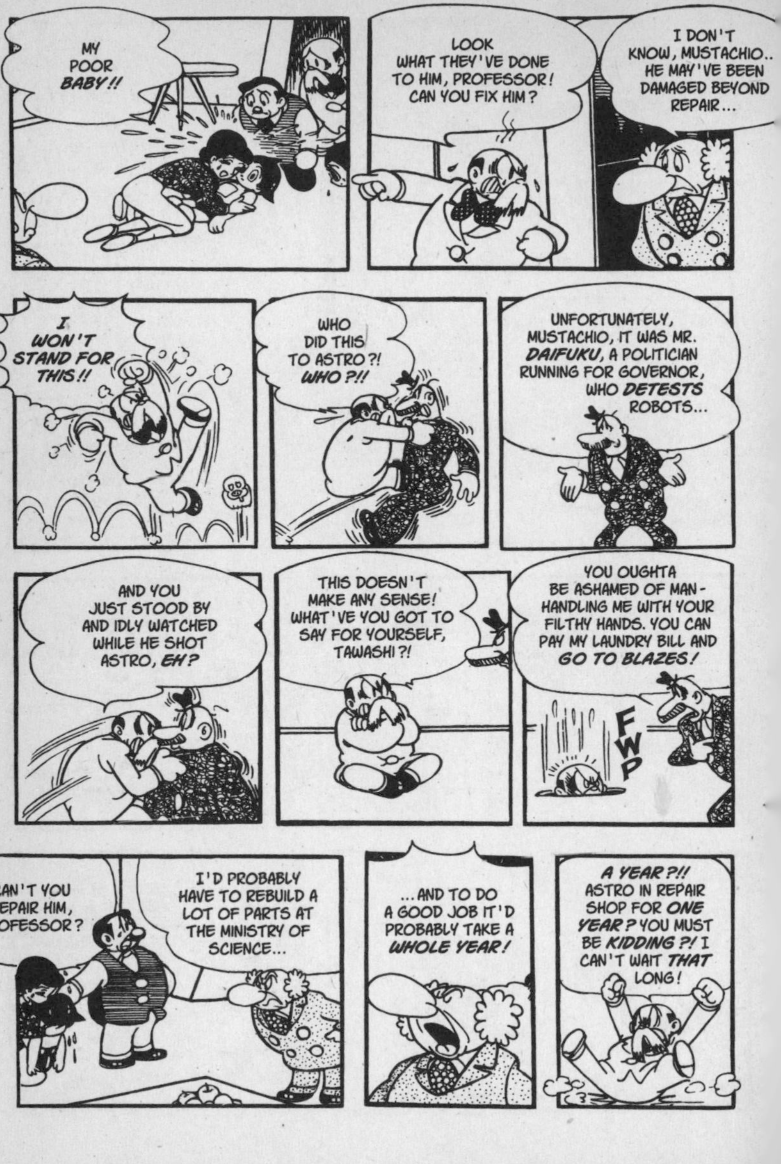
MY POOR BABY!!
LOOK WHAT THEY'VE DONE TO HIM, PROFESSOR! CAN YOU FIX HIM?
I DON'T KNOW, MUSTACHIO.. HE MAY'VE BEEN DAMAGED BEYOND REPAIR...
I WON'T STAND FOR THIS!!
WHO DID THIS TO ASTRO?! WHO?!!
UNFORTUNATELY, MUSTACHIO, IT WAS MR. DAIFUKU, A POLITICIAN RUNNING FOR GOVERNOR, WHO DETESTS ROBOTS...
AND YOU JUST STOOD BY AND IDLY WATCHED WHILE HE SHOT ASTRO, EH?
THIS DOESN'T MAKE ANY SENSE! WHAT'VE YOU GOT TO SAY FOR YOURSELF, TAWASHI?!
YOU OUGHTA BE ASHAMED OF MAN-HANDLING ME WITH YOUR FILTHY HANDS. YOU CAN PAY MY LAUNDRY BILL AND GO TO BLAZES!
FWP
CAN'T YOU REPAIR HIM, PROFESSOR?
I'D PROBABLY HAVE TO REBUILD A LOT OF PARTS AT THE MINISTRY OF SCIENCE...
...AND TO DO A GOOD JOB IT'D PROBABLY TAKE A WHOLE YEAR!
A YEAR?!! ASTRO IN REPAIR SHOP FOR ONE YEAR? YOU MUST BE KIDDING?! I CAN'T WAIT THAT LONG!

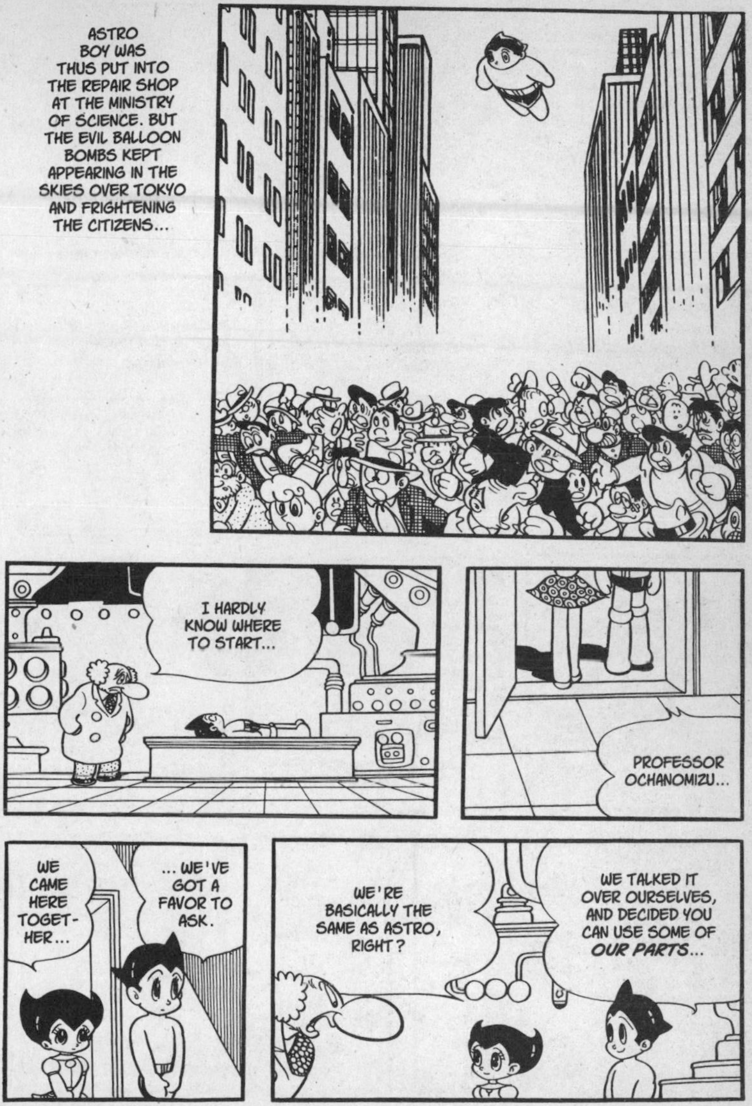
ASTRO BOY WAS THUS PUT INTO THE REPAIR SHOP AT THE MINISTRY OF SCIENCE. BUT THE EVIL BALLOON BOMBS KEPT APPEARING IN THE SKIES OVER TOKYO AND FRIGHTENING THE CITIZENS...
I HARDLY KNOW WHERE TO START...
PROFESSOR OCHANOMIZU...
WE CAME HERE TOGET-HER...
... WE'VE GOT A FAVOR TO ASK.
WE'RE BASICALLY THE SAME AS ASTRO, RIGHT?
WE TALKED IT OVER OURSELVES, AND DECIDED YOU CAN USE SOME OF *OUR PARTS*...

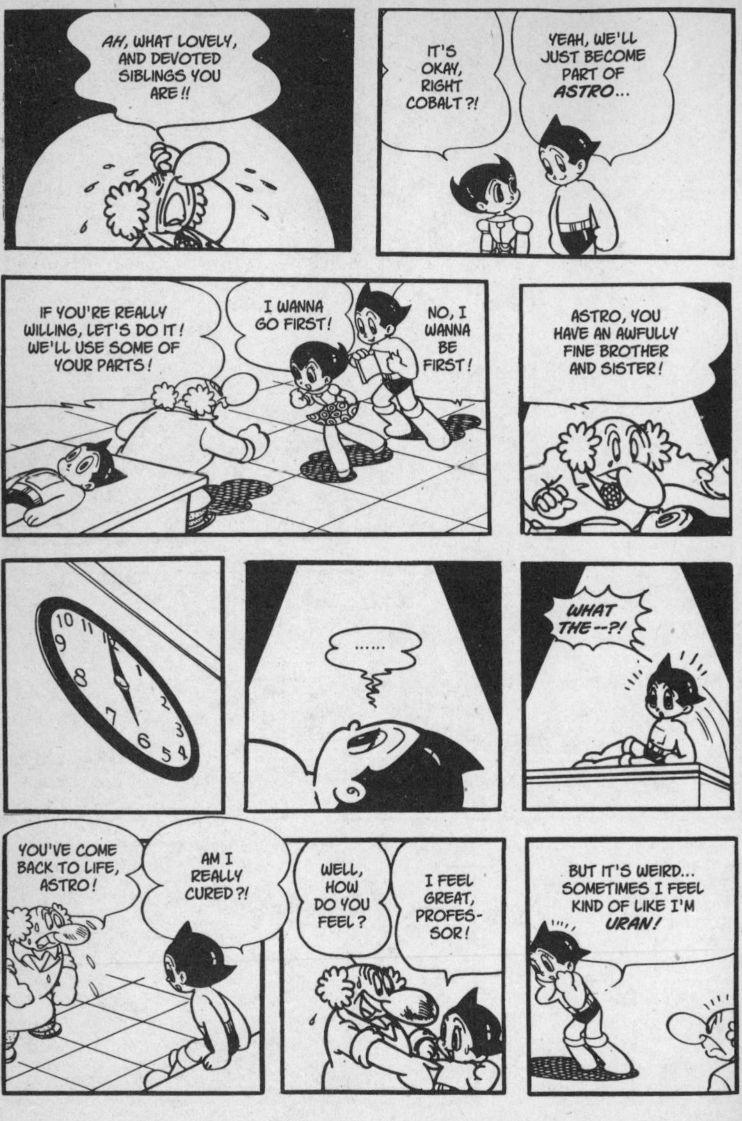
AH, WHAT LOVELY, AND DEVOTED SIBLINGS YOU ARE!!
IT'S OKAY, RIGHT COBALT?!
YEAH, WE'LL JUST BECOME PART OF ASTRO...
IF YOU'RE REALLY WILLING, LET'S DO IT! WE'LL USE SOME OF YOUR PARTS!
I WANNA GO FIRST!
NO, I WANNA BE FIRST!
ASTRO, YOU HAVE AN AWFULLY FINE BROTHER AND SISTER!
......
WHAT THE--?!
YOU'VE COME BACK TO LIFE, ASTRO!
AM I REALLY CURED?!
WELL, HOW DO YOU FEEL?
I FEEL GREAT, PROFES-SOR!
BUT IT'S WEIRD... SOMETIMES I FEEL KIND OF LIKE I'M URAN!

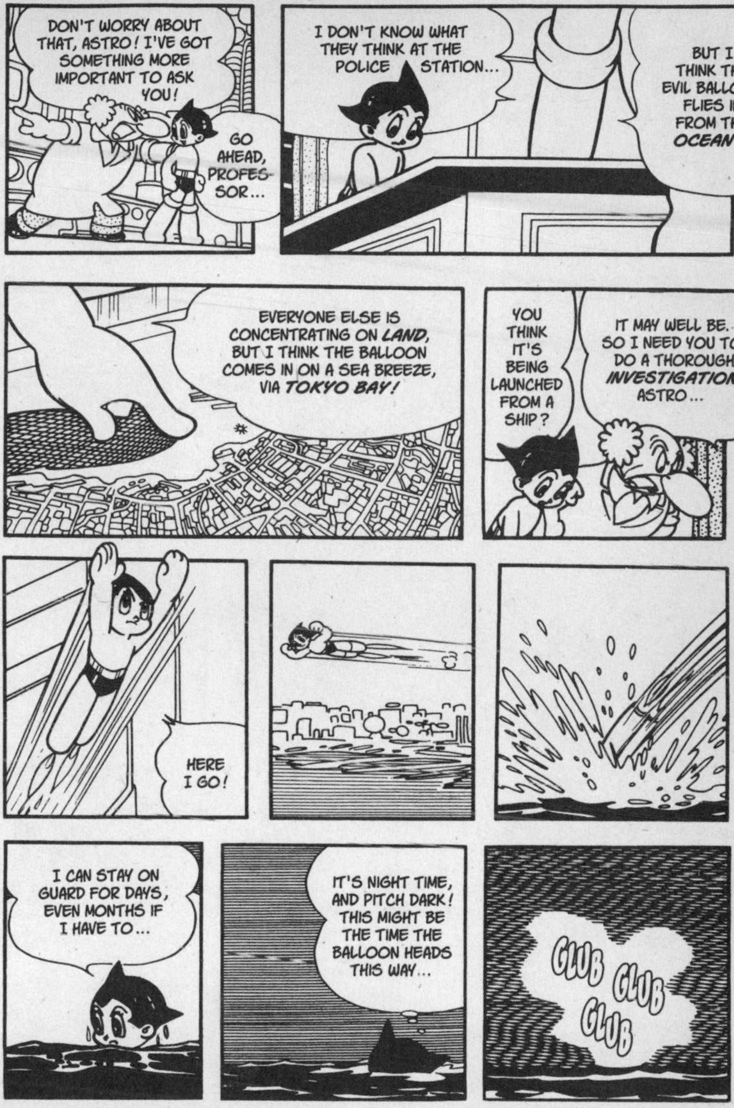
DON'T WORRY ABOUT THAT, ASTRO! I'VE GOT SOMETHING MORE IMPORTANT TO ASK YOU!
GO AHEAD, PROFESSOR...
I DON'T KNOW WHAT THEY THINK AT THE POLICE STATION...
BUT I THINK THE EVIL BALLOON FLIES IN FROM THE OCEAN...
EVERYONE ELSE IS CONCENTRATING ON LAND, BUT I THINK THE BALLOON COMES IN ON A SEA BREEZE, VIA TOKYO BAY!
YOU THINK IT'S BEING LAUNCHED FROM A SHIP?
IT MAY WELL BE. SO I NEED YOU TO DO A THOROUGH INVESTIGATION, ASTRO...
HERE I GO!
I CAN STAY ON GUARD FOR DAYS, EVEN MONTHS IF I HAVE TO...
IT'S NIGHT TIME, AND PITCH DARK! THIS MIGHT BE THE TIME THE BALLOON HEADS THIS WAY...
GLUB GLUB GLUB

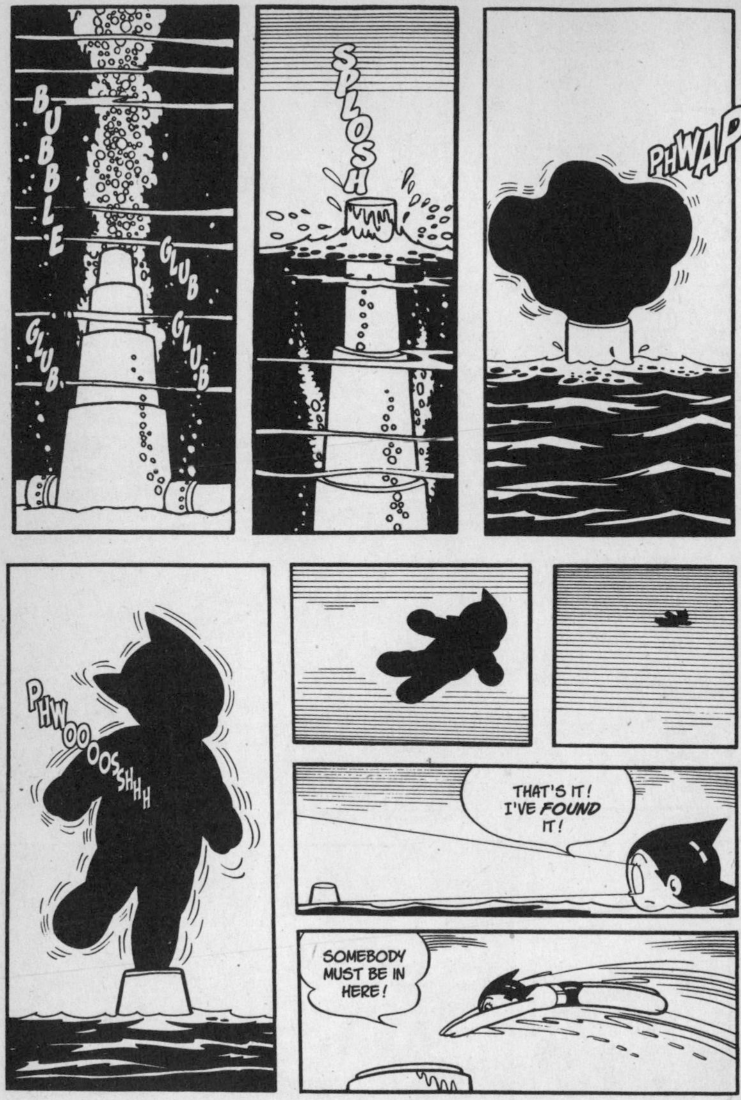
BUBBLE
GLUB
GLUB
GLUB
SPLOSH
PHWAP
PHWOOOOSSHHH
THAT'S IT! I'VE *FOUND* IT!
SOMEBODY MUST BE IN HERE!

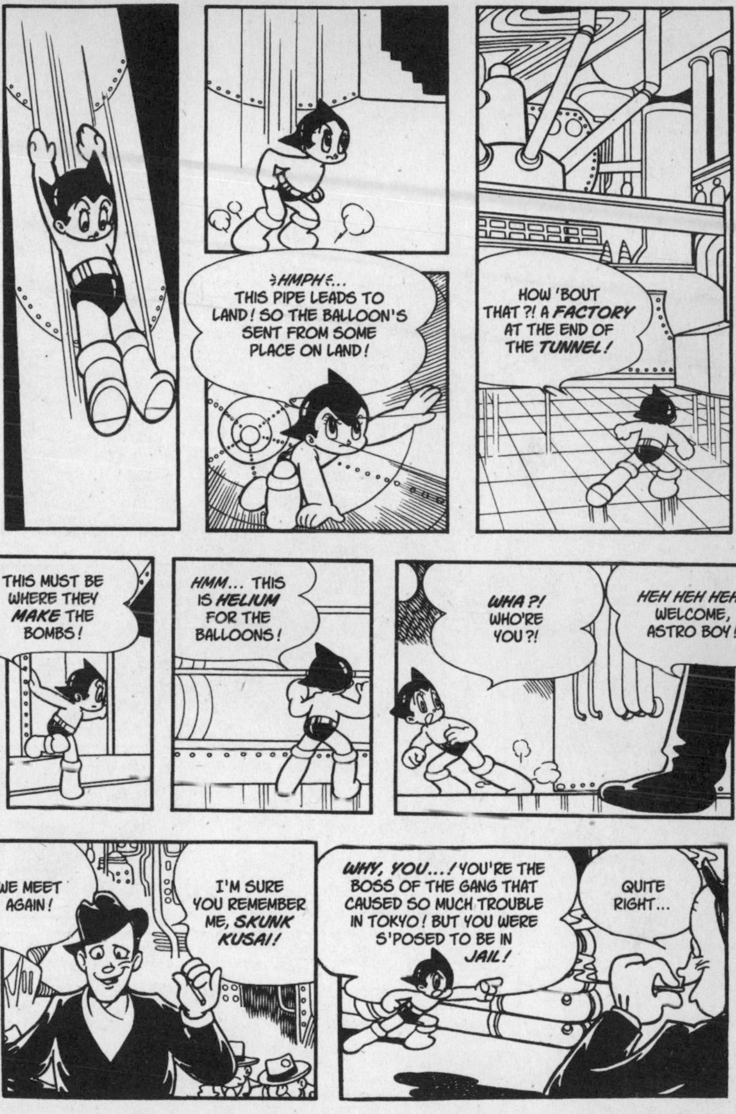

≡HMPH≡... THIS PIPE LEADS TO LAND! SO THE BALLOON'S SENT FROM SOME PLACE ON LAND!
HOW 'BOUT THAT?! A FACTORY AT THE END OF THE TUNNEL!
THIS MUST BE WHERE THEY MAKE THE BOMBS!
HMM... THIS IS HELIUM FOR THE BALLOONS!
WHA?! WHO'RE YOU?!
HEH HEH HEH! WELCOME, ASTRO BOY!
WE MEET AGAIN!
I'M SURE YOU REMEMBER ME, SKUNK KUSAI!
WHY, YOU...! YOU'RE THE BOSS OF THE GANG THAT CAUSED SO MUCH TROUBLE IN TOKYO! BUT YOU WERE S'POSED TO BE IN JAIL!
QUITE RIGHT...

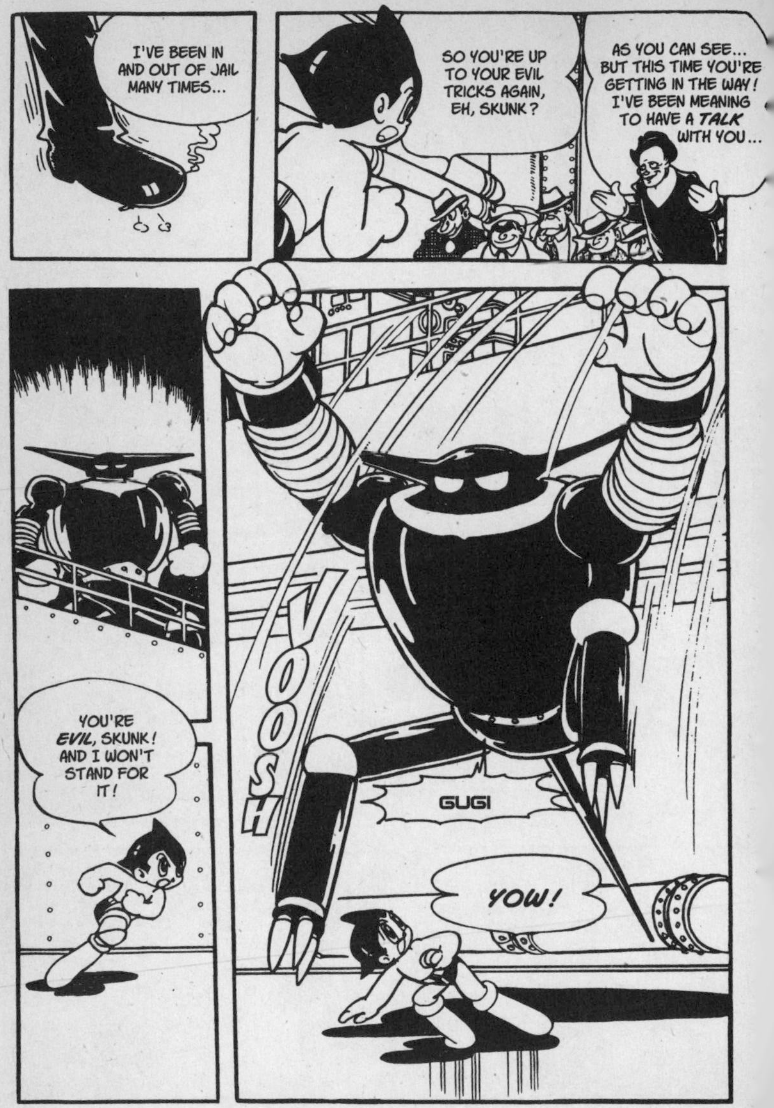

I'VE BEEN IN AND OUT OF JAIL MANY TIMES...
SO YOU'RE UP TO YOUR EVIL TRICKS AGAIN, EH, SKUNK?
AS YOU CAN SEE... BUT THIS TIME YOU'RE GETTING IN THE WAY! I'VE BEEN MEANING TO HAVE A TALK WITH YOU...
YOU'RE EVIL, SKUNK! AND I WON'T STAND FOR IT!
VOOOSH
GUGI
YOW!

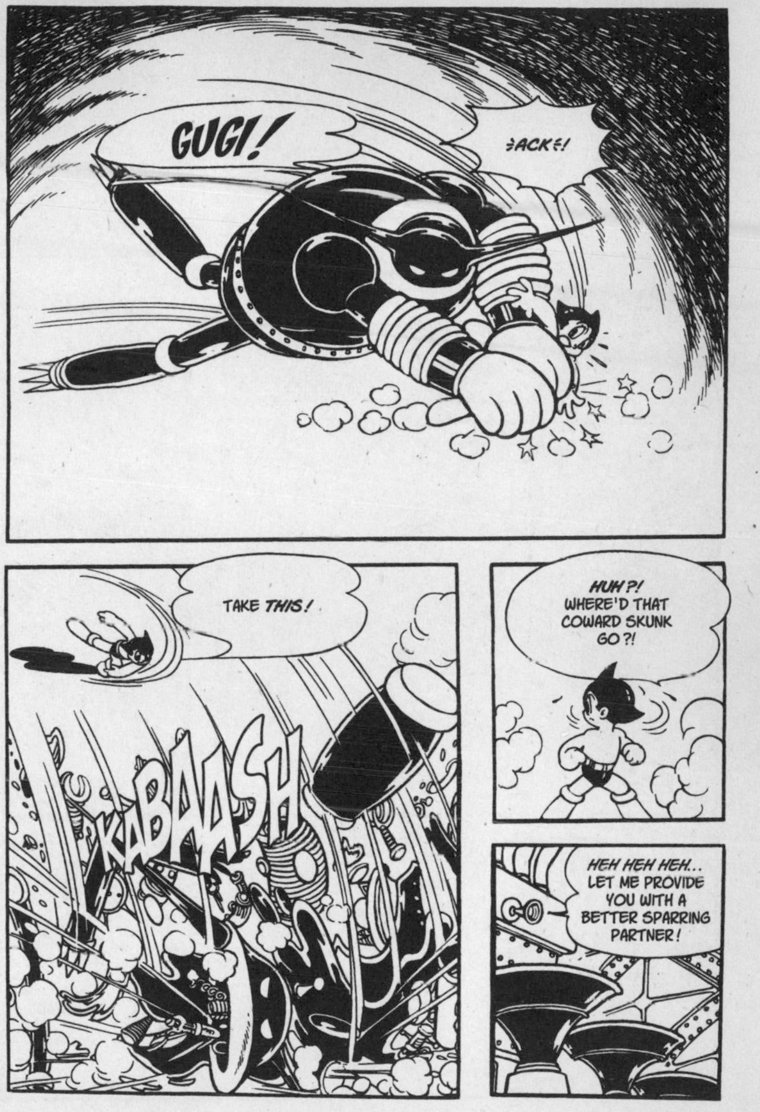
GUGI!
ACK!
TAKE THIS!
KABAASH
HUH?! WHERE'D THAT COWARD SKUNK GO?!
HEH HEH HEH... LET ME PROVIDE YOU WITH A BETTER SPARRING PARTNER!

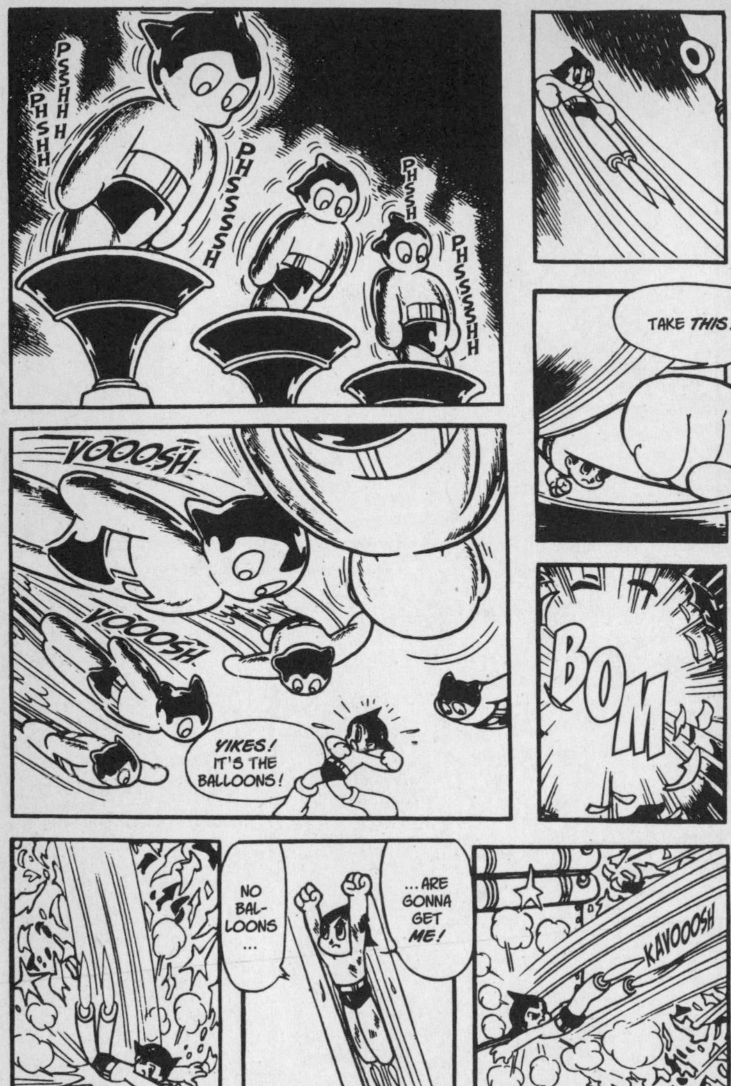
PSSHHH
PHSHH
PHSSSSSH
PHSSH
PHSSSSHH
VOOOSH
VOOOSH
YIKES! IT'S THE BALLOONS!
TAKE *THIS*!
BOM
NO BAL-LOONS ...
... ARE GONNA GET *ME*!
KAVOOOSH

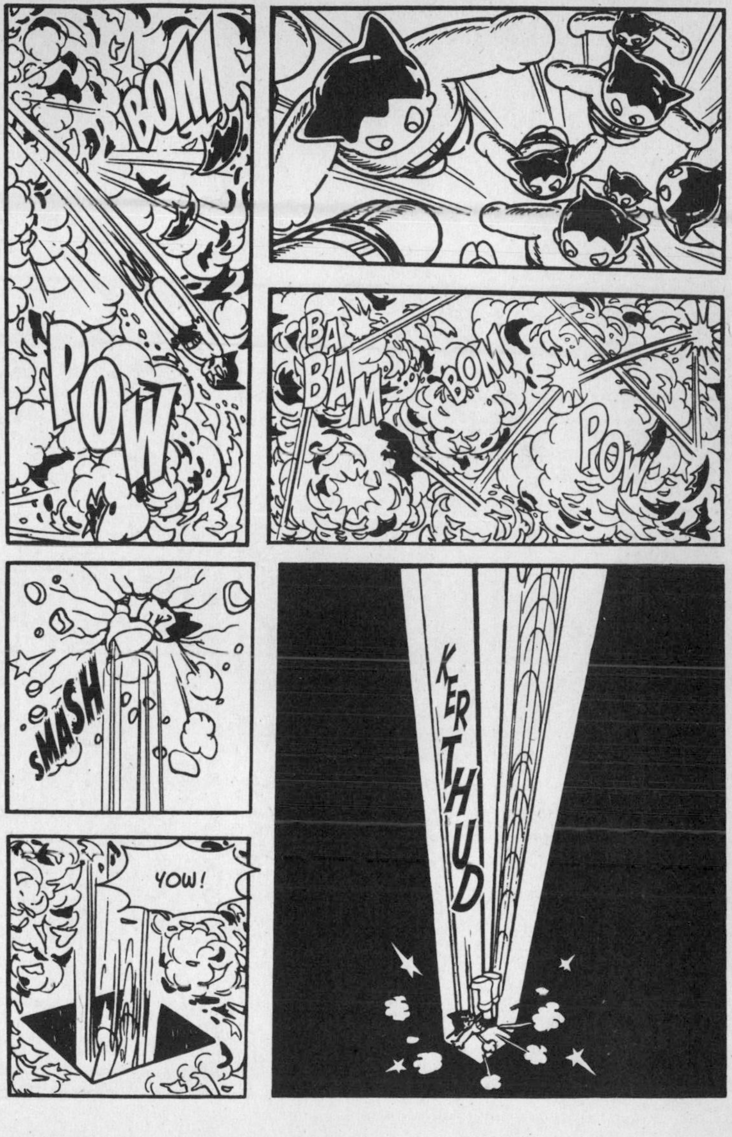
BOM
POW
BA
BAM
BOM
POW
SMASH
KERTHUD
YOW!

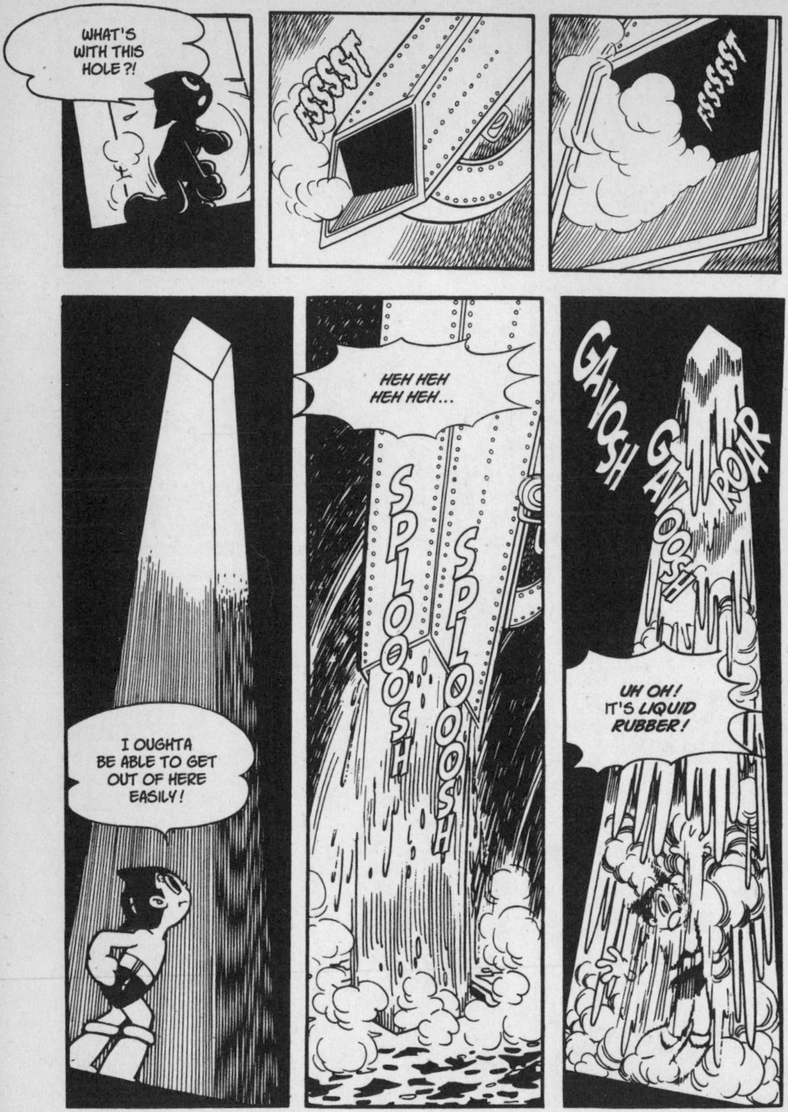

WHAT'S WITH THIS HOLE?!
FSSSST
FSSSST
I OUGHTA BE ABLE TO GET OUT OF HERE EASILY!
HEH HEH HEH HEH...
SPLOOOSH
SPLOOOSH
GAVOSH
GAVOOSH
ROAR
UH OH! IT'S LIQUID RUBBER!

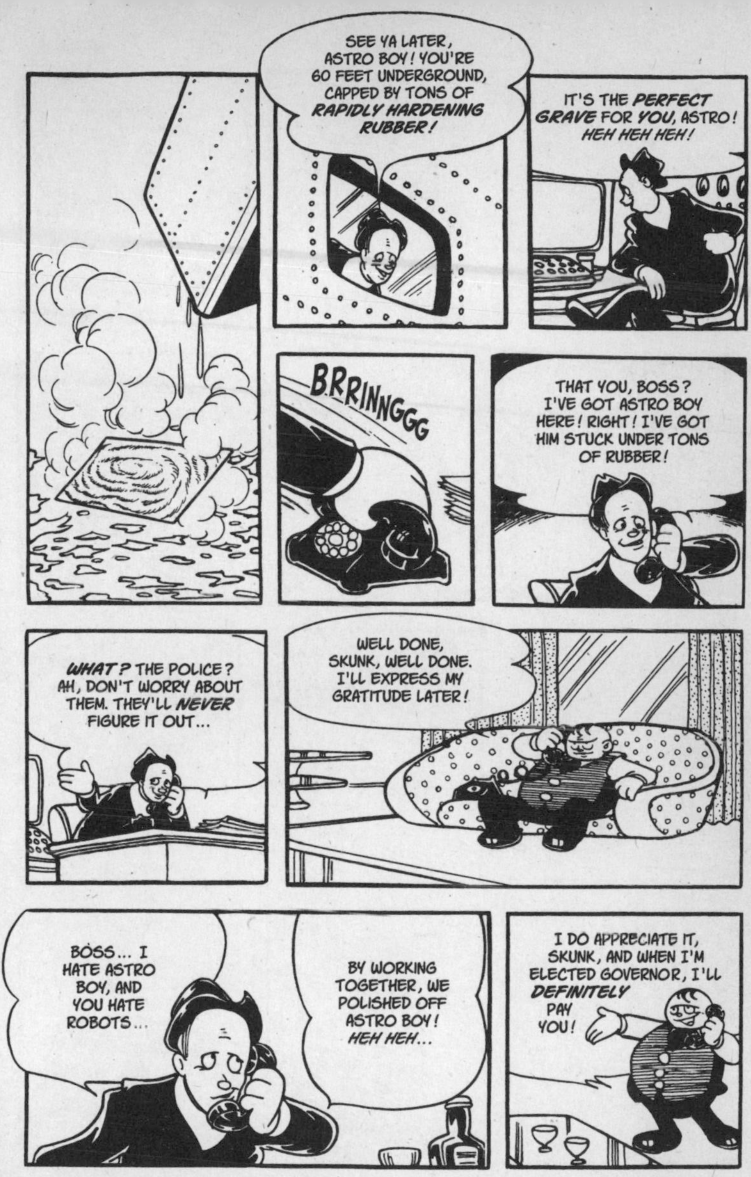
SEE YA LATER, ASTRO BOY! YOU'RE 60 FEET UNDERGROUND, CAPPED BY TONS OF *RAPIDLY HARDENING RUBBER!*
IT'S THE *PERFECT GRAVE* FOR *YOU,* ASTRO! *HEH HEH HEH!*
B.RRINNGGG
THAT YOU, BOSS? I'VE GOT ASTRO BOY HERE! RIGHT! I'VE GOT HIM STUCK UNDER TONS OF RUBBER!
WHAT? THE POLICE? AH, DON'T WORRY ABOUT THEM. THEY'LL *NEVER* FIGURE IT OUT...
WELL DONE, SKUNK, WELL DONE. I'LL EXPRESS MY GRATITUDE LATER!
BOSS... I HATE ASTRO BOY, AND YOU HATE ROBOTS...
BY WORKING TOGETHER, WE POLISHED OFF ASTRO BOY! *HEH HEH...*
I DO APPRECIATE IT, SKUNK, AND WHEN I'M ELECTED GOVERNOR, I'LL *DEFINITELY* PAY YOU!

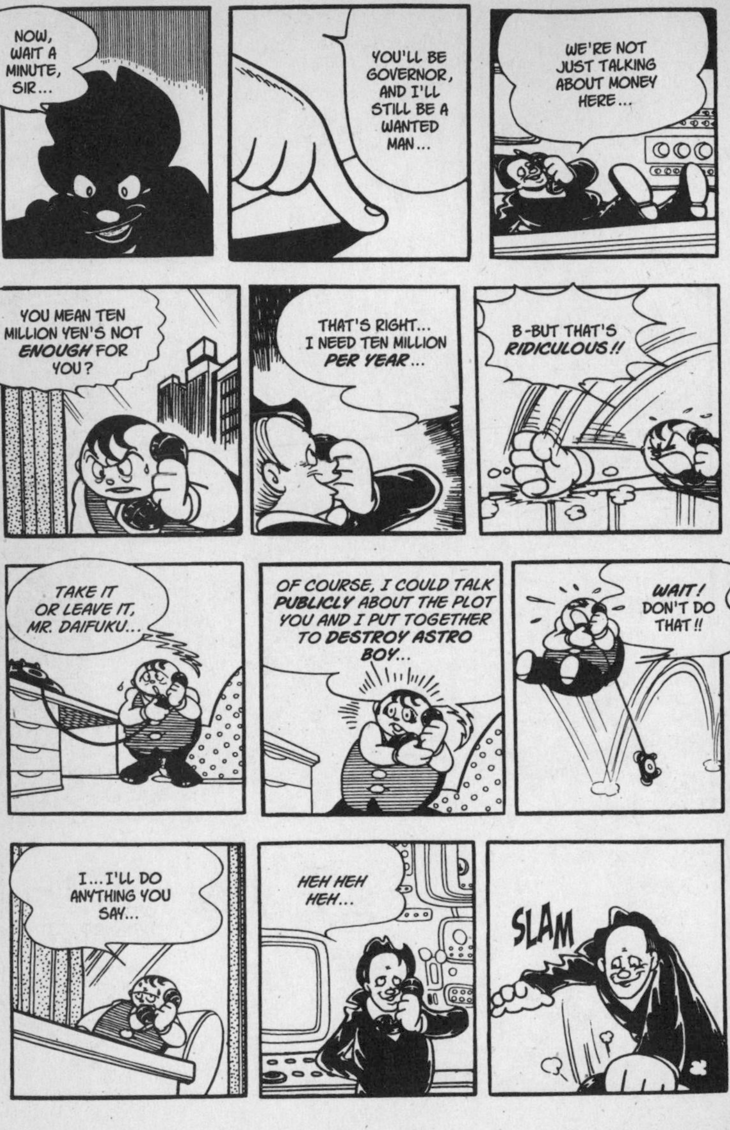
NOW, WAIT A MINUTE, SIR...
YOU'LL BE GOVERNOR, AND I'LL STILL BE A WANTED MAN...
WE'RE NOT JUST TALKING ABOUT MONEY HERE...
YOU MEAN TEN MILLION YEN'S NOT *ENOUGH* FOR YOU?
THAT'S RIGHT... I NEED TEN MILLION *PER YEAR*...
B-BUT THAT'S *RIDICULOUS!!*
TAKE IT OR LEAVE IT, MR. DAIFUKU...
*OF COURSE, I COULD TALK **PUBLICLY** ABOUT THE PLOT YOU AND I PUT TOGETHER TO **DESTROY ASTRO BOY**...*
WAIT! DON'T DO THAT!!
I...I'LL DO ANYTHING YOU SAY...
HEH HEH HEH...
SLAM

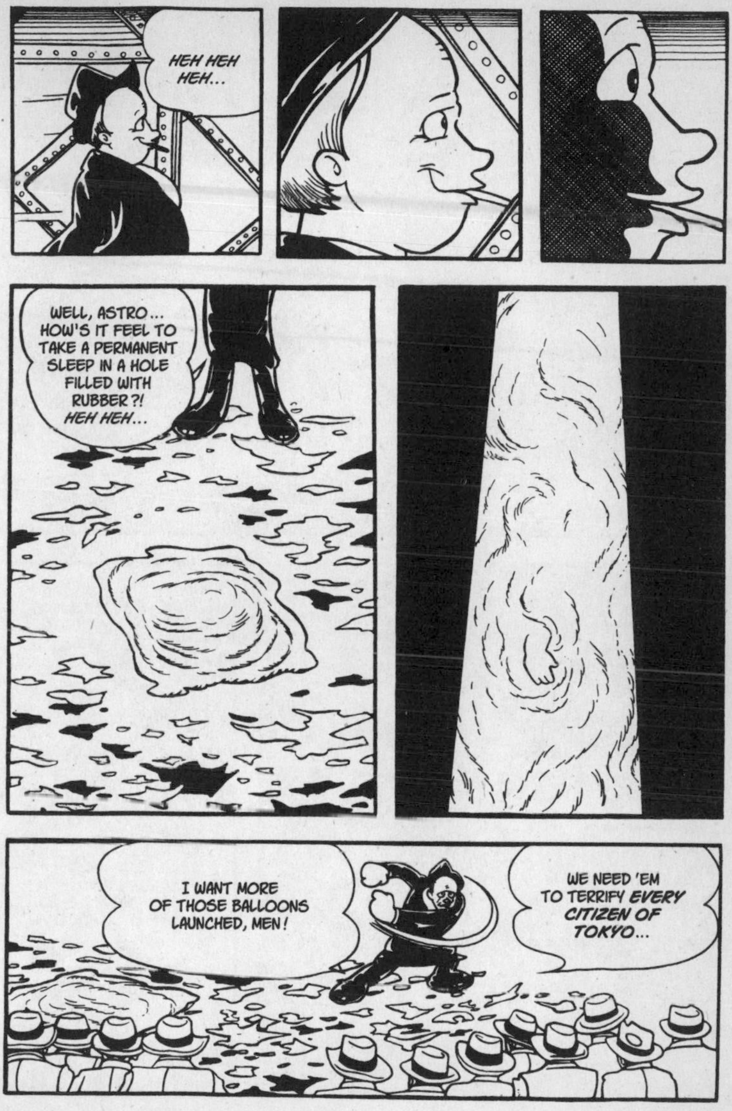
HEH HEH HEH...
WELL, ASTRO... HOW'S IT FEEL TO TAKE A PERMANENT SLEEP IN A HOLE FILLED WITH RUBBER?! HEH HEH...
I WANT MORE OF THOSE BALLOONS LAUNCHED, MEN!
WE NEED 'EM TO TERRIFY EVERY CITIZEN OF TOKYO...

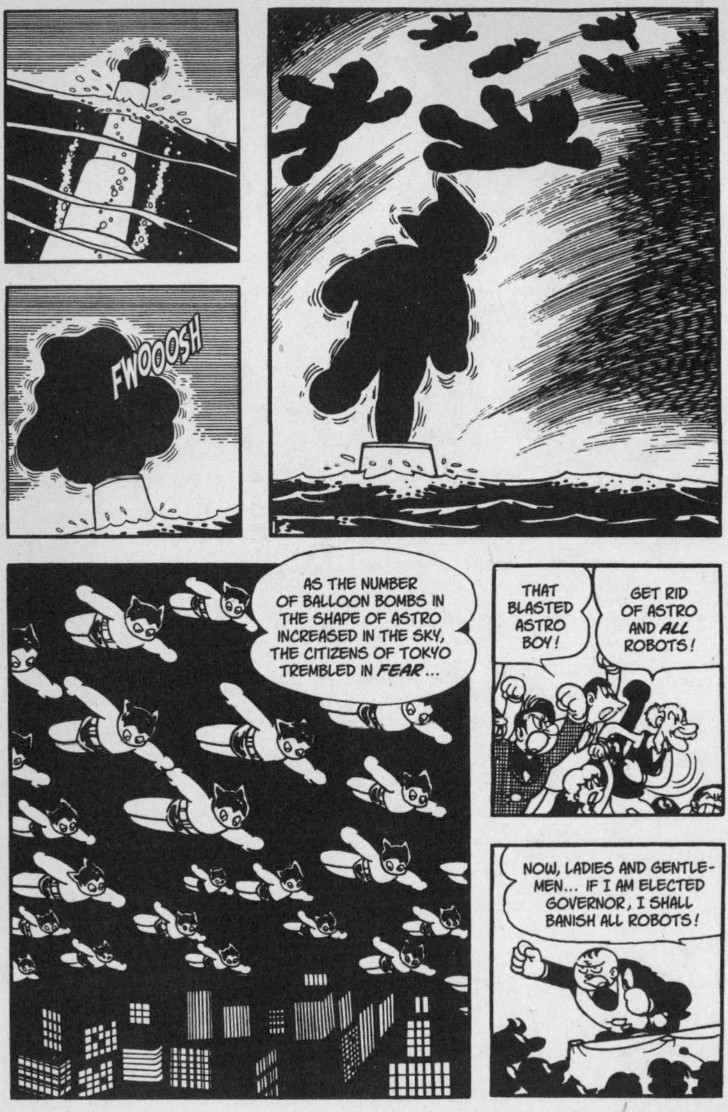
FWOOOSH
AS THE NUMBER OF BALLOON BOMBS IN THE SHAPE OF ASTRO INCREASED IN THE SKY, THE CITIZENS OF TOKYO TREMBLED IN *FEAR*...
THAT BLASTED ASTRO BOY!
GET RID OF ASTRO AND *ALL* ROBOTS!
NOW, LADIES AND GENTLE-MEN... IF I AM ELECTED GOVERNOR, I SHALL BANISH ALL ROBOTS!

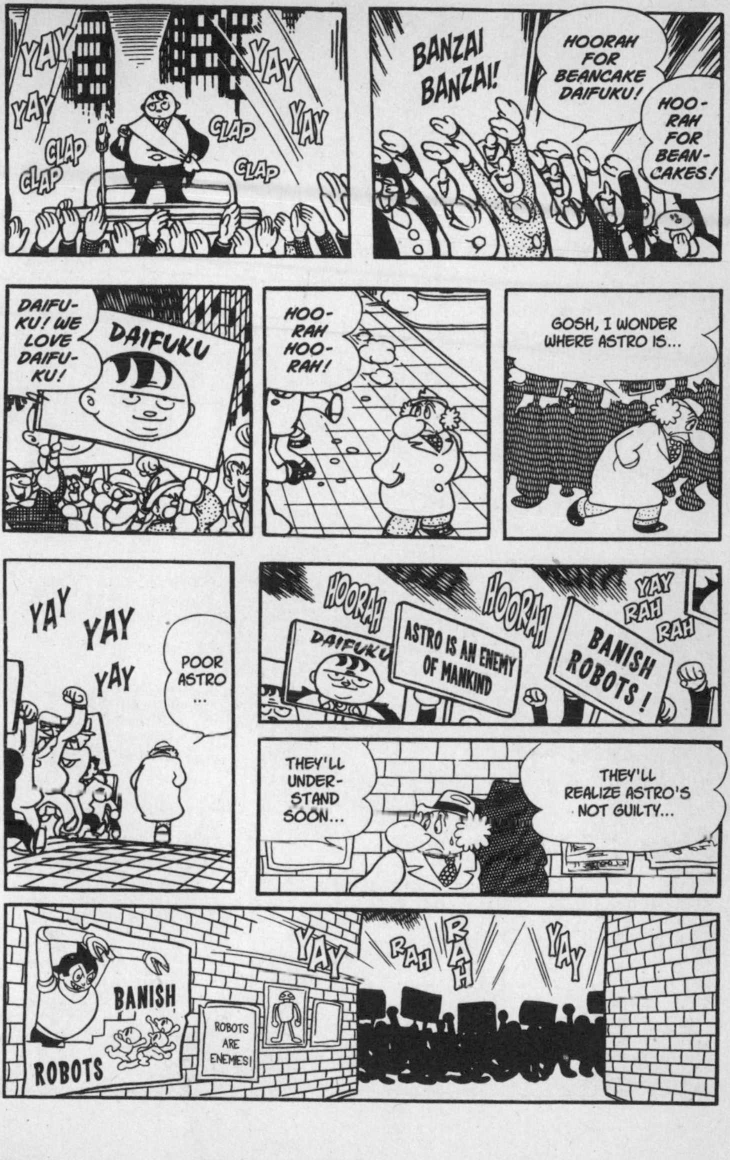
YAY
YAY
CLAP
CLAP
CLAP
YAY
CLAP
YAY
BANZAI BANZAI!
HOORAH FOR BEANCAKE DAIFUKU!
HOO-RAH FOR BEAN-CAKES!
DAIFU-KU! WE LOVE DAIFU-KU!
DAIFUKU
HOO-RAH HOO-RAH!
GOSH, I WONDER WHERE ASTRO IS...
YAY
YAY
YAY
POOR ASTRO ...
HOORAH
DAIFUKU
ASTRO IS AN ENEMY OF MANKIND
HOORAH
BANISH ROBOTS!
YAY RAH RAH
THEY'LL UNDER-STAND SOON...
THEY'LL REALIZE ASTRO'S NOT GUILTY...
BANISH
ROBOTS
ROBOTS ARE ENEMIES!
YAY
RAH
RAH
YAY

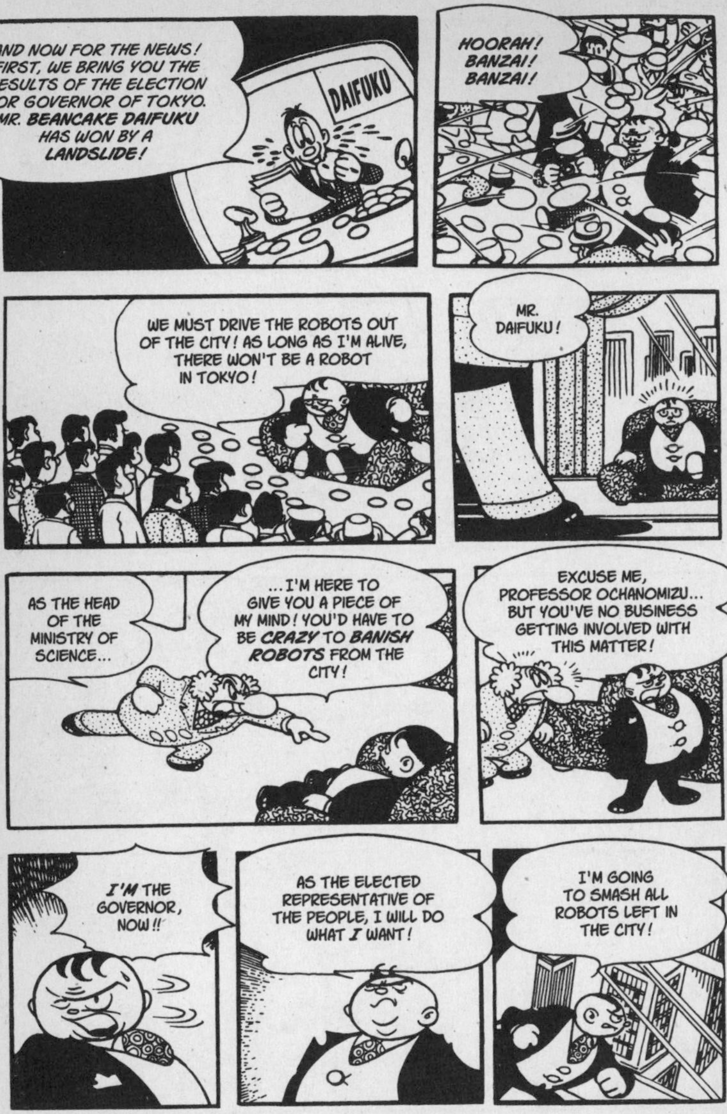
AND NOW FOR THE NEWS! FIRST, WE BRING YOU THE RESULTS OF THE ELECTION FOR GOVERNOR OF TOKYO. MR. BEANCAKE DAIFUKU HAS WON BY A LANDSLIDE!
DAIFUKU
HOORAH! BANZAI! BANZAI!
WE MUST DRIVE THE ROBOTS OUT OF THE CITY! AS LONG AS I'M ALIVE, THERE WON'T BE A ROBOT IN TOKYO!
MR. DAIFUKU!
AS THE HEAD OF THE MINISTRY OF SCIENCE...
...I'M HERE TO GIVE YOU A PIECE OF MY MIND! YOU'D HAVE TO BE CRAZY TO BANISH ROBOTS FROM THE CITY!
EXCUSE ME, PROFESSOR OCHANOMIZU... BUT YOU'VE NO BUSINESS GETTING INVOLVED WITH THIS MATTER!
I'M THE GOVERNOR, NOW!!
AS THE ELECTED REPRESENTATIVE OF THE PEOPLE, I WILL DO WHAT I WANT!
I'M GOING TO SMASH ALL ROBOTS LEFT IN THE CITY!

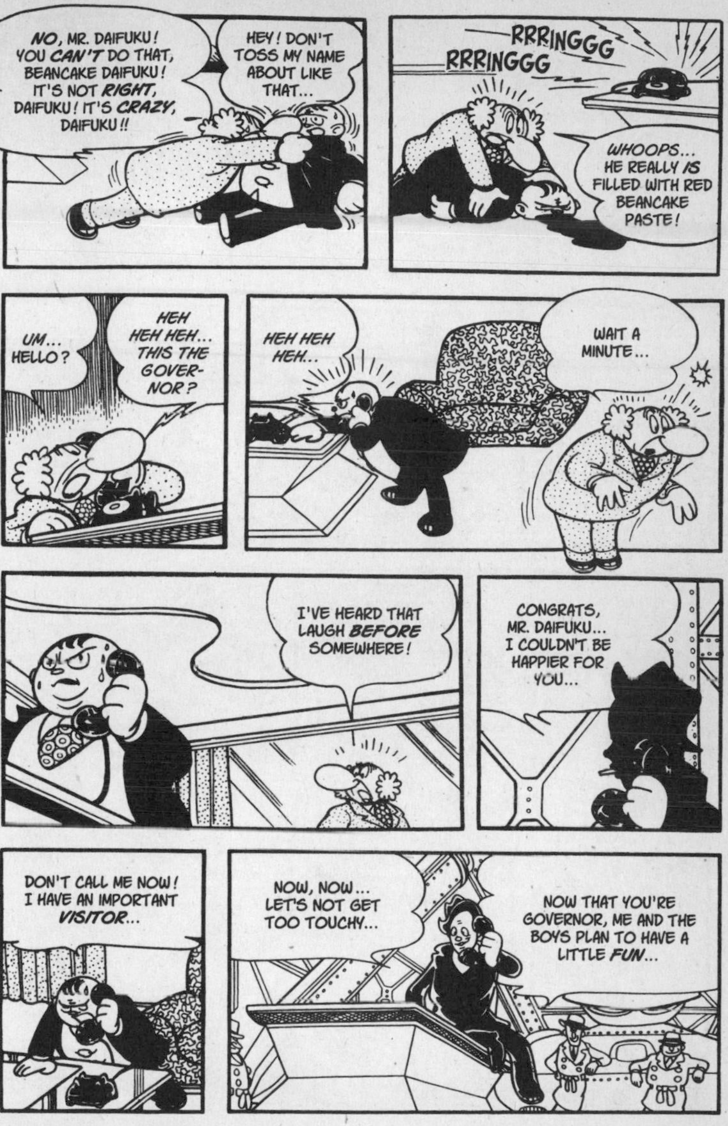
NO, MR. DAIFUKU! YOU CAN'T DO THAT, BEANCAKE DAIFUKU! IT'S NOT RIGHT, DAIFUKU! IT'S CRAZY, DAIFUKU!!
HEY! DON'T TOSS MY NAME ABOUT LIKE THAT...
RRRINGGG
RRRINGGG
WHOOPS... HE REALLY IS FILLED WITH RED BEANCAKE PASTE!
UM... HELLO?
HEH HEH HEH... THIS THE GOVERNOR?
HEH HEH HEH...
WAIT A MINUTE...
I'VE HEARD THAT LAUGH BEFORE SOMEWHERE!
CONGRATS, MR. DAIFUKU... I COULDN'T BE HAPPIER FOR YOU...
DON'T CALL ME NOW! I HAVE AN IMPORTANT VISITOR...
NOW, NOW... LET'S NOT GET TOO TOUCHY...
NOW THAT YOU'RE GOVERNOR, ME AND THE BOYS PLAN TO HAVE A LITTLE FUN...

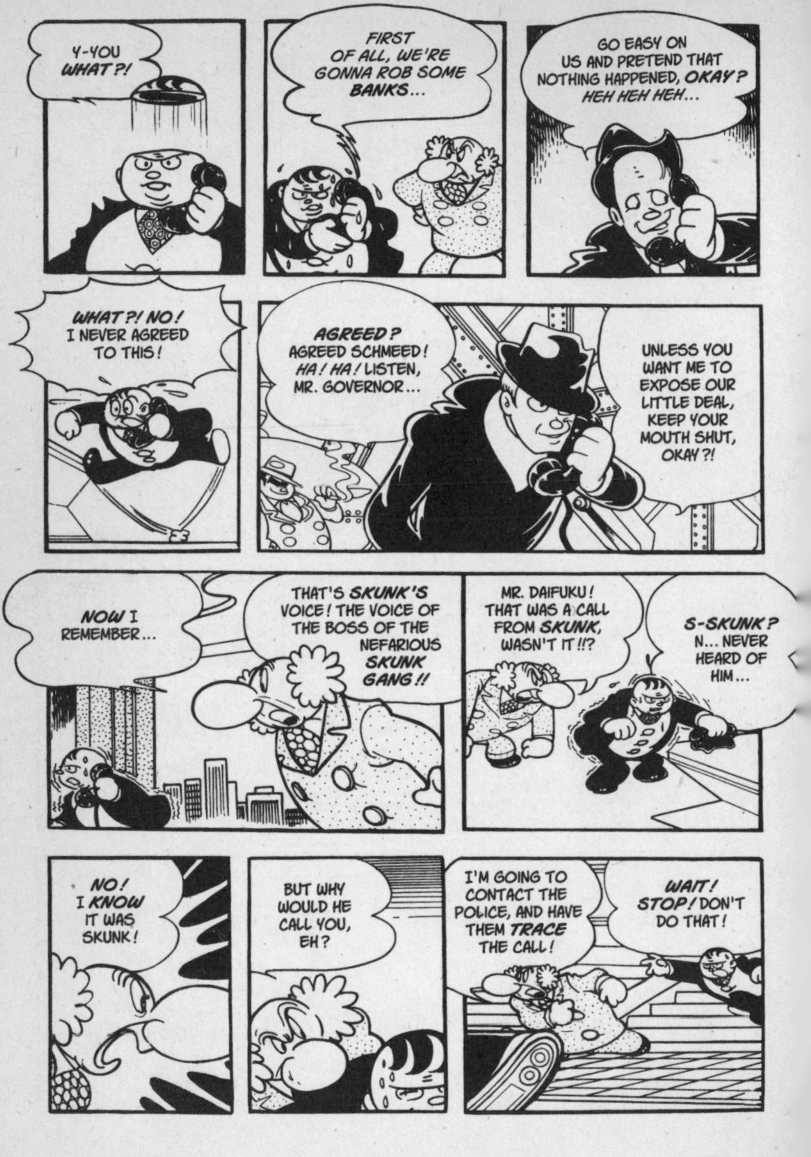
Y-YOU WHAT?!
FIRST OF ALL, WE'RE GONNA ROB SOME BANKS...
GO EASY ON US AND PRETEND THAT NOTHING HAPPENED, OKAY? HEH HEH HEH...
WHAT?! NO! I NEVER AGREED TO THIS!
AGREED? AGREED SCHMEED! HA! HA! LISTEN, MR. GOVERNOR...
UNLESS YOU WANT ME TO EXPOSE OUR LITTLE DEAL, KEEP YOUR MOUTH SHUT, OKAY?!
NOW I REMEMBER...
THAT'S SKUNK'S VOICE! THE VOICE OF THE BOSS OF THE NEFARIOUS SKUNK GANG!!
MR. DAIFUKU! THAT WAS A CALL FROM SKUNK, WASN'T IT!!?
S-SKUNK? N... NEVER HEARD OF HIM...
NO! I KNOW IT WAS SKUNK!
BUT WHY WOULD HE CALL YOU, EH?
I'M GOING TO CONTACT THE POLICE, AND HAVE THEM TRACE THE CALL!
WAIT! STOP! DON'T DO THAT!

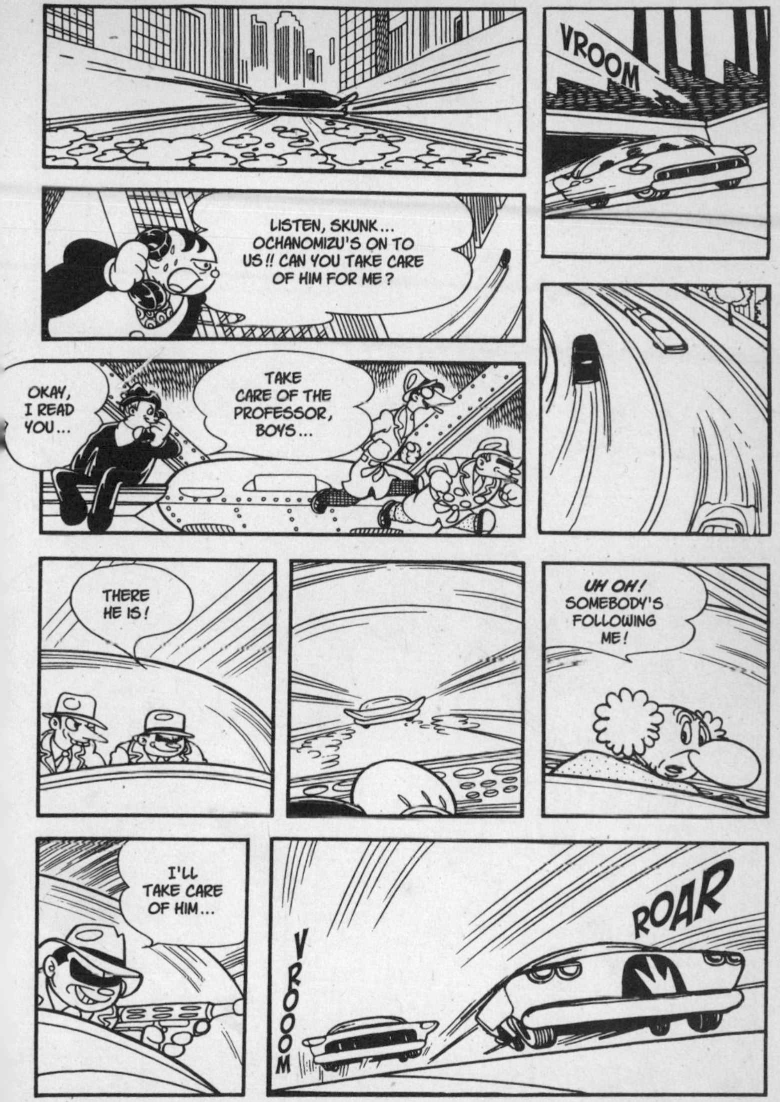
VROOM
LISTEN, SKUNK... OCHANOMIZU'S ON TO US!! CAN YOU TAKE CARE OF HIM FOR ME?
OKAY, I READ YOU...
TAKE CARE OF THE PROFESSOR, BOYS...
THERE HE IS!
UH OH! SOMEBODY'S FOLLOWING ME!
I'LL TAKE CARE OF HIM...
VROOOOM
ROAR

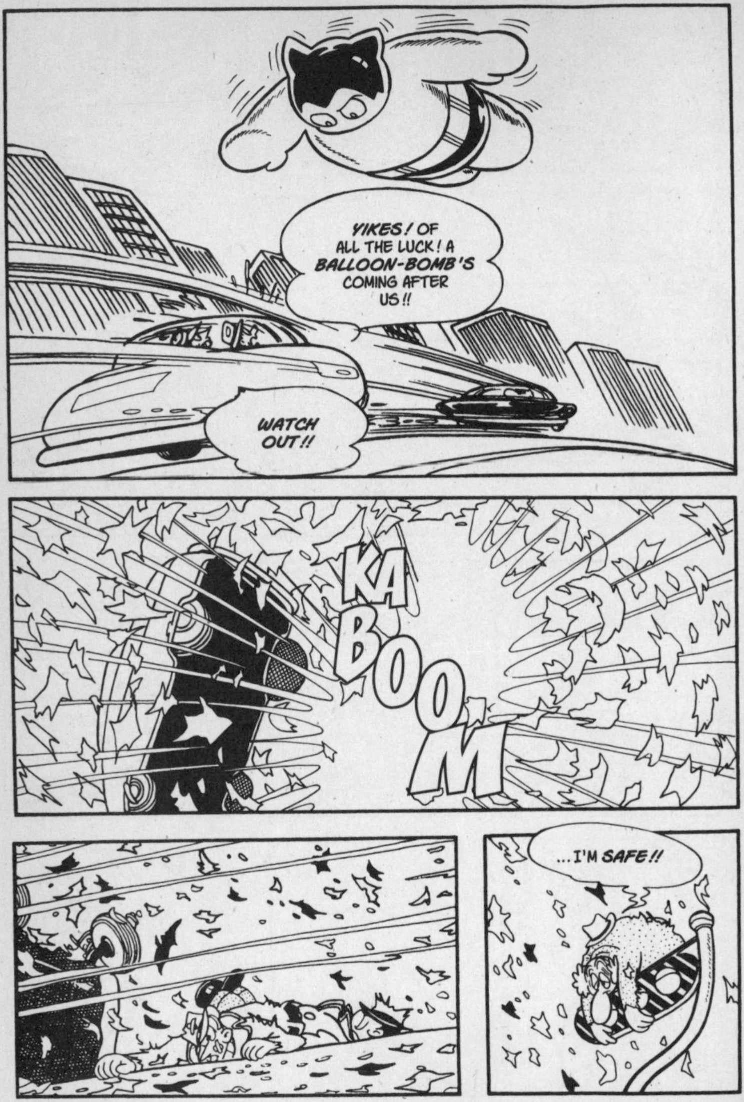
YIKES! OF ALL THE LUCK! A BALLOON-BOMB'S COMING AFTER US!!
WATCH OUT!!
KA BOOOM
...I'M SAFE!!

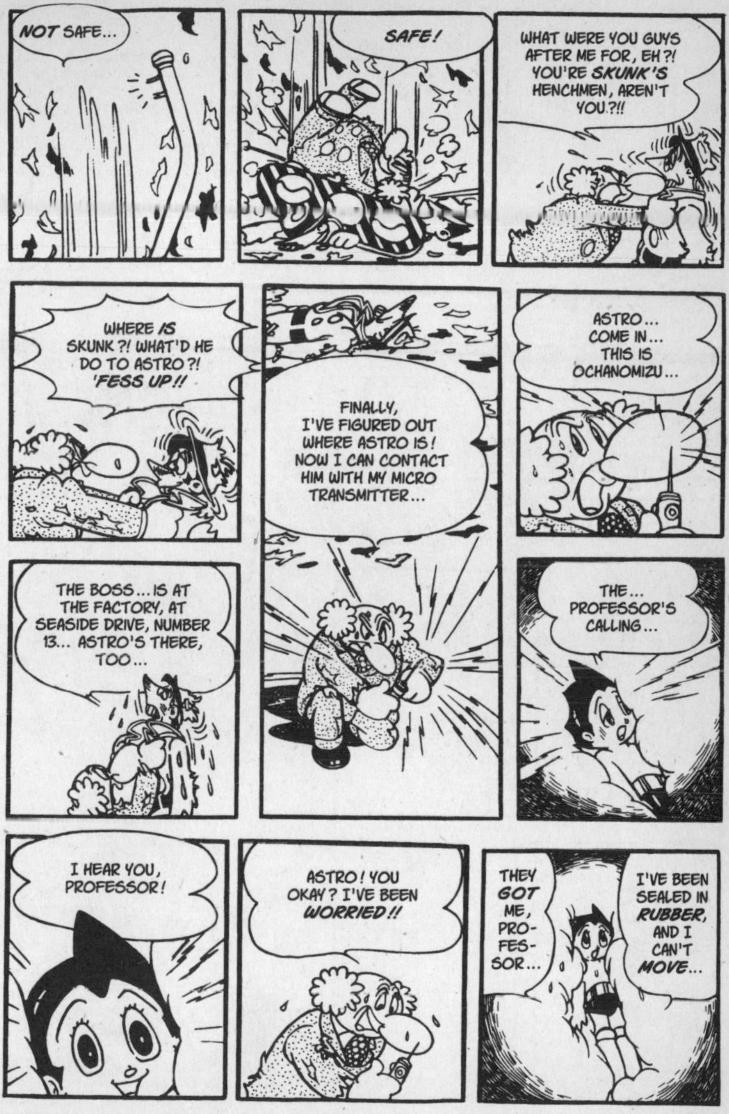
NOT SAFE...
SAFE!
WHAT WERE YOU GUYS AFTER ME FOR, EH?! YOU'RE SKUNK'S HENCHMEN, AREN'T YOU?!!
WHERE IS SKUNK?! WHAT'D HE DO TO ASTRO?! 'FESS UP!!
THE BOSS... IS AT THE FACTORY, AT SEASIDE DRIVE, NUMBER 13... ASTRO'S THERE, TOO...
FINALLY, I'VE FIGURED OUT WHERE ASTRO IS! NOW I CAN CONTACT HIM WITH MY MICRO TRANSMITTER...
ASTRO... COME IN... THIS IS OCHANOMIZU...
THE... PROFESSOR'S CALLING...
I HEAR YOU, PROFESSOR!
ASTRO! YOU OKAY? I'VE BEEN WORRIED!!
THEY GOT ME, PRO-FES-SOR...
I'VE BEEN SEALED IN RUBBER, AND I CAN'T MOVE...

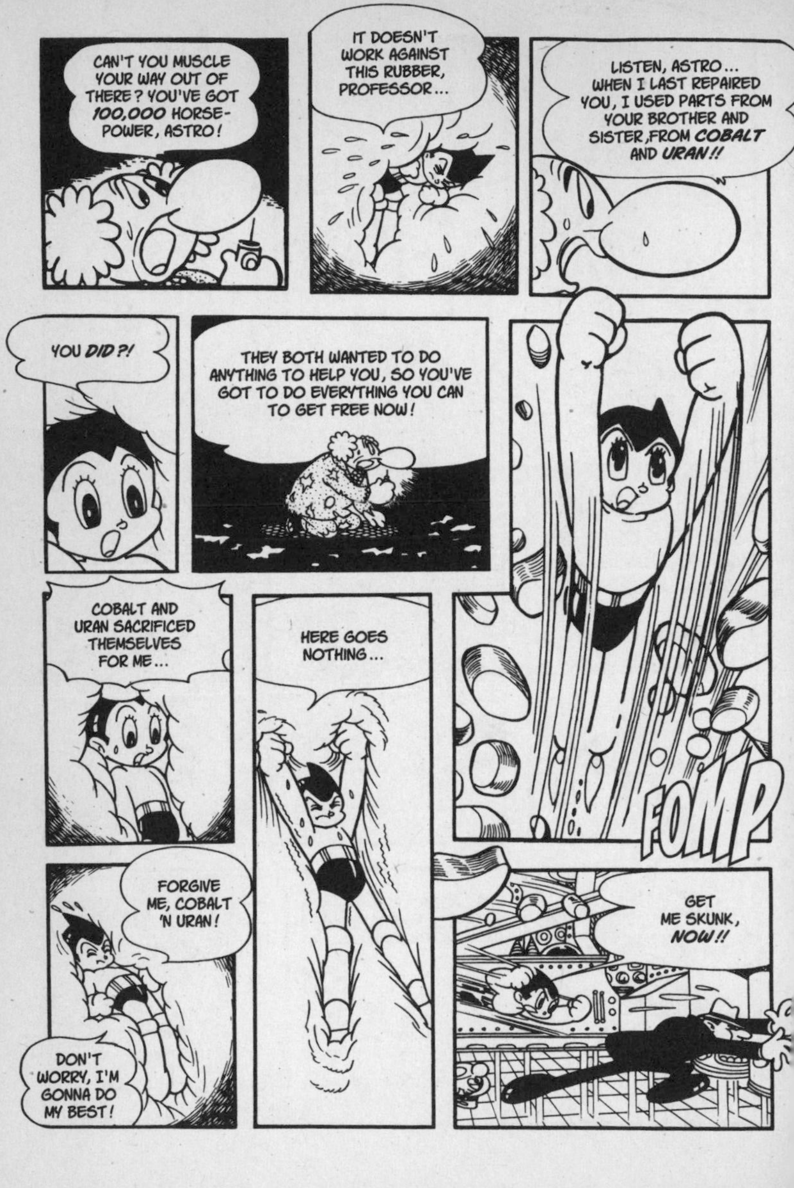
CAN'T YOU MUSCLE YOUR WAY OUT OF THERE? YOU'VE GOT *100,000* HORSE-POWER, ASTRO!
IT DOESN'T WORK AGAINST THIS RUBBER, PROFESSOR...
LISTEN, ASTRO... WHEN I LAST REPAIRED YOU, I USED PARTS FROM YOUR BROTHER AND SISTER, FROM *COBALT* AND *URAN!!*
YOU *DID?!*
THEY BOTH WANTED TO DO ANYTHING TO HELP YOU, SO YOU'VE GOT TO DO EVERYTHING YOU CAN TO GET FREE NOW!
COBALT AND URAN SACRIFICED THEMSELVES FOR ME...
FORGIVE ME, COBALT 'N URAN!
DON'T WORRY, I'M GONNA DO MY BEST!
HERE GOES NOTHING...
FOMP
GET ME SKUNK, *NOW!!*

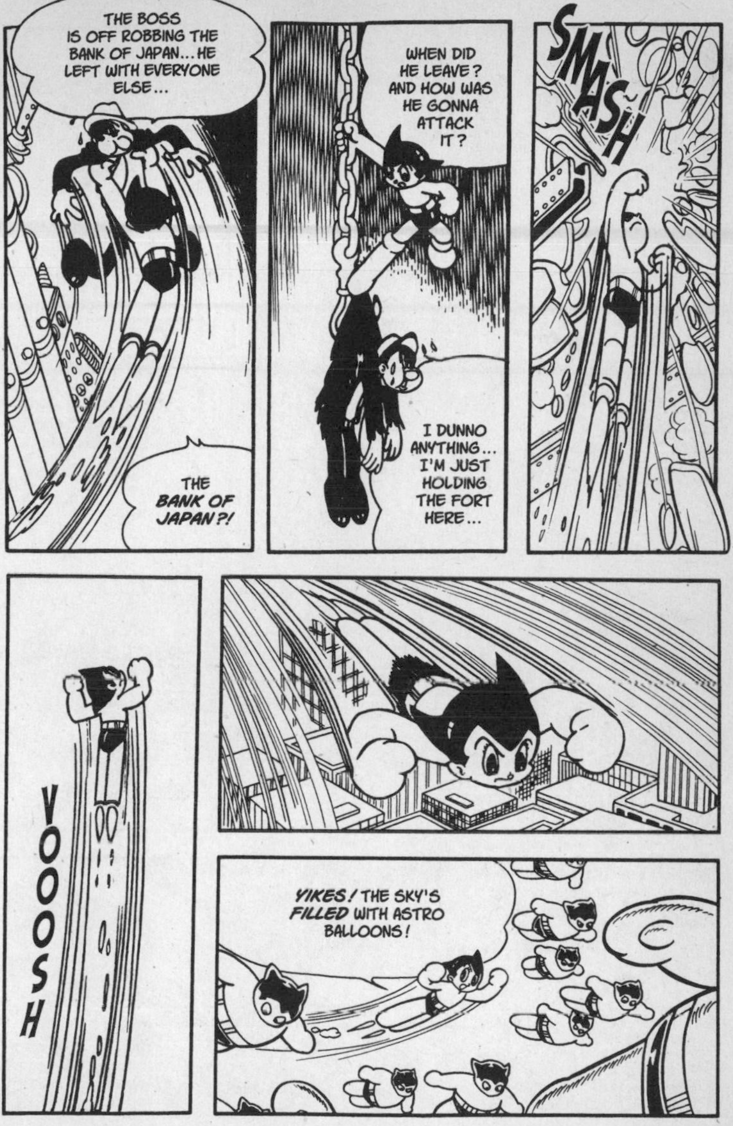
THE BOSS IS OFF ROBBING THE BANK OF JAPAN... HE LEFT WITH EVERYONE ELSE...
THE BANK OF JAPAN?!
WHEN DID HE LEAVE? AND HOW WAS HE GONNA ATTACK IT?
I DUNNO ANYTHING... I'M JUST HOLDING THE FORT HERE...
SMASH
VOOOSH
YIKES! THE SKY'S FILLED WITH ASTRO BALLOONS!

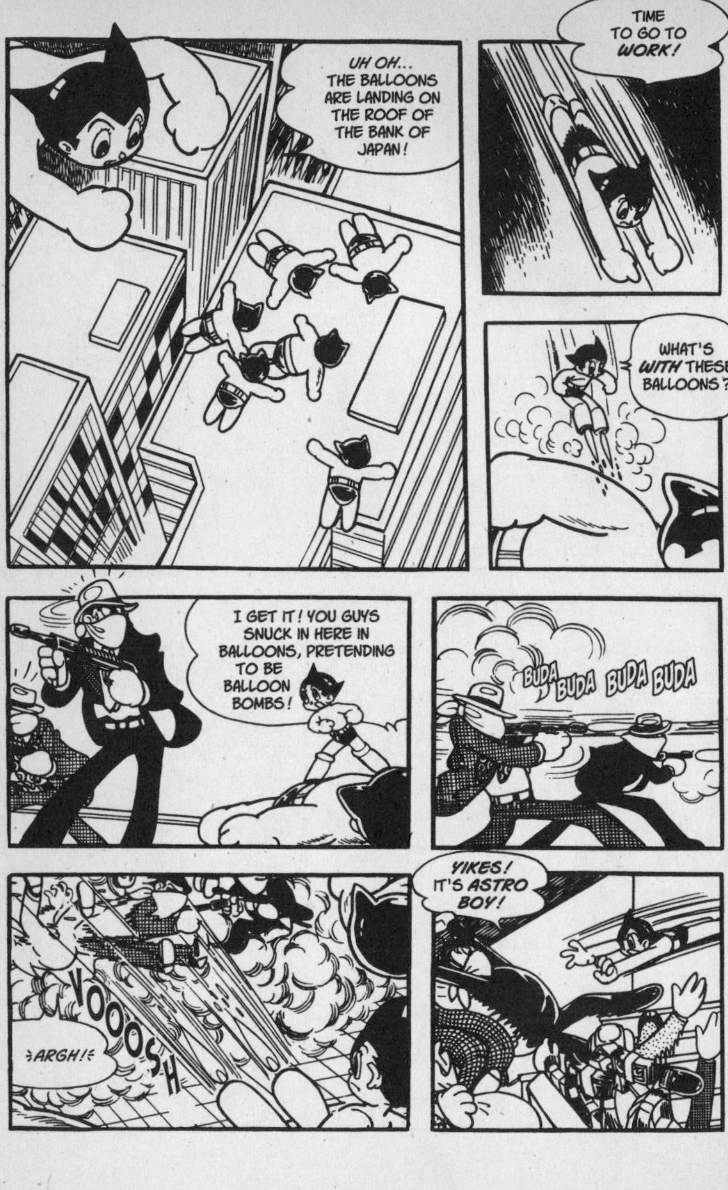
UH OH... THE BALLOONS ARE LANDING ON THE ROOF OF THE BANK OF JAPAN!
TIME TO GO TO WORK!
WHAT'S WITH THESE BALLOONS?
I GET IT! YOU GUYS SNUCK IN HERE IN BALLOONS, PRETENDING TO BE BALLOON BOMBS!
BUDA BUDA BUDA BUDA
VOOOSH
ARGH!
YIKES! IT'S ASTRO BOY!

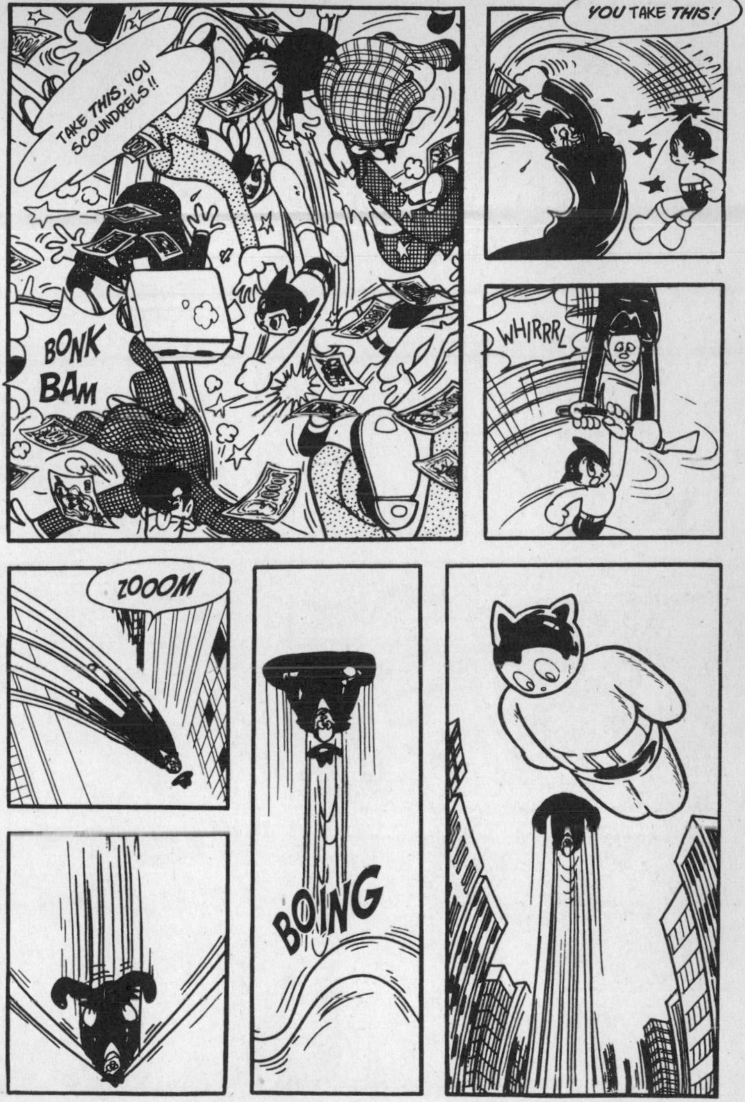
TAKE THIS, YOU SCOUNDRELS!!
BONK
BAM
YOU TAKE THIS!
WHIRRRL
ZOOOM
BOING

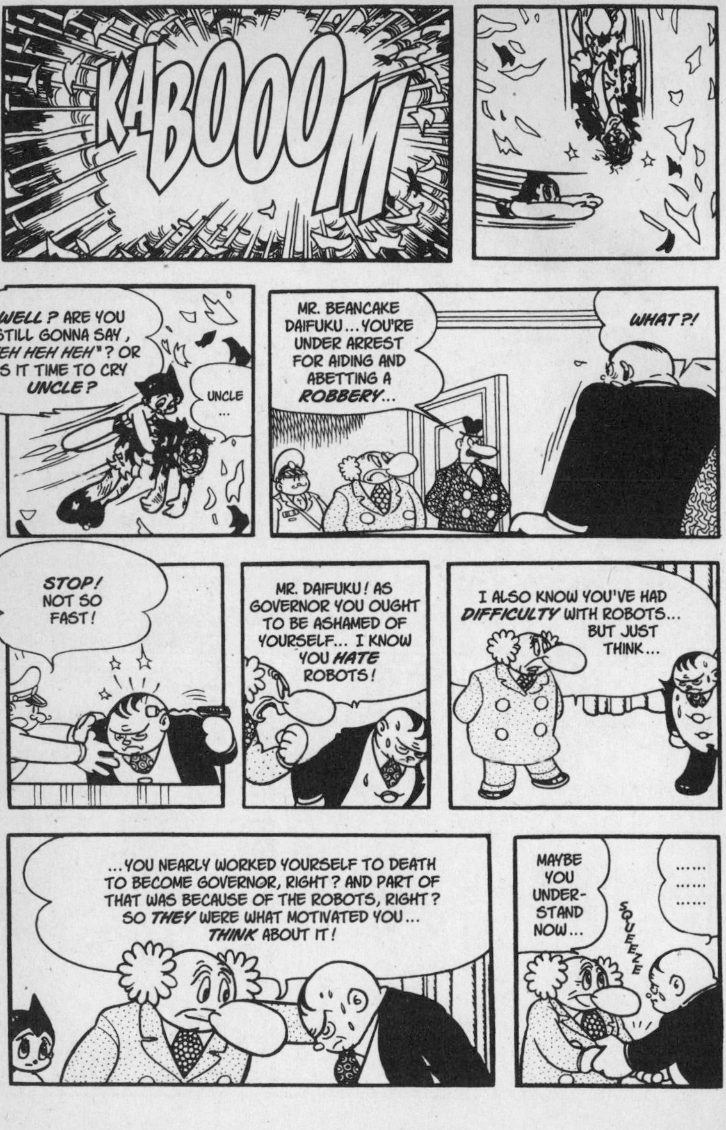
KABOOOM
WELL? ARE YOU STILL GONNA SAY, "HEH HEH HEH"? OR IS IT TIME TO CRY UNCLE?
UNCLE ...
MR. BEANCAKE DAIFUKU... YOU'RE UNDER ARREST FOR AIDING AND ABETTING A ROBBERY...
WHAT?!
STOP! NOT SO FAST!
MR. DAIFUKU! AS GOVERNOR YOU OUGHT TO BE ASHAMED OF YOURSELF... I KNOW YOU HATE ROBOTS!
I ALSO KNOW YOU'VE HAD DIFFICULTY WITH ROBOTS... BUT JUST THINK...
...YOU NEARLY WORKED YOURSELF TO DEATH TO BECOME GOVERNOR, RIGHT? AND PART OF THAT WAS BECAUSE OF THE ROBOTS, RIGHT? SO THEY WERE WHAT MOTIVATED YOU... THINK ABOUT IT!
MAYBE YOU UNDER-STAND NOW...
SQUEEZE
....

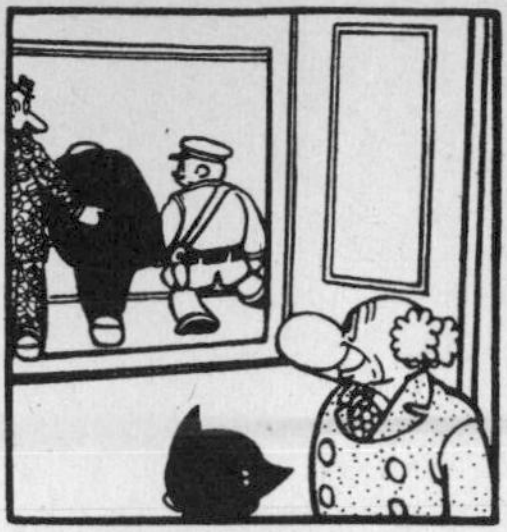

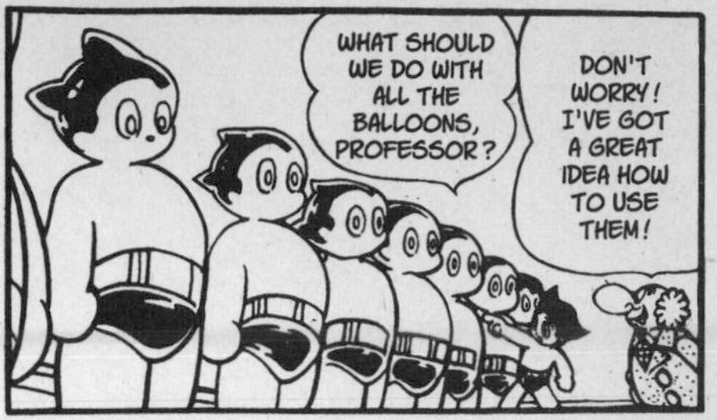
WHAT SHOULD WE DO WITH ALL THE BALLOONS, PROFESSOR?
DON'T WORRY! I'VE GOT A GREAT IDEA HOW TO USE THEM!

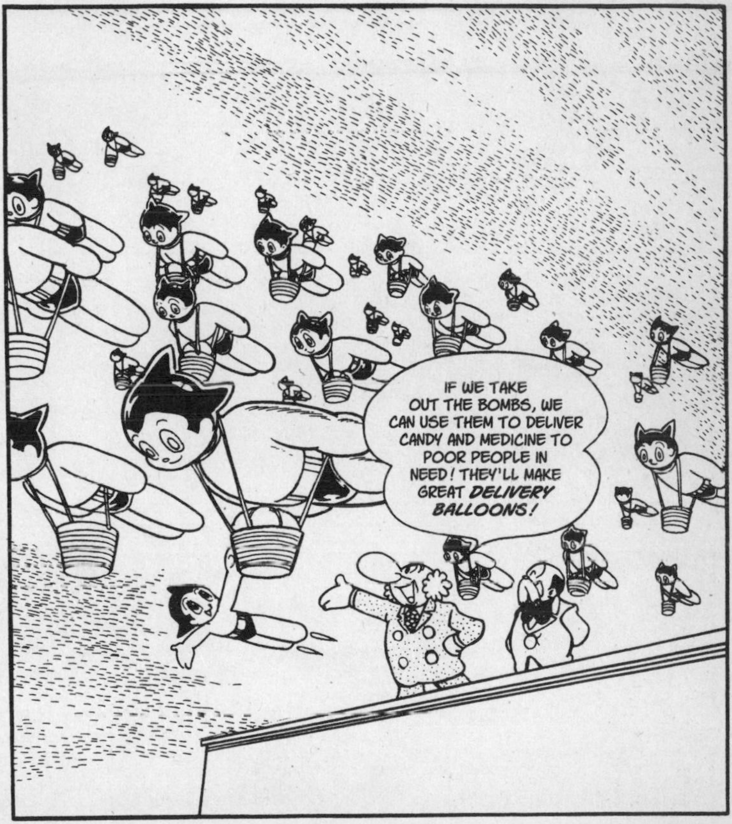
IF WE TAKE OUT THE BOMBS, WE CAN USE THEM TO DELIVER CANDY AND MEDICINE TO POOR PEOPLE IN NEED! THEY'LL MAKE GREAT *DELIVERY BALLOONS!*

THE END

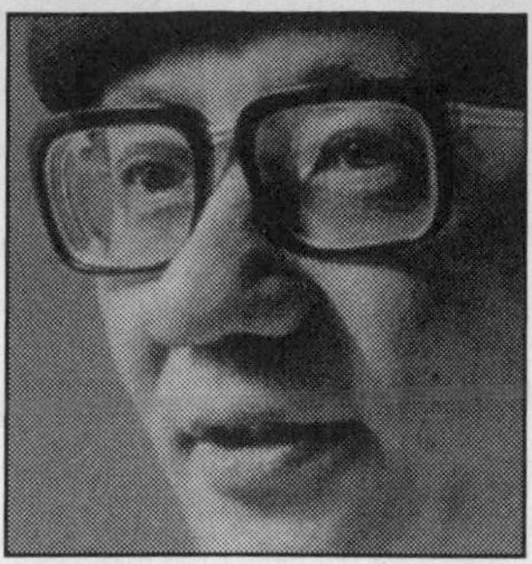

Osamu Tezuka was born in the city of Toyonaka, in Osaka, Japan, on November 3, 1928, and raised in Takarazuka, in Hyogo prefecture. He graduated from the Medical Department of Osaka University and was later awarded a Doctorate of Medicine.

In 1946 Tezuka made his debut as a manga artist with the work *Ma-chan's Diary*, and in 1947 he had his first big hit with *New Treasure Island*. In over forty years as a cartoonist, Tezuka produced in excess of an astounding 150,000 pages of manga, including the creation of *Metropolis*, *Mighty Atom* (a.k.a. *Astro Boy*), *Jungle Emperor* (a.k.a. *Kimba the White Lion*), *Black Jack*, *Phoenix*, *Buddha*, and many more.

Tezuka's fascination with Disney cartoons led him to begin his own animation studio, creating the first serialized Japanese cartoon series, which was later exported to America as *Astro Boy* in 1963. Tezuka Productions went on to create animated versions of *Kimba the White Lion* (*Jungle Emperor*) and *Phoenix*, among others.

He received numerous awards during his life, including the Bungei Shunju Manga Award, the Kodansha Manga Award, the Shogakukan Manga Award, and the Japan Cartoonists' Association Special Award for Excellence. He also served a variety of organizations. He was a director of the Japan Cartoonists' Association, the chairman of the Japan Animation Association, and a member of the Manga Group, Japan Pen Club, and the Japan SF Authors' Club, among others. Tezuka became Japan's "comics ambassador," taking Japan's comics culture to the world. In 1980, he toured and lectured in America, including a speech at the United Nations.

Regarded as a national treasure, Osamu Tezuka died on February 9, 1989 at the age of 60. In April 1994, the Osamu Tezuka Manga Museum opened in the city of Takarazuka, where he was raised. His creations remain hugely popular in Japan and are printed in many languages throughout the world, where he is acclaimed as one of the true giants of comics and animation, his work as vital and influential today as it was half a century ago.

"Comics are an international language," Tezuka said. "They can cross boundaries and generations. Comics are a bridge between all cultures."

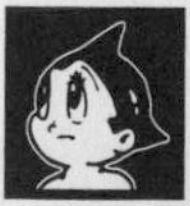

OSAMU TEZUKA'S ORIGINAL

ASTRO BOY®

JET-POWERED! SUPER-STRONG!
EVIL-ROBOT-BASHING!
ALIEN-INVASION-SMASHING!

Each volume retails for $9.95!
New volumes available every month!

AVAILABLE AT YOUR LOCAL COMICS SHOP OR BOOKSTORE
To find a comics shop in your area,call 1-888-266-4226 • For more information or to order direct:
On the web: www.darkhorse.com • E-mail: mailorder@darkhorse.com • Phone: 1-800-862-0052 or (503) 652-9701
Mon.-Sat. 9 A.M. to 5 P.M. Pacific Time

Volume 1
1-56971-676-5

Volume 2
1-56971-677-3

Volume 3
1-56971-678-1

Volume 4
1-56971-679-X

Volume 5
1-56971-680-3

Volume 6
1-56971-681-1

Volume 7
1-56971-790-7

Volume 8
1-56971-791-5

Volume 9
1-56971-792-3

Volume 10
1-56971-793-1

Volume 11
1-56971-812-1

Volume 12
1-56971-813-X

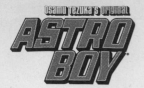

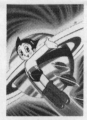

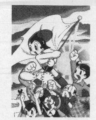

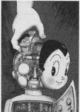

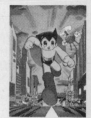

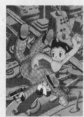

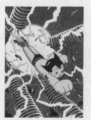

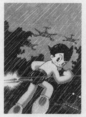

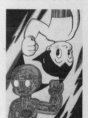

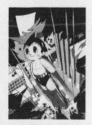

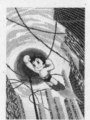

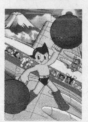

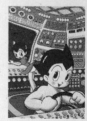

AKIRA
Katsuhiro Otomo
BOOK 1
ISBN: 1-56971-498-3 $24.95
BOOK 2
ISBN: 1-56971-499-1 $24.95
BOOK 3
ISBN: 1-56971-525-4 $24.95
BOOK 4
ISBN: 1-56971-526-2 $27.95
BOOK 5
ISBN: 1-56971-527-0 $27.95
BOOK 6
ISBN: 1-56971-528-9 $29.95

APPLESEED
Masamune Shirow
BOOK ONE
ISBN: 1-56971-070-8 $16.95
BOOK TWO
ISBN: 1-56971-071-6 $16.95
BOOK THREE
ISBN: 1-56971-072-4 $17.95
BOOK FOUR
ISBN: 1-56971-074-0 $17.95

BLACK MAGIC
Masamune Shirow
ISBN: 1-56971-360-X $16.95

BLADE OF THE IMMORTAL
Hiroaki Samura
BLOOD OF A THOUSAND
ISBN: 1-56971-239-5 $14.95
CRY OF THE WORM
ISBN: 1-56971-300-6 $14.95
DREAMSONG
ISBN: 1-56971-357-X $14.95
ON SILENT WINGS
ISBN: 1-56971-412-6 $14.95
ON SILENT WINGS II
ISBN: 1-56971-444-4 $14.95
DARK SHADOWS
ISBN: 1-56971-469-X $14.95
HEART OF DARKNESS
ISBN: 1-56971-531-9 $16.95
THE GATHERING
ISBN: 1-56971-546-7 $15.95
THE GATHERING II
ISBN: 1-56971-560-2 $15.95
BEASTS
ISBN: 1-56971-741-9 $14.95

BUBBLEGUM CRISIS
Adam Warren • Toren Smith
GRAND MAL
ISBN: 1-56971-120-8 $14.95

CANNON GOD EXAXXION
Kenichi Sonoda
VOLUME 1
ISBN: 1-56971-745-1 $15.95

CARAVAN KIDD
Johji Manabe
VOLUME 1
ISBN: 1-56971-260-3 $19.95
VOLUME 2
ISBN: 1-56971-324-3 $19.95
VOLUME 3
ISBN: 1-56971-338-3 $19.95

THE DIRTY PAIR
Adam Warren • Toren Smith
BIOHAZARDS
ISBN: 1-56971-339-1 $12.95
DANGEROUS ACQUAINTANCES
ISBN: 1-56971-227-1 $12.95
A PLAGUE OF ANGELS
ISBN: 1-56971-029-5 $12.95
SIM HELL
ISBN: 1-56971-742-7 $13.95
FATAL BUT NOT SERIOUS
ISBN: 1-56971-172-0 $14.95

DOMINION
Masamune Shirow
ISBN: 1-56971-488-6 $16.95

DOMU: A CHILD'S DREAM
Katsuhiro Otomo
ISBN: 1-56971-611-0 $17.95

GHOST IN THE SHELL
Masamune Shirow
ISBN: 1-56971-081-3 $24.95

GUNSMITH CATS
Kenichi Sonoda
BONNIE AND CLYDE
ISBN: 1-56971-215-8 $13.95

MISFIRE
ISBN: 1-56971-253-0 $14.95
THE RETURN OF GRAY
ISBN: 1-56971-299-9 $17.95
GOLDIE VS. MISTY
ISBN: 1-56971-371-5 $15.95
BAD TRIP
ISBN: 1-56971-442-8 $13.95
BEAN BANDIT
ISBN: 1-56971-453-3 $16.95
KIDNAPPED
ISBN: 1-56971-529-7 $16.95
MR. V
ISBN: 1-56971-550-5 $18.95
MISTY'S RUN
ISBN: 1-56971-684-6 $14.95

INTRON DEPOT
Masamune Shirow
INTRON DEPOT 1
ISBN: 1-56971-085-6 $39.95
INTRON DEPOT 2: BLADES
ISBN: 1-56971-382-0 $39.95

LONE WOLF AND CUB
Kazuo Koike & Goseki Kojima
VOLUME 1: THE ASSASSIN'S ROAD
ISBN: 1-56971-502-5 $9.95
VOLUME 2: THE GATELESS BARRIER
ISBN: 1-56971-503-3 $9.95
VOLUME 3: THE FLUTE OF THE FALLEN TIGER
ISBN: 1-56971-504-1 $9.95
VOLUME 4: THE BELL WARDEN
ISBN: 1-56971-505-X $9.95
VOLUME 5: BLACK WIND
ISBN: 1-5671-506-8 $9.95
VOLUME 6: LANTERNS FOR THE DEAD
ISBN: 1-56971-507-6 $9.95
VOLUME 7: CLOUD DRAGON, WIND TIGER
ISBN: 1-56971-508-4 $9.95
VOLUME 8: CHAINS OF DEATH
ISBN: 1-56971-509-2 $9.95
VOLUME 9: ECHO OF THE ASSASSIN
ISBN: 1-56971-510-6 $9.95
VOLUME 10: HOSTAGE CHILD
ISBN: 1-56971-511-4 $9.95